Blockchain and AI Technology in the Industrial Internet of Things

Subhendu Kumar Pani
Krupajal Computer Academy, India & Biju Patnaik University of Technology, India

Sian Lun Lau
Sunway University, Malaysia

Xingcheng Liu
Sun Yat-sen University, China

A volume in the Advances in Data Mining and
Database Management (ADMDM) Book Series

Published in the United States of America by
IGI Global
Engineering Science Reference (an imprint of IGI Global)
701 E. Chocolate Avenue
Hershey PA, USA 17033
Tel: 717-533-8845
Fax: 717-533-8661
E-mail: cust@igi-global.com
Web site: http://www.igi-global.com

Library of Congress Cataloging-in-Publication Data

Names: Pani, Subhendu Kumar, 1980- editor. | Hota, Chittaranjan, editor. |
   Qu, Guangzhi, editor. | Lau, Sian Lun, 1976- editor. | Liu, Xingcheng,
   1964- editor.
Title: Blockchain and AI technology in the industrial internet of things /
   Subhendu Kumar Pani, Chittaranjan Hota, Guangzhi Qu, Sian Lun Lau, and
   Xingcheng Liu, editors.
Description: Hershey, PA : Engineering Science Reference, an imprint of IGI
   Global, [2021] | Includes bibliographical references and index. |
   Summary: "With blockchain technology and artificial intelligence fueling
   the concept and growth of the Industrial Internet of Things, this book
   investigates the intersection of information science, computer science,
   and electronics engineering as it ushers in a new era for industrial and
   manufacturing companies"-- Provided by publisher.
Identifiers: LCCN 2020028048 (print) | LCCN 2020028049 (ebook) | ISBN
   9781799866947 (hardcover) | ISBN 9781799874799 (softcover) | ISBN
   9781799866954 (ebook)
Subjects: LCSH: Blockchains (Databases) | Internet of things.
Classification: LCC QA76.9.B56 B53 2021 (print) | LCC QA76.9.B56 (ebook)
   | DDC 005.74--dc23
LC record available at https://lccn.loc.gov/2020028048
LC ebook record available at https://lccn.loc.gov/2020028049

This book is published in the IGI Global book series Advances in Data Mining and Database Management (ADMDM)
(ISSN: 2327-1981; eISSN: 2327-199X)

British Cataloguing in Publication Data
A Cataloguing in Publication record for this book is available from the British Library.

For electronic access to this publication, please contact: eresources@igi-global.com.

Advances in Data Mining and Database Management (ADMDM) Book Series

David Taniar
Monash University, Australia

ISSN:2327-1981
EISSN:2327-199X

MISSION

With the large amounts of information available to organizations in today's digital world, there is a need for continual research surrounding emerging methods and tools for collecting, analyzing, and storing data.

The **Advances in Data Mining & Database Management (ADMDM)** series aims to bring together research in information retrieval, data analysis, data warehousing, and related areas in order to become an ideal resource for those working and studying in these fields. IT professionals, software engineers, academicians and upper-level students will find titles within the ADMDM book series particularly useful for staying up-to-date on emerging research, theories, and applications in the fields of data mining and database management.

COVERAGE

- Customer Analytics
- Text Mining
- Educational Data Mining
- Profiling Practices
- Factor Analysis
- Database Testing
- Quantitative Structure–Activity Relationship
- Web Mining
- Web-based information systems
- Neural Networks

IGI Global is currently accepting manuscripts for publication within this series. To submit a proposal for a volume in this series, please contact our Acquisition Editors at Acquisitions@igi-global.com or visit: http://www.igi-global.com/publish/.

Titles in this Series

For a list of additional titles in this series, please visit:
http://www.igi-global.com/book-series/advances-data-mining-database-management/37146

Data Science Advancements in Pandemic and Outbreak Management
Eleana Asimakopoulou (Independent Researcher, Greece) and Nik Bessis (Edge Hill University, UK)
Engineering Science Reference • © 2021 • 255pp • H/C (ISBN: 9781799867364) • US $225.00

Industry Use Cases on Blockchain Technology Applications in IoT and the Financial Sector
Zaigham Mahmood (University of Northampton, UK & Shijiazhuang Tiedao University, China)
Engineering Science Reference • © 2021 • 400pp • H/C (ISBN: 9781799866503) • US $245.00

Analyzing Data Through Probabilistic Modeling in Statistics
Dariusz Jacek Jakóbczak (Koszalin University of Technology, Poland)
Engineering Science Reference • © 2021 • 331pp • H/C (ISBN: 9781799847069) • US $225.00

Applications of Big Data in Large- and Small-Scale Systems
Sam Goundar (British University Vietnam, Vietnam) and Praveen Kumar Rayani (National Institute of Technology, Durgapur, India)
Engineering Science Reference • © 2021 • 377pp • H/C (ISBN: 9781799866732) • US $245.00

Developing a Keyword Extractor and Document Classifier Emerging Research and Opportunities
Dimple Valayil Paul (Department of Computer Science, Dnyanprassarak Mandal's College and Research Centre, Goa University, Goa, India)
Engineering Science Reference • © 2021 • 229pp • H/C (ISBN: 9781799837725) • US $195.00

Intelligent Analytics With Advanced Multi-Industry Applications
Zhaohao Sun (Papua New Guinea University of Technology, Papua New Guinea)
Engineering Science Reference • © 2021 • 392pp • H/C (ISBN: 9781799849636) • US $225.00

Handbook of Research on Automated Feature Engineering and Advanced Applications in Data Science
Mrutyunjaya Panda (Utkal University, India) and Harekrishna Misra (Institute of Rural Management, Anand, India)
Engineering Science Reference • © 2021 • 392pp • H/C (ISBN: 9781799866596) • US $285.00

Challenges and Applications of Data Analytics in Social Perspectives
V. Sathiyamoorthi (Sona College of Technology, India) and Atilla Elci (Hasan Kalyoncu University, Turkey)
Engineering Science Reference • © 2021 • 324pp • H/C (ISBN: 9781799825661) • US $245.00

701 East Chocolate Avenue, Hershey, PA 17033, USA
Tel: 717-533-8845 x100 • Fax: 717-533-8661
E-Mail: cust@igi-global.com • www.igi-global.com

Table of Contents

Detailed Table of Contents

Chapter 1
    Manpreet Kaur, Chandigarh University, Gharaun, India & Guru Nanak Dev Engineering
        College, Ludhiana, India
    Shikha Gupta, Chandigarh University, Gharaun, India

Blockchain technologies are drawing attention after the success of cryptocurrency. Due to the inherent features, such as decentralization, transparency, security, immutability, and integrity, they have already become the prime choice of researchers and scientists. Blockchain is among the most disruptive innovations which have the potential to reshape the behavior of many businesses and industries. Blockchain applications are based on DLT in which public ledger can be accessed by everyone by eliminating the need of third party. Although the power of AI allows the intelligence and decision-making powers of machines in the same way as humans, it relies on a unified model for training and validating datasets. However, the unified nature of AI poses many threats to data privacy and data tempering. Thus, the unique features of blockchain technology makes its application attractive in almost every field including financial services, healthcare, IoT, and many more. This chapter presents a comprehensive overview on blockchain and its integration with AI to explore numerous capabilities.

Chapter 2
    Ranjana Sikarwar, Amity University (AUMP) Gwalior, USA

IoT is not the only buzzword proliferating in the technological world nowadays; blockchain, the underlying tech behind Bitcoin cryptocurrency, is also becoming more ubiquitous and mainstream in the world market. Blockchain and IoT are the perfect pair and seem to flourish together as there is an immense need of data security for the enormous data produced by IoT sensors. The integration of two technologies going hand-in-hand can make IoT objects more reliable and secure in the network. Many companies will exploit the integration of blockchain-based IoT systems in the near future as blockchain is more commendable. In the blockchain-based IoT systems, nodes deployed in the blockchain technology are more or less likely the devices connected in the IoT systems network. Blockchain-enabled IoT systems ease business processes and enhance transparency for improved customer experiences.

Rinki Sharma, Ramaiah University of Applied Sciences, Bangalore, India

Over the years, the industrial and manufacturing applications have become highly connected and automated. The incorporation of interconnected smart sensors, actuators, instruments, and other devices helps in establishing higher reliability and efficiency in the industrial and manufacturing process. This has given rise to the industrial internet of things (IIoT). Since IIoT components are scattered all over the network, real-time authenticity of the IIoT activities becomes essential. Blockchain technology is being considered by the researchers as the decentralized architecture to securely process the IIoT transactions. However, there are challenges involved in effective implementation of blockchain in IIoT. This chapter presents the importance of blockchain in IIoT paradigm, its role in different IIoT applications, challenges involved, possible solutions to overcome the challenges and open research issues.

Mevlut Ersoy, Suleyman Demirel University, Turkey
Asım Sinan Yüksel, Suleyman Demirel University, Turkey
Cihan Yalcin, Suleyman Demirel University, Turkey

Internet of Things (IoT) security and privacy criteria are seen as an important challenge due to IoT architecture. In this study, the security of the IoT system that is created with devices integrated into the embedded system by means of various sensors has been ensured by using a single cryptographic structure. The data transmitted between the nodes in the IoT structure is transmitted to the central node using the Blockchain data structure. The transmitted data is verified at central nodes and the energies consumed between nodes during the transmission phase is detected. An infrastructure has been developed for how blockchain technology can be used in the IoT structure. In this study, an experimental environment was developed and comparative analysis were made in terms of energy consumption and data transfer rates.

Shagun Sharma, Chitkara University Institute of Engineering and Technology, Chitkara University, Punjab, India
Ashok Kumar, Chitkara University Institute of Engineering and Technology, Chitkara University, Punjab, India
Megha Bhushan, School of Computing, DIT University, India
Nitin Goyal, Chitkara University Institute of Engineering and Technology, Chitkara University, Punjab, India
Sailesh Suryanarayan Iyer, Rai School of Engineering, Rai University, Ahmedabad, India

Technology is revolutionizing and making positive as well as negative impacts on social animals. The social animal's behavior gets affected due to instant change in their lives. A concept of blockchain technology or distributed ledger transforms the way of their living. This technology is well known for its immutable and distributed architecture. The government focuses on such technologies rather than centralized network so that they can avoid central server banking crimes. These technologies allow social animals to stay secured and updated in an online process of information transfer. These are very famous for bitcoin, ripple, and ether transactions; however, mentioned transactions are just applications of distributed ledger. This chapter discusses the features, pros, cons, challenges, and future scope of distributed ledger. Further, it discusses the applications of blockchain technology in different sectors like identity management, smart cities, privacy protection, travel industry, electronic voting, finance, health industry, smart contracts, and hospitality.

Chapter 6

Ambika N., Department of Computer Applications, Sivananda Sarma Memorial RV College, Bangalore, India

IoT is used in industrial setup to increase security and provide ease to the user. The manual efforts decrease in this environment. The previous work concentrates on capturing images and transmitting the encrypted image. It uses the Merkle root and blockchain to make the transmission reliable. The suggestion increases reliability to the previous work. The system uses the Merkle root to endorse the key to the transmitting devices. The work increases reliability by 2.58% compared to the previous contribution.

Chapter 7

Anchitaalagammai J. V., Velammal College of Engineering and Technology, India
Kavitha S., Velammal College of Engineering and Technology, India
Murali S., Velammal College of Engineering and Technology, India
Hemalatha P. R., Velammal College of Engineering and Technology, India
Subanachiar T., Velammal College of Engineering and Technology, India

Blockchains are shared, immutable ledgers for recording the history of transactions. They substitute a new generation of transactional applications that establish trust, accountability, and transparency. It enables contract partners to secure a deal without involving a trusted third party. The internet of things (IoT) is rapidly changing our society to a world where every "thing" is connected to the internet, making computing pervasive like never before. It is increasingly becoming a ubiquitous computing service, requiring huge volumes of data storage and processing. The stable growth of the internet of things (IoT) and the blockchain technology popularized by cryptocurrencies has led to efforts to change the centralized nature of the IoT. Adapting the blockchain technology for use in the IoT is one such efforts. This chapter focuses on blockchain-IoT research directions and to provide an overview of the importance of blockchain-based solutions for cloud data manipulation in IoT.

Chapter 8

Aprajita Shriwastawa, Galgotias University, India
Nitya Singhal, Galgotias University, India
S. Prakash, Galgotias University, India

Blockchain is an emerging technology of the new generation. Safety and protection of the data have been the prime concern of people. Digitalization has paved the way for the generation of trillions of data every second. With these developing lives of people, blockchain is the solution. The authors discuss the applications of blockchain in various aspects of life along with the introduction of digital currency. The means and norms are considered for digital money transfer and generation of end-to-end encrypted code for the sake of high-end security. They discuss the framework that can be used by the organizations to develop a new form of the internal network. Finally, the suggestion for future work and development along with all the cons is shown.

Chapter 9
    A. K. M. Bahalul Haque, North South University, Bangladesh
    Bharat Bhushan, Sharda University, India

Blockchain gets its name from being a series of blocks that are linked together to form a chain. Once the information has been added to the chain, it cannot be changed. There are several consensus protocols, and each of them is chosen based on the type of blockchain and the system requirements. With the rapid urbanization of the world, several economic, social, and environment-related issues have been raised. Smart cities are an emerging concept that holds the solution to these urban problems. Blockchain is such an innovation that can promote the development of smart cities. Along with its application in the internet of things, smart cities, and logistics, blockchain truly is state-of-the-art technology. Here, the authors aim to provide an in-depth look into this relatively new technology, beginning with blockchain's fundamentals and then covering the applications, issues, and future scope.

Chapter 10
    Kamalendu Pal, City, University of London, UK

The manufacturing industry inclines to worldwide business operations due to the economic advantage of product design and development. In this way, globalized manufacturing supply chains make their management and control more difficult. As a distributed ledger technology that ensures transparency, trust, traceability, and cybersecurity, blockchain technology promises to ease some global manufacturing operation problems. This chapter presents blockchain technology basics and analyses the issues (e.g., traceability, cybersecurity, flexibility, and smart contracts) related to the blockchain-based manufacturing information system. Next, the chapter presents related research work in the manufacturing industry in recent years. It also includes a classification mechanism for manufacturing information systems based on specific properties. It is followed by discussing the critical issues that need to consider in designing industry-specific reference information system architecture. Finally, the chapter discusses the scope of future research.

Chapter 11
    Charles Tim Batista Garrocho, Federal University of Ouro Preto, Brazil
    Célio Márcio Soares Ferreira, Federal University of Ouro Preto, Brazil
    Carlos Frederico Marcelo da Cunha Cavalcanti, Federal University of Ouro Preto, Brazil
    Ricardo Augusto Rabelo Oliveira, Federal University of Ouro Preto, Brazil

The industrial internet of things is expected to attract significant investment to the industry. In this new environment, blockchain presents immediate potential in industrial IoT applications, offering several benefits to industrial cyber-physical systems. However, works in the blockchain literature target environments that do not meet the reality of the factory and do not assess the impact of the blockchain on industrial process requirements. Thus, this chapter presents an investigation of the evolution of industrial process automation systems and blockchain-based applications in the horizontal and vertical integration of the various systems in a supply chain and factories. In addition, through an investigation of experimental work, this work presents issues and challenges to be faced for the application of blockchain in industrial processes. Evaluations and discussions are mainly focused on aspects of real-time systems in machine-to-machine communication of industrial processes.

Chapter 12

Sini Anna Alex, Ramaiah Institute of Technology, India
Anita Kanavalli, Ramaiah Institute of Technology, India
Drishya Ramdas, Ramaiah Institute of Technology, India

In the world of cutting-edge technology, a buzzword that has been thrown around quite often is blockchain. It has gained prominence in a wide array of fields ranging from the money transfer industry to that of the healthcare sector. The primordial reason for this varied use is the concept of smart contract that makes it intangible and less susceptible to errors. Using this platform of blockchain, the authors propose an avant-garde method of contributing donations to charities through a pivotal body, namely the trust. This application is paramount in the sense that it binds the advancements made on the technological frontier with the social aspect of life, that is, charities in the form of NGO's or other such beneficiaries. This enforces the scrupulous way of donating, ensuring that the money does not get consumed by outsiders or any third-party bodies because ultimately, safeguarding the needs and necessities of the lesser privileged folks is the primary goal, which should be addressed with immediate effect.

Chapter 13

ruwandi Madhunamali, Sabaragamuwa University of Sri Lanka, Sri Lanka
K. P. N. Jayasena, Sbaragamuwa University of Sri Lanka, Sri Lanka

The epidemic crises place massive burdens on our economies. The risk of food supplies is also pushing massive stress on food vendors around the world. There are big problems associated with supply chains framework. Farmers do not receive payment upon delivery of their supplies. The buyers do not have access to finance that will enable them to pay farmers on time. To solve this problem, the authors proposed a dairy production system integration with blockchain and IoT. Blockchain is a decentralized digital ledger technology that allows network participants to trust each other and interact. The dairy product system can check the temperature of the product in real-time by using the website application. Moreover, customers can get notifications when the policy found problems related to temperature values. The blockchain database confirms the information security of the system by using the proof of work algorithm to create the transactions and the blocks. Therefore, the proposed methods can use sensitive data with reasonable time consumption, and no block creation fees are needed.

A decade earlier, the basic guiding theory of the blockchain was implemented. It took a few years for
the technology to be widely recognized outside the computer science sector in industry and academic
communities. Since then, several scientific institutions have taken up the topic. Through this chapter, the
authors focus not only on the working mechanism of the technology but also towards the use cases in
varied industries. Blockchain implementations are an effective way to actively move business expertise to
study goals that support both technical growth and testing through analysis, design, and research approach.

The central problem to be addressed in this research is to investigate how blockchain technology can
be used in today's food supply chains to deliver greater traceability of assets. The aim is to create a
blockchain model in the dairy supply chain that can be implemented across any food supply chains and
present the advantages and limitations in its implementation. Blockchain allows monitoring all types
of transactions in a supply chain more safely and transparently. Acceptance of blockchain in the supply
chain and logistics is slow right now because of related risks and the lack of demonstrable models. The
proposed solution removes the need for a trusted centralized authority, intermediaries and provides
records of transactions, improving high integrity, reliability, and security efficiency and protection. All
transactions are registered and maintained in the unchangeable database of the blockchain with access
to a shared file network.

Preface

INTRODUCTION

Blockchain and artificial intelligence (AI) in industrial internet of things is an emerging field of research at the intersection of information science, computer science, and electronics engineering. The radical digitization of industry coupled with the explosion of the internet of things (IoT) has set up a paradigm shift for industrial and manufacturing companies. There exists a need for a comprehensive collection of original research of the best performing methods and state-of-the-art approaches in this area of blockchain, AI, and the industrial internet of things in this new era for industrial and manufacturing companies. Blockchain Technologies are drawing maximum attention after success of cryptocurrency. Due to the inherent features, such as decentralization, transparency, security, immutability, and integrity, it has already become the prime choice of researchers and scientists. Blockchain is among the most disruptive innovations which have the potential to reshape the behavior of many businesses and industries.

This edited book, Blockchain and artificial intelligence (AI) in industrial internet of things, compares different approaches to the industrial internet of things and explores the direct impact blockchain and AI technology have on the betterment of the human life. The chapters provide the latest advances in the field and provide insights and concerns on the concept and growth of the industrial internet of things. While including research on security and privacy, supply chain management systems, performance analysis, and a variety of industries, this book is ideal for professionals, researchers, managers, technologists, security analysts, executives, practitioners, researchers, academicians, and students looking for advanced research and information on the newest technologies, advances, and approaches for blockchain and AI in the industrial internet of things. Researchers and practitioners working in the fields of Blockchain, machine learning and artificial intelligence will greatly benefit from this book, which will be a good addition to the state-of-the-art approaches collected for Internet of things. It will also be very beneficial for those who are new to the field and need to quickly become acquainted with the best performing methods. With this book they will be able to compare different approaches and carry forward their research in the most important areas of this field, which has a direct impact on the betterment of human life by maintaining the security of our society. No other book is currently on the market which provides such a good collection of state-of-the-art methods for Blockchain and AI -based models for Internet of things, as it is a newly emerging field and research in Blockchain and artificial intelligence is still in the early stage of development.

ORGANIZATION OF THE BOOK

The 15 chapters of this book present scientific concepts, frameworks and ideas on Blockchain and artificial intelligence (AI) in industrial internet of things across different domains. The Editorial Advisory Board and expert reviewers have ensured the high caliber of the chapters through careful refereeing of the submitted chapters. For the purpose of coherence, we have organized the chapters with respect to similarity of topics addressed; ranging from issues pertaining to Blockchain for Industrial Internet of Things (IIoT), Blockchain a ledger for IOT enabled secure systems and blockchain-based image encryption.

In Chapter 1, "Blockchain Technology for Convergence: An Overview, Applications, and Challenges" Manpreet Kaur and Shikha Gupta present the comprehensive overview on blockchain and its integration with AI to explore numerous capabilities. Blockchain is among the most disruptive innovations which have the potential to reshape the behavior of many businesses and industries. Blockchain applications are based on DLT in which public ledger can be accessed by everyone by eliminating the need of third party. Although the power of AI allows imitating intelligence and decision-making powers of machines in a same way as humans, rely on a unified model for training and validating datasets. However, the unified nature of AI poses many threats to data privacy and data tempering. Thus, the unique features of blockchain technology make its application an attractive in almost every field including financial services, health care, IoT and many more.

In Chapter 2, "Blockchain: A Ledger for IoT-Enabled Secure Systems," Ranjana Sikarwa discusses the integration of technologies going hand-in-hand can make IOT objects more reliable and secure in the network. IOT is not the only buzzword proliferating in the technological world nowadays however Blockchain the underlying tech behind Bitcoin cryptocurrency is also becoming more ubiquitous and mainstream of the world's market. Blockchain and IOT the perfect pair seems to flourish together as there is an immense need of data security for the enormous data produced by IOT sensors. Many companies will exploit the integration of IOT systems in near future as blockchain is more commendable. In the blockchain based IOT systems nodes deployed in the blockchain technology are more or less likely the devices connected in the IOT systems network. Blockchain enabled blockchain based IOT systems embarks the ease of business processes, enhancing transparency for improved customer experience.

In Chapter 3, "Blockchain for Industrial Internet of Things (IIoT)" Rinki Sharma presents the importance of Blockchain in IIoT paradigm, its role in different IIoT applications, challenges involved, possible solutions to overcome the challenges and open research issues. Over the years, the industrial and manufacturing applications have become highly connected and automated. The incorporation of interconnected smart sensors, actuators, instruments and other devices helps in establishing higher reliability and efficiency in the industrial and manufacturing process. This has given rise to numerous Industrial Internet of Things (IIoT). Since IIoT components are scattered all over the network, real-time authenticity of the IIoT activities becomes essential. Blockchain technology is being considered by the researchers as the decentralized architecture to securely process the IIoT transactions. However, there are challenges involved in effective implementation of Blockchain in IIoT.

In Chapter 4, "Adaptation of Blockchain Architecture to the Internet of Things and Performance Analysis," Mevlut Ersoy, Asım Yüksel, Cihan Yalcin focuses on the role Energy saving via smart contracts and comparative analysis has been performed towards how blockchain technology can be used and the literature has been supported with this direction. Internet of Things (IoT) technologies are used for the benefits and welfare of humanity. Issues such as speed and energy saving in data acquisition have also taken precedence in such technological processes. Due to architectural structure of internet of things, security mechanisms could not meet the desired data security criteria. Using blockchain with internet of things idea have been developed for this gap. An IoT system has been created through various sensors integrated in an embedded system and the data was transmitted with blockchain data structure. Data obtained from the internet of things has been authenticated.

In Chapter 5, "Is Blockchain Technology Secure to Work On?" Shagun Sharma, Ashok Kumar, Megha Bhushan, Nitin Goyal, Sailesh Iyer discuss about the features, pros, cons, challenges and future scope of distributed ledger. Further, it discusses about the applications of Blockchain Technology in different sectors like Identity Management, smart cities, privacy protection, travel industry, electronic-voting, finance, health industry, smart contracts, and hospitality. Now days the technology is revolutionizing and making positive as well as negative impact on social animals. The social animal's behavior gets affected due to instant change in their lives. A concept of Blockchain Technology or distributed ledger transforms the way of their living. This technology is well known for its immutable and distributed architecture. The Government focuses on such technologies rather than centralized network so that they can avoid central server banking crimes. These technologies allow social animals to stay secured and updated in an online process of information transfer. These are very famous for bitcoin, ripple and ether transactions, however, mentioned transactions are just applications of distributed ledger.

In Chapter 6, "A Reliable Blockchain-Based Image Encryption Scheme for IIoT Network," Ambika N. discusses the transmission reliability by using the Merkle root, and the issue that the blockchain is used in Industrial setup to increase security and provide ease to the user. The manual efforts decrease in this environment. The previous work concentrates on capturing images and transmitting the encrypted image. The system uses the Merkle root to endorse the key to the transmitting devices. The work increases reliability by 2.58% compared to the previous contribution.

In Chapter 7, "Current Trends in Integrating the Blockchain With Cloud-Based Internet of Things," Anchitaalagammai J. V., Kavitha S., Murali S., Hemalatha P. R., and Subanachiar T. focus on blockchain-IoT research directions and to provide an overview of importance blockchain based solution for cloud data manipulation in IoT. Blockchains are shared, immutable ledgers for recording the history of transactions. They substitute a new generation of transactional applications that establish trust, accountability, and transparency. It enables contract partners to secure a deal without involving a trusted third party. The Internet of Things (IoT) is rapidly changing our society to a world where every "thing" is connected to the Internet, making computing pervasive like never before. It is increasingly becoming a ubiquitous computing service, requiring huge volumes of data storage and processing.

In Chapter 8, "Blockchain: Emerging Digital Currency and Need of the Modern Industrialization," Aprajita Shriwastawa, Nitya Singhal, S. Prakash describe about the framework which can be used by the organizations to develop a new form of the internal network. Blockchain is an emerging technology of the new generation. Safety and protection of the data have been the prime concern of people. Digitalization has paved the way for the generation of trillion of data every second. With these developing lives of people, Blockchain is the solution.

In Chapter 9, "Blockchain in a Nutshell State-of-the-Art Applications and Future Research Directions," A. K. M. Bahalul Haque and Bharat Bhushan discuss an in-depth look into this relatively new technology, beginning with blockchain's fundamentals and then covering the applications, issues, and future scope. Blockchain gets its name from being a series of blocks that are linked together to form a chain. Once the information has been added to the chain, it cannot be changed. There are several consensus protocols, and each of them is chosen based on the type of blockchain and the system requirements. With the rapid urbanization of the world, several economic, social, and environment-related issues have been raised. Smart cities are an emerging concept that holds the solution to these urban problems.

In Chapter 10, "Applications of Secured Blockchain Technology in Manufacturing Industry," Kamalendu Pal presents related research work in the manufacturing industry in recent years. It also includes a classification mechanism for manufacturing information systems based on specific properties. It followed by discussing the critical issues that need to consider in designing industry-specific reference information system architecture. Finally, the chapter discusses the scope of future research.

In Chapter 11, "Blockchain-Based Industrial Internet of Things for the Integration of Industrial Process Automation Systems," Charles Garrocho, Célio Ferreira, Carlos Cavalcanti, Ricardo Oliveira discuss issues and challenges to be faced for the application of blockchain in industrial processes. The industrial Internet of Things is expected to attract significant investment to the industry.

In Chapter 12, "Blockchain in Philanthropic Management: Trusted Philanthropy With End-to-End Transparency," Sini Anna Alex, Anita Kanavalli, Drishya Ramdas discuss avant-garde method of contributing donations to charities through a pivotal body namely the trust. This application is paramount in the sense that, it binds the advancements made on the technological frontier with the social aspect of life, that is charities in the form of NGO's or other such beneficiaries. This enforces the scrupulous way of donating, ensuring that the money does not get consumed by outsiders or any third-party bodies because ultimately, safeguarding the needs and necessities of the lesser privileged folks is our primary goal which should be addressed with immediate effect.

In Chapter 13, "Blockchain and IoT Integration in Dairy Production to Survive the COVID-19 Situation in Sri Lanka," Ruwandi Madhunamali and K. P. N. Jayasena emphasize dairy production system integration with block-chain and IoT. Block-chain is a decentralized digital ledger technology that allows network participants to trust each other and interact. The dairy product system can check the temperature of the product in real-time by using the website application. Moreover, customers can get notifications when our policy found. problems related to temperature values. The blockchain database, confirm the information security of our system by using the proof of work algorithm to create the transactions and the blocks. Therefore, proposed methods can use with sensitive data with reasonable time consuming, and no block creation fees are needed.

In Chapter 14, "The Role of Blockchain Technology and Its Usage in Various Sectors in the Modern Age," Amrit Sahani, Sushree Priyadarshini, Suchismita Chinara focus not only on the working mechanism of the technology but as well as we are heading towards the uses cases in varied industries. Blockchain implementations are an effective way to actively move business expertise to study goals that support both technical growth and testing through analysis, design and research approach.

In Chapter 15, "Blockchain and IoT-Based Diary Supply Chain Management System for Sri Lanka," K. Pubudu Jayasena and Poddivila Marage Nimasha Madhunamali discuss blockchain model in the dairy supply chain that can be implemented across any food supply chains and present the advantages and limitations in its implementation. The central problem to be addressed in this research is to investigate how blockchain technology can be used in today's food supply chains to deliver greater traceability of assets.

The book is a collection of the 15 chapters by eminent professors, researchers, and industry people from different countries. The chapters were initially peer reviewed by the editorial board members, reviewers, and industry people who themselves span many countries. The chapters are arranged so that all the chapters have the basic introductory topics and the advances as well as future research directions, which enable budding researchers and engineers to pursue their work in this area.

Blockchain and artificial intelligence (AI) in industrial internet of things are so diversified that it cannot be covered in single book. However, with the encouraging research contributed by the researchers in this book, we (contributors), Editorial members, and reviewers tried to sum up the latest research domains, development in the data analytics field, and applicable areas. First and foremost, we express heartfelt appreciation to all authors. We thank them all in considering and trusting this Edited Book as the platform for publishing their valuable work. We also thank all authors for their kind co-operation extended during the various stages of processing of the manuscript. This edited book will serve as a motivating factor for those researchers who have spent years working as crime analysts, data analysts, statisticians, and budding researchers.

Subhendu Kumar Pani
Krupajal Computer Academy, India & Biju Patnaik University of Technology, India

Sian Lun Lau
Sunway University, Malaysia

Xingcheng Liu
Sun Yat-sen University, China

Chapter 1
Blockchain Technology for Convergence:
An Overview, Applications, and Challenges

Manpreet Kaur

(iD) https://orcid.org/0000-0001-5346-2602

Chandigarh University, Gharaun, India & Guru Nanak Dev Engineering College, Ludhiana, India

Shikha Gupta

Chandigarh University, Gharaun, India

ABSTRACT

Blockchain technologies are drawing attention after the success of cryptocurrency. Due to the inherent features, such as decentralization, transparency, security, immutability, and integrity, they have already become the prime choice of researchers and scientists. Blockchain is among the most disruptive innovations which have the potential to reshape the behavior of many businesses and industries. Blockchain applications are based on DLT in which public ledger can be accessed by everyone by eliminating the need of third party. Although the power of AI allows the intelligence and decision-making powers of machines in the same way as humans, it relies on a unified model for training and validating datasets. However, the unified nature of AI poses many threats to data privacy and data tempering. Thus, the unique features of blockchain technology makes its application attractive in almost every field including financial services, healthcare, IoT, and many more. This chapter presents a comprehensive overview on blockchain and its integration with AI to explore numerous capabilities.

INTRODUCTION

Nowadays, blockchain is considered as one of the most quickly-growing technologies and it has been becoming increasingly popular due to its unique features. Satoshi Nakamoto (Nakamoto, 2009) demonstrated the method in which blockchain technology, a cryptographically secured P2P connected network, could effectively be utilized to get rid of various issues related with transaction management in chronological

DOI: 10.4018/978-1-7998-6694-7.ch001

order and to prevent the double spending problem. Blockchain technologies are continuously surprising the world to a great extent because of the successful accomplishment of Bitcoin (Dinh et al., 2018). Dinh et.al (Dinh et al., 2018) defined blockchain as a public open database that is spread across several nodes which not necessarily trust each other and these nodes adopt append-only data structure i.e. new data and transaction can only added on to blockchain but previous data remain intact. This chapter also concluded that the most of the devices on the blockchain give their consent on an ordered chain of block where each block individually a set of transactions, therefore referred blockchain as a log of ordered transactions (Zhang et al., 2019). Since its prevalence began in 2008, blockchain evolving continuously due to its disruptive nature and it will certainly reshape the method of interacting people, automate payments, trace and track transactions (Makridakis et al., 2018). A survey published in (McKendrick, 2017), has termed it as a disruptive technology due to its revolutionary nature that can change current era of internet.

EVOLUTION OF BLOCKCHAIN

Blockchain technology has been proven as one of the biggest innovations of this century. As shown in Table 1 it has four phases of its evolution. In first phase financial transactions based on DLT to be executed with Bitcoin. In second phase, smart contracts came into existence which are self-executing

Table 1. Evolution of Blockchain

Generation	Description	Use cases	Year
First Generation	Store and transfer of value	Bitcoin, Ripple, Dash)	(1991)-2008)
Second Generation	Programmable via smart contracts	Ethereum	(2008-2013)
Third Generation	Enterprise Blockchains	Hyperledger R3 Corda & Ethereum Quorum	(2013-2015)
Next Generation	Highly scalable with high concurrency	RChain	2015 onwards

programs when certain conditions are satisfied. In third phase, blockchain are shifting towards decentralized internet thus there is a need for Distributed Applications (DAPP) which are open end platforms that have front end and smart contracts. In the final phase, blockchain needs an integrated approach to coordinate all the services and infrastructures provided to meet business requirements (Srivastava et al., 2018).

BLOCKCHAIN TERMINOLOGY

Blockchain consists of three important concepts namely ***Blocks, Nodes*** and ***Miners.***

Block

The block in a Blockchain is an elementary component. A block is a bunch of transactions that have been added to the Blockchain (Li et al., 2017). The first block in a blockchain is known as Genesis Block. Figure 1. shows typical block structure, there are two components of a block one is block header and another is block body. Block header represents the unique identity of a specific block and consists of following elements:

1. Block Hash (a 256-bit number) associated with current block.
2. Previous Block Hash (a 256-bit number) of ancestor block.
3. Tree Root Hash is hash of the root of Merkle Tree.
4. Nonce (an arbitrary number used only once) used in PoW algorithm.
5. Timestamp is approximate time when block is created/found,
6. Meta Data contains other related information.

Figure 1. Sample block structure

Block Header		
Block Hash	Tree Root Hash	Nonce
Previous Block Hash	Timestamp	Other Meta Data
Block Data		
Transaction Counter	Total Block Value	Total Block Transaction Fee
TX_1	TX_2	TX_n
Sender Address	Sender Address	Sender Address
Value	Value	Value
TX_1 Fee	TX_2 Fee	TX_n Fee
Receiver Address	Receiver Address	Receiver Address

Block Data includes transaction counter and transactions along following elements:

1. Transaction Counter
2. Total Block Value
3. Total Transaction Fee

Every transaction in Block contains following information:

1. Transaction Number or ID
2. Sender Address
3. Value associated with transaction
4. Transaction Fee usually in cryptocurrency
5. Receiver Address

Figure 2 demonstrates two subsequent blocks in blockchain.

Figure 2. Two subsequent blocks in blockchain

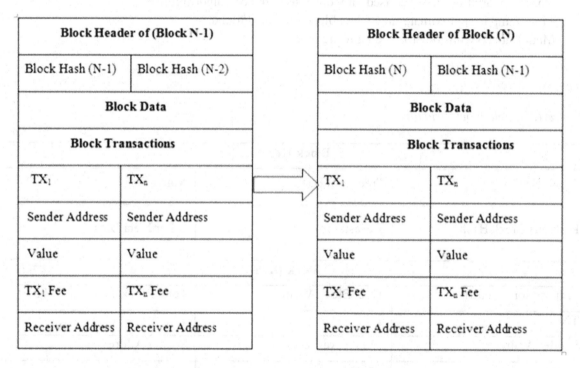

Nodes

A node in blockchain system could be any device such as computers, laptops or even bigger servers. These nodes constitute the significant component in a blockchain framework. All the active nodes.which are a part of a blockchain at a time holds a copy of its current state of data and they constantly exchange the latest blockchain data with each other so that all nodes get updated with latest identical copies (Jimi, 2018). These nodes are able to store, share and maintain the integrity of blockchain data, hence forms a strong pillar for blockchain system to exist.

Miners

These are the special nodes that are willing to share their computational power to add new blocks to the blockchain. There are number of miner nodes in a blockchain network and whenever a new transaction or block is being mined then all these miners are in competition to efficiently solve a computationally demanding mathematical puzzle associated with that newly initiated candidate block. The solution discovered by this method is known as the Proof of Work. This verification is the evidence that miner consumed a considerable amount of time and resources to solve this difficult puzzle. Miners may get some incentives in terms of transaction charges or cryptocurrency for the creation of this new block.

Blockchain and Distributed Ledger Technology (DLT)

DLT/Blockchain is a special type of open source transparent and self-regulating database that is replicated and synchronized over multiple locations in order to perform and keep track of transactions (Deshpande, 2017). Every participant of a blockchain network maintains a copy of this database. Additionally, a general agreement, taking into consideration the majority of the network participants is governed by participants itself without involving any third party intervention, is also established on the current instance of the blockchain that is stored by all the participants of the network. Each instance of such a DLT, stored by each participant of the network, gets updated simultaneously without provision for retroactive transformations in the records (Hassan et al., 2019). Thus, DLT/Blockchain can provide an advancement in productivity, trustworthiness and data reconciliation across all ledger participants (Deshpande, 2017).

THE CAPABILITIES OF BLOCKCHAIN

Blockchain is simply a dispersed repository of trustworthy digital records stored and updated among peers. A distributed ledger can be a digital system used for recording and tracking of monetary or non-monetary transactions. This ledger is different from centralized ledgers in two aspects. First, information is shared by all the nodes of network, with changes to the ledger reflected simultaneously for all holders of the ledger. Second, the information is certified by a cryptographic signature. These two properties making distributed ledger a robust structure to provide a transparent and authentic record of transactions (Deshpande, 2017). In other words, it extends the capabilities of conventional Internet of information and communications to afresh era that could be called "Internet of Value". That new era of Internet that facilitates fund transfer between two parties without any financial institutions, exchange of stocks, maintaining notary services such as real estate titles, creating or executing smart contacts, improving supply chains along with the conventional email or file transfer (Makridakis et al., 2018). Blockchain is capable to offer:

1. **Trustworthiness and Privacy**: Every new block which itself is a set of transactions, can only become part of blockchain when that block is able to get approval from most of the nodes in the network. This approval that is a result of satisfactory validations performed on that block, assures that block data is secured by cryptographic functions. Thus, promotes trust among participating nodes. Although every node can access the blocks in a Blockchain but every block serves the purpose anonymously, so the identity of the sender is yet not be decrypted.

2. **Immutability and transparency**: Hash values are unique for every block. Every block contains its own hash address and hash address of its preceding block. If any node attempts to change block data then it has to alter data everywhere as blocks are spread all over the network. Additionally, it has to change all foremost blocks as change in one block will generate different hash value making all subsequent blocks to be invalid. Hence every subsequent block strengthens the verification of previous block in blockchain. Therefore, data on the blockchain will never be altered in an existing block making it irreversible, temper-proof and promotes transparency.

3. **Disintermediation**: The record of transactions is maintained by all the participating nodes individually (Makridakis et al., 2018). Therefore, any two nodes are capable to initiate an exchange without the necessity of a trusted third party to certify the transactions or to verify the records (Zhang et al., 2019).

4. **Reduced costs and faster speeds**: The transaction fees are usually not applicable as there are absence of intermediate parties say banks or other centralized authorities (Makridakis et al., 2018). Sometimes transaction fee is much reduced from existing financial institution charges if included with transaction. The user can decide whether to offer transaction fees for speeding up their transaction. As if fee is associated with a transaction then more miners will come to validate that transaction and transaction get validated fast.

WORKING OF BLOCKCHAIN

Blockchain technology has the major potential to enable the paradigm shift from Internet of information sharing to Internet of Value, makes it to be called as disruptive technology that can bring revolutionary changes in a way of doing business for a wide range of industries, products and services (Chen et al., 2018). One of the greatest challenge for business owner is to guide their companies to fully explore the emerging capacities of this technology and to develop new applications and innovative products and services at reasonable prices to better satisfy existing and emerging needs (Makridakis et al., 2018). As shown in Figure 3 the process to add a new block requires six steps explained as follows:

Step 1: A node starts a transaction by first creating and then digitally signing it with its private key (created via cryptography).

Step 2: A transaction can represent various actions in a Blockchain. A new block to represent that transaction or set of transactions is then created.

Step 3: A new transaction is propagated (flooded) to all participating nodes to validate that transaction based on predefined scripts. Normally, blockchain need multiple nodes to verify a transaction.

Step 4: Special nodes called miner nodes are responsible to validate new transaction or block and store it onto distributed ledger. Miners get into a competition to resolve a cryptographic hash algorithm oriented complex mathematical problem or puzzle. The solution to this problem, known as Proof of Work (PoW), is a evidence that miner utilized significant computing efforts. Miners may entitled with some incentive for mining that could be either in form of cryptocurrency or transaction charges.

Step 5: Once a transaction is validated, it is appended in a block, then new instance of blockchain is again propagated into network to provide the latest information about a block. On this step, a transaction is getting its first confirmation.

Step 6: This latest block is then stored on distributed ledger and subsequent blocks links with this block via a hash pointer. At this point, the transaction receives its second confirmation and the block gets its first confirmation. Whenever a new block is being created its associated transactions get reconfirmations. Normally, a network requires six confirmations for considering a transaction to be final.

Figure 3. Steps followed to add a new block in a Blockchain

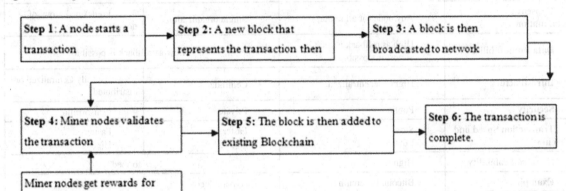

VI. TYPES OF BLOCKCHAIN

When various nodes from different geographical locations across the globe wants to communicate or exchange cryptocurrency, without even having knowledge about one another, blockchain are utilized in this type communication to ensure end to end transmission. Some nodes shows byzantine behavior(an arbitrary behavior) in which node either forwarding no block or different blocks to different nodes, but the most of them are trustworthy. Altogether, the nodes continue to maintain a shared repository of its global instances and execute transactions that can alter these instances. Thus, blockchain could be unique data structure which stores past instances and transactions. All these participating nodes give their consent on state of transactions and their order in blockchain (Dinh et al., 2017).

Blockchain systems are broadly classified as permissioned or private that are only accessible to authorized or designated users and permissionless or public that are publicly accessible for all users through internet.

Three types of Blockchain exists namely (Salah et al., 2018):

1. Public
2. Private
3. Consortium

Table 2 displays comparison and classification of blockchain (Dib et al., 2018).

Table 2. Blockchain Classification

	Public	**Private**	**Consortium**
Access	Anyone	Single organization	Multiple organizations
Participants	Anonymous and without Permissions	Known entities and with permissions	
Consensus Determination	Any node (or all miners)	Single organization	Predefined group of nodes
Data Immutability	High as rollback is almost impossible	Low as rollback is possible	
Infrastructure	Highly decentralized	Centralized	Partially Centralized or distributed
Security	Public	Private	Consortium
Transaction Speed and Efficiency	Slow; Low	Faster; High	Faster; High
Network Scalability	High	Low to medium	
Example	Bitcoin, Ethereum	Hyperledger	R3's Corda

A .Public or Permissionless Blockchain

A public blockchain is an open network in which all transactions are visible to all participants and everyone could take part in consensus mechanism. These chains are designed to be fully decentralized, without any single node provided with full control on transactions. Public blockchain are highly immutable, since transactions are recorded on large group of participants. Finally, these blockchain take significant time to propagate transactions and blocks due to high size of network. Hence transaction productivity is limited and latency is high (Zheng et al., 2017). Sometimes, block reward is also associated with public blockchain.

B. Private or Permissioned Blockchain

The second type of chains are private blockchain, possess a number of significant differences from public blockchain. Interested nodes require membership or permissions to participate in the network. Since transactions are private, they are only available to designated participants. Only those nodes that are associated with particular enterprise would be allowed to take part in consensus mechanism (Salah et al., 2018). Private blockchain are termed as centralized network as the enterprises that owns the blockchain have full control over all participants. Private blockchain are of great value to such enterprises who want to collaborate and share data, without making available their sensitive business data accessible to all participants as in public blockchain. Although, these blockchain are highly efficient, but they are not fully immutable due to their limited size (Zheng et al., 2017). Private blockchain may or may not have a reward involved with it.

C. Consortium or Federated Blockchain

Consortium blockchain are utilized by a predefined group of enterprises (Salah et al., 2018). The groups are usually formed based on the mutual interests of participating organizations (Li et al., 2018). Similar to private blockchain, these blockchains are executed as permissioned systems with only a group of pre-approved nodes would participate in consensus process, making them partially decentralized (Dib et al., 2018). The consortium blockchain are comparatively faster than public blockchain because of the limited size of participants with pre-specified permissions. Additionally, these blockchain consume less energy due to limited number of miners making them more efficient and fast (Zheng et al., 2017).

VII. APPLICATION AREAS OF BLOCKCHAIN

A. Smart Contracts

The concept of smart contracts came into existence with Ethereum. Each node participating in blockchain has a local virtual machine that is called EVM (Ethereum Virtual Machine) in Ethereum. Smart Contract is code or group of programs that run on EVM (Dib et al., 2018). In other words, smart contract is a collection of self-executing computer instructions to ensure mutual consent between non-trusting parties (Finck, 2019). Their deployment and execution are automatically invoked by miner nodes as a part of blockchain transactions. Usually, it requires significant amount of time and computational power to execute these contracts, so miners may get reward for this job (Alharby et al., 2018). A Smart Contract, in simple terms, is a digital form of a legal contract that facilitates negotiations between non trusted entities without human intervention (Finck, 2019). Trust among participating entities is created by public availability of code. Automatic execution eliminates the need for a trusted intermediary (Hu et al., 2019)[50]. Smart contracts exhibit following features:

(i) *Self-Governance*: Participating nodes agree on the decisions and hence need for mediators and bias related to them could be dispensed of.
(ii) *Trust*: All fundamental documents and records are stored on a open ledger that is publically accessible, thus cannot be demolished or lost.
(iii) *Backup*: As data is replicated on multiple nodes participating in the network it provides data safety and security.
(iv) *Savings*: Smart contracts by eliminating the need for a mediator cutting the significant cost.

Thus smart contracts due to their inherent capabilities can be used in real estate for registration of land possession and property rights, intellectual property. Ethereum and Hyperledger Fabric are two most popular blockchain platform for creating smart contracts (Alharby et al., 2018).

B. Banking

Blockchain banking applications can minimize the huge expenditure incurred by avoiding the need to have mediators to verify payments and enforces secure trading (Makridakis et al., 2018). Blockchain are always supported by increased levels of safety and security while exchanging data, information, and funds. It also facilitates users to take benefit of the transparency of network infrastructure with reduced operational costs with support of decentralization. As with blockchain it is always possible to trace every possible historic record of significant worth that was exchanged between parties in past, will guarantee to provide assurance and authenticity throughout the financial operation. These characteristics of blockchain makes them reliable, favorable and prominent solution for the banking and financial industry. Corda is a good example of blockchain banking application powered by R3 startup and other renowned organizations (Makridakis et al., 2018).

C. Health Care

Blockchain has the capabilities to revolutionize the healthcare management of patients by exploring huge breakthrough in the healthcare ecosystem. With the support of blockchain, patients have full control on their health related information. They would be able to grant or revoke privileges to their personal sensitive data. So blockchain could be termed as a patient-empowered platform (Meinert et al., 2018). In a healthcare system, smooth information exchange and quick access of comprehensive set of patient's records would allow doctors to diagnose and treat patient in a more accurate way without delay in waiting their previous history (Meinert et al., 2018). Day by day patient records are growing in size which requires appropriate usage of assets to explore maximum useful insights discovered through it. Hence blockchain based health application is an integrated approach to provide patient consent as well as access to authorized people making it a cost-effective solution.

D. Retail

The blockchain has the potential to drastically change the retail supply chains by managing the supply data, autonomous transactions and chain of custody information. The systems supported by blockchain can helps in establishing trust between retail supply chain stakeholders. A number of leading retailers such as eBay, Walmart and Open Bazaar have already exploited the potential of blockchain enabled solutions. This means the trade is being done with no mandatory fees and without any central organization to monitor trade (Makridakis et al., 2018). Subsequently, blockchain provides assistance to retailers to keep tracking of entire history of product through a supply chain, facilitating them with better command over products they are going to sell. In a nutshell, blockchain applications could assist retailers through improved inventory management, tracking provenance, ensuring product authenticity, eliminating processing charges and enhancing customer loyalty or reward programs (Cognizant, 2017).

E. Education

Education system is still in preliminary phase to reap the entire benefits of technology as a powerful tool for revolution in existing teaching learning environment (USDofE, 2017). Blockchain technology has promising features to explore numerous possibilities to assist instructors, to maintain sound relationship between student and teacher and to provide authentic learning experience. In present scenario, some universities and institutes have applied this technology for the purpose of credential or identity verification, automatic credit transfer and intellectual property protection. However, researchers assumes that this technology has many other features yet to explore that can dramatically minimize data management cost by eliminating many manual processes (Blockchain-Based Applications in Education, n.d.).

Blockchain-enabled platform helps to maintain the authenticity of academic records such as transcripts, certificates, degrees and personal records of learners or instructors. Many academic organizations have utilized private blockchain environment to provide authorized access to specified users only (Arenas & Fernandez, 2018)[24]. All the educational records stored at single shared ledger will not only enables easy access but also improve the accountability and transparency of those records. Therefore, Blockchain is in position to reinvent the education sector.

F. Internet of Things (IoT)

Blockchain has emerged as an effective solution for solving scalability, confidentiality, security and trustworthiness issues of IoT. A Blockchain technology uses a cryptographic algorithm and hashing techniques which ensures confidentiality and security of data on network that is of prime concern of IoT industry. The tamper resistant and decentralized approach of blockchain makes it suitable for monitoring a huge number of connected devices and supports transaction processing and management (Restuccia et al., 2018). By integrating the blockchain with IoT devices can significantly reduce the installation and maintenance costs of servers for an IoT network. This decentralized nature would eliminate central point of failure, thus application of blockchain in IoT ecosystem can offer better environment for devices to execute. The distributed ledger is appropriate to ensure smooth and secure data transfer in IoT network (Panarello et al., 2018).

G. Voting System

Voting has always been viewed as an democratic exercise adopted by citizens to express their opinion to formally select a candidate. In all democratic practices, security of an election is an issue of national security (Hjálmarsson et al., 2018). The solution is to create trustworthy blockchain-enabled digital voting system. By generating a transaction to represent every vote, this blockchain-enabled system could keep track of number of votes. As system utilizes public database, all stakeholders can formally validate the final results because they can count the votes themselves. This platform allows voters to remain anonymous to preserves privacy of voter (Hardwick et al., 2018). Adapting to advanced democratic strategies to make the open political decision process less expensive, quicker and simpler is need of hour. This additionally permit voters to communicate their viewpoint on specific legislative proposals (Hjálmarsson et al., 2018).

VII. BLOCKCHAIN AND AI TECHNOLOGY CONVERGENCE

It is hard to deny that both Blockchain and AI are two prominent technologies that can speed up pace of innovation and redefine existing technological paradigm. By converging blockchain with AI could help leverage many advantages of AI through creation of trusted AI ecosystem. AI has the potential to improve underlying architecture of blockchain while blockchain can enable AI to be more coherent and easy to understand.

A. MAJOR CHALLENGES IN AI

AI needs huge volumes of data and availability of getting error free and reliable data is point of concern in AI as in this technology the whole power lies in quality of data being fed to algorithms or models to discover patterns, learning and to make intelligent decisions (Makridakis et al., 2018). So, blockchain can solve this problem of AI by providing public access to data on which these models could be trained by storing that data on blockchain while preserving the integrity and authenticity of data (Artificial Intelligence and Privacy, 2018)[27]. Secondly, data silos being accessed by AI machines making it non beneficial to share this kind of data and can lead to poor decision making wastage of resources. These data silos thus impacting profitability are putting major issue towards exploring AI capabilities (Alienor, 2018)[29]. Meanwhile, blockchain is becoming increasing accepted for enabling users to share data and conduct transaction free of cost, faster and in a secure manner anonymously and without being their information altered. Thirdly, personal user data is getting more worth day by day and while handling huge amount of user data in AI could lead to widespread invasion of user privacy. Blockchain offers a secure way to generate ownership and to gain more control over the data. Additionally, AI black-box suffers from explainability problem. How AI has reached a particular decision is biggest question to build trust in user (Choudhary, 2019). With immutability feature of blockchain, it is possible to decode the decision logic taken by AI. Moreover, AI acquires a centralized control on data and computing power that is only possible by huge investment to get access of data and to process that data. Blockchain could address this challenge by providing decentralized control through distributed ledger technology to enable anyone across the world to create and utilize AI models effectively. Thus transforming AI from retrieving data from paid big data sources to an open end environment where everyone allows to contribute freely. Furthermore, AI has the ability to help blockchain frameworks by upgrading their security and scalability, by performing as a computerized arbitrator and administration component, for privacy-preserving customized systems. Blockchain, on the other hand, can serve AI frameworks by empowering decentralized computational powers, providing data sharing foundations, serving a basis for a path followed by AI to reach at certain inference along with controlling untrusting participants (Pandl et al., 2020). The integration of these two promising technologies is drawing in countless business people and researchers these days. However, the way toward coupling of these two innovations is not that simple as it appears. Blockchain technology is decentralized and its participating nodes are all heterogeneous in nature. Additionally, if Blockchain is public and open-sourced, it will become crucial for AI outputs to concentrate as a point. AI-based systems used in present scenario, however, notwithstanding the demanded security measures and robustness guarantees necessary to govern a blockchain solution.

B. MAJOR CHALLAENGES IN BLOCKCHAIN

As a nascent technology Blockchain adoption presents numerous challenges that could be easily resolved with AI. Blockchain requires mining of blocks which is an undeniable job which requires huge amount of energy. AI combined with machine learning algorithms has already proven to be energy efficient in optimization of energy consumption. Thus, combining AI with blockchain could significantly result in reduced investments in mining hardware (Andoni et al., 2019). Another issue faced by blockchain systems is scalability as blockchain networks are constantly growing at a pace of 1 MB every 10 minutes (Zhou et al., 2020). AI can introduce entirely new decentralized learning model such as sharding technique to divide the blockchain network into easily manageable smaller networks and federated learning to make system more efficient (Habib ur Rehman et al., 2020). Making personal data increasingly secure perpetually prompts it being sold, bringing about creation of data marketplaces could be another issue being faced (Wolfson, 2018). Thus, users will rely on AI machines to grant access and track data usage. Additionally security (more evidents in public blockchain) and privacy threats in blockchain can however, be reduced greatly by implementing homomorphic encryption algorithms that are performed directly on encrypted data (Zhang et al., 2019). Also, the environment executing the coupling of these two innovations, however, request a increased computational power. Furthermore, as every immature innovation must be provided with standardization for a significant number of global adoptions. As blockchain is still in development phase, which implies that there has been an absence of uniform standards that are vital for any new innovation acceptance. Due to lack of these global legacy specifications, it would become difficult to achieve desired level of interpretability in different blockchain networks. However, its integration with existing technology could be considered as the possible solution. Lastly, due to the poor understanding of blockchain technology, numerous businesses who need to utilize the blockchain are generally doubtful about the feasibility of the innovation (Hileman & Rauchs, 2017).

VIII. FUTURE PROSPECTS

Blockchain-AI convergence is inevitable as both these technologies deals with data and its value. Blockchain enables secure sharing of dataset or anything with value, while AI can discover patterns insights from dataset to generate value. This decentralized AI would rely on distributed, digitally signed, shared datasets stored on blockchain to perform analytics and making decisions without intermediaries (Salah et al., 2018). In turn, Blockchain could use AI to monetize user-controlled data and create marketplace for AI models. Using blockchain, users are empowered with full control over their data in terms of granting and revoking privileges. In current scenario, monetization is done by central authorities but blockchain enables users to monetize their own data and data thus produced can be used for development of AI models. The integrated approach holds many exciting opportunities that can revolutionize the world by providing a reliable innovation-empowered system that is virtually temper-resistant and provide solid insightful decisions (Monrat et al., 2019).

IX. CONCLUSION

It is quite certain that blockchain has a caliber to disrupt almost every possible existing sector. Blockchain technology ends up being a perfect choice for building new trust models by offering anonymity, persistence, fault tolerance, security and minimal cost decentralized management without third party mediators (Shi et al., 2019). In this chapter, we focused our research in two phases. In first phase, we present overview of blockchain consisting of introduction, evolution, related terminology, working of blockchain and its various types. We also demonstrate typical blockchain applications. In next phase, we identify the possible opportunities and better results by coupling blockchain with AI and summarize major challenges to these two techniques. Some possible future directions are shown to explore some new possibilities in this convergence. This integration will not only open new opportunities for more effective secure solutions that will eventually protect users from prime breaches and vulnerabilities, but will also permit a user to take back ownership and control on their personalized information. We would like to explore our research in meaningful embedding of these two technologies that could propel to a substantially higher level of opportunities and results.

REFERENCES

Alharby, M., Aldweesh, A., & Moorsel, A. v. (2018). Blockchain-based Smart Contracts: A Systematic Mapping Study of Academic Research. *International Conference on Cloud Computing, Big Data and Blockchain (ICCBB)*, 1-6. 10.1109/ICCBB.2018.8756390

Alienor, L. (2018). *What is Data Silo and Why it is Bad for Your Organisation*. Retrieved from https://www.plixer.com/blog/data-silo-what-is-it-why-is-it-bad/

Andoni, M., Robu, V., Flynn, D., Abram, S., Geach, D., Jenkins, D., McCallum, P., & Peacock, A. (2019, February). Blockchain technology in the energy sector: A systematic review of challenges and opportunities. *Renewable & Sustainable Energy Reviews*, *100*, 143–174. doi:10.1016/j.rser.2018.10.014

Arenas, R., & Fernandez, P. (2018). CredenceLedger: A Permissioned Blockchain for Verifiable Academic Credentials. *Proceedings of the 2018 IEEE International Conference on Engineering, Technology and Innovation (ICE/ITMC)*, 1–6. 10.1109/ICE.2018.8436324

Artificial Intelligence and Privacy. (2018). *Datatilsynet (Norwegian Data Protection Authority)*. Available at: https://www.datatilsynet.no/globalassets/global/english/ai-and-privacy.pdf

Blockchain-Based Applications in Education: A Systematic Review. (n.d.). College of Computing and Informatics, Saudi Electronic University.

Chen, G., Xu, B., Lu, M., & Chen, N.-S. (2018). Exploring blockchain technology and its potential applications for education. *Smart Learning Environments.*, *5*(1), 1. Advance online publication. doi:10.118640561-017-0050-x

Choudhary, D. (2019). *Human Bias in AI*. Retrieved from https://www.infosys.com/services/incubating-emerging-technologies/offerings/Documents/human-bias.pdf

Cognizant. (2017). *Retail: Opening the Doors to Blockchain*. Available at: https://www.cognizant.com/whitepapers/retail-opening-the-doors-to-blockchain-codex2879.pdf

Dasoriya, R., Rajpopat, J., Jamar, R., & Maurya, M. (2018). The Uncertain Future of Artificial Intelligence. *2018 8th International Conference on Cloud Computing, Data Science & Engineering (Confluence)*, 458-461. 10.1109/CONFLUENCE.2018.8442945

Deshpande, A. (2017). *Distributed ledger technologies/blockchain: Challenges, opportunities and the prospects for standards*. British Standards Inst. Available: https://www.bsigroup.com/LocalFiles/zh-tw/InfoSec-newsletter/No201706/download/BSI_Blockchain_D LT_Web.pdf

Dib, O., Brousmiche, K.-L., Durand, A., Thea, E., & Hamida, E. (2018). Consortium Blockchains: Overview, Applications and Challenges. *International Journal On Advances in Telecommunications, IARIA, 2018*, 51–64.

Dinh & Thai. (2018). AI and Blockchain: A Disruptive Integration. *Computer, 51*(9), 48-53.

Dinh, T. T., Wang, J., Chen, G., Liu, R., Ooi, B. C., & Tan, K.-L. (2017). Blockbench: A framework for analyzing private blockchains. *Proceedings of the 2017 ACM International Conference on Management of Data*, 1085-1100. 10.1145/3035918.3064033

Dinh, T. T. A., Liu, R., Zhang, M., Chen, G., Ooi, B. C., & Wang, J. (2018, July 1). Untangling Blockchain: A Data Processing View of Blockchain Systems. *IEEE Transactions on Knowledge and Data Engineering, 30*(7), 1366–1385. doi:10.1109/TKDE.2017.2781227

Dorri, A., Steger, M., Kanhere, S. S., & Jurdak, R. (2017, December). BlockChain: A distributed solution to automotive security and privacy. *IEEE Communications Magazine, 55*(12), 119–125. doi:10.1109/MCOM.2017.1700879

Finck, M. (2019, May). Smart contracts as a form of solely automated processing under the GDPR. *International Data Privacy Law, 9*(2), 78–94. doi:10.1093/idpl/ipz004

Habib ur Rehman, M., Salah, K., Damiani, E., & Svetinovic, D. (2020). *Towards Blockchain-Based Reputation-Aware Federated Learning*. Academic Press.

Han, M., Li, Z., He, J. S., Wu, D., Xie, Y., & Baba, A. (2018). A Novel Blockchain-based Education Records Verification Solution. *Proceedings of the 19th Annual SIG Conference on Information Technology Education*, 178–183. 10.1145/3241815.3241870

Hardwick, F. S., Akram, R. N., & Markantonakis, K. (2018). *E-voting with blockchain: An e-voting protocol with decentralisation and voter privacy*. Available: https://arxiv.org/abs/1805.10258

Hassan, F., Ali, A., Latif, S., Qadir, J., Kanhere, S., Singh, J., & Crowcroft, J. (2019). *Blockchain And The Future of the Internet: A Comprehensive Review*. Available online: https://www.researchgate.net/publication/331730251_Blockchain_And_The_Future_of_the_Internet_A_Comprehensive_Review

Hileman, G., & Rauchs, M. (2017) Global Blockchain Benchmarking Study. SSRN *Electron. J.* doi:10.2139srn.3040224

Hjálmarsson, F. Þ., Hreiðarsson, G. K., Hamdaqa, M., & Hjálmtýsson, G. (2018). Blockchain-Based E-Voting System. *2018 IEEE 11th International Conference on Cloud Computing (CLOUD)*, 983-986. 10.1109/CLOUD.2018.00151

How to Breakdown Data Silos. (n.d.). *Problems and Solutions*. Retrieved from https://status.net/articles/data-silos-information-silos/

Hu, Y., Liyanage, M., Manzoor, A., Thilakarathna, K., Jourjon, G., & Seneviratne, A. (2019). *Blockchain-based Smart Contracts - Applications and Challenges*. Retrieved from: https://arxiv.org/abs/1810.04699

Internet Security & the Trust Working Group. (2018). Big data, machine learning, consumer protection and privacy. ITU. Available at: https://www.itu.int/en/ITU-T/extcoop/figisymposium/2019/Documents/Presentations/Big%20data,%20Machine%20learning,%20Consumer%20protection%20and%20Privacy.pdf

Jimi, S. (2018). Blockchain: What are nodes and masternodes? *Medium.* https://medium.com/coinmonks/blockchain-what-is-a-node-or-masternode-and-what-does-it-do-4d9a4200938f

Li, X., Jiang, P., Chen, T., Luo, X., & Wen, Q. (2017). A survey on the security of blockchain systems. *Future Generation Computer Systems.*

Li, Z., Kang, J., Yu, R., Ye, D., Deng, Q., & Zhang, Y. (2018). Consortium blockchain for secure energy trading in industrial internet of things. *IEEE Transactions on Industrial Informatics, 14*(8), 3690–3700.

Lu, Q., & Xu, X. (2017, November/December). Adaptable blockchain-based systems: A case study for product traceability. *IEEE Software, 34*(6), 21–27. doi:10.1109/MS.2017.4121227

Makridakis, S., Polemitis, A., & Giaglis, G. (2018). *Blockchain: The Next Breakthrough in the Rapid Progress of AI. Robot Autom Eng J.*

Marwala, T., & Xing, B. (2018). *Blockchain and Artificial Intelligence.* ArXiv, volume=abs/1802.04451.

McKendrick, J. (2017). *Blockchain as Blockbuster: Still Too Soon to Tell.* But Get Ready, Forbes.

Meinert, E., Alturkistani, A., Foley, K., Osama, T., Car, J., Majeed, A., Van Velthoven, M., Wells, G., & Brindley, D. (2018). *Blockchain Implementation in Health Care: Protocol for a Systematic Review.* . doi:10.2196/10994

Monrat, A. A., Schelén, O., & Andersson, K. (2019). Survey of Blockchain from the Perspectives of Applications, Challenges and Opportunities. *IEEE Access.* . doi:10.1109/ACCESS.2019.2936094

Nakamoto, S. (2009). *Bitcoin: A Peer-to-Peer Electronic Cash System.* https://metzdowd.com

Panarello, A., Tapas, N., Merlino, G., Longo, F., & Puliafito, A. (2018). Blockchain and IoT Integration: A Systematic Survey. *Sensors (Basel), 18*(8), 2575. doi:10.339018082575 PMID:30082633

Pandl, K. D., Tiebes, S., Schmidt-Kraepelin, M., & Sunyaev, A. (2020). *On the convergence of artifcial intelligence and distributed ledger technology: A scoping review and future research agenda.* arXiv preprint arXiv:2001.11017.

Restuccia, F., d'Oro, S., Kanhere, S., Melodia, T., & Das, S. (2018). *Blockchain for the Internet of Things: Present and Future.* Available online: https://www.researchgate.net/publication/329044700_Blockchain_for_the_Internet_of_Things_Present_and_Future

Salah, K., Habib ur Rehman, M., Nizamuddin, N., & Al-Fuqaha, A. (2018). Blockchain for AI: Review and Open Research Challenges. *IEEE Access.* doi:10.1109/ACCESS.2018.2890507

Sgantzos, K., & Grigg, I. (2019). Artificial Intelligence Implementations on the Blockchain. Use Cases and Future Applications. *Future Internet, 11*(8), 170. doi:10.3390/fi11080170

Shi, P., Wang, H., Yang, S., Chen, C., & Yang, W. (2019). Blockchain-based trusted data sharing among trusted stakeholders in IoT. *Software, Practice & Experience*, spe.2739. Advance online publication. doi:10.1002pe.2739

Srivastava, A., Bhattacharya, P., Singh, A., & Mathur, A. (2018). *A Systematic Review on Evolution of Blockchain Generations.* Academic Press.

Szabo, N. (n.d.). *Formalizing and Securing Relationships on Public Networks*. Available online: http://ojphi. org/ojs/index.php/fm/article/view/548/469

USDofE. (2017). *Reimagining the Role of Technology in Education: 2017 National Education Technology Plan Update*. U.S. Department of Education. Retrieved From: https://tech.ed.gov/files/2017/01/NETP17.pdf

Wang, K., Dong, J., Wang, Y., & Yin, H. (2019). Securing Data With Blockchain and AI. *IEEE Access: Practical Innovations, Open Solutions*, 7, 77981–77989. doi:10.1109/ACCESS.2019.2921555

Waseem, A. (2017, September 30). Blockchain Technology: Challenges and Future Prospects. *International Journal of Advanced Research in Computer Science*, 08(9), 642–644. doi:10.26483/ijarcs.v8i9.4950

Wolfson, R. (2018, November). Diversifying Data With Artificial Intelligence And Blockchain Technology. *Forbes*. Retrieved from: https://www.forbes.com/sites/rachelwolfson/2018/11/20/diversifying-data-with-artificial-intelligence-and-blockchain-technology/#338157b74dad

Wood, G. (2014). Ethereum: A secure decentralised generalised transaction ledger. Ethereum Project Yellow Paper, 151, 1–32.

Zhang, R., Xue, R., & Liu, L. (2019). Security and privacy on blockchain. ACM Computing Survey. doi:10.1145/3316481

Zheng, Z., Xie, S., Dai, H.-N., Chen, X., & Wang, H. (2017). *An Overview of Blockchain Technology: Architecture*. Consensus, and Future Trends. doi:10.1109/BigDataCongress.2017.85

Zhou, Q., Huang, H., & Zheng, Z. (2020). *Solutions to Scalability of Blockchain: A Survey*. IEEE Access. doi:10.1109/ACCESS.2020.2967218

Chapter 2
Blockchain:
A Ledger for IoT–Enabled Secure Systems

Ranjana Sikarwar

Amity University (AUMP) Gwalior, USA

ABSTRACT

IoT is not the only buzzword proliferating in the technological world nowadays; blockchain, the underlying tech behind Bitcoin cryptocurrency, is also becoming more ubiquitous and mainstream in the world market. Blockchain and IoT are the perfect pair and seem to flourish together as there is an immense need of data security for the enormous data produced by IoT sensors. The integration of two technologies going hand-in-hand can make IoT objects more reliable and secure in the network. Many companies will exploit the integration of blockchain-based IoT systems in the near future as blockchain is more commendable. In the blockchain-based IoT systems, nodes deployed in the blockchain technology are more or less likely the devices connected in the IoT systems network. Blockchain-enabled IoT systems ease business processes and enhance transparency for improved customer experiences.

1. INTRODUCTION

Blockchain and Internet of Things (IoT), has emerged as top cutting-edge technologies (Riya Thakore et al, 2019) and the most captivating concept of the technological era transforming the future of the digital world. IoT enabled objects are smart capable of sharing data and talking online. These devices connect and communicate through internet sends data to the centralized storage like cloud server for exchanging information which may pose threat to the security of the system due to the cyber-attacks and may violate the privacy of the large responsive data produced. So blockchain technology provides a confidential mechanism of exchanging information using a distributed/P2P model (Riya Thakore et al, 2019) in order to accomplish privacy, authentication, and transparency. Blockchain an open, distributed ledger where data is resistant to modification typically managed by a peer-to-peer network using an inter-node communication protocol and validates new blocks in the chain. Blockchain is considered as secure by design. It can reshape and elevate the global infrastructure of the technologies connected with each other through the internet.

DOI: 10.4018/978-1-7998-6694-7.ch002

Let us first understand the basic concepts of IoT and blockchain before going in to the details of transformation caused by the merging of two most popular technologies.

1.1 What is IoT?

To understand the basics of IoT consider the example of a smart phone which can now be used for many purposes like listening to music online, playing games, watching movies, mobile banking, checking emails, sharing data with peers, online reservation etc. But few years back cell phones were used only for the purpose of making calls and sending text messages. They were not smart because were not connected to the internet. But cell phones have become smart phones because they can send or receive data through internet. This is the indispensable theory how objects or devices can become smarter using internet.

Classification of Internet of things can be done as follows:

- **Devices that collect data and act on it**
- Things like smart cars, connected medical devices, watches, etc that receive data from sensors and act in stimuli to that data.
- **Things that aggregate data and send it**
- For example, sensors for monitoring the temperature, moisture and Gas sensors that detect and respond to changes in an environment.
- **Things that perform both functionalities**

Dielectric Soil Moisture Sensors used in IoT farming collect data about moisture levels to know the amount of water required by the crops.

1.2 IoT Architecture

IoT systems need to follow a definite process framework enabling the devices involved in the IOT network to sense the physical environment and respond to the stimuli from the real-world without intervention of humans. Thus, the IoT framework is built for the IoT systems comprising of four stages or layers.

Stage 1(Sensors/Actuators) – Devices involved in the IoT network must be embedded with sensors and actuators has the ability to sense, emit, accept and process signals (Balraj, 2018).

Stage 2(Data Acquisition Systems) - Data Acquisition Systems collect data from the sensors, transform into digital streams for further processing and analysis.

Stage 3(Edge IT/Analytics) – After the IoT data is aggregated, digitized by the Data Acquisition systems it needs further processing and analysis before it is transferred to the data center or cloud. The hardware and the software gateways in the edge IT network pre-process and analyze the data before it enters the data center.

Stage 4(Data Center/Cloud) – Data received from Edge IT center is sent to the cloud for further processing analytics, management, and security control of devices(JR Fuller,2016).

1.3 Challenges in Current IoT Solutions

As current IoT architecture is a centralized one there is a need for proper authentication, trust, and standardization to ensure security in the IoT ecosystem in which vast volume of data is generated by the IoT devices. IoT ecosystem has a centralized architecture where all data is stored and analyzed in the cloud servers thus making data more prone to the Byzantine failure. Thus performance of the system is affected due to increasing number of devices in the network leading to operational delays and redundant data transfers. Blockchain can be used to keep record of data produced by the sensors and avoids duplication with any other malicious data. In a blockchain network; no third party is employed for establishing the trust. Using the client-server model will be an expensive business due to high infrastructure costs, maintenance costs, and low inter-operability because of low data aggregation capability(Riya Thakore et al, 2019). To overcome such challenges for IoT a decentralized architecture will lower all such costs reduced redundancy, services are improved, Byzantine fault resistant. In an IoT based architecture cloud is the center of storing all the data and a single point of failure which can bring down the whole network. Blockchain uses a distributed ledger to remove a single source of failure in the network.

1.4 Applications of IoT

The top trending applications of IoT are smart appliances, smart energy meters, wearable devices, connected cars, and smart health devices. These devices are mainly used in environmental monitoring, surveillance, smart cities, smart homes, and industrial equipments. Some of these applications are briefly described below (Deepa Pavithran, 2020):

A. Smart Homes – Smart home products consist of different appliances like smart-bulbs, air conditioners, washing machines, and refrigerators(Deepa Pavithran et al.,2020), etc. which are promised to save time, energy, and money. This enhances the security of the house and makes life easier by switching on and off appliances remotely to avoid accidents (Johannes Lambrechts, 2016). Detection of windows and doors openings to prevent intruders.

B. Wearables – Wearable IoT devices are small in size embedded with sensors and software which track and collect data and later pre-processes to extract important insights about the user. These devices broadly cover health monitoring, fitness, and entertainment. Wearable application needs to be highly energy-efficient, small in size as a prerequisite for IoT technology.

C. Smart Cities – A smart city is another powerful application of IoT equipped with devices capable of sending and receiving signals through internet. Smart surveillance, automated transportation, smart energy management systems, environment monitoring, etc. are IoT enabled areas of application for smart cities. Smart parking system comprises of sensors to detect vehicles and use web applications to find free available space for parking in the city. (Amandeep Suter, 2019). Smart cities use intelligent technologies to achieve an energy-efficient and environment friendly infrastructure.

D. Smart Metering - Smart Grids, Tank level monitoring, water flow (Johannes Lambrechts, 2016) measurement, monitoring, and optimization of performance in solar energy etc are all applications of real-time IoT applications.

E. Smart Environment – Air pollution control, forest fire detection, snow level monitoring, landslide and avalanche prevention i.e. monitoring of soil moisture, vibrations and earth density to detect dangerous patterns in land condition.

2. WHAT IS BLOCKCHAIN?

The term Blockchain was first coined in the year 1991 by a group of practitioners who wanted to invent a tool for time stamping digital documents so that they are not altered or backdated. Blockchain technology nowadays is gaining popularity after the invention of Bitcoin, the first digital currency. Blockchain was introduced in the year 2008 by a person or a group named Satoshi Nakamoto in 2008 after the invention of cryptocurrency Bitcoin ("Bitcoin: A P2P Electronic Cash System") (S.Nakamoto2008). Typically it is type of a payment rail, a chain of blocks or growing record lists linked together using cryptography. Blockchain is composed of two parts – Blocks, consists of set of transaction and Chain, which consist of blocks in a specific sequence linked to hash values of previous blocks, a timestamp and transaction data represented in the form of a Merkle tree. Some of the challenges IT is facing are decentralization, poor interoperability, privacy, security vulnerabilities which will be overcome by blockchain technology. Blockchain technically is a distributed ledger, cryptographically secured decentralized database which allows for the secure transfer of data between parties (Chrisjan Pauw, 2018) and records every transaction made on a network. The ledger is distributed over a network of nodes which can either be a public network or a private network.

Blockchain allows peer-to-peer transactions, discarding the need of intermediaries.

The two fields that are going to be influenced by it are:

- It creates a decentralized system with peer-to-peer interaction and abandons the necessity of central servers.
- It creates a fully transparent and open to all databases, and prevents overriding of data by individuals using it for their own working.

This technology has the fields mentioned below.

1. **Consensus:** It's an agreed upon protocol by all participating members of the network. Provides the proof of work (POW) and verifies the ledger updation in the networks.
2. **Ledger:** Provides the detailed system of records of transaction within networks.
3. **Cryptography:** Ensures encryption of data in ledger and networks and maintains data integrity also only authorized user can decrypt the information.
4. **Smart contract:** Also known as Chain code is used to verify and validate the participant's terms of business agreement on the network (Hemlata Kohad, 2020).

2.1 Why IoT Needs Blockchain?

IoT needs to implement blockchain for many reasons like security, automation and cost reduction as billions of IoT devices sends data to the centralized cloud architecture currently and in the coming years also. As traditional IoT systems send data to the centralized architecture which has limited reliability, opens billions of weak points hampering network security and will become very expensive and slow if the middleman has to authenticate and check each and every micro transaction between the devices in the network(Chrisjan Pauw, 2018).

Blockchain at its core is a cryptographically secured, decentralized, distributed ledger that removes the involvement of third party and allows for the secure transfer of data between parties(Chrisjan Pauw,

2018). Blockchain makes all the transactions directly and records all transactions cryptographically so that they are not changed or altered once recorded.

Some of the reasons are listed below for the use of blockchain in IoT.

2.1.1 Security for IoT

IoT network comprised of many devices connected to the internet exposed to cyberattacks and hacks.

According to a Gartner Research report, the number of installed IoT devices will reach 20.4 billion by the year 2020(Ashok Kumar Das et al., 2018).

These devices will be more vulnerable to cyberattacks without blockchain. Blockchain is the best solution to protect IoT against hacks and cyberattacks as it records the transaction. Blockchain technology promises to be the missing link enabling peer-to-peer contractual behaviour without any third party to certify the IoT transaction. It answers the challenge of reliability, single point of failure, time stamping, record, privacy, trust, and security (https://www.i-scoop.eu/internet-of-things-guide/blockchain-iot).

2.1.2 Automation to Reduce Costs

As the technology is growing quickly nowadays there is no need to perform certain tasks manually, blockchain enables the automation to complete those processes. A smart contract is one of the aspects of blockchain which can be used for automation in industrial sector. Smart contracts in blockchain network once created allow devices to function autonomously by creating agreements (Chrisjan Pauw, 2018) governed, executed, upheld and carried-out by the blockchain instead of an individual person.

It allows peer-to-peer communication and can automatically deduct monies owed and handles transaction without human intervention. Like a traditional contract, it defines rules and regulations and enforces obligations.

2.2 Types of Blockchain

There are two types of blockchains primarily private and public. Other variations are also available like hybrid and consortium blockchains as shown in fig 1.

1. **Public Blockchains** – A public blockchain is an open-source, non-restrictive system where everyone can read or write data. Anyone can become an authorized node of the network by signing into a blockchain platform through internet. All transactions are fully transparent means that any participating node in the blockchain network is authorized to access current and previous records verify transactions or do proof-of-work for an incoming block and perform mining. Public blockchains are used basically for mining and exchanging Cryptocurrencies. Example – Bitcoin, Ethereum, Litecoin (Mohammad Wazid et. al, 2020).

2. **Private Blockchains** – A private blockchain is a restrictive or permissioned where all the participants are known and trusted. This is useful when blockchain is used within an organization or enterprise where all participants belong to the same network. Examples- Hyperledger and R3 Corda. Mainly used in supply chain management, voting, asset ownership, etc. Example – Multichain and Hyperledger projects (Fabric, Sawtooth, Corda etc).

3. **Hybrid Blockchains –** It uses the features of both public and private blockchain. In a hybrid blockchain system one can have a private permission-based system as well as a public permission-less system (Mohammad Wazid et al.,2020). Only selected data or records from the blockchain can be made public while others are kept as confidential in the private network. Examples include Dragonchair a hybrid blockchain.
4. **Consortium Blockchain –** A consortium blockchain is a semi-decentralized type governed by a group rather than a single entity. Participants in consortium blockchain may include banks, government organizations, etc. Examples of consortium blockchains are Energy web Foundation, R3, etc.

Figure 1. Types of Blockchain

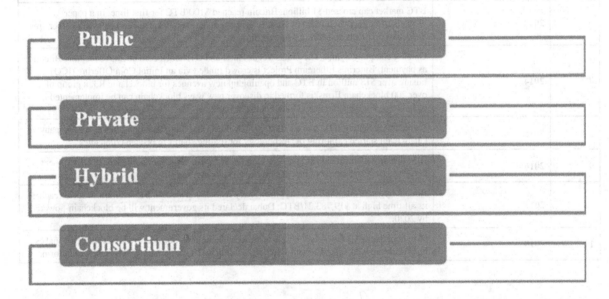

2. 3 History of Blockchain

Some of the most notable and significant incidents in the subsequent development of Blockchain are shown below in Table 1. (Sam Daley 2019, March 16).

2.4 Advantages of Using Blockchain Technology:

1. Allows for scalability, data is resistant to malicious attacks because data is on distributed network of nodes and, greater automation,
2. Cheaper transfers, no third-party needed to administer the transactions.
3. Also prevent overrides by individuals that want to use the data for their own benefit (Chrisjan Pauw, 2018).
4. Security of the network is maintained due to decentralized, cryptographically- secured network.
5. There is no single point of failure thus doesn't bring the whole network down in contrast with a centralized network, single point of failure disables the entire network.

Table 1. History of Blockchain

S.No	Year	Inventions
1	**2008**	"Bitcoin: A Peer to Peer Electronic Cash System." Concept by Satoshi Nakamoto.
2	**2009**	First Bitcoin (BTC) transaction took place between computer scientist Hal Finney and Satoshi Nakamoto successfully.
3	**2010**	Laszlo Hanycez a programmer from Florida undergoes the first purchase using Bitcoin. He transacted 10,000 BTC's, costing about $60 at the time. Current worth is $80 million.
4	**2011**	1 BTC = $1USD, the cryptocurrency compatibility with the US dollar. Electronic Frontier Foundation, Wiki leaks and other organizations considered Bitcoin as donations.
5	**2012**	Blockchain and cryptocurrency are advertised in television shows like *The Good Wife*, injecting blockchain into pop culture. *Bitcoin Magazine* launched by early Bitcoin developer Vitalik Buterin.
6	**2013**	BTC market cap crossed $1 billion. Bitcoin reached $100/BTC for first time. In a paper "Ethereum Project" published by Buterin propounding that blockchain can be used in other areas like smart contracts apart from using as Bitcoin.
7	**2014**	Gaming company Zynga, The D Las Vegas Hotel and Overstock.com all start accepting Bitcoin as payment. Buterin's Ethereum Project is crowd funded via an Initial Coin Offering (ICO) raising over $18 million in BTC and opening up new avenues for blockchain. R3, a group of over 200 blockchain firms, is formed to discover new ways blockchain can be implemented in technology. PayPal announces Bitcoin integration.
8	**2015**	Marketers accepting BTC outrun 100,000. NASDAQ and San-Francisco blockchain company Chain team started exploring the technology for trading shares in private companies.
9	**2016**	IBM declares a blockchain strategy for cloud-based business solutions. Japanese Government perceived the consistency of blockchain and Cryptocurrencies.
10	**2017**	Bitcoin hyped to $1,000/BTC. Cryptocurrency market cap went to $150 billion. Bitcoin reaches its all-time high at $19,783.21/BTC. Dubai declared its government will be blockchain-powered by 2020.
11	**2018**	Face book started a blockchain group and revealed about its cryptocurrency Libra. IBM shakes hand with big banks like Citi and Barclays and initiated a blockchain-based banking platform.

2.5 Working of Blockchain

Blockchain keeps the track of the transactions in chunks of block which are linked using cryptography. Cryptography is a technique in which data communication is made secure by encrypting it thus preventing third parties by sniffing to the private messages. Every related block consists of the necessary information as the hash of the preceding block, hash of current block, timestamp, other information and transactions for that block. When an owner node generates an agreement, it transmits it to all the nodes connected in the system. The node receiving this transaction validates the generated transaction and creates proof of work. In a blockchain proof-of-work is generating data, solving mathematical problems successfully and hence adding the new block to the chain. The winning node of the goodness of proof of work will distribute it to all other nodes and append the block to the chain. The transaction incorporates the public key of the next owner and is digitally signing a hash of transaction of the sender. All the other nodes of the distributed network can validate the genuineity of the transaction (Deepa Pavithran et al,2020).

Figure 2. Working of Blockchain
https://ipspecialist.net/how-blockchain-technology-works

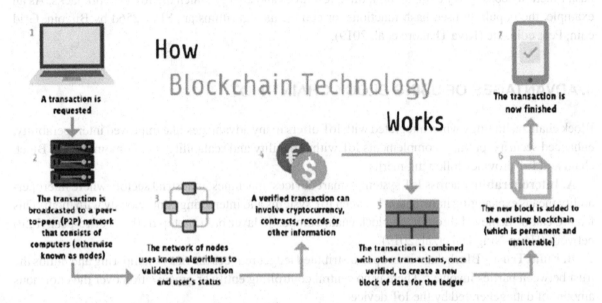

3. DESIGNING OF OPTIMIZED BLOCKCHAIN FOR IOT

The architecture of the blockchain in IoT must be designed to regulate the traffic generated by the nodes in the network. Blockchain system must provide security to protect the data from threats and cyberattacks. It must be designed to provide scalability, transparency, concurrency, etc.

3.1 Architecture

Wireless Sensor Networks – A large collection of sensors in a communication network called nodes with each individual node capable of communication, sensing, actuation, computing with constrained power requirements.

   Agent Node – A special node in blockchain responsible for deploying the smart contract in the network.
   Blockchain Network – A tiered coordinated blockchain system.

3.2 Cryptographic Algorithms Used

To maintain the privacy in the network, transaction is decrypted by the nodes containing sender's public key. To keep up the integrity of data changes or any kind of manipulations may refuse exact decoding. The use of private keys will provide security. Some of the most secure and powerful PKC schemes used are RSA and Elliptic Curve Diffie - Hellman Exchange recommended by NIST. RSA is considered to be energy draining for nodes, steady, computation -intensive thus inappropriate to use. Also Ephemeral Key Exchange has heavy overhead and computation thus not suitable for deployment. So considering the above limitations a simplified RSA, Elliptic Key cryptography is used which shows comparatively enhanced performance on resource constraint devices. A weak mathematical model used can easily tear down the system. The hash functions used in blockchain are very important in their working. A powerful hash function needs heavy computation, time, resources and energy which the IoT network lacks. As an example, the popularly used hash functions for consensus algorithms are SHA-256d by Bitcoin, Grid coin, Peer coin, etc (Riya Thakore et al, 2019).

4. ADVANTAGES OF USING BLOCK CHAIN IN IOT

Block chain technology when integrated with IoT offers many advantages like improved interoperability, enhanced security, privacy, complements IoT with reliability and scalability. The combination of Block chain and IoT provides following merits.

A. Interoperability across IoT systems, smart devices, machines, industrial sectors where interoperability means exchanging information between IoT systems and interacting continuously with them. This feature can be achieved through the block chain composite layer built on top of the peer-to-peer (P2P) network (Hong-Ning Dai et. al, 2019).

B. Build Trust – Blockchain is an open distributed ledger reduces the risk of tampering and builds the trust between parties involved. There is no central controlling entity or organization over the enormous amount of data generated by the IoT devices.

C. Improved Security – Blockchain integrated with IoT provides security against cyber attacks. Real-time threat detection can be detected using machine-learning approaches.

D. Data Exchange for Digital currency – Data is exchanged for the digital currency in a more reliable way using Block chain with IoT.

E. Reduced Costs – Blockchain allows IoT companies to reduce the costs by removing processing overheads of IoT gateways.

F. Increased speed of Transactions – Block chain ensures fast processing of transactions and increased interaction among billions of connected devices.

5. BLOCKCHAIN BASED IOT PLATFORMS

1) IoT Chain

This platform also knows as ITC is specifically designed for IoT devices uses distributed ledger technology to solve IoT security to operate as decentralized network. In the coming years most of the electronics will have some level of smart technology embedded in it to connect and share data. To communicate in the network these devices will require an IoT operating system. This technology can be implemented at the chip level with IoT chain to become a good-to-use platform for such devices in the IoT ecosystem. The IoT Chain is a digital token of the project and wanted to be the basic network for the Internet of Things. This project was developed by the Chinese team of developers who started in 2017 emphasized on the processing of micro operations. The project was initiated with the notion of creating platforms for the communication of "smart devices". This type of network is used in the area of artificial intelligence.

2) IOTA

IOTA is the first blockchain based IoT platform (crypto project) using DAG (Directed Acyclic Graph) particularly made for Internet of Things which provides data transfer layer for connected devices with transaction settlement. This project completely eliminates the idea of paying miner's fee. IOTA is distributed ledger technology (DLT) and in an IOTA network, a new transaction will be added to the chain only ahead of last two transactions.

Figure below compares traditional blockchain data structure with DAG based IOTA.

Figure 3. Blockchain Vs IOTA (Tangle/DAG)

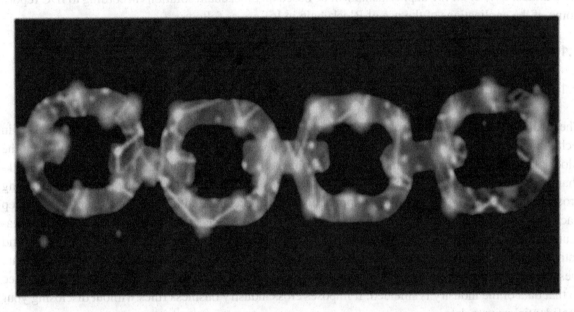

IOTA Tangle platform is a decentralized, block less network integrated with Hyper ledger Fabric systems which is cryptographic where users validate transactions of other users instead of verification by the third party. It is advantageous as it provides scalability and avoids the payment of transaction fees to miners. These features are beneficial in an IoT network (Chrisjan Pauw, 2018) where billions of micro-transactions are processed between the devices regularly extending to fee-less payments, encrypted transaction payload and public/private message chains. When a smart-contract is executed a call is made to this platform to save the output of its execution and for the transactions between the IOTA Wallet holders.

3) Walton Chain

The word Walton in Walton Chain is derived from the name of Charlie Walton who was the inventor of RFID technology. The term Walton can be elaborated as WALTON = Wisdom, Alters Label, Trade, Organization. One block in Walton chain can accommodate up to 255 transaction records. The communication mode used in IoT devices is RFID and the electronic transaction is carried out on the blockchain architecture. This combined technology tracks the products using RFID identification at every step of distribution and production. The data linked with each item is stored on an immutable blockchain which in turn promises its accuracy. Walton chain gave the idea of Value internet of Things to introduce the merged concept of their proprietary RFID chips with blockchain technology. The Software used is the Walton chain protocol and another one is Walton coin.

6. APPLICATIONS OF BLOCKCHAIN IN IOT

The merging of IoT and Blockchain technologies will allow sharing and access of data privately within their network and in this way helps to create a scalable and decentralized ecosystem for IoT devices. By 2019 almost 20% of all IoT deployments will be based on blockchain solutions according to IDC report. Some of the applications of the use of Blockchain in IoT are as follows:

6.1 Application Areas of Blockchain Based IOT

6.1.1. Pharmaceutical Industry

The challenge faced by pharmaceutical sector is the counterfeiting of medicines. The use of Blockchain technology with IoT protects the drug manufacturing process by allowing the stakeholders to keep the Blockchain network updated with real-time on-going activities in the manufacturing process. As block-chain works as a distributed, transparent ledger it is easy to observe and watch the drug manufacturing process and supply. One of the real life applications of Blockchain and IoT is Mediledger that can keep track of all the legalities involved in the medicines. It is an open decentralized network for the pharmaceutical industry. The Mediledger network helps the pharma industry to keep record of transactions and data to exhibit adherence to the regulations and enhances security. It provides permission-based private messaging for the exchange of data between the business partners. It protects the business intelligence so that data of the industry is shielded. It imposes cross industry business rules without disclosing your confidential private data.

6.1.2. Smart Homes Industry

The use of Blockchain technology in IoT used in smart homes enhances the security of the data generated by the IoT devices which are operated remotely from the smart phones.

Blockchain used in IoT can enhance the security of Smart Homes overcoming the drawbacks of centralized infrastructure. As an example, an Australian telecommunication and media company has implemented biometric security to protect the data generated by the smart devices at home from being manipulated. By injecting the Blockchain technology in IoT devices data is accessed only by the authorized persons of home.

6.1.3. Supply chain and Logistics

Supply chain and logistics industry faces a lot of issues in the delay in delivery of the items as there are a number of partners involved in the supply chain network. As IoT- enabled devices are used to keep track of the transport of products at every stage. Transparency of the whole transaction is maintained with blockchain. IoT sensors (for ex motion sensors, GPS, temperature sensor, etc) gives collects and keeps record of the shipment status. The data collected from the IoT sensors is stored in the Blockchain network as useful information for transparency to provide updates to all the participating members in the smart contracts so that they can get the real-time updated information. The combination of Blockchain and IoT adds reliability to the supply chain network. Also they improve the traceability of the goods.

6.1.4. Automotive Industry

Automotive industry also accompanies digitization like other sectors. Therefore, industries promote fully automated vehicles with IoT-enabled sensors in them. These vehicles are IoT & Blockchain enabled helps different involved users to share sensitive information easily and fast. For ex NetObjex is a blockchain automated traffic control. It works in collaboration with PN which is a parking sensor company that performs for real time vehicle detection and for searching vacant available parking slots in the parking area. Also the payments of these are done using crypto-wallets.

6.1.5. Cooperatively Owned Self-Driving Cars

A Blockchain based service can be used in self-driving vehicle sharing among a group of individuals who can enter into an agreement regarding vehicle sharing and its maintenance among themselves. Cooperative groups can form contracts with other groups and share usage of vehicles with other peer groups.

7. IoT Companies Using Blockchain

1. **HELIUM** – Helium is a San Francisco, California based company, recently demonstrated its first successful blockchain transaction. It is the world's first decentralized machine network which uses blockchain to connect low-power IoT machines (like routers and microchips) to the internet. The company uses radio technology for empowering its wireless internet infrastructure (blockchain-based). The team of the company has performed the first successful blockchain-based transaction and is planning to implement their nodes across California, Boston and UK to test their peer-to-peer decentralized network(Sam Daley 2019, March 16).

2. **CHRONICLED** – It uses the combination of Blockchain based IoT devices for an point-to-point supply chain solutions. The company uses IoT based consignments with embedded sensors to produce the real-time shipping information for pharmaceutical and food supply industries. Group of people which are part of the medicine industry or food supply shipping task are updated of custody chain by using blockchain in their IoT devices.

3. **ARCTOUCH** – The company has developed and built blockchain-based software for wearables, smart TV'S, voice assistants etc. Arctouch has developed decentralized apps(DApps) for many companies using IoT devices. As a real-life use-case, many blockchain DApps are built to connect smart devices like Amazon, Alexa and Facebook Messenger (Sam Daley 2019, March 16).

4. **FILAMENT** – This company is located in Reno, Nevada. Filament designed blockchain suite called Blocklet which emphasizes on reinforcing data security in IoT devices for industries. As a use case in real-life Filament developed the Blocklet USB Enclave. The blockchain based device can plug into an USB port and can implement any projects on blockchain(Sam Daley, 2019).

5. **HYPR –** HYPR is located in New York which uses decentralized network to provide security for ATM'S, cars, locks and homes. The systems of centralized databases are more susceptible to cyber attacks storing millions of passwords. HYPR uses decentralized network to secure the important information using biometric protocols like unique facial, eye, voice and palm recognition tools for IoT devices.

CONCLUSION

This chapter provides a detailed description of uses and advantages of implementing Blockchain technology in Internet of Things. The importance of Blockchain technology in IoT has been addressed in depth which may overcome many of the challenges faced by IoT network. With the increase in the number of IoT devices in the network issues of scalability and security arises which can be overcome by the Blockchain network. Blockchain uses distributed model and ensures privacy, security, transparency, scalability, and protection against cyberattacks. This chapter covers the blockchain working, its types, companies using blockchain, and advantages of combining blockchain with IoT.

REFERENCES

Ali, A., & Jan, S. (n.d.). [*A Comparative Analysis of Blockchain Architecture and Its Applications: Problems and Recommendations*. Academic Press.]. *Nadeem, & Alghamdi.*

Balraj. (2018). *Crypto currency: Everything You Need to Know about It*. Retrieved May 13, 2020, from https://pepnewz.com/2018/02/24/cryptocurrency-everything-need-know

Bharani. (2019). *What is IoT (Internet of Things)? IoT Architecture*. Retrieved May 13, 2020, from https://www.edureka.co/blog/what-is-iot

Blockchain and the Internet of Things: the IoT blockchain opportunity and challenge. (n.d.). Retrieved May 13, 2020 from https://www.i-scoop.eu/internet-of-things-guide/blockchain-iot

Dai, Zheng, & Zhang. (2019). Blockchain for Internet of Things: A Survey. *IEEE Internet of Things Journal.*

Daley. (2019). *Blockchain and IoT: 8 examples making our future smarter*. Retrieved May 13, 2020 from https://builtin.com/blockchain/blockchain-iot-examples

Das, Zeadally, & He. (n.d.). Taxonomy and analysis of security protocols for Internet of Things. *Future Generation Computer Systems.*

Fuller, J. R. (2016). *The 4 stages of an IoT architecture*. Retrieved May 13, 2020, from https://techbeacon.com/enterprise-it/4-stages-iot-architecture

Gura, N., Patel, A., Wander, A., Eberle, H., & Shantz, S. C. (2004). Comparing Elliptic Curve Cryptography and RSA on 8-bit CPUs. *Proceedings of the International Workshop on Cryptographic Hardware and Embedded Systems.*

Habib, M., Mehmood, T., Ullah, F., & Ibrahim, M. (2009). Performance of WiMAX Security Algorithm (The Comparative Study of RSA Encryption Algorithm with ECC Encryption Algorithm). *Proceedings of the 2009 International Conference on Computer Technology and Development, 2*, 108-112.

Kohad, H. (2020). Scalability Issues of Blockchain Technology. *International Journal of Engineering and Advanced Technology*.

Lambrechts & Sinha. (2016). *Micro sensing Networks for Sustainable Cities: Pollution as a Key Driving Factor*. https://link.springer.com/chapter/10.1007/978-3-319-28358-6_1

Nakamoto, S. (2008). *Bitcoin: A Peer-to-Peer Electronic Cash System*. https://bitcoin.org/bitcoin.pdf

NIST. (n.d.). https://www.nist.gov

Pauw, C. (2018). *How Significant Is Blockchain in Internet of Things?* https://cointelegraph.com/news/how-significant-is-blockchain-in-internet-of-things

Pavithran, Shaalan, Al-Karaki, & Gawanmeh. (2020). Towards building a blockchain framework for IoT. *Cluster Computing*.

Rivest, R. L., Shamir, A., & Adleman, L. (1978). A method for obtaining digital signatures and public-key cryptosystems. *Communications of the ACM, 21*(2), 120–126. doi:10.1145/359340.359342

Shrestha, R., & Kim, S. (2019). *Integration of IoT with blockchain and homomorphic encryption: Challenging issues and opportunities*. Elsevier BV.

Suter, A. (2019). *How is the Internet Of Things Making Life Safer?* Retrieved May 13, 2020 from https://techstory.in/internet-of-things-making-life-safe

Thakore, R., Vaghashiya, R., Patel, C., & Doshi, N. (2019). Blockchain - based IoT: A Survey. *Proceedings of the 2nd International Workshop on Recent advances on Internet of Things: Technology and Application Approaches (IoT-T&A 2019) 2019*.

Wazid, M., Das, A. K., Shetty, S., & Jo, M. (2020). A Tutorial and Future Research for Building a Blockchain-Based Secure Communication Scheme for Internet of Intelligent Things. *IEEE Access: Practical Innovations, Open Solutions*.

Zhao, S., Li, S., & Yao, Y. (2019). *Blockchain Enabled Industrial Internet of Things Technology. IEEE Transactions on Computational Social Systems*.

Chapter 3
Blockchain for Industrial Internet of Things (IIoT)

Rinki Sharma

Ramaiah University of Applied Sciences, Bangalore, India

ABSTRACT

Over the years, the industrial and manufacturing applications have become highly connected and au-tomated. The incorporation of interconnected smart sensors, actuators, instruments, and other devices helps in establishing higher reliability and efficiency in the industrial and manufacturing process. This has given rise to the industrial internet of things (IIoT). Since IIoT components are scattered all over the network, real-time authenticity of the IIoT activities becomes essential. Blockchain technology is being considered by the researchers as the decentralized architecture to securely process the IIoT transactions. However, there are challenges involved in effective implementation of blockchain in IIoT. This chapter presents the importance of blockchain in IIoT paradigm, its role in different IIoT applications, challenges involved, possible solutions to overcome the challenges and open research issues.

1.1 INTRODUCTION

Industrial Internet of Things (IIoT) refers to the connected industrial applications such as asset monitor-ing, remote control of machinery and automated quality control systems, to name a few. Apart from these applications, connected cars, buildings and industries also play significant role in IIoT. This segment further spans over smart - retail, - supply chain, - cities, - energy and - agriculture (Schneider, 2017). Such wide array of IIoT applications face numerous challenges in terms of security and scalability. Billions of such connected online devices increase the attack surfaces and give rise to numerous weak areas through which the IIoT systems can be hacked. Current IIoT architecture also has characteristics such as centralized design, the legacy client-server model-based communication, lack of multi-vendor interoperability, and personal identifiable data stored and managed by entities that require trust. These characteristics of IIoT make it vulnerable to attacks and difficult to scale (Sengupta, Ruj & Bit, 2020).

Use of blockchain in IIoT environments would help in achieving a tamper proof record of IIoT ac-tivities that is auditable in real-time. Blockchain enables in achieving decentralized architecture (thus

DOI: 10.4018/978-1-7998-6694-7.ch003

eliminating single point of attack), distributed network, peer-to-peer communication model and ability to securely process transactions without involving infrastructure costs and risks of centralized model. Blockchain for IIoT can register, certify and track partnership between multiple parties through a supply chain, and verify it in a secure encrypted environment. It can maintain a truly decentralized and trusted ledger of all the transactions in the network. Blockchain allows to maintain a tamper proof record of IIoT device history, particularly for applications where information generation and exchange needs to be trustworthy (Huang et al., 2019).

While blockchain provides numerous advantages to IIoT, there are challenges in successful and effective implementation of blockchain in IIoT. Scalable and deployable blockchain based IIoT solutions still face numerous challenges such as distributed consensus algorithms and data analytics, with privacy preservation. The key challenge is that blockchain is computationally intensive, while the devices in IIoT platform (such as sensors and edge devices) are battery powered, with minimal data storage and processing power. In case of mobile nodes (as in the connected car environment) problem of intermittent connectivity persists. Private key generation and sharing also is a challenge (Zheng et al., 2018).

Numerous blockchain based IIoT solutions and applications have been proposed and developed by the researchers. However, wide adoption of the solutions is an issue in resource constrained IIoT environments. In this chapter, a comprehensive survey and review of the available blockchain based solutions for IIoT is presented. The limitations and challenges of blockchain implementation in different IIoT sectors is discussed. Based on this study, open issues and research avenues for adoption of blockchain technology in IIoT are presented.

The rest of this chapter is structured as follows. Section 2 presents brief introduction of IIoT and its applications. Section 3 introduces the role of blockchain in IIoT and its characteristics that blockchain useful for IIoT. The role of blockchain in different IIoT applications is also emphasized. While blockchain is important for IIoT, its implementation in IIoT poses numerous challenges. The challenges in adoption of blockchain in IIoT are discussed in Section 4. The research opportunities to support blockchain for IIoT are presented and discussed in Section 5. Section 6 concludes the chapter.

1.2 Industrial Internet of Things (IIoT)

The idea behind Internet of Things (IoT) is to enable the devices communicate and take appropriate action without human intervention thus achieving certain level of automation. Industry 4.0, the fourth industrial revolution, combines the customary industrial and manufacturing platforms with contemporary smart communication technology. Use of technology to connect and automate the industry and manufacturing process, obtain data and carry out analytics to augment these processes further, Industrial Internet of Things (IIoT) is used. The authors in (Weyer, Schmitt, Ohmer & Gorecky 2015) distribute the Industry 4.0 operation into three central paradigms as follows, with the aim of achieving reliable and productive industrial environment:

1.   Smart product: This paradigm takes control of the resources and orchestrates the manufacturing process to its end
2.   Smart machine: This paradigm represents the cyber physical system (CPS) wherein the conventional industrial and manufacturing process transitions into the production lines that are self-organizing, flexible, adaptable and distributed.

3. Augmented operator: This paradigm adds flexibility and capability to the human operator working in the industrial system.

The IIoT is a CPS comprising of machines, computers and people enabling intelligent industrial operations using advanced data analytics to realize transformational business outcomes. Over the years, industrial systems have increased in complexity, leading to inefficient productivity when operated using traditional systems. Present day devices are equipped with sensors, storage, bandwidth and computational power, which allows these industrial machines to be constantly monitored on a large scale. With the help of cloud computing, these devices can be remotely controlled and monitored. Hence IIoT plays a crucial role in present day industrial operations. In most of the cases, IIoT primarily comprises of a network of sensors communicating over wireless medium to each other, or a sink node, or cloud, from where the data can be accessed remotely. Mobility and density of these sensors may lead to increase in network complexity and deterioration in its performance (Sharama, Shankar, & Rajan 2014). Security of data and devices is also a cause of concern in IIoT. However, despite of complexity of implementation and operation, IIoT has gained tremendous popularity in industrial operations.

Some of the industrial application popular for IIoT are:

1. Healthcare
2. Vehicular networks
3. Oil and gas industry
4. Manufacturing
5. Smart building
6. Power industry
7. Smart agriculture
8. Retail and supply chain

This section presents some of the industries to have incorporated the IIoT concepts for enhanced productivity and operation, and the challenges faced by these industries where blockchain can play a crucial role.

Healthcare

IIoT is being actively used in the healthcare industry for applications such as remote patient monitoring, patient rehabilitation, medical waste management, patient fitness and activity tracking, robotic surgery, and in tracing, supply, distribution, monitoring and management of drugs. Numerous smart healthcare devices and systems are commercially available for these purposes (Tyagi, Agarwal & Maheshwari, 2016) and (Sharma, Gupta, Suhas, & Kashyap, 2014).

Vehicular Networks

Autonomous and connected vehicles are equipped with sensors, processing modules and communication units for intra - and inter - vehicle communication. The vehicles communicate with roadside infrastructure and surrounding vehicles for cooperative driving, positioning and navigation. Vehicles form temporary networks known as vehicular ad-hoc networks (VANETs) a subset of mobile ad-hoc networks (MANETs) and communicate over wireless medium with nearby vehicles or roadside units. The topology of MANETs and VANETs is dynamic highly dynamic in nature, leading to connection impairment and interference (Gopinath, Kumar, & Sharma, 2013). Some of the important applications of vehicular networks in IIoT are platooning, road condition updates, e-toll, location-based advertising, retail promotion, infotainment and crowdsensing data (Thriveni, Kumar, & Sharma, 2013).

Oil and Gas Industry

Exploration of oil and gas reservoirs requires high end technology and scientific data. Customary practices involved expensive and unpredictable process of drilling and exploration based on geologist's analysis of the mapping of seafloor. Also, the vast data available on the status and condition of drilling tools, machinery, oil wells, drilling rig was difficult to store and process due to unavailability of sufficient storage and processing resources (Berge, 2018).

Present day oil and gas exploration involves the use of modern sensors, analytics and feedback control systems for enhanced connectivity, monitoring, control and automation (Lu, Guo, Azimi & Huang, 2019). With incorporation of IoT and availability of technological advances such as high bandwidth communication channels, wireless sensors, cloud storage, data analytics and intelligent networking, the process of predictability and exploration of oil and gas reservoirs has become efficient.

Manufacturing

Manufacturing processes can be made more reliable and efficient by integrating IoT. Smart sensors provide optimized asset and inventory management. Constant monitoring of manufacturing process help in achieving agile and energy efficient operations along with reduced machine downtime and operational costs. Some of the advantages achieved by incorporating IoT in manufacturing industry are reduction in operational cost, shorter time-to-market, mass customization, increased safety and reliability (Kiel, Arnold & Voigt, 2017).

Smart Building

Commercial and non-commercial buildings consume volumes of electricity and generate green-house gas emissions. The strategies developed to enhance energy efficiency of the buildings such as improving building insulation and providing better building control systems is difficult to be integrate in old buildings as they were not designed to be energy efficient (Kastner, Kofler, Jung, Gridling, & Weidinger, 2014). IoT plays a major role in efficient energy consumption by these buildings with the help of sensors, actuators and wireless communication. Heating, cooling, air-conditioning, escalators and lighting used in the buildings can be efficiently controlled with the help of sensors depending on the presence of people in the building (Jain, Kaushik, & Jayavel, 2017).

Smart Agriculture

With the help of IoT, smart agriculture helps the farmers with efficient decision making about crops based on weather and soil conditions. Some of the applications of IoT in agriculture are study of climatic conditions, precision farming, smart greenhouse, crop management and data analytics (Brewster, Roussaki, Kalatzis, Doolin, & Ellis, 2017). IoT solutions offer real-time monitoring of weather conditions such as temperature, humidity and rainfall. Based on this information farmers make suitable farming decisions. Precision farming makes the practice of farming more precise and controlled. Precision farming techniques such as livestock management, irrigation management, inventory monitoring, field observation and vehicle tracking increase the farming process manifolds. Solar powered IoT sensors help in real-time monitoring of greenhouse regarding light, temperature, pressure and humidity levels (Gill, Chana, & Buyya, 2017). Data collected by the sensors is stored and analyzed for long term prediction and decision making.

Retail and Supply Chain

Radio Frequency Identification (RFID) tags and sensors are being used in retail and supply chain to make informed decisions about goods and customers. In large retail houses IoT aids location, movement, accounting and stocking of inventory. Based on the sale of certain products, customer-centric decisions can be made to improve sales and customer experience (Jayaram, 2016). The generated consumer data is analyzed to decide the manufacturing status of certain product based on customer demand.

As seen from the above study, the role of IoT present day industry operation is crucial to attain enhanced production and operation efficiency while reducing the machine downtime. While integration of IoT in industrial applications provides numerous advantages, its features such as complex networks, heterogeneous data, support for diverse IoT devices and systems, and decentralization of IoT systems gives rise to the following challenges:

1. Interoperability is difficult to achieve due to heterogeneity among systems and devices.
2. IoT devices primarily comprise of sensor nodes. These nodes are resource constrained with limited processing and battery power.
3. IoT networks are comprises of a mix of static and mobile nodes communicating primarily over a wireless channel. There could be hundreds of diverse IoT sensors and devices communicating over network at a time using different wireless communication protocols. This forms a complex network architecture.

IoT systems are vulnerable to privacy and security as these devices are controlled and communicated through remotely. As the IoT network is decentralized, heterogeneous and comprises of resource constrained mobile nodes communicating over wireless medium, it becomes even more vulnerable to security attacks. Complex authentication and encryption processes are difficult to implement on resource constrained IoT nodes.

1.3 Role of Blockchain in IIoT

The blockchain technology was primarily used for cryptocurrency and secure financial transactions. Over the years, there have been attempts to explore and consider the use of blockchain for other industrial applications. Blockchain is a digital ledger of economic transactions, secured through cryptographic methods. It can be programmed to record the transaction of anything of value. A blockchain is a distributed and decentralized database of transactions that have been executed or shared among the participating nodes. The authors in (Zheng, Xie, Dai, Chen, & Wang, 2018) list decentralization, anonymity, chronological order of data, distributed security, transparency, immutability and stability of trustless environments as the advantages of blockchain. Since it is a distributed ledger, instead of single database or organization keeping transaction records, the records can be made available to other computers anonymously.

1.3.1. Characteristics of Blockchain Helpful for IIoT

- *Distributed database:* Every participating node in the blockchain has access to entire database. Therefore, no single entity has a control over the database. This increases the reliability of the records on database as it can be verified by any node.
- *Transparency:* As the database is distributed, the transactions are visible to everyone. These transactions are indelible once validated by the network.
- *Irreversible records:* If a transaction needs to be changed, then every other block in the chain need to be amended. This makes manipulation of records impossible.
- *Peer-to-peer communication:* In blockchain, all participating nodes are peers, unlike client-server architecture prevalent over Internet. There is no central node in the network. Therefore, very node is capable of communicating with every other node.

With all the above said advantages, blockchain is being considered highly beneficial for secure and trustworthy transactions in IIoT. This section presents the application of blockchain in different aspects of IIoT.

1.3.2 Blockchain for Healthcare

Management of patient data: Remote sharing and exchange of patient health records is vulnerable to security and reliability concerns. The incidents of mismatched patient records can be drastically reduced with the use of blockchain. Conventionally, the patient health records have remained fragmented. Blockchain facilitates the integration of patient health records by providing a structure for securely sharing the data with stakeholders. The stakeholders can access the patient records authentically, securely and reliably. The accessed data can be stored in the cloud for remote access in future. With the use of blockchain, the records of numerous patients can be monitored to identify the spread of diseases over a particular age group or region (Esposito et al, 2018) and (Ekblaw, Azaria, Halamka, & Lippman, 2016).

Drug supply chain: Drug supply and drug counterfeiting are the major issues faced by the pharmaceutical industry. In blockchain, every transaction in the block is timestamped and immutable thus making is easy to track them. The ability of tracking the products by using blockchain allows the pharmaceutical companies to monitor their supply chain to track and detect counterfeit medicines (Clauson, Breeden, Davidson, & Mackey, 2018) and (Jamil, Hang, Kim, & Kim, 2019).

1.3.3 Blockchain for Vehicular Networks

Secure message dissemination: Connected and autonomous vehicular networks are essential for intelligent transportation. In VANETs, the vehicular nodes can join and leave the network dynamically as in MANETs. This dynamic nature of the network also permits the entry of malicious nodes into the network. These malicious nodes can propagate false and untrustworthy information over the network. To overcome this issue of malicious data exchange, blockchain is being considered to support secure and trustworthy message dissemination. The blockchain can store and manage the history of trustworthiness of the messages exchanged and trust levels of the vehicular nodes propagating the messages, as a distributed and reliable solution (Mendiboure, Chalouf, & Krief, 2020) and (Shrestha, Bajracharya, Shrestha, & Nam, 2020).

1.3.4 Blockchain for Oil and Gas Industry

Digitized transactions: Oil and gas companies manage sale of crude oil and land worth millions of dollars. Conventional methods of maintaining records of such transactions has been cumbersome, prone to forgery and illicit activities. The use of blockchain is considered to bring enhanced security, transparency and efficiency in this industry (Berge, 2018) and (Ajao, Agajo, Adedokun, & Karngong, 2019).

Improved trust among parties: A private blockchain network can store the track record of employee and contractor certifications. This can be used to in future by the stakeholders before engaging in any transactions (Lu, Huang, Azimi, & Guo, 2019).

1.3.5 Blockchain for Manufacturing

Enhanced reliability and efficiency of manufacturing process: Incorporating blockchain in the manufacturing process enables the manufacturers with streamlining manufacturing operations, gaining better visibility into the supply chain and tracking the assets with precision. Blockchain is considered to enhance transparency and trust at different stages of manufacturing process such as supply chain monitoring, material provenance, counterfeit detection, identity management, asset tracking, quality assurance and regulatory compliance (Abeyratne & Monfared, 2016).

1.3.6 Blockchain for Smart Building

Efficient power management and billing: With the use of sensors and IoT, smart buildings can control power consumption based on the presence of people in the building. In case of absence of occupants in some area of the building, the power can be turned off, thus saving energy. A building may have different sections having different occupants. Based on the usage by the occupants of different sections of the building, billing can be controlled (Miglani, Kumar, Chamola, & Zeadally, 2020). This helps in efficiently controlling the usage of energy and billing.

1.3.7 Blockchain for Smart Agriculture

Agricultural produce traceability: Farmers, consumers and other stakeholders can maintain and obtain reliable information origins, produce and harvest of the agricultural produce. This enables consumers to trace the journey of the produce and keep a tab on its freshness, leading to timely food consumption and reducing food wastage (Caro, Ali, Vecchio, & Giaffreda, 2018) and (Salah, Nizamuddin, Jayaraman, & Omar, 2019).

Secure transactions and crop insurance: Enables farmers to sell their crops at fair price and benefit from agro commerce and micro-financing. Crop insurance involves communication of information regarding produce, its location and other basic compliance information with carriers. With better visibility about the crops, the participants can obtain reliable information about price, location, quality and state of the product (Tripoli & Schmidhuber, 2018) and (Kim & Laskowski, 2018).

1.3.8 Blockchain for Retail and Supply Chain

Retail and supply chain tracking: By integrating blockchain to the retail and supply chain industry the products can be tracked all the way from manufacturer to consumer. This ensures reliability in supply chain while overcoming the problem of counterfeiting of products. The production details are published in the blockchain by the manufacturer. The transit, logistics and retail details are further updated at the end of logistics partner, warehouse and retailer respectively (Azzi, Chamoun & Sokhn, 2019).

1.4 Challenges With Adoption of Blockchain Technology in IIoT

The IIoT nodes are mainly sensors or other small devices that are resource constrained in terms of storage and computational power. Therefore, adoption of blockchain technology becomes challenging in IIoT, despite of its advantages. Some the main challenges faced by adoption of blockchain in IIoT are as follows (Khan & Salah, 2018) and (Golatowski et al., 2019):

Scalability: The blockchain ledger increases with every transaction. More the number of nodes involved in the blockchain, larger will be the size of the ledger. As IIoT nodes are resource constrained, storage and computation of big ledgers is difficult. This also puts a limit on scale of the blockchain.

Storage: As all the nodes in a blockchain are peers, and there is no central entity to store transaction details and device IDs, this information has to be stored at the nodes itself. For resource constrained IIoT nodes this is a challenge.

Security: While blockchain is secure and robust against hacks, the IIoT applications running over the blockchain platform may not be secure. These connected devices stand huge risk of identity and data theft, device manipulation, data falsification and network manipulation. This calls for the need of mechanisms to identify and prevent the attacks on the IIoT systems.

Processing: Blockchain uses complex encryption and authentication mechanisms. Most of the participating nodes in blockchain may not be equipped with appropriate processing and computation resources required for such complex computations.

Intermittent connectivity: Mobile IoT devices require reliable bidirectional signaling between the IoT devices. Node mobility leads to breakages in connection leading to loss of data or delay in data transfer.

Bandwidth: The surge in the number of IoT devices and the data exchanged between them leads to bottleneck in the network. Reliable data exchange at required data rate requires sufficient bandwidth.

Time - critical applications: Time - critical applications such as healthcare, industrial control, mobility automation and real - time media need high bandwidth, data rate and low latency.

1.5 Research Opportunities to Support Blockchain for IIoT

As discussed in the Section 1.4, while the implementation of blockchain brings in numerous advantages to the field of IIoT, it brings in many challenges as well. This Section presents the research carried out in this field and available research opportunities.

1.5.1 Artificial Intelligence for Blockchain Based IIoT

In spite of blockchain being secure and robust against attacks, the IIoT applications running over blockchain may not be secure. AI can be used to perceive any threats that the blockchain based IIoT system could be vulnerable to. With AI, the application data can be traced and anomalies, fraud, delays and other external events can be detected (Golatowski et al., 2019).

Intelligent AI and ML algorithms are used to detect the presence of attacks in early stages in the IIoT applications and take appropriate action to prevent the damage, such as isolating the attacked component of the blockchain platform to keep the rest of it safe.

To support scalability, AI can increase the block creation rate in case of increasing number of transactions so that the throughput can be increased at the cost of longer confirmation times (Dinh & Thai, 2018).

1.5.2 Security in Blockchain Based IIoT

While the blockchain is secure and robust, the IIoT applications running over it may not be fully secure. Increasing number of connected IIoT devices also increase the number of threats and vulnerabilities of these devices. Attackers exploit these vulnerabilities through various tools and malicious codes. IIoT devices face threats that can be primarily classified under four different categories: Intruder attacks, Denial of Service (DoS), physical attacks and attacks on privacy (Rizvi, Kurtz, Pfeffer, & Rizvi, 2018).

Researchers are working on developing solutions to defend these attacks. In (Ometov et al., 2019) propose the adoption of multi-factor authentication such that multiple heterogenous factors can be combined to control access to IIoT devices and networks. For this, enablers such as hardware tokens, memorable passwords/PINs, fingerprint/palm/eye scanner, facial recognition, voice recognition, data from wearables and behavioral patterns are used. Authors in [38] emphasize the use of AI and ML to identify, predict and defend the security risks for IIoT devices and network. Authors in (Krishnan, Najeem & Achuthan, 2017) have developed a software defined networking (SDN) based framework for securing IoT networks. SDN is considered to be appropriate for providing security to IoT network due to its ability to securely connect millions of connected IoT devices, program dynamically for enforcing custom policies and applications, constant network security monitoring and dynamic network configuration to avoid malicious activity.

1.5.3 SDN and NFV for Blockchain Based IIoT

IIoT involves large number of devices with heterogenous characteristics. The participating devices and related applications have different data rate, throughput and latency requirements. As the participating devices in IIoT are diverse in terms of their capabilities (processor, memory and storage), have different performance requirements, and support different communication standards, traditional networking methods are not suitable for these networks. Use of SDN and NFV can help in achieving cost effective scaling and versatility of IIoT networks. NFV helps in reducing the CAPEX and OPEX cost of the network by sharing the network infrastructure for different services and applications (Ananth & Sharma, 2017) and ((Ananth & Sharma, 2016). It also provides customizability to the network through network slicing and subnet isolation.

As the network scales network bandwidth requirements also increase. SDN can dynamically configure network bandwidth based on network traffic and performance requirements of time-critical applications. Multiple paths can be used for route the data and load balancers can be used for faster data processing (Sharma & Reddy, 2019).

Mobile IIoT applications such as mobile ad-hoc networks (MANETs) and vehicular ad-hoc networks (VANETs) undergo network connectivity issues due to node mobility. Highly dynamic nature of these networks calls for dynamic allocation of network resources for QoS provisioning. The use of SDN in a VANET is explored in (Ku et al., 2014) and (Zhu, Cao, Pang, He, & Xu, 2015).

1.5.4 Big Data for Blockchain Based IIoT

IIoT applications generate thousands of Gigabytes of data per day. Huge digital data is generated by both humans and machines in diverse fields. Volumes of data is used in IIoT to streamline and optimize industrial functions, and to attain transparency in supply chain process. Big data is used to address specific problems in logistics processes (Teslya & Ryabchikov, 2017). In vehicular networks, big data produced from sensors is used to monitor weather and traffic conditions, study driving patterns, advertising and forecasts, and for vehicle diagnostics. The concern is safety and reliability of big data. This is where blockchain plays an important role. Multiple independent nodes in the IIoT blockchain can confirm ledger addition, and detect inconsistent and inaccurate records (Tariq et al., 2019). However, all of these devices are not capable of storing and processing the data. Therefore, advanced, efficient and robust techniques are required to handle such big data in terms of its acquisition, transmission, storage, computation, analytics and processing.

1.5.5 Bandwidth Enhancement for Mobile IIoT

As the IIoT applications gain popularity, data surge for these applications has led to bottleneck in the network. In mobile IIoT applications such as MANETs and VANETs, the node position changes rapidly and continuously. This makes it difficult to maintain the network connectivity. Many researchers are working on increasing the capacity and data rate of wireless communication channels. To increase the distance of wireless communication, contemporary wireless standards and devices use directional antenna (Nitsche et al., 2014). Directional antenna is used to direct energy and extend communication range in these networks (Sharma, Kadambi, Vershinin & Mukundan, 2015) and (Perahia & Gong, 2011). Antenna directivity combined with dual polarization increases network bandwidth, data rate and network throughput to maintain quality provisioning in highly dynamic mobile networks (Sharma, Kadambi, Vershinin & Mukundan, 2015) and (Rinki, 2014). Apart from mobile nodes, time - critical applications such as healthcare, industrial control, mobility automation and real - time media that need high bandwidth, data rate and low latency also get benefitted by dual polarized directional antenna (DPDA) based solutions. Present day wireless standards such as IEEE 802.11 ab, ad and 5G and 6G wireless communication technologies make use of antenna directivity and MIMO (Perahia & Gong, 2011) and (Zhang et al., 2019).

1.6 CONCLUSION

The way of carrying out operations in different industries has changed tremendously with IoT. Increase of IIoT applications calls for secure, reliable and robust IIoT communication. Blockchain technology's decentralized and distributed architecture plays a crucial role in securing IIoT communication and transactions. This chapter presents the role of Blockchain on in present day IIoT applications. The chapter presented the popular IIoT applications and the importance of blockchain in securing these applications. The challenges of adopting blockchain in IIoT are also discussed. A great deal of research is taking place to overcome these challenges. The research opportunities and open research issues in complete adoption of blockchain in IIoT are discussed with the aim to help the researchers in this domain.

REFERENCES

Abeyratne, S. A., & Monfared, R. P. (2016). Blockchain ready manufacturing supply chain using distributed ledger. *International Journal of Research in Engineering and Technology, 5*(9), 1–10. doi:10.15623/ijret.2016.0509001

Ajao, L. A., Agajo, J., Adedokun, E. A., & Karngong, L. (2019). Crypto hash algorithm-based blockchain technology for managing decentralized ledger database in oil and gas industry. *J—Multidisciplinary Scientific Journal, 2*(3), 300-325.

Ananth, M. D., & Sharma, R. (2016, December). Cloud management using network function virtualization to reduce capex and opex. In *2016 8th International Conference on Computational Intelligence and Communication Networks (CICN)* (pp. 43-47). IEEE. 10.1109/CICN.2016.17

Ananth, M. D., & Sharma, R. (2017, January). Cost and performance analysis of network function virtualization based cloud systems. In *2017 IEEE 7th International Advance Computing Conference (IACC)* (pp. 70-74). IEEE. 10.1109/IACC.2017.0029

Azzi, R., Chamoun, R. K., & Sokhn, M. (2019). The power of a blockchain-based supply chain. *Computers & Industrial Engineering, 135*, 582–592. doi:10.1016/j.cie.2019.06.042

Berge, J. (2018, April). Digital Transformation and IIoT for Oil and Gas Production. In *Offshore Technology Conference*. Offshore Technology Conference. 10.4043/28643-MS

Brewster, C., Roussaki, I., Kalatzis, N., Doolin, K., & Ellis, K. (2017). IoT in agriculture: Designing a Europe-wide large-scale pilot. *IEEE Communications Magazine, 55*(9), 26–33. doi:10.1109/MCOM.2017.1600528

Caro, M. P., Ali, M. S., Vecchio, M., & Giaffreda, R. (2018, May). Blockchain-based traceability in Agri-Food supply chain management: A practical implementation. In 2018 IoT Vertical and Topical Summit on Agriculture-Tuscany (IOT Tuscany) (pp. 1-4). IEEE. doi:10.1109/IOT-TUSCANY.2018.8373021

Clauson, K. A., Breeden, E. A., Davidson, C., & Mackey, T. K. (2018). Leveraging blockchain technology to enhance supply chain management in healthcare: an exploration of challenges and opportunities in the health supply chain. *Blockchain in Healthcare Today, 1*(3), 1-12.

Dinh, T. N., & Thai, M. T. (2018). Ai and blockchain: A disruptive integration. *Computer, 51*(9), 48–53. doi:10.1109/MC.2018.3620971

Ekblaw, A., Azaria, A., Halamka, J. D., & Lippman, A. (2016, August). A Case Study for Blockchain in Healthcare:"MedRec" prototype for electronic health records and medical research data. In *Proceedings of IEEE open & big data conference (Vol. 13*, p. 13). Academic Press.

Esposito, C., De Santis, A., Tortora, G., Chang, H., & Choo, K. K. R. (2018). Blockchain: A panacea for healthcare cloud-based data security and privacy? *IEEE Cloud Computing, 5*(1), 31–37. doi:10.1109/MCC.2018.011791712

Gill, S. S., Chana, I., & Buyya, R. (2017). IoT based agriculture as a cloud and big data service: The beginning of digital India. *Journal of Organizational and End User Computing, 29*(4), 1–23. doi:10.4018/JOEUC.2017100101

Golatowski, F., Butzin, B., Brockmann, T., Schulz, T., Kasparick, M., Li, Y., ... Aydemir, Ö. (2019, May). Challenges and research directions for blockchains in the internet of things. In *2019 IEEE International Conference on Industrial Cyber Physical Systems (ICPS)* (pp. 712-717). IEEE. 10.1109/ICPHYS.2019.8780270

Gopinath, T., Kumar, A. R., & Sharma, R. (2013, April). Performance evaluation of TCP and UDP over wireless ad-hoc networks with varying traffic loads. In *2013 International Conference on Communication Systems and Network Technologies* (pp. 281-285). IEEE. 10.1109/CSNT.2013.66

Huang, J., Kong, L., Chen, G., Wu, M. Y., Liu, X., & Zeng, P. (2019). Towards secure industrial IoT: Blockchain system with credit-based consensus mechanism. *IEEE Transactions on Industrial Informatics, 15*(6), 3680–3689. doi:10.1109/TII.2019.2903342

Jain, M., Kaushik, N., & Jayavel, K. (2017, February). Building automation and energy control using IoT-Smart campus. In *2017 2nd International Conference on Computing and Communications Technologies (ICCCT)* (pp. 353-359). IEEE. 10.1109/ICCCT2.2017.7972303

Jamil, F., Hang, L., Kim, K., & Kim, D. (2019). A novel medical blockchain model for drug supply chain integrity management in a smart hospital. *Electronics (Basel), 8*(5), 505. doi:10.3390/electronics8050505

Jayaram, A. (2016, December). Lean six sigma approach for global supply chain management using industry 4.0 and IIoT. In *2016 2nd international conference on contemporary computing and informatics (IC3I)* (pp. 89-94). IEEE.

Kastner, W., Kofler, M., Jung, M., Gridling, G., & Weidinger, J. (2014, September). Building Automation Systems Integration into the Internet of Things The IoT6 approach, its realization and validation. In *Proceedings of the 2014 IEEE Emerging Technology and Factory Automation (ETFA)* (pp. 1-9). IEEE. 10.1109/ETFA.2014.7005197

Khan, M. A., & Salah, K. (2018). IoT security: Review, blockchain solutions, and open challenges. *Future Generation Computer Systems, 82*, 395–411. doi:10.1016/j.future.2017.11.022

Kiel, D., Arnold, C., & Voigt, K. I. (2017). The influence of the Industrial Internet of Things on business models of established manufacturing companies–A business level perspective. *Technovation, 68*, 4–19. doi:10.1016/j.technovation.2017.09.003

Kim, H. M., & Laskowski, M. (2018). Agriculture on the blockchain: Sustainable solutions for food, farmers, and financing. In *Supply Chain Revolution*. Barrow Books.

Krishnan, P., Najeem, J. S., & Achuthan, K. (2017, August). SDN framework for securing IoT networks. In *International Conference on Ubiquitous Communications and Network Computing* (pp. 116-129). Springer.

Ku, I., Lu, Y., Gerla, M., Gomes, R. L., Ongaro, F., & Cerqueira, E. (2014, June). Towards software-defined VANET: Architecture and services. In *2014 13th annual Mediterranean ad hoc networking workshop (MED-HOC-NET)* (pp. 103-110). IEEE.

Lu, H., Guo, L., Azimi, M., & Huang, K. (2019). Oil and Gas 4.0 era: A systematic review and outlook. *Computers in Industry, 111*, 68–90. doi:10.1016/j.compind.2019.06.007

Lu, H., Huang, K., Azimi, M., & Guo, L. (2019). Blockchain technology in the oil and gas industry: A review of applications, opportunities, challenges, and risks. *IEEE Access: Practical Innovations, Open Solutions, 7*, 41426–41444. doi:10.1109/ACCESS.2019.2907695

Mendiboure, L., Chalouf, M. A., & Krief, F. (2020). Survey on blockchain-based applications in internet of vehicles. *Computers & Electrical Engineering, 84*, 106646. doi:10.1016/j.compeleceng.2020.106646

Miglani, A., Kumar, N., Chamola, V., & Zeadally, S. (2020). Blockchain for Internet of Energy management: Review, solutions, and challenges. *Computer Communications, 151*, 395–418. doi:10.1016/j.comcom.2020.01.014

Nitsche, T., Cordeiro, C., Flores, A. B., Knightly, E. W., Perahia, E., & Widmer, J. C. (2014). IEEE 802.11 ad: Directional 60 GHz communication for multi-Gigabit-per-second Wi-Fi. *IEEE Communications Magazine, 52*(12), 132–141. doi:10.1109/MCOM.2014.6979964

Ometov, A., Petrov, V., Bezzateev, S., Andreev, S., Koucheryavy, Y., & Gerla, M. (2019). Challenges of multi-factor authentication for securing advanced IoT applications. *IEEE Network, 33*(2), 82–88. doi:10.1109/MNET.2019.1800240

Perahia, E., & Gong, M. X. (2011). Gigabit wireless LANs: An overview of IEEE 802.11 ac and 802.11 ad. *Mobile Computing and Communications Review, 15*(3), 23–33. doi:10.1145/2073290.2073294

Rinki, S. (2014). *Simulation studies on effects of dual polarisation and directivity of antennas on the performance of MANETs* (Doctoral dissertation). Coventry University.

Rizvi, S., Kurtz, A., Pfeffer, J., & Rizvi, M. (2018, August). Securing the Internet of Things (IoT): A security taxonomy for IoT. In *2018 17th IEEE International Conference On Trust, Security And Privacy In Computing And Communications/12th IEEE International Conference On Big Data Science And Engineering (TrustCom/BigDataSE)* (pp. 163-168). IEEE.

Salah, K., Nizamuddin, N., Jayaraman, R., & Omar, M. (2019). Blockchain-based soybean traceability in agricultural supply chain. *IEEE Access: Practical Innovations, Open Solutions, 7*, 73295–73305. doi:10.1109/ACCESS.2019.2918000

Schneider, S. (2017). The industrial internet of things (iiot) applications and taxonomy. *Internet of Things and Data Analytics Handbook*, 41-81.

Sengupta, J., Ruj, S., & Bit, S. D. (2020). A Comprehensive survey on attacks, security issues and blockchain solutions for IoT and IIoT. *Journal of Network and Computer Applications*, *149*, 102481. doi:10.1016/j.jnca.2019.102481

Sharama, R., Shankar, J. U., & Rajan, S. T. (2014, April). Effect of Number of Active Nodes and Inter-node Distance on the Performance of Wireless Sensor Networks. In *2014 Fourth International Conference on Communication Systems and Network Technologies* (pp. 69-73). IEEE. 10.1109/CSNT.2014.22

Sharma, R., Gupta, S. K., Suhas, K. K., & Kashyap, G. S. (2014, April). Performance analysis of Zigbee based wireless sensor network for remote patient monitoring. In *2014 Fourth International Conference on Communication Systems and Network Technologies* (pp. 58-62). IEEE. 10.1109/CSNT.2014.21

Sharma, R., Kadambi, G. R., Vershinin, Y. A., & Mukundan, K. N. (2015, April). Dual Polarised Directional Communication based Medium Access Control Protocol for Performance Enhancement of MANETs. In *2015 Fifth International Conference on Communication Systems and Network Technologies* (pp. 185-189). IEEE. 10.1109/CSNT.2015.104

Sharma, R., Kadambi, G. R., Vershinin, Y. A., & Mukundan, K. N. (2015, April). Multipath Routing Protocol to Support Dual Polarised Directional Communication for Performance Enhancement of MANETs. In *2015 Fifth International Conference on Communication Systems and Network Technologies* (pp. 258-262). IEEE. 10.1109/CSNT.2015.105

Sharma, R., & Reddy, H. (2019, December). Effect of Load Balancer on Software-Defined Networking (SDN) based Cloud. In *2019 IEEE 16th India Council International Conference (INDICON)* (pp. 1-4). IEEE.

Shrestha, R., Bajracharya, R., Shrestha, A. P., & Nam, S. Y. (2020). A new type of blockchain for secure message exchange in VANET. *Digital Communications and Networks*, *6*(2), 177–186. doi:10.1016/j.dcan.2019.04.003

Tariq, N., Asim, M., Al-Obeidat, F., Zubair Farooqi, M., Baker, T., Hammoudeh, M., & Ghafir, I. (2019). The security of big data in fog-enabled IoT applications including blockchain: A survey. *Sensors (Basel)*, *19*(8), 1788. doi:10.339019081788 PMID:31013993

Teslya, N., & Ryabchikov, I. (2017, November). Blockchain-based platform architecture for industrial IoT. In *2017 21st Conference of Open Innovations Association (FRUCT)* (pp. 321-329). IEEE. 10.23919/FRUCT.2017.8250199

Thriveni, H. B., Kumar, G. M., & Sharma, R. (2013, April). Performance evaluation of routing protocols in mobile ad-hoc networks with varying node density and node mobility. In *2013 International Conference on Communication Systems and Network Technologies* (pp. 252-256). IEEE. 10.1109/CSNT.2013.60

Tripoli, M., & Schmidhuber, J. (2018). *Emerging Opportunities for the Application of Blockchain in the Agri-food Industry*. FAO and ICTSD: Rome and Geneva. Licence: CC BY-NC-SA, 3.

Tyagi, S., Agarwal, A., & Maheshwari, P. (2016, January). A conceptual framework for IoT-based healthcare system using cloud computing. In *2016 6th International Conference-Cloud System and Big Data Engineering (Confluence)* (pp. 503-507). IEEE. doi:10.1109/CONFLUENCE.2016.7508172

Weyer, S., Schmitt, M., Ohmer, M., & Gorecky, D. (2015). Towards Industry 4.0-Standardization as the crucial challenge for highly modular, multi-vendor production systems. *IFAC-PapersOnLine, 48*(3), 579–584. doi:10.1016/j.ifacol.2015.06.143

Zhang, Z., Xiao, Y., Ma, Z., Xiao, M., Ding, Z., Lei, X., Karagiannidis, G. K., & Fan, P. (2019). 6G wireless networks: Vision, requirements, architecture, and key technologies. *IEEE Vehicular Technology Magazine, 14*(3), 28–41. doi:10.1109/MVT.2019.2921208

Zheng, Z., Xie, S., Dai, H. N., Chen, X., & Wang, H. (2018). Blockchain challenges and opportunities: A survey. *International Journal of Web and Grid Services, 14*(4), 352–375. doi:10.1504/IJWGS.2018.095647

Zheng, Z., Xie, S., Dai, H. N., Chen, X., & Wang, H. (2018). Blockchain challenges and opportunities: A survey. *International Journal of Web and Grid Services, 14*(4), 352–375. doi:10.1504/IJWGS.2018.095647

Zhu, M., Cao, J., Pang, D., He, Z., & Xu, M. (2015, August). SDN-based routing for efficient message propagation in VANET. In *International Conference on Wireless Algorithms, Systems, and Applications* (pp. 788-797). Springer. 10.1007/978-3-319-21837-3_77

APPENDIX

List of abbreviations:

5G Fifth Generation

6G Sixth Generation

AI Artificial Intelligence

CAPEX Capital Expenditure

CPS Cyber Physical System

DoS Denial of Service

DPDA Dual Polarized Directional Antenna

ID Identifier

IIoT Industrial Internet of Things

IoT Internet of Things

MANET Mobile Ad-hoc Network

MIMO Multi Input Multi Output

ML Machine Learning

NFV Network Function Virtualization

OPEX Operational Expenditure

PIN Personal Identification Number

QoS Quality of Service

RFID Radio Frequency Identification

SDN Software Defined Networking

VANET Vehicular Ad-hoc Network

Chapter 4
Adaptation of Blockchain Architecture to the Internet of Things and Performance Analysis

Mevlut Ersoy
Suleyman Demirel University, Turkey

Asım Sinan Yüksel
Suleyman Demirel University, Turkey

Cihan Yalcin
Suleyman Demirel University, Turkey

ABSTRACT

Internet of Things (IoT) security and privacy criteria are seen as an important challenge due to IoT architecture. In this study, the security of the IoT system that is created with devices integrated into the embedded system by means of various sensors has been ensured by using a single cryptographic structure. The data transmitted between the nodes in the IoT structure is transmitted to the central node using the Blockchain data structure. The transmitted data is verified at central nodes and the energies consumed between nodes during the transmission phase is detected. An infrastructure has been developed for how blockchain technology can be used in the IoT structure. In this study, an experimental environment was developed and comparative analysis were made in terms of energy consumption and data transfer rates.

INTRODUCTION

IoT devices consist of different sensors and technologies in today's conditions. They collect data from certain environments, communicate with each other and create information services for the users. Within the context of IoT, an estimated 10-11 billion devices are assumed to be interconnected. These devices

DOI: 10.4018/978-1-7998-6694-7.ch004

do not have autonomous defense skills against malicious approaches. The immature IoT standards are the main reason for this. Besides that, hardware and software modules that are used in IoT devices are non-standardized. Design, development, distribution processes are not hierarchical. Efforts to define a global security mechanism to secure the IoT devices and data transfers have also become a difficult problem to solve due to the diversity of resources on the Internet of Things. To solve this problem, the Internet of Blockchain-Based Things has been developed.

The rapid increase of the network devices and increasing number of cyber-attacks during the data transfer has revealed the necessity to develop solutions for this area. Numerous insecure IoT devices with heterogeneous nature and high computing power make them easy and attractive targets for attackers (Khan & Salah, 2018). The most up-to-date standardization and research activities are aimed at solving various security problems of IoT devices (Khorov et al., 2020). Most connected devices are easily exposed to security threats and attacks such as botnets during data transfer and these threats have proven that these devices have easily exploitable vulnerabilities (Wang et al., 2020). Due to the resource shortage and vulnerability in wireless communication, Advanced security infrastructures are needed for distributed computing systems that do not have a central control unit. (Kumar et al., 2014). The Denial of Service (DoS) and Distributed Denial of Service (DDoS) attacks are the types of attacks that mostly affect wireless networks. There is a lot of work involved to protect against these types of attacks. (Abramov & Herzberg, 2011, Aldaej, 2019). The addition of these protection systems to IoT structures provides significant disadvantages in terms of resource use. For this reason, protection systems added to IoT structures should be in infrastructures to eliminate such disadvantages. Likewise, the blockchain needs to be transformed into a heterogeneous system, such as users and verifiers, with clear role separations (Popov et al., 2019).

Transport and security protocols have great importance that ensure reliable and secure communication. There has been increasing interest to blockchain for security and privacy policies in the Internet of Things (Dorri et al., 2017). Blockchain is a technical framework that allows users to collectively protect the reliable database in a decentralized manner. In a blockchain system, data is generated and saved in units of the nodes. Sequential nodes are combined in a chronological order to create a chained data structure. All user nodes participate in the maintenance, repository, and validity of the data. More than half of users must approve the genesis of the new block. Data is broadcasted to all user nodes to create a network-wide synchronization (Dai et al., 2017). The neighbors of the nodes receive an identity and hash value with this broadcast. More nodes mean receiving higher validation and stronger security as a result. (Akyildiz & Jornet, 2010).The security and end-user privacy issues increase and become stricter in IoT, due to the asymmetric nature of the communications between sensors and the ordinary Internet hosts (Sahraoui & Bilami, 2014). For this reason, the use of blockchain has been proposed to contribute to the security and privacy issues of IoT applications.

In this study, the speed and energy usage of IoT with Blockchain have been analyzed. These analyzes have been compared with the non-blockchain structure in a second experiment under the same circumstances. In the developed experimental environment, Raspberry Pi 3 B + board was used as an embedded system. The IoT infrastructure has been installed with "Docker" in the Rasbian operating system. The data has been gathered with three different sensors; it was encrypted in the blockchain structure and transferred to neighbor nodes. The data from the previous node has been added to the blockchain structure by validating the hash value and transmitted to the other node. It is ensured that the collected data has been transmitted to the central node in a correct and complete manner. A separate structure without blockchain was established with the same transmission infrastructure and transmission of data to the central node was also provided in this experimental environment.

As a result of the analysis, securely transmitted data with the blockchain structure in the wireless sensor network has been analyzed for energy usage. In these analyzes, it has been determined that less energy is used in WSN structures where blockchain is not used and 17% more energy consumption is realized in data transmissions performed with Proof of Work (PoW) in the blockchain structure. Additionally, IoT and blockchain combination has been considered as a daily life utilization. The research topics and challenges that need to be addressed to provide; reliable, efficient, and scalable IoT security solutions are summarized. The main motivation for this study is to combine the two main technologies and reveal the energy consumption by providing the maximum level of safety.

MATERIALS AND METHODS

The Internet of Things is characterized by small but very frequent volumes of information. Packet transfers in the IoT infrastructure are usually done by the methods required by a certain protocol. Since the packet structures of these protocols are standard, it causes unnecessary packet transfers in the transmission of small-sized data. This will cause unnecessary energy consumption in the IoT infrastructure. The represented network which has embedded devices with objects or sensors that are connected via a private or public network. The devices in IoT can be remotely controlled to perform the requested functionality. Information sharing between smart devices can be done through a network using standard communication protocols. The future importance of IoT is also evident due to applications in daily life. (Khan & Salah, 2018).

Internet of Things

The intensive use of computer networks has resulted in the development of communication systems and protocols, which may meet different needs and applications. The Internet of Things (IoT) is the name given to the entire communication systems that collect data from billions of devices and enable the data to be broadcast over the internet. The purpose of these systems is to provide information to people over the data collected for a particular region. In this way, while improving our lives and working conditions; our homes, vehicles, work areas, and cities can turn into smart interactive spaces. In outdoor and indoor environments, every sector in which there is a human and technology factor is within the scope of the IoT.

The Internet of Things (IoT) is a technology that enables the embedded system devices communicate with each other and exchange data between unique communication channels. The development of IoT is becoming increasingly tailored to the needs of humanity. It is widely used in vehicles, health care, wearable devices, retail sales, logistics, manufacturing, agriculture, utilities, appliances, etc. (Fernández & Fraga, 2018). Internet of Things concept covers the systems that exchange data between them without the need for human interference. An important function of The Internet of Things is to gather data to cause better decision-making or control. The data life cycle includes the following stages: capture, storage, sharing, maintenance, publishing, archiving, and cleanup (Tseng et al., 2020). To meet the expectations, and needs of people through technological devices that are used the Internet connection, these systems gather the data in a certain environment and communicate with each other, and create the information service for the users. The main idea of this notion is to cooperate with the devices using the addressing systems and use the obtained data meaningful way and make it ready for analysis on virtual platforms. The Internet of Things consists of eight main components as shown in Figure 1.

Figure 1. Internet of Things Components (Christoph, 2009)

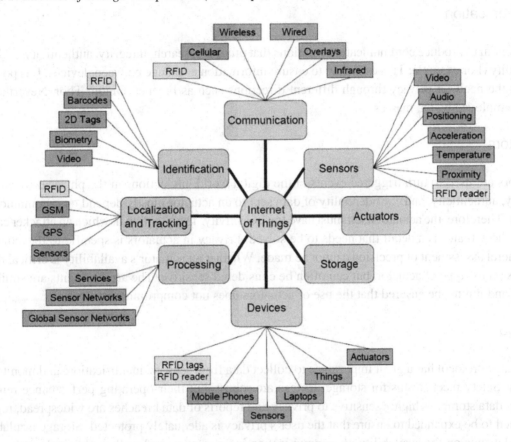

Devices

In the Internet of Things environment, devices are needed to interact with people within the physical world. The integrity of the devices means a tool doesn't contain malware. The originality of a device is often seen as the connecting endpoint. Privacy on a device is the third party's commitment to ensuring that the devices cannot access their internal data. This is normally provided in the case of device integrity. The availability of a device depends on the integrity and reliability of the devices as well as the availability of the communication part connecting the device.

Sensors

Sensors utilized in sensing and perceiving the physical world transfer the data they capture to the digital world. The integrity of the sensor data is a current research goal that must be addressed. Sensor data privacy is a weak need; because the attacker can physically place his own sensor and can detect the same values. Therefore, within the sensor itself, the necessity for sensor privacy is low, and therefore, the need for privacy is based on communication privacy. Stealth in sensors mainly targets the perceived physical world. The availability of sensors mostly depends on the communication infrastructure. Regulations to protect the privacy of people who are currently unaware of the most frequenting sensors need to be done.

Communication

It is essential to produce communication solutions that provide research, integrity, authenticity, and confidentiality (For example; TLS or IPSec) to ensure information exchange between devices. It is possible to meet the need for privacy through different directions such as Freenet, Onion, Thor. Nevertheless, it's not employed by the masses.

Actuators

Actuators are used to turn triggered events in the digital world into actions in the physical world. The integrity, authenticity, and confidentiality of data sent to an actuator mostly depend on communication security. Therefore, the actuator itself must have low sensitivity. The situation in which an attacker cannot control the actuator is a detail that needs to be solved. Privacy in actuators is specific to the situation, so a general assessment of precision cannot be made. Whether an actuator's availability is critical or not depends on the type of actuator, but can often be considered sensitive. The arrangements are similar to sensors and it must be ensured that the use of actuators does not compromise privacy.

Storage

The storage protocol has a great importance to collect data from sensors, identification, and monitoring systems. Safety mechanisms for storage devices are robust, but their operating performance remains poor. As data storage is highly sensitive to privacy and reports of data breaches are widespread, regulations need to be expanded to ensure that the user's privacy is adequately protected. Storage availability mostly depends on the availability of communication infrastructure and well-established mechanisms for storage backup.

Processing

Integrity in data processing is based on the integrity of the device and the integrity of the communication. Besides, the correct design and correct implementation of algorithms for data processing are of great importance. As the machine can often be abiding by actuator actions, it is also a delicate situation in that the actuator can receive incorrect commands. Processing only depends on the originality of the device; hence it depends on the originality of the communication. The nature of confidentiality in the process is not only enthusiastic to the integrity of the device; It also depends on the integrity of the communication in "Case of Distributed Transaction". The processing phase is critical to privacy and storage.

Tracking

Localization and monitoring steps are applied for locating and tracking in the physical world. The integrity of localization and monitoring is essentially based on communication integrity. Also, the integrity of the reference signals used in localization forms various anchor points. Likewise, originality also depends on the communication and device integrity. Privacy and localization, as well as the privacy of tracking data, are of critical importance to ensure the user's privacy. In this context, privacy means that an attacker cannot reveal localization data and therefore basically relies on communication privacy. Privacy in localization data;

It means that the attacker is not able to reveal the identity of the person or reveal the object to which localization data was attached.
It means localization and monitoring is not possible without clearing agreement or knowledge.

The availability of localization is important to ensure that reference signals for localization are robust and cannot be manipulated by the attacker.

Identification

Identity enables the data collected from the outside world to be separated by processing, monitoring, storage, and communication between other devices. It shares the same sensitivities as the identification, localization, and tracking clause. The only difference is that it also has high precision in integrity. The attacker can easily manipulate the identification process as well as manipulate the localization process. This is mainly due to an attacker's localization technologies (e.g., GSM) and technological advances (e.g., RFID or biometric) where manipulation is even easier.

From a security perspective, the main disadvantage of IoT applications and platforms is that they rely on a centralized cloud. A decentralized, blockchain-based approach tackles most of the problems associated with the central cloud approach. Some experts point out that blockchain can provide a minimal level of security for IoT devices. There is no single point of failure or vulnerability in the blockchain (Kshetri, 2017).

Internet of Things Management

Node-Red is a web-based visual development tool that is used to connect hardware and API (Application Programming Interface) on the Internet of things applications. The data flow in Node-Red is used with nodes that are interconnected by connection cable tools. The user interface consists of a flow editor with customizable templates. Admins can manage the flows which can be categorized. After a flow is created or modified, the admin saves the stream to the server and begins distributing it back to the Node-Red server (Giang et al., 2015). The flows in the nodes inherit the flow logic from their base class. (Johnston et al., 2004). Furthermore, the nodes are implemented based on observer design patterns. These nodes are subclasses of event organizers API and to maintain their subscriber list, the dataflow spread through to lower nodes. Input nodes can subscribe to external services; they can start "HTTP" requests, listen to data on specified ports, and run them. When the data is processed from an external service with "function," the node calls the "send ()" method with a "JavaScript" object (Blackstock & Lea, 2014).

It is possible to mark the nodes as "Device Nodes", "Server Nodes" or "Mobile Nodes." A server node may require assistance such as; specific programming languages on the platforms, the processing power of a server hosted in the clouds, data storage, or server connectivity outside of the firewall. Node without device ID can be contemplated as mobile node and it can be hosted on the devices or server. It can perform a heuristic scan based on user preferences or determine the best placement of a node. Similarly, a flow pattern can be expanded including different node types. The connections between the nodes and whole local connections work on the same execution engine. However, it can include data transfer between devices/ servers over a local/ wide area network.

Blockchain

Blockchain is a chronological database that operates on a distributed network of multiple nodes or computers that follow the data transactions. It is called "Blockchain" because of the ways in which transactions are recorded and verified. In Blockchain technology, all transactions are verified by all, and cryptographically signed with a hash value (Singh et al., 2020). The Information about a definite number of transactions is organized and encrypted into "blocks". Each new block, node, or computer is validated when a consensus is reached over the network. Blockchain and most distributed ledger technologies concern that contradictions are related to security, privacy, scalability, continuity, and energy consumption. Another approach is to integrate the blockchain with other digital technologies such as the Internet of Things, Artificial Intelligence, Deep Learning, Robotics, or Additive Manufacturing (Lemieux et al., 2019). Distributed Ledger Technology is shown in Figure 2.

Transactions in the blockchain that keep the list of constantly growing transaction records are called, "Block." The first block structure is called the "Genesis Block" shown in Figure 3 (Taş & Kiani, 2018).

The cryptographic algorithms and/or passwords provide the security and accuracy of the blocks. Each block contains the cryptographic password of the previous block in its content and checks the authenticity of the file. The cryptographic encryption process is called "Cryptographic Hashing" which is a short definition of the "Hash" process. The hash function encodes an entry of any length into a uniform (Uniform String) text string according to the specified algorithm. The generated hash code changes even for each addition of a bit. Thus, a block that is recorded in the distributed ledger and added to the chain becomes unalterable. The block structure is shown in the Figure 4 (Sousa et al., 2018).

Cryptography

Cryptography is the collection of mathematical methods used to capture personal information and make it unreadable by unwanted parties. Each block has its own unique identity. In case of any retrospective attempt to be made within the block since the generated hash code, it will change itself and not comply with the existing hash code in the next block. Depending on the encryption algorithm, it cannot be returned to the original structure of the data by unwanted people who do not have the spousal key even if the data has been seized. The data can be transformed to the original state only by verifying the unique keys owned by the sender and the recipient.

Figure 2. Distributed Ledger Technology (Garderen, 2016)

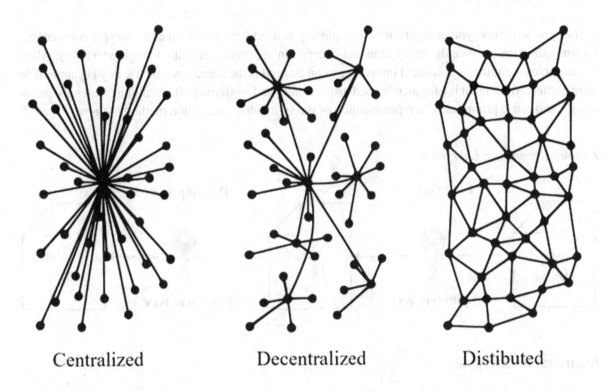

Centralized   Decentralized   Distibuted

Figure 3. Genesis Blog

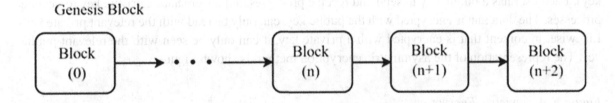

Genesis Block

Figure 4. Blockchain Structure (Sousa et al., 2018)

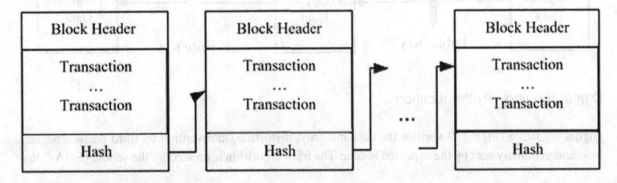

Symmetric Encryption

In the symmetric encryption algorithms, a single key is used for encryption and decryption processes. Its strength is speed since the encryption and decryption are processed with a single secret key. All of the incoming, sending, and content information can be read if the secret- symmetric key is captured by third parties. Although it is a frequently used method, alter and re-sharing after sending creates a separate burden and cause problems. The representation of the symmetric encryption method is shown Figure 5.

Figure 5. Symmetric Encryption

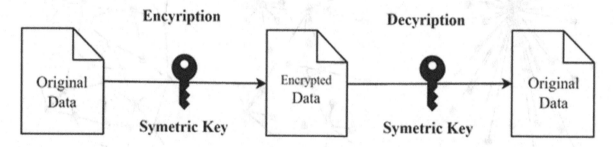

Asymmetric Encryption

In the asymmetric encryption algorithms, two different keys are used for encryption and decryption processes. One of the keys is for encryption (public key) and the other key is for decryption (private key). Each user has a public key to send and receive processes and never share a private key to decode processes. The data that is encrypted with the public key, can only be read with the relevant private key. Likewise, in content that is encrypted with a private key, it can only be seen with the relevant public key. The representation of the asymmetric encryption method is shown Figure 6.

Figure 6. Asymmetric Encryption

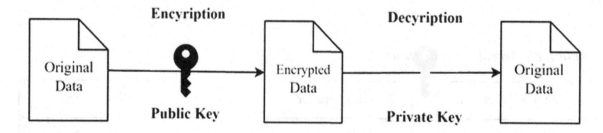

Digital Signing - Authentication

Digital signature (Figure 7) verifies the data integrity, distortion, intervention by third parties, packet loss, and genuinely sent by the expected sender. The hash algorithm is created by the sender (SHA-256)

Figure 7. Digital Signature-Verification Steps

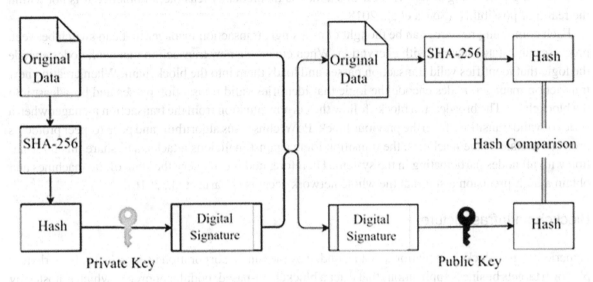

and encrypted with its private key and send to the recipient's public key. By comparing the hash code that is, created by the recipient's hash code of the sender, the recipient can find out whether it came from the right place and the receiver decrypts it with its own private key. If there is a content mismatch when comparing two hash codes (summary value), it is concluded that the user is not the recipient/ sender who created the content and signed the summary value, or it means that the message content was interfered while the data transfer.

Merkle Tree

The Merkle Tree structure is used for the secure and fast verification in case of exceeding the size of data transfer, and it is a standardized model of major platforms and providers using blockchain. It separates the hash values similar to the tree model in the binary structure and keeps the hashes of the hash values that have been divided into small pieces in order. Each divided data value passes through the hash function to generate its own hashes. This process is directly proportional to the size of the data sent and continues until it is reduced to the maximum data size that can be carried. At this stage, the leaves (Merkle Leaf) combine the hashes of each conjugate that is divided and obtain a new hash. This process continues until it reaches (Merkle Root) the root.

Blockchain Security Services

In order for the attackers to seize the system, they must capture the majority of the nodes in the network. The distributed nature of the nodes greatly reduces this possibility. Hash functions are actively used in the blockchain, and altering a single transaction in the system will require calculating all the blocks in the chain as well. This strives will require tremendous processing power. For each block to be changed in the chain, the other nodes will need to be persuaded and PoW calculations will also need to be performed. This is defined as a 51% attack because all nodes in the network will need to have at least 51%

of the mining processing power. Even if this attack is theoretically feasible, in practice it is not within the realm of possibility. (Sousa et al., 2018).

Each computing resource can be thought of as a single transaction manager that can switch between processes and states secured with encryption. When creating a new transaction manager, nodes encode the logic that identifies valid transaction passes and loads them into the blockchain. When creating new transaction manager, nodes encode the logic that identifies valid transaction passes and broadcast into the blockchain. The broadcasted blocks follow the current situation from the transaction manager when a series of valid transitions from the previous block. PoW, consensus algorithms and peer-to-peer protocols protect the state of the machines, the transition logic against malicious attacks, and share this information with all nodes participating in the system. Therefore, nodes can query the state of the machines and obtain a high-precision result that the whole network accepts (Azaria et al., 2016).

Blockchain Infrastructure

Hyperledger is a blockchain platform that is funded by the Linux Corporation in early 2016. Hyperledger platform targets business applications that offer a blockchain-based modular approach which is hosted by IBM. The aim is to build universal and flexible blockchain platform. Hyperledger produces and develops a range of business blockchain technologies such as distributed ledger frameworks, smart contract engines, utility libraries, and sample applications. (Saghiri et al., 2020). It also supports a wide range of smart contracts as a basic design. A key feature of this system is its expandable nature and its multi-services that provide infrastructure tools to create blockchain in particular. It allows the use of multiple smart contracts to manage the blockchain (Sousa et al., 2018). Blocks are preserved by the reconciliation mechanism and the cryptographic hashes against the interventions (Androula et al., 2018). The blockchain can remain attached to the model with or without permission. Without permission, records can be maintained by DLT (Distributed Ledger Technology) decentrally and anonymously. (Cachin, 2016). In an unauthorized chain, anyone can participate without having a specific identity. On the other hand, public blockchains operate between a blockchain among several known and defined participants. An authorized blockchain, the group of assets that does not rely on each other with a common goal (Transactions for Fund, Goods, or Information Exchange), it provides an interaction guarantee of getting a road between (Androula et al., 2018). Consensus-based PoW contains a local currencies for economic incentive (Chain.co, 2014). PoW involves that solving cryptographic puzzle and consumes resources to control the production of new blocks. The Proof of Work task requires miners to find a nonce value to be included in the block so that the hash value of the new block is less than a target value. Also, the difficulty can be adjusted over time to control the block generation rate. After the creation of the generated block, it is published to other nodes. After receiving the new block, the other nodes can validate the PoW by recalculating the hash value and comparing it with the hash value contained in the received block. (Dedeoğlu et al., 2020)

The Fabric Protocol is responsible for creating blocks to the distributed ledger and the services in which block is annexed to the ledger. All these processes are described in the steps below (Figure 8):

Step 1: Clients create a co-mission activity and send message to conjugates for validation. This message is used to call a chain code function. This is done by only if chaincode includes to chaincode ID and timestamps.

Step 2: The approved conjugates are simulating the co-mission actions and sign a compromise agreement. If the client is agreeably authorized, it can process by implementing the access control policies of the chain. After that the transactions are executed according to the current situation. The conjugates transmit the result of this occurrence to the client (it is allowed or rejected to read and write permissions the nodes associated with their current state). This is done with the validator conjugates signature and there is no additional updates are made at this point to ledger.

Step 3: Clients can collect and combine co-mission functions. The clients approves the conjugates signature if the read and write results of the clusters match with conjugates. If these conditions are met, clients create an "envelope" containing an approved literacy permission which includes an approved channel ID and signatures. The channel is the point within the fabric network that provides a special blockchain data section. Each conjugate shares the channel's specific registry that the envelope represents a transaction.

Step 4: The processors suggest co-mission action to broadcast. The service provider does not read the contents of the envelope. It collects the envelopes from all channels in the network only and creates the approved chain blocks which contain these envelopes.

Step 5: The envelope blocks are delivered to conjugates in the channel Envelopes within the blocks are checked and validated whether there is a change in conjugates status for the permission variables to ensure and fulfill approval policies. For this purpose, while the reading set simulates an operation, it contains a series of version keys that allow the reading of the conjugates (Step 2). The hinge on the accomplishment of these confirmations, the motion tender subsumed in the envelopes are marked as valid or invalid.

Step 6: The conjugates enclose the received block to the blockchain of the channel. The permission sets are dedicated to the conjugates current state for each accepted transaction. An event is triggered to broadcast the client that a transaction has been added precisely to the channel's blockchain, and it is decided that the transaction be considered valid or invalid. It is noted that invalid transactions are also added to the ledger, but this does not apply to conjugates. This also brings the advantage of making it possible to detect malicious clients because their actions are also recorded.

Figure 8. Hyperledger Transaction Processing Protocol (Sousa et al., 2018)

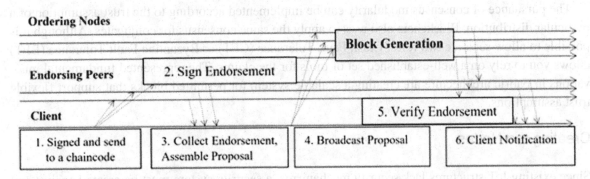

The substantial aspect of the fabric protocol is the verification comparison (step 2) and the verification of validation (step 5) can be done in distinct conjugates. The same operation can also confirm by distinct spouses; it will produce the same output. (Androulaki et al., 2018) The blockchain is similar to a "Reliable" computer service through a distributed protocol operated by connected nodes over the internet. The service represents or creates an asset in which all nodes have some stake. The nodes share the goal of running service, but they don't necessarily trust each other for more. In an unauthorized blockchain, anyone can run a node by spending CPU cycles and it can exhibit an example of "operational security." On the other hand, the authorized model can typically generate identities and establish a compromise protocol with these nodes.

A Fabric network supports multiple blockchains models that are connected to the same service. In such networks, each blockchain is called a channel and may have different conjugates as its members. The channel can be thought as a part of the blockchain network but the consensus is not coordinated between these channels. The total transaction order is separated from the others in each channel.

Beginning of the Process

Each chain code can define its own permanent entries during the process. The ledger with reading permission also includes a security infrastructure for authentication and authorization because the transaction is applied. It supports registration and transaction authorization through public-key certificates. The privacy of the chain code that occurs through in-band encryption. In simpler terms in order to connect to the network, each conjugate must obtain a registration certificate from the registration system, which is part of the membership services. It is substantial to get necessary transaction certificates and capacitate a peer to be able to connect and operate to network. The chain code that exists for smart contracts is provided with symmetric key encryption. Transactions are executed with a specific key that can be used for all spouses with a registration certificate for blockchain (Cachin, 2016).

Fabrics architecture validates a new execution sequence to distribute entrusted code in an unrelied environment. It divides the process flow into three steps to run in different entities in the system:

Step 1: Take action (process), check the accuracy, confirm.
Step 2: Providing service through a compromise protocol regardless of transaction semantics.
Step 3: To grant transaction confirmation based on trust assumptions that are specific to applications that may affect the time and outcome conditions due to co-time.

The pursuance of consensus modularity can be implemented according to the trust assumption of a particular distribution. Blockchain also uses to apply the same consensus for conjugates. Although it is possible to allow separate two roles; Crash Fault Tolerance (CFT) or Byzantine Fault Tolerance (BFT) allows you to rely on a well-established set of tools for the claims. The represented fundamental innovations in Fabric architecture are creating a scalable system for permitted blocks that support flexible trust assumptions.

Creating the Nodes

Since existing IoT structures lack security mechanisms, a security system must be created against any cyber-attack even in the smallest data communication. In the developed system, blockchain has been used to record the transmission of data distributed between the nodes. These nodes ensure that the data cannot be changed and tampered with. It will not be possible to change or obtain the data recorded from the blockchain structure without seizing all nodes of the chain.

Nodes were created on Raspberry Pi 3B + embedded systems using Node-red and dissociated by different VLANs by setting static IPs. All devices (Raspberry Pi 3B +) were added as peers by creating a Perishable Network in Hyperledger Composer. The sensor data sent over with Node-Red included to the blockchain over IBM Watson. The provided data, read over from the IBM Watson through the Hyperledger Playground interface.

The energies of Raspberry Pi embedded system nodes are provided with an adapter with 5V/2,5A DC features. The wattmeters are connected to the nodes to detect energy expenditures which can be found easily on the market. These Watt Meters were checked in two different experimental groups.

Data transmission was provided without using blockchain in the first experimental group. It was determined that how much energy was consumed with Raspberry Pi embedded systems and how long the sent data is transmitted.

The second group was subjected to the same experiments using the blockchain. Tests have been carried out to ensure that the data is going to the correct address, whether the data has been altered or manipulated, and whether the data has been securely transferred to the central node. According to the results obtained; data transfer rates, temperature, and sensor data were analyzed. Additionally, the energy consumptions were compared in the established project.

FINDINGS

In blockchain integrated IoT system; Linux open-source Blockchain Application Hyperledger Fabric and Hyperledger Composer were used. Performance analyses have been made on energy consumption and data transmission speeds. Each device has an enclosure active fans to avoid temperature. GPIO pins, active network connection, embedded lights, and two sensors connected on each device. Also, devices have been sending sensor data every 5 seconds. It should be stated that the sensors which have been used in this context are the general-purpose sensors used in the market.

In Figure 9, "Energy Consumption Without Using Blockchain" shown in blue, and "Energy Consumption With Using Blockchain" shown green below. When the blockchain integration was achieved, integrated fans were embedded on the Raspberry Pi enclosure box to prevent congealment and shutdown due to heating. Upward movements (Peak) of the fans fed from the device's adapter and GPIO pins can be monitored in energy consumption.

Figure 10 shows the energy consumption with and without integration to blockchain. The part indicated by the blue lines is sensor data which is sent periodically to blockchain via Node-Red. The green lines show the sensor data without integrating to blockchain.

The incrementation of power consumption when using blockchain decreased to affordable differences in data transfer analysis when considering the security crisis. Transfer speeds, which differ according to the used smart contracts, provide a solution to the problem of not being preferred due to slowness regarding end-users by using Practical Byzantine Fault Tolerance (PBFT).

CONCLUSION

As the number of interconnected devices on the Internet of Things increases, user's expectations increase accordingly. With the lack of self-defense capability, a rapidly increased number of devices, and immature security standards are becoming harder to establish a security standard on the Internet of

Figure 9. Blockchain Integrated Post-Energy Consumption

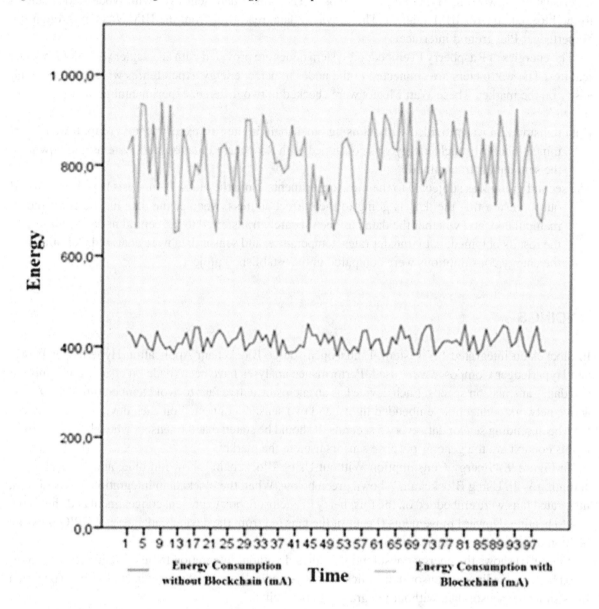

Things. On the other hand, blockchain technology which became popular in recent years has brought innovation expectations in this field. Unfortunately, we could not be using this technology efficiently. The idea to combine two major technologies that are expected to affect public, private, and especially academic sectors can eliminate the efficiency and security deficiencies. As long as the technology and intermediary programs that have offered the business markets only by large companies, "structure that is free and easily accessible to users" cannot be reached within this time.

The blockchain that is known as breaking news in the data security sector originally includes the security sectors of the future. The potential security, privacy, and anonymity principles of blockchain when considering the age of speed, will minimize the people's actions which are shifting into multiple

Figure 10. Transfer Speed with and without Blockchain

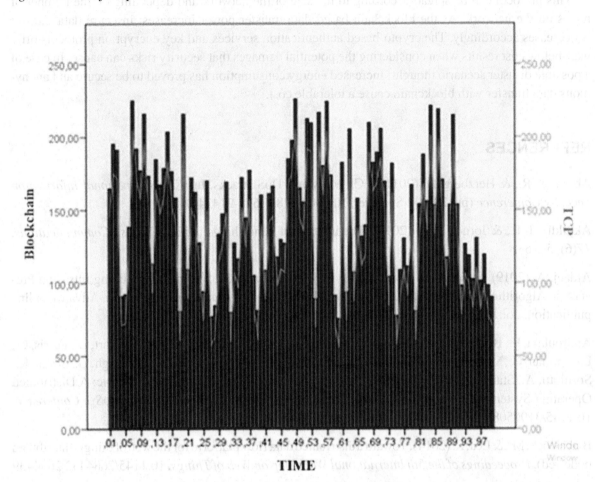

efforts on behalf of individuals using this technology. The blockchain's potential has sufficient quality to save users from more than one workload. Besides that using blockchain architecture on the Internet of Things system, the difficulty of meeting the prerequisites, and its presentation on a single platform (Linux) poses a problem for the end-users. The system's hardware infrastructures were created physically and grouped on the Node-Red. Temperature, humidity, motion, proximity, distance sensing, gas, rain, wetness measurement, vibration, and inclination sensors are separately grouped and added to Raspberry Pi 3 B+ cards. It has been observed that when more than two sensors actively provide data to the blockchain, it brings energy-induced long freezes and temperature problems on the processor side on Raspberry Pi cards.

Crypto-based authentication services and key encryption protocols offer significant advantages in terms of security and privacy. As an advantage, blockchain-based cybersecurity systems are much more difficult to seize than other solutions. As the blockchain-based data transfer power increases, insecure data transfer decreases accordingly. Even if the blockchain-based Internet of Things System offers well security solutions for the Internet of Things, blocks and blockchain have no such ability to solve security issues automatically/individually.

This protocol can be spread according to the size of the network and depending on the number of nodes on the network. As the blockchain-based data transfer power increases; insecure data transfer is decreases accordingly. The crypto-based authentication services and key encryption protocols offer well-below cost results when considering the potential damages that security risks can cause. In case of a possible disaster scenario thought; Increased energy consumption has proved to be secure and anonymous data transfer with blockchain cause a tolerable cost.

REFERENCES

Abramov, R., & Herzberg, A. (2011). TCP ack storm DoS attacks. In *IFIP International Information Security Conference* (pp. 29-40). Springer. 10.1007/978-3-642-21424-0_3

Akyildiz, I. F., & Jornet, J. M. (2010). The internet of nano-things. *IEEE Wireless Communications*, *17*(6), 58–63.

Aldaej, A. (2019). Enhancing Cyber Security in Modern Internet of Things (IoT) Using Intrusion Prevention Algorithm for IoT (IPAI). *IEEE Access : Practical Innovations, Open Solutions*. Advance online publication. doi:10.1109/ACCESS.2019.2893445

Androulaki, E., Barger, A., Bortnikov, V., Cachin, C., Christidis, K., De Caro, A., Enyeart, D., Ferris, C., Laventman, G., Manevich, Y., Muralidharan, S., Murthy, C., Nyugen, B., Sethi, M., Singh, G., Smith, K., Sorniotti, A., Stathakopoulou, C., Vukolic, M., ... Yellick, J. (2018). Hyperledger Fabric: A Distributed Operating System for Permissioned Blockchains. *Proceedings of the Thirteenth EuroSys Conference.* 10.1145/3190508.3190538

Blackstock, M., & Lea, R. (2014). Toward a distributed data flow platform for the web of things (distributed node-red). *Proceedings of the 5th International Workshop on Web of Things.* 10.1145/2684432.2684439

Cachin, C. (2016). Architecture of the hyperledger blockchain fabric. In *Workshop on distributed cryptocurrencies and consensus ledgers* (*Vol. 310*, p. 4). Academic Press.

Chain.co. (2014). https://chain.com/docs/1.2/protocol/papers/whitepaper

Dai, F., Shi, Y., Meng, N., Wei, L., & Ye, Z. (2017, November). From Bitcoin to cybersecurity: A comparative study of blockchain application and security issues. In *2017 4th International Conference on Systems and Informatics (ICSAI)* (pp. 975-979). IEEE. 10.1109/ICSAI.2017.8248427

Dedeoglu, V., Jurdak, R., Dorri, A., Lunardi, R. C., Michelin, R. A., Zorzo, A. F., & Kanhere, S. S. (2020). Blockchain technologies for iot. In *Advanced Applications of Blockchain Technology* (pp. 55–89). Springer.

Dorri, A., Kanhere, S. S., & Jurdak, R. (2017, April). Towards an optimized blockchain for IoT. In *2017 IEEE/ACM Second International Conference on Internet-of-Things Design and Implementation (IoTDI)* (pp. 173-178). IEEE.

Fernández-Caramés, T. M., & Fraga-Lamas, P. (2018). A Review on the Use of Blockchain for the Internet of Things. *IEEE Access : Practical Innovations, Open Solutions*, *6*, 32979–33001.

Garderen, P. V. (2016). *Introduction to Blockchain and Recordkeeping, Recordkeeping Roundtable*. http://www.interpares.org/display_file.cfm?doc=ip1_dissemination_ss_van-garderen_rr_2016.pdf

Giang, N. K., Blackstock, M., Lea, R., & Leung, V. C. (2015). Developing iot applications in the fog: A distributed dataflow approach. In *2015 5th International Conference on the Internet of Things (IOT)* (pp. 155-162). IEEE. 10.1109/IOT.2015.7356560

Johnston, W. M., Hanna, J. P., & Millar, R. J. (2004). Advances in dataflow programming languages. *ACM Computing Surveys, 36*(1), 1–34. doi:10.1145/1013208.1013209

Khan, M. A., & Salah, K. (2018). IoT security: Review, blockchain solutions, and open challenges. *Future Generation Computer Systems, 82*, 395–411. doi:10.1016/j.future.2017.11.022

Khorov, E., Lyakhov, A., Ivanov, A., & Akyildiz, I. F. (2020). Modeling of real-time multimedia streaming in Wi-Fi networks with periodic reservations. *IEEE Access : Practical Innovations, Open Solutions, 8*, 55633–55653.

Kshetri, N. (2017). Can blockchain strengthen the internet of things? *IT Professional, 19*(4), 68–72.

Kumar, E. S., Kusuma, S. M., & Kumar, B. V. (2014, April). An intelligent defense mechanism for security in wireless sensor networks. In *2014 International Conference on Communication and Signal Processing* (pp. 275-279). IEEE

Lemieux, V. L., Hofman, D., Batista, D., & Joo, A. (2019). Blockchain technology & recordkeeping. *ARMA International Educational Foundation, May, 30*.

Meghdadi, M., Özdemir, S., & Güler, İ. (2008). Kablosuz Algılayıcı Ağlarında Güvenlik: Sorunlar ve Çözümler. *Bilişim Teknolojileri Dergisi, 1*(1).

Popov, S. (2016). *The tangle*. Academic Press.

Saghiri, A. M. HamlAbadi, K. G., & Vahdati, M. (2020). The internet of things, artificial intelligence, and blockchain: implementation perspectives. In Advanced applications of blockchain technology (pp. 15-54). Springer, Singapore.

Sahraoui, S., & Bilami, A. (2014, May). Compressed and distributed host identity protocol for end-to-end security in the IoT. In *2014 International Conference on Next Generation Networks and Services (NGNS)* (pp. 295-301). IEEE.

Singh, S. K., Rathore, S., & Park, J. H. (2020). Blockiotintelligence: A blockchain-enabled intelligent IoT architecture with artificial intelligence. *Future Generation Computer Systems, 110*, 721–743.

Sousa, J., Bessani, A., & Vukolic, M. (2018). A byzantine fault-tolerant ordering service for the hyperledger fabric blockchain platform. In *2018 48th annual IEEE/IFIP international conference on dependable systems and networks (DSN)* (s. 51-58), IEEE. 10.1109/DSN.2018.00018

Taş, O., & Kiani, F. (2018). Blok zinciri teknolojisine yapılan saldırılar üzerine bir inceleme. *Bilişim Teknolojileri Dergisi, 11*(4), 369–382. doi:10.17671/gazibtd.451695

Wang, Q., Zhu, X., Ni, Y., Gu, L., & Zhu, H. (2020). Blockchain for the IoT and industrial IoT: A review. *Internet of Things, 10*, 100081.

Chapter 5
Is Blockchain Technology Secure to Work On?

Shagun Sharma

Chitkara University Institute of Engineering and Technology, Chitkara University, Punjab, India

Ashok Kumar

iD https://orcid.org/0000-0003-3279-5111

Chitkara University Institute of Engineering and Technology, Chitkara University, Punjab, India

Megha Bhushan

iD https://orcid.org/0000-0003-4309-875X

School of Computing, DIT University, India

Nitin Goyal

Chitkara University Institute of Engineering and Technology, Chitkara University, Punjab, India

Sailesh Suryanarayan Iyer

Rai School of Engineering, Rai University, Ahmedabad, India

ABSTRACT

Technology is revolutionizing and making positive as well as negative impacts on social animals. The social animal's behavior gets affected due to instant change in their lives. A concept of blockchain technology or distributed ledger transforms the way of their living. This technology is well known for its immutable and distributed architecture. The government focuses on such technologies rather than centralized network so that they can avoid central server banking crimes. These technologies allow social animals to stay secured and updated in an online process of information transfer. These are very famous for bitcoin, ripple, and ether transactions; however, mentioned transactions are just applications of distributed ledger. This chapter discusses the features, pros, cons, challenges, and future scope of distributed ledger. Further, it discusses the applications of blockchain technology in different sectors like identity management, smart cities, privacy protection, travel industry, electronic voting, finance, health industry, smart contracts, and hospitality.

DOI: 10.4018/978-1-7998-6694-7.ch005

INTRODUCTION

Over the period of time, the population in urban areas has increased rapidly. As stated by a report of United States (Dunphy & Petitcolas, 2018), in the past 30 years, there is an increase of 2.5 billion people who shifted to urban areas and by 2050 more than 70% of the world's population will migrate to urban areas. In Africa and Asia, the urbanization rate is higher than other regions of the world. During 2001-2015, the urbanization rate of China has increased from 38% to 56%. This has improved the level of some of the facilities like electronic-voting (e-voting), healthcare, transport facility, smart cities and so on and so forth. These facilities have brought some issues and challenges with them. For instance, due to increase in data fissure, centralized networks have led to an increase in fraud of identity, privacy issues and damage in reputation management. These issues cause shortage of ownership and control. In order to deal with these issues, Blockchain Technology having a Peer to Peer (P2P) architecture and a support for urbanization and smart cities come into being. The digital identity also come into existence after development of Bitcoin, as it supports Distributed Ledger Technology (DLT) which does not require middle authority to validate the transactions. Bitcoin, which had been first implemented using Blockchain Technology, was invented by Satoshi Nakamoto in 2008 (Xie et al., 2019). Due to these characteristics of a Blockchain Technology, the transactions are maintained in nodes. Further, this technology has cryptographic data structure which is developed through hashing algorithm and involving DLT in it. It is a distributed, immutable and publicly available database. The transactions are documented in DLT in such a way that any node can access, transmit and verify these transactions. Many features like transparency, pseudonymity, distribution, decentralization and security could be achieved by implementing DLT on smart cities. Transparency means, anyone can easily access the transactional records on the network easily. Pseudonymity means applying the hashing algorithm on the real-world identity instead of making it available to others over the network. Decentralization means, the DLT could help systems to run in a P2P network reliably without third party support. Whereas, security is defined in terms of confidential data, integrity and authorization.

The aim behind Blockchain Technology was to update the Cryptocurrency transactions with protection from cyber-attacks in mind. When any kind of transaction is carried out, all the data pertaining to it gets stored in global ledger. A new block is added to the global ledger to keep record of the data. Further, each block contains hash of the previous block and a Merkle root. As Blockchain Technology is based on P2P network, it is suitable for easy communication between the nodes, where every node is equally responsible for the participation and contains the hashed information about all the transactions done over the network. There is an absence of centralized server in this network and information is consumed and produced by each peer. All peers are involved in the procedure of information exchange over the network. And the global ledger is liable for transferring information between the peers reliably. These peers get a unique digital pseudonym, during the transaction, and it is produced by using an asymmetric cryptography. Intercommunications between peers are always accepted after completion of a transaction and it adds a block containing source address, destination peer address, message to be transferred and signatures of the members of the transaction.

To solve the issues of distributed data synchronization, Blockchain Technology contains some aspects like algorithm, encryption/decryption, business model along with mathematics by emerging node to node networks within distributed ledger (Niranjanamurthy et al., 2019).

The rest of the chapter is organized as follows. The definition, types and key elements of Blockchain Technology are described in background section. Literature review section comprises of the related work in the field of Blockchain Technology. Summary of state-of-the-art section gives the brief summary about features, pros, cons and applications of the Blockchain Technology. Further, research gaps and future scopes section describes the research gaps identified from existing literature pertaining to the area of Blockchain Technology. Lastly, the results are given in conclusion section.

BACKGROUND

This section comprises of definition, types and key elements of Blockchain Technology.

A. Blockchain Technology

It is a structure of data, which involves the DLT, and is made up of encrypted sequence of transactions where encryption is done by cryptographic hashing algorithm (Dunphy & Petitcolas, 2018). It is a public database consisting of decentralized and immutable data(Xie et al., 2019). The data pertaining to each transaction is recorded and any peer involved in the transaction is privileged to validate and access the information. The data is saved on first come first serve basis or chronological order i.e. a record validated first is inserted first into the Blockchain(Niranjanamurthy et al., 2019). Blockchain works in a distributed manner, without the need of central authority while dealing with Cryptocurrency(Feng et al., 2019).

B. Types of Blockchain Technology

Blockchain Technology is divided into three types (Feng et al., 2019; Miraz & Donald, 2018; Niran-janamurthy et al., 2019; Xie et al., 2019).

1. Public Blockchain Technology
2. Private Blockchain Technology
3. Hybrid Blockchain Technology

1. PUBLIC BLOCKCHAIN TECHNOLOGY

This is the kind of Blockchain Technology, on which most of the projects rely on (Feng et al., 2019).

Figure 1 shows the structure of Public Blockchain Technology.

In this any member can engage, validate, access and make the information transaction (Feng et al., 2019; Niranjanamurthy et al., 2019). All the transactional data and records are available to everyone over the network (Miraz & Donald, 2018). It requires a key component called incentive layer, which is responsible for adding business incentives to the Blockchain arrangement (Swati & Prasad, 2018). Public Blockchain is costly as compared to consortium Blockchain(Kang et al., 2018) and it doesn't need any involvement of third party for the procedure of joining of a fresh user in the chain (Ferrag et al., 2018). This is well-known for digital currency transactions (Hjálmarsson et al., 2018). Applications of such Blockchain Technology are Bitcoin and Ethereum (Bodkhe et al., 2019; Niranjanamurthy et al., 2019).

Figure 1. Public Blockchain Technology

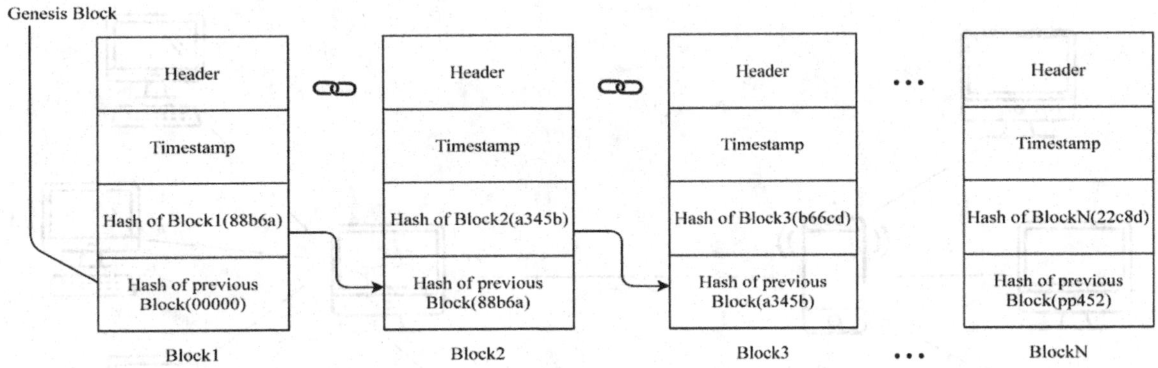

2. PRIVATE BLOCKCHAIN TECHNOLOGY

The private Blockchain has a centralized architecture and it is owned by an authority or a company (Xie et al., 2019). It is just contrary to Public Blockchain(Feng et al., 2019), where the authorization for write and read is reserved, centralized to the authority and limited to a random amount. It is limited and only authorized nodes are involved in the chain(Niranjanamurthy et al., 2019). It permits only those nodes to join the network which are trustworthy and have read and write permission (Miraz & Donald, 2018; Swati & Prasad, 2018). In this type of Blockchain, the miners are handled by the middle authority (Ferrag et al., 2018). The authorization can be approved by particular peers, which are involved in the process of Blockchain(Hjálmarsson et al., 2018) and thus limits the read and write permissions. It can be implemented better in the area of tourism industries (Bodkhe et al., 2019). It guarantees the security and safety because each peer in the network is authorized to access data and validate the final count without depending on another node (Hardwick et al., 2018).

Figure 2 shows Private Blockchain Technology

3. HYBRID BLOCKCHAIN TECHNOLOGY

A Hybrid Blockchain is useful in the business domain to keep track of the transactions (Xie et al., 2019). It is different from public Blockchain because it only allows approved companies to take part in the chain procedure. All pre-defined peers manage the whole network of Blockchain(Feng et al., 2019) and the authority of reading the records is generally permissionless or limited to valid users only, and consequently considered as moderately decentralized. It contains public or private information (Niranjanamurthy et al., 2019). Hyperledger and R3CEV are the examples of hybrid Blockchain(Feng et al., 2019; Niranjanamurthy et al., 2019). In this, write permission works like private Blockchain, where, the read permission could be treated as publicly open (Miraz & Donald, 2018).

Figure 3 shows hybrid Blockchain Technology.

Figure 2. Private Blockchain Technology

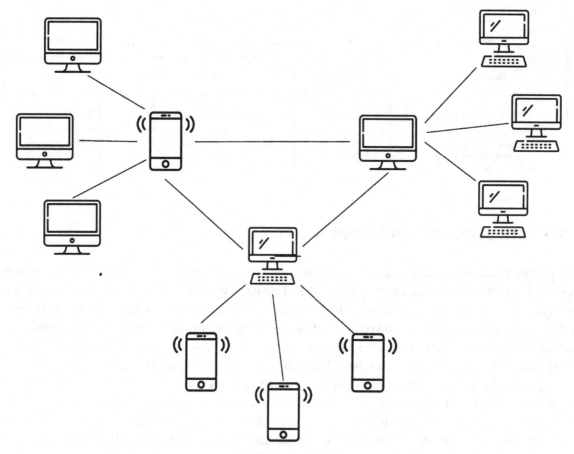

C. The key Elements of Blockchain Technology (Dunphy & Petitcolas, 2018; Feng et al., 2019; Niranjanamurthy et al., 2019; Xie et al., 2019) are as Follows

1.   Transparent- It shows transactional record to everyone.
2.   Decentralized- It enables the system to work on P2P network without involving central authority.
3.   Autonomous- Any node can update the transaction and access the records.
4.   Distributed- The information about the records will be updated over the network in a P2P manner.
5.   Open source- Blockchain Technology is open to each node, in which, information can be verified publicly.
6.   Contractual- The procedure of consensus can be accomplished by running the protocols of Blockchain Technology without using the middle authority. And these protocols define that the processes of Blockchain Technology will work without human involvement.
7.   Anonymous- It is used to solve the trust challenges among the peers by using peer's Blockchain address only.
8.   Democratic – In this, the decision of acceptance and rejection of new block is done by all the peers of the Blockchain together.

Figure 3. Hybrid Blockchain Technology

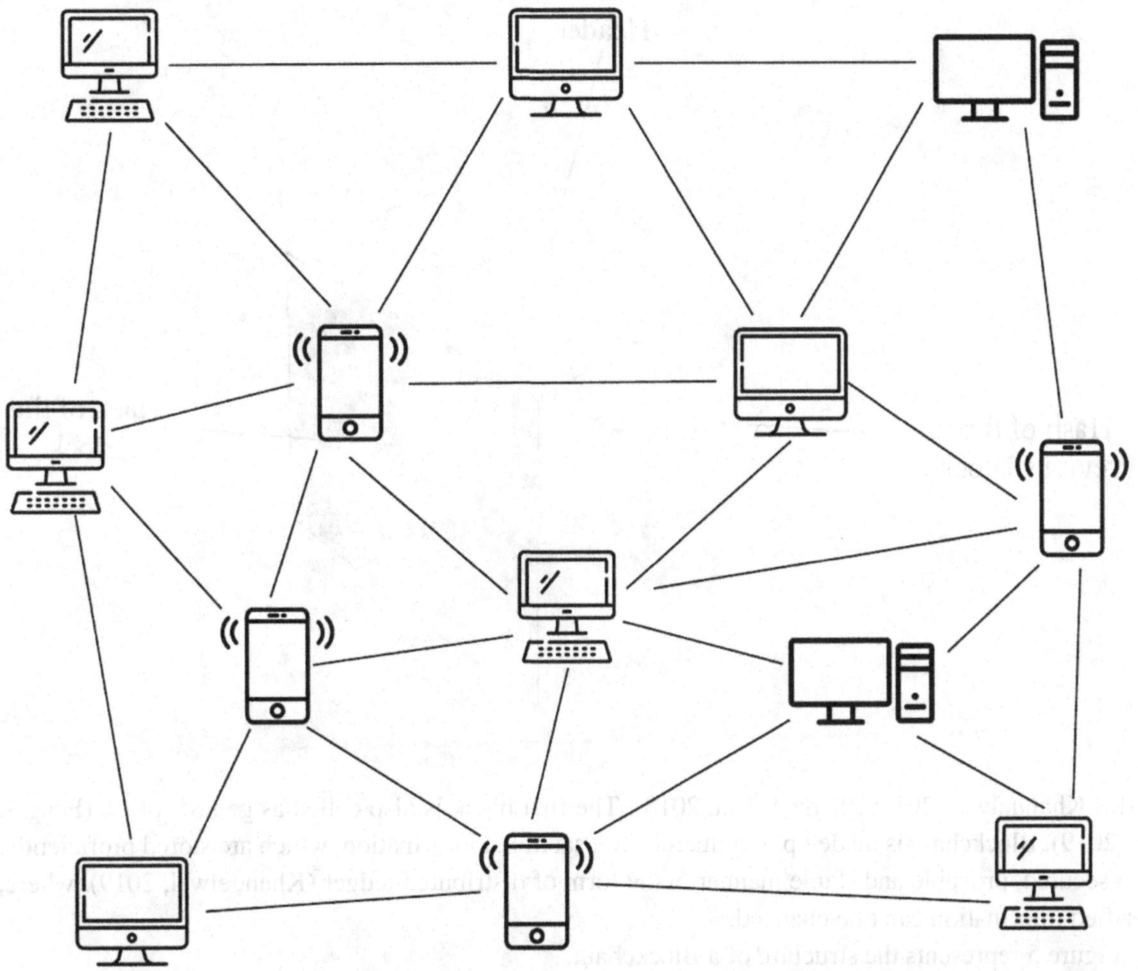

9. Pseudonymity- Real world identity of each peer is hidden by enabling public availability of encrypted address. This feature can work perfectly if real identity needs to be secret.

D. Structure of Blockchain Technology

A Blockchain is made up of sequence of blocks (Miraz & Donald, 2018). These blocks are systematically organized to keep track of the records (Xie et al., 2019). Figure 4 represents the structure of a block.

Blockchain is also named as DLT in which each block refers to the previous block (Swati & Prasad, 2018)as shown in Figure 5.

During information transaction procedure, the distributed ledger will store the information in a constantly list (Ferrag et al., 2018) and block is made up of timestamp, header, hash of the block and hash of the previous block (Feng et al., 2019), all the blocks are connected in such a form that it will create a linked list (Ferrag et al., 2018) timestamp contains sequence of transactions, header consists of the data about Id, size of the block and hash of the predecessor block (Feng et al., 2019; Ferrag et al.,

Figure 4. Structure of a block

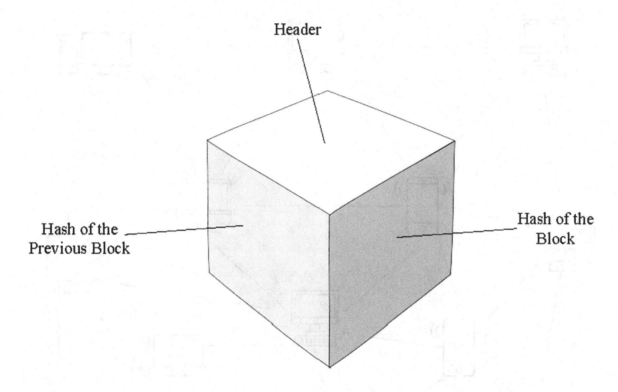

2018; Khandelwal, 2019; Zhang & Lin, 2018). The first block is also called as genesis block (Feng et al., 2019). Blockchain is made up of numerous transactional information, which are stored proficiently, in a secured, provable and stable manner in the form of distributed ledger (Khandelwal, 2019), where, verified information can't be changed.

Figure 5 represents the structure of a Blockchain.

LITERATURE REVIEW

In this section, literature related to Blockchain Technology for smart cities, e-voting, healthcare, Identity Management (IdM) and pharmaceutics are discussed.

It has been observed in (Dunphy & Petitcolas, 2018) that DLT are not the proper solution for IdM and has shown the strong as well as weak points of implementing DLT on IdM. This technology lacked in the storage of private data of particular entities and due to this, Blockchain Technology faced numerous issues. As a solution, General Data Protection Regulation (GDPR) allowed to keep private data on data controllers and processors.

A complete survey of applying DLT on smart cities and introduction of contextual knowledge is provided in (Xie et al., 2019), in accordance with healthcare, grid, citizens, transportation and Supply Chain Management (SCM) in smart cities. The issues including privacy, security, storing power, efficacy and cost were also discussed. Many aspects like cloud computing, machine learning, edge computing and Internet of Things (IoT) were also discussed. Further, it described the behavior of Blockchain Technol-

Figure 5. Structure of a Blockchain

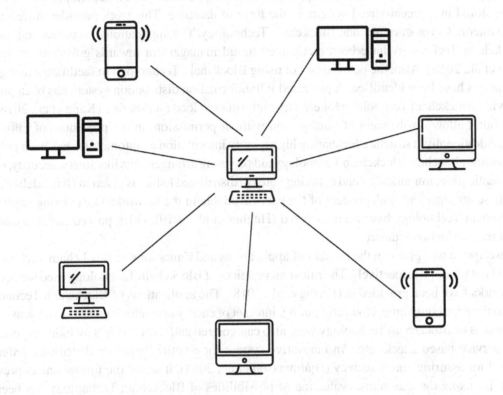

ogy when it finds the solutions for the challenges in smart cities. Existing visions and secrecy problems with Blockchain Technology were provided in (Feng et al., 2019). It provided the mechanism of solving anonymity and operational privacy problems in terms of DLT. The implementation of these mechanisms was also done to attain the secrecy prevention.

Without the use of middle authority, Blockchain Technology allows peers to do and validate the transactions (Niranjanamurthy et al., 2019). Strength, Weakness, Opportunities and Threats (SWOT) analysis has been done and how Blockchain Technology works along with the features and limitations were also described. The advantages of Blockchain Technology include better quality information, strength, consistency, integrity and immutability. The use of DLT in context with protected interchange transactions was described in (Miraz & Donald, 2018) where an effective effort is made on authorized facets. The design, development and implementation of hybrid Blockchain Technology were also studied in the perspective of information interchange. The complete architecture, concepts of Blockchain Technology and how these concepts can be implemented in travel industry is described in (Swati & Prasad, 2018). Hotel and airline rentals were considered as applications of Blockchain Technology. A number of changes made by the implementation of Blockchain Technology to avoid fraud protection, data security and online transactions in travel industry is also described. The results concluded that DLT can be implemented on many aspects like privacy services, status systems, public services and IoT. An analysis on Blockchain Technology and Cryptocurrency was done in (Yuan & Wang, 2018). A detailed six- layer reference exemplary of Blockchain Technology structure has been given along with advantages, ecologies, applications, and basics of Cryptocurrency. A survey was done on the issues faced by Blockchain

Technology in context with Blockchain applications (Tasatanattakool & Techapanupreeda, 2018). The data was stored in a decentralized system, in the form of database. This work provided differentiation between bitcoin Cryptocurrency and Blockchain Technology. The applications, solutions and use cases of Blockchain Technology have been recognized to aid management towards government amenities (Alketbi et al., 2018). Also, the possibilities of using Blockchain Technology to facilitate smart government services have been identified. A protected P2P information distribution system has been proposed by applying Blockchain Technology for effective information load and sharing (Kang et al., 2018). This system didn't allow involvement of third person without permission, in the procedure of information sharing. Additionally, a structure for sharing high quality information in automobiles has been proposed.

An outline about how Blockchain Technology aids e-voting arrangements like safety, security, concurrent authentication, immutability and counting votes in distributed ledger is given in (Khandelwal, 2019) where these arrangements independent of the peers available in the network. The existing applications of Blockchain Technology have been analyzed (Hughes et al., 2019) which proved major possibilities to profit the production industries.

A description was given on the number of applications and limitations of Blockchain Technology to adopt and not to adopt, respectively. The rules and practices of Blockchain Technology used for designing IoT networks have been provided in (Ferrag et al., 2018). The applications of Blockchain Technologies related to the edge computing, cloud computing, internet of energy and vehicles were also discussed. The threat models of Blockchain Technology were also categorized and these models included cryptanalytic threats, service-based attacks etc. An innovative system for e-voting based on distributed ledger was developed for assuring voters secrecy (Hjálmarsson et al., 2018), it stated the limitations in prevailing systems. By using these systems, evaluation of possibilities of Blockchain Technology has been seen in context with e-voting.

According to (Kshetri & Voas, 2018), Blockchain Technology was in emerging situation as it is yet not described so much, further, this technology was inappropriate to use current framework of e-voting system. BloHost (Bodkhe et al., 2019) i.e. Blockchain Enabled Smart Tourism and Hospitality Management framework was proposed to initiate single wallet Cryptocurrency payments and help vacationers to communicate with shareholders. It used distributed ledger, in which no confirmations and verifications of money were needed. Further, it provided an amazing experience to travelers. The existing issues in applicational concept of Blockchain Technology i.e. copyright space in cardinal atmosphere and how these challenges can be solved using distributed ledger are outlined in (Savelyev, 2018). Further, it was claimed that Blockchain Technology can present long scheduled limpidity in concept of copyright space and allows handling of risks by giving control to digital copy. In context with scarceness, the distributed ledger and Cryptocurrency were used for the implementation to decrease the issue of poverty (Barrutia Barreto et al., 2019) in America and Caribbean. A comprehensive examination of prospective of tourism, distributed ledger and Cryptocurrency was collected. By using these implementations, number of endeavors was made by country management and corporations to grow business of tourism in such type of regions, in which traditional possessions and biodiversity were yet not discovered perfectly.

Crypto-voting is an e-voting system (Fusco et al., 2018), which was built by using Blockchain Technology implemented on Shamirs secrecy sharing method. This system was used to incorporate between actions of voting and organizational processes. This technology included sharing of ID's (authorizations), set of voting documents, priority calculation, conclusion publications and many more. It improved the inspection of voting process and procedures of traceability without the interruption of central authority. A distributed node to node system (Mehta et al., 2019) was proposed to deal with the problem of incorrect image acknowledgment for the photographs that were uploaded in stock pictures web-applications. This system was implemented and validated using Ethereum test chain, to get the information about how much this system was reliable, impartial and realistic. It did not allow anyone to upload the images on the websites which were somewhere altered and similar to already uploaded images. It also rejected the new upload of images by looking at same hashes and vigorous keen contracts of Ethereum, it prevented the actual authorization of real photographers.

An e-voting protocol was proposed by using DLT (Hardwick et al., 2018). It allowed the voter to make changes in their vote (within a given period of time). The capability and effectiveness of Blockchain Technology were also discovered. A Healthchain tool was proposed to preserve the private data of the patient by enabling encryption in such a manner for access resist (Xu et al., 2019). In this context, a user can give authorization to a particular doctor and control key administration. This tool introduced the process of deletion and alteration of data to prevent health clashes. As the data of a patient could be stored in different hospital's databases, a distributed ledger called MedBlock (Fan et al., 2018) was proposed to maintain the EMRs (Electronic Medical Data) of a patient to avoid the privacy concerns. It also demonstrated the data security by integrating private key cryptography and authorization control rules. A protocol for e-voting has been proposed (Pawar et al., 2019) to attain the cost effective and protected method of voting in which privacy is of utmost importance to monitor. Due to the encoding nature, it is difficult to rule the access of the votes.

Researchers have described the working of Ethereum and solidity (Wohrer & Zdun, 2018), and defined six patterns which reported privacy and sharing problems during the coding of smart contracts. It resulted into decentralized implementation delivered by Ethereum. An architecture based on Blockchain Technology has been proposed for the hospitality, business and manufacturing (Filimonau & Naumova, 2020). Many technological and official issues were also analyzed which need to be solved. The economic infrastructure has been discussed to improve the effectiveness and efficacy by using Blockchain Technology(Zhao & Duncan, 2018). It also listed- pros, cons, and attacks on distributed ledger. Further, it generated a set of applications in many areas like government sector, code preservation and risk in software etc.

Authors have explored the potential of distributed ledger in case of data sharing in a trustful environment (Hawlitschek et al., 2018). This system transformed the communications among nodes in which degree of trust is necessary. The advantages and disadvantages of distributed ledger were summarized in (Gatteschi et al., 2018). It resulted that this technology is not an ideal solution for every sector because it can vary its advantages and disadvantages based on the change in the field i.e. IT sector, financial sector etc. A PHI (Personal Health Information) sharing protocol based on Blockchain Technology was developed to focus on electronic health system (Zhang & Lin, 2018). In this system, two types of Blockchain were used i.e. consortium and private Blockchain to record the information of data sharing. A study was conducted in (Calvaresi et al., 2019) about the implementation of Blockchain Technology in tourism. It also provided the theoretical overview, conventions, characteristics, limitations and challenges of distributed ledger.

SUMMARY OF STATE OF THE ART

This section presents a summary of the existing research works in the area of Blockchain Technology.

Table 1 shows a comparative analysis of state-of-the-art in terms of year of publication, features, pros, cons and applications.

Table 1. Summary of features, pros, cons and applications of Blockchain Technology

Articles	Year	Features	Pros	Cons	Applications
(Dunphy & Petitcolas, 2018)	2018	• Decentralized	-	• For storage of personal data it needs GDPR	• IdM
(Xie et al., 2019)	2019	• Trust free • Transparency • Pseudonymity • Democracy • Data protection • Computerization • Decentralization	• Dual chain storage arrangement	• Scalability challenges	• Smart cities • Smart contracts • Transport
(Feng et al., 2019)	2019	• Independent • Distributed • Immutability • Contractual	• Data protection administration • Accessibility of private data	• Time consuming due to waiting delay • Weighty storage • No hold up for audit	• Cryptocurrency • IoT • SCM
(Niranjanamurthy et al., 2019)	2019	• Immutability • Traceability • Transparency • Provable • Non repudiable • Protected • Distributed	• High class information • Robustness • Consistency • Procedure veracity • Auditing facility	• Late performance • Signature confirmation for each transaction is tough	• Cryptocurrency • Business • Smart administration • Health • Smart home
(Miraz & Donald, 2018)	2018	• Distributed • Immutability	• Scalability • Localization of information	• Handling settlements, trade and payments	• Protected stock exchange transaction • Cryptocurrency • Smart contracts
(Swati & Prasad, 2018)	2018	• Decentralized • Persistent • Secrecy • Audit ability •	• Absence of middlemen	• Complexity of challenges • Performance issues • Large network size	• Travel Industry (IdM, Scam anticipation)
(Kang et al., 2018)	2018	• Distributed • Decentralized • Immutable	• Trustworthy • Protected messaging between vehicles	• Information allotment challenges • More cost • Restricted resources	• Smart contracts • Repute organization • Vehicular protection
(Ferrag et al., 2018)	2018	• Transaction privacy • Privacy protection • Immutability • Audit ability • Veracity • Authorization • Transparency • Error tolerance	• Mobility • Ease of access • Concurrency • Light weight • Transparency	• Scalability problem • Network blocking • Power usage is high	• Bitcoin • Edge computing • Internet of cloud • Internet of energy • Internet of vehicles
(Hjálmarsson et al., 2018)	2018	• Immutability • Provable • Distributed consensus	• Voter privacy • Web browsers support for voting systems	• Safety problems • Veracity problem in e-voting • High congestion in network • 51% attack	• e-voting based on smart contracts
(Bodkhe et al., 2019)	2019	• Transparency • Creditability • Distributed ledger	• Prevented extra booking • Belongings tracking • Rewards scheme • Protected transaction • Industrial ratings • Travel ID authentication	• Mining procedure is expensive • Scalability problems	• Healthcare • Businesses • Education • Smart grids • IoT • Governance
(Hardwick et al., 2018)	2018	• Immutability	• More transparency • In built confidentiality • Security • Consistency	-	• e-voting
(Khandelwal, 2019)	2019	• Information modification is almost impossible, once it has been inserted to Blockchain.	• Secrecy • Consistency • Larger transparency • Immutability	• Complex and difficult • Protection problems	• e-voting
(Zhang & Lin, 2018)	2018	• Distributed • Immutable	• Maintain growing list of information	• Scalability issues • Accessibility of data problems	• Biomedical • Healthcare
(Yuan & Wang, 2018)	2018	• Distributed • Decentralized • Independent • Computerized	• Good co-ordination and co-operation • P2P transaction	-	• Smart devices • Decentralized allotment economy • Shipment transport • Enterprise administration and knowledge computerization

continued on following page

Table 1. Continued

Articles	Year	Features	Pros	Cons	Applications
(Tasatanattakool & Techapanupreeda, 2018)	2018	• Distributed • Decentralized	-	• Patients information can be lost • Information can be generated for illegitimate purpose	• e-voting • Smart contracts • Eplug • Filament(IoT)
(Alketbi et al., 2018)	2018	• Data integrity • Consistency • Realism	• Accessibility • Information secrecy	• Man In The Middle Attack (MITMD) • Sybil attack • Timing issues • Illegitimate actions • 51% attack • System hack	• Currency (money transfer, electronic payments) • Contracts (feature, loans, smart contract and smart property) • Social applications (health, art, govt.)
(Hughes et al., 2019)	2019	• Immutable • Time stamped • Append only • Protected • Transparent and open	• Fewer cost for tiny networks • Transactional transparency is good	• More cost latency • Flexibility challenges • Secrecy hack	• Finance • Logistics • Supply chain
(Kshetri & Voas, 2018)	2018	• Immutable	• Protected voting information • Support huge voter involvement • Provided progress in identity confirmation • Removal of duplicity • Precision and transparent to voters	• Complexity challenges	• Blockchain enabled e-voting (BEV)
(Savelyev, 2018)	2018	• Transparency • Idleness • Immutability • Disintermediation	• Resistant and transparent to cyber attacks	• Meta data and digital information storage problems • Copyright challenges • Network problems • Permissible problems	• Copyright protection in images
(Barrutia Barreto et al., 2019)	2019	• Settlement and financial payments in smart contracts, can be modified involuntarily	-	-	• Cryptocurrency • Finance
(Fusco et al., 2018)	2018	• Slide is the main feature in crypto voting system	• Remotely management of voting	• Architectural challenges	• Electronic government • Electronic learning • Electronic inclusion • Electronic culture • Electronic health
(Mehta et al., 2019)	2019	-	• Permanent information of deal • Transparency • Belief • Immutability • High accessibility • Information security • Cost savings	• Instant raise in storage space • Scalability challenges	• Image sharing • Smart contracts
(Xu et al., 2019)	2019	• Transparent and open in nature	-	• Information security • Information privacy	• Network scenario • Healthcare
(Fan et al., 2018)	2018	• Open nature • Provable	• MedBlock handled patients information	• Information storage challenges	• Healthcare
(Pawar et al., 2019)	2019	• More ease of use • Provable • Transparency • Immutability • Distributed ledger • Decentralized network • Better security	• Protected and secure • Anonymous for voters privacy • Avoided information loss • Dual voting challenges are avoided	• Time challenges • Cost problems	• e-voting
(Wohrer & Zdun, 2018)	2018	• Immutability	-	• Not suitable for storing the large amount of data • Poor performance for high frequency and less latency transactions	• Cryptocurrency
(Filimonau & Naumova, 2020)	2020	• Distributed database	• Tracks electric power allocation in remote/rural/poor areas	• Challenges in food traceability, food production control • Food supply chain transparent problems	• Hospitality • Electronic marketing
(Zhao & Duncan, 2018)	2018	• Robust • Less latency mechanism	• Advanced effectiveness of business infrastructure • Code protection	• Denial of Service (DOS) attack is harmful to performance and functionality	• Cryptocurrency
(Hawlitschek et al., 2018)	2018	• Immutability • Trust free	• Absence of middle authority	• Privacy protection problems • Difficult to identify whether transactional database is consistent, protected and correct or not.	• Payment and transaction systems • Electronic commerce
(Gatteschi et al., 2018)	2018	• Immutable • Publicly provable	• Trust between parties • Transparency is guaranteed • Data can't be deleted or changed • Computerization	• High power consumption • Data replication requires more space/storage • Privacy challenges • Slow procedure	• Smart contracts • Health sciences • Education
(Calvaresi et al., 2019)	2019	• Decentralization	• Advantages still depend upon the sector	• Belief and security challenges	• Tour and travel industry

RESEARCH GAPS AND FUTURE SCOPES

In Blockchain Technology, there is a need to address the issues related to waiting delay problems (Feng et al., 2019). Further, a survey is also required to focus on the use of Blockchain Technology in case of electronic healthcare (Tasatanattakool & Techapanupreeda, 2018) so that external entities could be benefitted with hospital and health industries medical data without getting the personal information about patients. It is also important to work on the privacy concerns, which arises due to the use of Blockchain Technology and further, needs to identify more available applications based on IoT (Alketbi et al., 2018).

CONCLUSION

The aim of this chapter is to identify "Whether the Blockchain Technology is secure to work on or not?". Due to the cons of Blockchain Technology, it is difficult to say that this technology is reliable and accurate to work on but as compared to its cons, it has more features, pros and applications, which enable people to work on Blockchain Technology. This technology allows social animals to stay secured and updated in an online process of information transfer. Additionally, researchers and students will get benefits from the information related to features, advantages, disadvantages along with the applications of Blockchain Technology.

REFERENCES

Alketbi, A., Nasir, Q., & Talib, M. A. (2018, February). Blockchain for government services—Use cases, security benefits and challenges. In *2018 15th Learning and Technology Conference (L&T)* (pp. 112-119). IEEE.

Barrutia Barreto, I., Urquizo Maggia, J. A., & Acevedo, S. I. (2019). Cryptocurrencies and blockchain in tourism as a strategy to reduce poverty. RETOS. *Revista de Ciencias de la Administración y Economía, 9*(18), 287–302.

Bodkhe, U., Bhattacharya, P., Tanwar, S., Tyagi, S., Kumar, N., & Obaidat, M. S. (2019, August). Blohost: Blockchain enabled smart tourism and hospitality management. In *2019 International Conference on Computer, Information and Telecommunication Systems (CITS)* (pp. 1-5). IEEE. 10.1109/CITS.2019.8862001

Calvaresi, D., Leis, M., Dubovitskaya, A., Schegg, R., & Schumacher, M. (2019). Trust in tourism via blockchain technology: results from a systematic review. In *Information and communication technologies in tourism 2019* (pp. 304–317). Springer. doi:10.1007/978-3-030-05940-8_24

Dunphy, P., & Petitcolas, F. A. (2018). A first look at identity management schemes on the blockchain. *IEEE Security and Privacy, 16*(4), 20–29. doi:10.1109/MSP.2018.3111247

Fan, K., Wang, S., Ren, Y., Li, H., & Yang, Y. (2018). Medblock: Efficient and secure medical data sharing via blockchain. *Journal of Medical Systems, 42*(8), 136. doi:10.100710916-018-0993-7 PMID:29931655

Feng, Q., He, D., Zeadally, S., Khan, M. K., & Kumar, N. (2019). A survey on privacy protection in blockchain system. *Journal of Network and Computer Applications, 126*, 45–58. doi:10.1016/j.jnca.2018.10.020

Ferrag, M. A., Derdour, M., Mukherjee, M., Derhab, A., Maglaras, L., & Janicke, H. (2018). Blockchain technologies for the internet of things: Research issues and challenges. *IEEE Internet of Things Journal, 6*(2), 2188–2204. doi:10.1109/JIOT.2018.2882794

Filimonau, V., & Naumova, E. (2020). The blockchain technology and the scope of its application in hospitality operations. *International Journal of Hospitality Management, 87*, 102383. doi:10.1016/j.ijhm.2019.102383

Fusco, F., Lunesu, M. I., Pani, F. E., & Pinna, A. (2018). Crypto-voting, a Blockchain based e-Voting System. In KMIS (pp. 221-225). doi:10.5220/0006962102230227

Gatteschi, V., Lamberti, F., Demartini, C., Pranteda, C., & Santamaria, V. (2018). To blockchain or not to blockchain: That is the question. *IT Professional, 20*(2), 62–74. doi:10.1109/MITP.2018.021921652

Hardwick, F. S., Gioulis, A., Akram, R. N., & Markantonakis, K. (2018, July). E-voting with blockchain: An e-voting protocol with decentralisation and voter privacy. In *2018 IEEE International Conference on Internet of Things (iThings) and IEEE Green Computing and Communications (GreenCom) and IEEE Cyber, Physical and Social Computing (CPSCom) and IEEE Smart Data (SmartData)* (pp. 1561-1567). IEEE.

Hawlitschek, F., Notheisen, B., & Teubner, T. (2018). The limits of trust-free systems: A literature review on blockchain technology and trust in the sharing economy. *Electronic Commerce Research and Applications, 29*, 50–63. doi:10.1016/j.elerap.2018.03.005

Hjálmarsson, F. Þ., Hreiðarsson, G. K., Hamdaqa, M., & Hjálmtýsson, G. (2018, July). Blockchain-based e-voting system. In *2018 IEEE 11th International Conference on Cloud Computing (CLOUD)* (pp. 983-986). IEEE. 10.1109/CLOUD.2018.00151

Hughes, L., Dwivedi, Y. K., Misra, S. K., Rana, N. P., Raghavan, V., & Akella, V. (2019). Blockchain research, practice and policy: Applications, benefits, limitations, emerging research themes and research agenda. *International Journal of Information Management, 49*, 114–129. doi:10.1016/j.ijinfomgt.2019.02.005

Kang, J., Yu, R., Huang, X., Wu, M., Maharjan, S., Xie, S., & Zhang, Y. (2018). Blockchain for secure and efficient data sharing in vehicular edge computing and networks. *IEEE Internet of Things Journal, 6*(3), 4660–4670. doi:10.1109/JIOT.2018.2875542

Khandelwal, A. (2019, February). Blockchain implimentation on E-voting System. In *2019 International Conference on Intelligent Sustainable Systems (ICISS)* (pp. 385-388). IEEE. 10.1109/ISS1.2019.8907951

Kshetri, N., & Voas, J. (2018). Blockchain-enabled e-voting. *IEEE Software, 35*(4), 95–99. doi:10.1109/MS.2018.2801546

Mehta, R., Kapoor, N., Sourav, S., & Shorey, R. (2019, January). Decentralised Image Sharing and Copyright Protection using Blockchain and Perceptual Hashes. In *2019 11th International Conference on Communication Systems & Networks (COMSNETS)* (pp. 1-6). IEEE. 10.1109/COMSNETS.2019.8711440

Miraz, M. H., & Donald, D. C. (2018, August). Application of blockchain in booking and registration systems of securities exchanges. In *2018 International Conference on Computing, Electronics & Communications Engineering (iCCECE)* (pp. 35-40). IEEE. 10.1109/iCCECOME.2018.8658726

Niranjanamurthy, M., Nithya, B. N., & Jagannatha, S. (2019). Analysis of Blockchain technology: Pros, cons and SWOT. *Cluster Computing, 22*(6), 14743–14757. doi:10.100710586-018-2387-5

Pawar, D., Sarode, P., Santpure, S., Thore, P., & Nimbalkar, P. (n.d.). *Secure Voting System using Blockchain*. Academic Press.

Savelyev, A. (2018). Copyright in the blockchain era: Promises and challenges. *Computer Law & Security Review, 34*(3), 550–561. doi:10.1016/j.clsr.2017.11.008

Swati, V., & Prasad, A. S. (2018, December). Application of Blockchain Technology in Travel Industry. In *2018 International Conference on Circuits and Systems in Digital Enterprise Technology (ICCSDET)* (pp. 1-5). IEEE.

Tasatanattakool, P., & Techapanupreeda, C. (2018, January). Blockchain: Challenges and applications. In *2018 International Conference on Information Networking (ICOIN)* (pp. 473-475). IEEE. 10.1109/ICOIN.2018.8343163

Wohrer, M., & Zdun, U. (2018, March). Smart contracts: security patterns in the ethereum ecosystem and solidity. In *2018 International Workshop on Blockchain Oriented Software Engineering (IWBOSE)* (pp. 2-8). IEEE. 10.1109/IWBOSE.2018.8327565

Xie, J., Tang, H., Huang, T., Yu, F. R., Xie, R., Liu, J., & Liu, Y. (2019). A survey of blockchain technology applied to smart cities: Research issues and challenges. *IEEE Communications Surveys and Tutorials, 21*(3), 2794–2830. doi:10.1109/COMST.2019.2899617

Xu, J., Xue, K., Li, S., Tian, H., Hong, J., Hong, P., & Yu, N. (2019). Healthchain: A blockchain-based privacy preserving scheme for large-scale health data. *IEEE Internet of Things Journal, 6*(5), 8770–8781. doi:10.1109/JIOT.2019.2923525

Yuan, Y., & Wang, F. Y. (2018). Blockchain and cryptocurrencies: Model, techniques, and applications. *IEEE Transactions on Systems, Man, and Cybernetics. Systems, 48*(9), 1421–1428. doi:10.1109/TSMC.2018.2854904

Zhang, A., & Lin, X. (2018). Towards secure and privacy-preserving data sharing in e-health systems via consortium blockchain. *Journal of Medical Systems, 42*(8), 140. doi:10.100710916-018-0995-5 PMID:29956061

Zhao, Y., & Duncan, B. (2018, July). The Impact of Crypto-Currency Risks on the Use of Blockchain for Cloud Security and Privacy. In *2018 International Conference on High Performance Computing & Simulation (HPCS)* (pp. 677-684). IEEE. 10.1109/HPCS.2018.00111

Chapter 6
A Reliable Blockchain– Based Image Encryption Scheme for IIoT Networks

Ambika N.

ⅈD https://orcid.org/0000-0003-4452-5514

Department of Computer Applications, Sivananda Sarma Memorial RV College, Bangalore, India

ABSTRACT

IoT is used in industrial setup to increase security and provide ease to the user. The manual efforts decrease in this environment. The previous work concentrates on capturing images and transmitting the encrypted image. It uses the Merkle root and blockchain to make the transmission reliable. The suggestion increases reliability to the previous work. The system uses the Merkle root to endorse the key to the transmitting devices. The work increases reliability by 2.58% compared to the previous contribution.

1. INTRODUCTION

Industrial Internet-of-things (IIoT) (Ambika, 2020) (Hossain & Muhammad, 2016) is an aggregation of assembling procedure, checking, and the executive's frameworks. The system manages the availability of industrial facilities like machines and board frameworks required for business activities. IIoT is the contribution of cutting-edge machines and sensors to different ventures. Some examples include aviation, wellbeing (Ambika N., 2020) (Arcelus, Amaya, Jones, Goubran, & Knoefel, 2007) (Chandel, Sinharay, Ahmed, & Ghose, 2016), vitality, and resistance. The framework breaks down leads to a dangerous crisis. In this way, this division requires concentrated consideration and an elevated level of security. It is used across businesses, beginning of the essential assembling segment to signify the magnitude of creation units. It comprises creation, plans of action, client relations, investigate activities, instruction, and overall techniques of advancement.

A blockchain (A & K, 2016) (Atlam & Wills, 2019) is a computerized record that contains the whole history of exchanges made on the system. The essential reason for its existence was to wipe out outsiders from cash exchanges by making dependable advanced money transactions. It is a collection

DOI: 10.4018/978-1-7998-6694-7.ch006

of connected obstructs that are combined by hash esteems. All data on the blockchain is perpetual and can't be changed. Many applications have used blockchain in their doings. IIoT is one of them. (Khan & Byun, 2020) is an encryption plot for an IIoT-arranged system processing framework introduced that depends on a blockchain. It begins with the introduction of the web administration of the blockchain for hubs of the system. There are many picture catching gadgets, and every device goes about as a hub. When a device receives the transaction, it commences the chain for preparing the proposed calculation for preliminary checks. It will check that the present time is not as much as that of the message circulation stage and whether the hub is enrolled or not. The Certificate Authority (CA) allocates a computerized personality to each device of the system. If the device has a cryptographically approved advanced testament, mapped by the CA, at that point, it can take an interest in the framework. After beginning checks, it will start with the encryption procedure for the transaction. A hashed exchange ID broadcasted to all the systems. The device that has received hashed ID are the third parties.

The proposal aims to increase reliability. The contribution uses the Merkle root method to generate endorsement keys. The devices register themselves with the auxiliary devices by sharing their credentials. It transmits the encrypted data and the hash value (by using blockchain) to the respective validating node. The endorsement keys calculated by auxiliary devices are attached to the received data before transmitting them. The endorsement keys are derived using the identity of the transmitted device and validating node.

The division of the work is into seven segments. We start by introducing the technologies to the user and a brief paragraph on the contribution. Various authors have provided their insight into the technology is made available in the second division. The third division provides the narration of the Merkle root. The fourth section details the contribution. The details of the analysis are in the fifth section. Future work suggestion is in the sixth segment. The seventh segment contains an outline of the work.

2. LITERATURE SURVEY

The design (Wan, Li, Imran, & Li, 2019) has four layers. The detecting layer comprises of different sorts of sensors and a microcomputer. These gadgets sense information and pre-process the gathered information. The Hub layer parses the transferred information, encodes them, packs them and burdens the equivalent into the database. The capacity layer stores the information gathered by them in the conveyed structure. It synchronizes the information. Firmlayer associates the information securing unit, circulated calculation and information stockpiling innovation. The application layer observes the network and takes care or circumstances like failure forecast. The blockchain utilizes Merkle root to play out its errand. SHA256 and Elliptical curve cryptography calculation is utilized to upgrade security.

The blockchain hubs(Zhao, Li, & Yao, 2019) can be sorted into full hub (FN) and lightweight hub (LN). Full hub can download and check all blocks and exchanges. It can go about as mining hub and make obstructs for the blockchain. Lightweight hub, due to the confine assets stores information on the blockchain. With it, the LN can interface peers running a FN to send and get exchanges. The messages are encoded in CoAP messages. The FN sends back a reaction that can be confirmed by LN by checking its own token while the LN continues to build the exchanges. In IIoT condition, a LN can build up associations with the various intrigued FN to help yield recovery, verification age, updates to the structure, and compromise.

(Zhang, Zhu, Maharjan, & Zhang, 2019), is an edge insight and blockchain enabled 5G IIoT organize for joining and planning appropriated heterogeneous edge assets for modern applications in a proficient and secure way. The creators have built up a cross-area sharing empowered ideal edge asset planning plan to limit the working expenses of the edge hubs while improving limit. In the blockchain enabled it arranges, to proficiently arrive at an edge asset exchange agreement, credit-separated exchange endorsement component for conveyed edge hubs are suggested. The cross-area includes crossing between various asset types and diverse IIoT systems. Three fundamental components of the deep reinforcement learning (DRL) methodology include state, activity, and grant. The state comprises the administration requests of assorted applications in various systems, and the accessible limit of heterogeneous assets of each edge hub. The activity is characterized as edge asset booking techniques, which allot heterogeneous edge assets for different kinds of modern applications created in various systems.

(Xu, et al., 2019), is a blockchain-based nonrepudiation administration provisioning methodology for IIoT situations. The blockchain is utilized as a proof recorder and an administration distribution intermediary. The necessary help program is cut into non-executable parts for conveyance by means of on-chain and off-chain diverts in independent strides. The procedure can lessen the weight of the blockchain and maintain a strategic distance from the program exposure chance. In addition, it implements proof entries of even off-chain practices. The system guarantees the genuine reasonableness of nonrepudiation scheme. The creators planned an assistance confirmation strategy dependent on homomorphic hash strategies, which can accurately approve administrations dependent on negligible lightweight on-chain proof instead of complete help program codes, supporting the centre usefulness of the model.

LightChain(Liu, Wang, Lin, & Xu, 2019) is a savvy manufacturing plant representing the structure of the blockchain framework. The framework comprises of four layers-API layer, LightChain layer, Cache layer, and Storage layer. The light chain layer is comprised of various approval systems to affirm the legitimacy and uprightness of pending (computerized signature approval and connection approval). An API layer offers interfaces for modern control applications. Cache layer is intended to quicken the reactions to different calls. The information stores the pending blocks, and helpful blocks. Capacity layer, ordinarily served by asset rich gadgets, gives determined capacity, administration to the upper layers.

Proof-of-Reputation-X (PoRX)(Wang, Liang, Chen, Kumari, & Khan, 2020) includes a notoriety module which can be incorporated in the PoX conventions. The quintessence of the blockchain accord is to keep up a similar status of the record on various hubs. In every agreement cycle, a certified hub is chosen to refresh the blockchain record. In blockchains the Standard of the agreement is to choose hubs who contribute decisively to the framework based on plentiful assets. Subsequently, with PoRX by the notoriety of hubs in the framework, it can lessen the trouble of PoX agreement, which stays away from the need of ASIC mining machines hazard and the danger of centralization. Identity-based Method incorporates - presumed development, obstruct start process, revelry cycle, motivating force component and Protocol Parameters Update Rule.

(Chen, et al., 2019), is a multi-bounce circulated calculation offloading answer. It considers the information handling undertakings and the digging assignments together for blockchain-engaged IIoT. To address the principal issue introduced, the creators have built up a game-hypothesis based disseminated calculation offloading technique to permit the information preparing undertakings and the mining errands to be offloaded to the Edge servers to accomplish worldwide asset enhancement. To address the subsequent issue introduced, they have defined the offloading issue as a multi-bounce calculation offloading game (MCOG) and plan a dispersed calculation by which the game can rapidly meet to a steady state.

The IIoT Bazaar expects to address these difficulties by applying a decentralized Blockchain organize and the various leveled, conveyed structure of a Fog Computing. Blockchain innovation is utilized to make a commercial centre for the trade of utilizations in which no outsiders should be trusted. The IIoT

Bazaar App is the connection between the Edge Devices in the field and the Technician. The experts utilize their cell phones, which have the IIoT Bazaar App introduced, to recognize, distinguish and associate with the Edge Devices. After effective confirmation, the specialists can introduce or uninstall applications utilizing drag and drop activities. Besides, the IIoT Bazaar App gives data about the current status of the Edge Devices and their cooperations with respect to application establishments and updates. The IoT Manager is the core of the design and essential issue of contact. The Dev Store is the interface for the engineers with the IIoT Bazaar biological system. The Warehouse stores the binaries.

In this work, an encryption plot for an IIoT-arranged system processing framework is introduced that depends on a blockchain. The procedure begins with the introduction of the web administration of the blockchain for hubs of the system. There are many picture catching gadgets, and every gadget goes about as a hub. At the point when a hub catches the picture and sends it to the chain for preparing, the proposed calculation will perform introductory checks. It will check that the present time is not as much as that of the message circulation stage and whether the hub is enlisted or not enrolled. The Certificate Authority (CA) allocates a computerized personality to each hub of the system. If the hub has a cryptographically approved advanced testament, mapped by the CA, at that point, it can take an interest in the framework. If the mentioned exchange is as of now prepared, at that point, it is overlooked. After beginning checks, it will begin the encryption procedure for the picture. This picture is prepared, and a hashed exchange ID will be distributed for each picture, which is the key to the whole plan.

The framework foundation(Huang, et al., 2019) is based on DAG-organized blockchain. Every element is a hub in the blockchain-based IIoT framework. There are four segments in the engineering. Remote sensors conveyed in a shrewd industrial facility to gather readings. Every sensor will produce a blockchain account when introduced. The key pair for every gadget is used to sign exchanges. Gateways get the solicitations from different sensors and communicate the exchanges in the knot, they exchange from legitimate sensors that are approved by the chief. The director can oversee the gadgets through propelling an exchange which records public keys of approved IoT gadgets. The knot arrangement is a public blockchain organize where any gathering can get into the system. The credit-based POW instrument to make the tradeoff between productivity and security is proposed. Hubs comply with the framework rules to send exchanges and will build the credit after sometime step by step.

, is a credit-based installment method to help quickness and successive vitality exchanging. Stackelberg games for credit-based advances are used to evaluate the work. All approved EAGs need to review and check exchange records in new squares. It requires some investment to complete the agreement procedure. The process is completed by comparing with the wallet address. At the token mentioning stage, the borrower can apply a token dependent on its credit. During vitality exchanging, the borrower utilizes vitality coins in wallet to complete installation. Every installment Based on the wallet is confirmed and recorded by the nearby credit bank. The credit bank puts the hash estimation of installment related information into prerecording. After a legitimacy span of the token, the borrower will get the most updated token including all hash estimations of the credit-based installment records.

A blockchain-empowered IIoT framework (Liu, Yu, Teng, Leung, & Song, 2019) comprising two sections is suggested. The IIoT arrangement creates exchanges of information and shares the same. The block chain framework manages the exchanges in a secure way. Two sorts of exchanges consistently are made by the savvy gadgets. These exchanges are handed-off to blockchain frameworks for putting away/getting the information into/from the circulated record. To deal with the exchanges created by the youth organize, a block is made, communicated to another block maker, and add the block to their nearby blockchain after an accord is reached on the new block.

An Anonymous Reputation System on a Proof-of-Stake blockchain (ARS-PS)(Liu, Alahmadi, Ni, Lin, & Shen, 2019) is suggested. The contribution permits retailers to build up notorieties by amassing inputs from shoppers. The proposed framework safeguards the commentator namelessness. The individual survey measurements are hidden and just the collected audit insights have been uncovered to people in general by breaking the job of the encryption key administration authority over different council individuals. The blockchain-based engineering that executes the proposed unknown notoriety framework to improve the framework straightforwardness is suggested. In the off-chain rating token stage, the proposed engineering lessens the on-chain stockpiling and calculation overhead.

BPIIoT(Bai, Hu, Liu, & Wang, 2019) is contained on-chain and off-chain organization. All exchanges are handled in the on-chain system (computerized signature). The off-chain organize manages the capacity, complex information preparing, and different issues that blockchain can't explain. The keen agreement is used as the administration agreement by purchasers and assembling assets, giving on-request fabricating administration. Two shrewd application cases, producing gear information sharing and support administration sharing from keen assembling, are executed to clarify the brilliant agreement for the hardware upkeep administration and status information sharing administration. The on-chain organize maintains a strategic distance from the support of outsiders by presenting Secure Multi-Party Computation (SMPC). Information inquiry and computation are dispersed on various hubs, which take an interest in the count without spilling data.

(Seok, Park, & Park, 2019), is a lightweight hash-based blockchain engineering for IIoT. The proposed blockchain organize comprises of "Cell hub" and "Capacity hub", and it works between the field layer and control layer. Field layer of the proposed design relates to level 0 and level 1 in Purdue model. The control layer relates to level 2 in Purdue model. For covering numerous heterogeneous gadgets in an expansion zone, the fields are isolated in a little territory, which is referenced as "Cell". The cell hub makes block of information assembled from associated gadgets and communicate to different hubs in the blockchain for block approval after block mining. After the block approval process, all hubs partaking in block approval sends the arrival message to the capacity hub for notice approving outcomes and afterward block update is prepared. The capacity hub is answerable for overseeing block update and record the board. In the block update process, the capacity hub adds the approved block. The entirety of the prepared exchange can be checked from the conveyed record in the capacity hub.

SCFMCLPEKS+ (Wu, Chen, Wang, & Wu, 2019) utilizes a bilinear guide, ace key, and hash work. The information proprietor's the halfway private key, information client's fractional concealed credential, and worker's incomplete private key DS are registered. Utilizing public, private, and mystery keys, the hidden entryway is determined. The worker's private solution and ciphertext utilization authenticate the check procedure. The proposition improves disconnected watchword speculating assault.

The creators have built up the first CLKS plot with multi-beneficiary watchword scan work (Lu, Li, & Zhang, 2019) for IIoTs. The plan stays away from the excessive bilinear matching. It gives protection catchphrase search. MARCKS plot contains four various elements, in particular: a credential generating center, a distributed storage worker, a sender, and different beneficiaries. The center is accountable for making a lot of shared framework boundaries and a framework ace key. It is likewise answerable for delivering a couple of fractional keys for the sender and every beneficiary. The sender creates and sends the accessible ciphertexts to the distributed storage worker. Each target beneficiary can recover these information ciphertexts by sending the disseminated storage worker an inquiry token determines from the pursuit watchword by utilizing the beneficiary's private key. Finally, the distributed storage worker abuses the pursuit token to find all coordinating ciphertexts that are then gotten back to the beneficiary.

The work (Zhou, et al., 2018) considers assault for Cui's multi-key total accessible encryption, where the aggressor can figure the other approved clients' keys from the unapproved inside client's key. The creators have presented a formalized meaning of record driven total watchword attainable encryption framework, which can be utilized for the IIoT information sharing and approved information search. They formalize two new security models on the Fc-MKA-KSE framework. One catches catchphrase ciphertext security, for example, the lack of definition against particular document picked catchphrase assault, and different catches the hidden entrance security, for example, the vagary against specific record watchword speculating assault. They build a catchphrase reachable encryption conspire in the record driven structure in IIoT sending. At that point, they actualize a model of the proposed plot and assess its presentation. The assessment shows that the ciphertext and secret entrance can figure on the sensor.

The creators planned safe station free certificateless public key encryption with various catchphrases (Ma, He, Kumar, Choo, & Chen, 2017) plot for IIoT sending. It uses two-cycle bunches with a similar request. It chooses a generator and guides it to produce bilinear matching. The framework has four elements- a cloud worker, an information proprietor, a beneficiary, and a credential obtaining unit. It is liable for producing a framework clue and incomplete private keys of both collectors and workers. Information Owner uses the collector's and worker's public solution to encode the information and the file of catchphrases contained in the facts. The information proprietor can store the encoded data and scrambled catchphrase lists in the cloud worker. The recipient is an informed client who acquires his/her incomplete private key from the credential unit. The beneficiary creates the secret entryway of watchwords that he/she wishes to look, sends it to the cloud worker. Cloud Server acquires its halfway private key from key unit. It is answerable for preparing information, for example, registering information, putting away information, and scanning information for the client. The work comprises of eight polynomial-time probabilistic calculations.

The creators develop a light-weight attainable public-key encryption conspire with forwarding protection (Chen, Wu, Kumar, Choo, & He, 2019). It accomplishes both forward preserves and searches effectiveness near that of some down to earth accessible symmetric encryption plans. It keeps away from the requirement for costly credential administration. SPE-FP demonstrates to be ciphertext vague in the irregular prophet model, and it additionally accomplishes forward security. An accessible encryption plot with concealed structure arranges the catchphrase attainable ciphertexts with carefully planned shrouded relations. It lists ciphertexts by the corresponding closed connection between public Head to the first ciphertext. The arrangement has four elements- Certificate Authority (CA), Cloud Server Provider (CSP), Data Owner (DO), and Data Receiver (DR). The correspondence among DO and DR is non-concurrent through a free-channel. There are two channels for corresponds among CSP and DR, where one is a public channel. DO is liable for producing and sending re-appropriated ciphertexts, which incorporate record ciphertexts, file ciphertexts, variant ciphertexts, and catchphrase ciphertexts. CSP entrusts with information stockpiling and recovery, which has practically boundless capacity and calculation limits. DR can give search inquiries by using a catchphrase secret entrance and afterward get all coordinating documents containing the relating watchword.

The information proprietor assembles the catchphrase lists and transfers the information along with the watchword lists to the haze hub (Yu, Chen, Li, Li, & Tian, 2019). The elements of IIoT can present some pursuit tokens called secret entryways to the haze hub looks through the redistributed information relating to catchphrases. The haze hub performs uniformity testing to figure out which parts of the ciphertext coordinate the secret entrance and afterward restores the coordinated share to the element as an output. SE arranges into two classes- symmetric accessible encryption (SSE) and public key encryption with catchphrase search (PEKS). It executes CPoR on a MacBook Pro with 2.3 GHz Intel Core i5 CPU and 8 GB RAM. The calculations run in C ventures upheld by the OpenSSL library. The work area has a 64-piece Win 10 working framework and 8 GB RAM, The processor is Intel Core i5-7400 CPU @ 3.00 GHZ, and the compiler is Visual Studio 2012. The Raspberry Pi 3 is outfitted with Cortex-A53 (ARMv8) 64-piece SoC @ 1.4 GHz CPU and Broadcom BCM2837B0, whose working framework is Raspbian.

The Visual Processing Hub (VPH) in mechanical observation networks (Muhammad, et al., 2018) gathers visual information from visual sensors as video outlines, bringing large volumes of video information. The creators tentatively demonstrated that the aftereffects of vital pictures are multiple times quicker than existing techniques for object discovery. The preliminaries for each casing caught by the visual camera are preliminary for the evacuation of foundation movement and accurate assessment. They estimate by figuring the adjustments in picture block esteems in neighboring casings. The proposed calculation has two significant segments- significant part means to utilize an ongoing 2D disordered guide to create PRNG appropriate for our proposed picture encryption, and the subsequent ones execute one round of stage dispersion measures for the keyframe viable. They utilize a randomized methodology, making it infeasible for assailants to master anything about the first information from the encoded outlines. A 2D strategic balanced sine map (LASM) gives efficiencies and high affectability to starting qualities and sophisticated turbulent conduct of its produced groupings. They set the underlying grades as mystery keys to make assaults ineffectual and futile. Coding the pixels of the keyframe begins with installing genuine disordered pieces into one channel of the sole keyframe. At that point, disarray and dissemination tasks intend to haphazardly change the pixel esteems and mix the pixel positions, individually.

The visual preparation center (VPH) gets visual data from sensors as a video outline in the keen medical care reconnaissance organizations, prompting critical measures of video data. The proposed extraction YOLOv3 calculation for keyframes (Khan, et al., 2020) is lightweight since it is used as a preparation picture dataset and describes to distinguish human presence from the recorded recordings. The utilized methodology proposes a technique to expand discovery accuracy while advancing a continuous cycle by displaying YOLOv3's jumping box, the most representative of single-stage finders. The precision of the model is 88-90% with 1-16 FPS (document every second) on the Intel Core i5-fifth era framework, which is more fitting in regards to the patient's observing in the keen medical services framework. Each communication or development of the patient is precisely distinguished with high exactness and inside the jumping boxes. This extraction cycle utilizes with deferent patients in different clinic wards into the savvy medical services arrangement, and as a came about keyframe. It essentially delivers keyframe from the keyframe extraction model is passed to the lightweight encryption model for additional protected activity. The recommended calculation has two parts. The primary segment that utilizes the most recent cosine transform-based turbulent arrangement (CTC) to produce PRNG proper for our proposed picture encryption and the subsequent one intends to perform three rounds of disarray – dissemination strategies for the keyframe.

The proposed framework (Ahmad, Larijani, Emmanuel, & Mannion, 2018) checks the number of inhabitants and sends information to the distributed computing stage ThingSpeak progressively. Protection attack is consistently a worry for video-based inhabitance observing frameworks when associated with the Internet. They have utilized the Intertwining Logistic guide, and results are likewise contrasted outcomes and NCA map. Analyses use a solitary overhead camera in the T10 office at Glasgow Caledonian University, UK. In the proposed framework, when individuals cross a virtual line, inhabitance (in/out) is estimated, and information transfer to the distributed computing stage, ThingSpeak. The person distinguished in an edge undergoes scrambling.

The proposed model (Elhoseny, et al., 2018) has four consistent cycles. The secret patient's information scrambles utilizing proposed hybrid encryption conspire that creates from both AES and RSA encryption calculations. It hides in a spread picture that uses either 2D-DWT-1L or 2D-DWT-2L and produces a stego-picture. The separated data undergoes unscrambling to recover the first information. The execution completes by using the MATLAB R2015a programming running on a PC with a 2.27 GHz Intel (R) Core (TM) I3 CPU, 8 GB RAM, and Windows 7 as the working framework. The outcomes dependent on six measurable boundaries containing the Peak Signal to Noise Ratio (PSNR Mean Square Error (MSE), Bit Error Rate (BER), Structural Similarity (SSIM), Structural Content (SC), and Correlation.

The calculation introduced joins two clamorous frameworks- Arnold's Cat guide and Duffing conditions (Boutros, Hesham, Georgey, & Abd El Ghany, 2017), for the two phases of confusion based picture encryption. For the disarray stage, pixels rearrangement utilizes an altered two-dimensional Arnold's Cat map. The proposed calculation is executed on Matlab R2016a to investigate its exhibition dependent on the usual security boundaries. The examination performance on three grayscale test pictures of various sizes- Lenna (512×512), Lenna (256×256), and Cameraman (256×256). Histogram examination is performed on the encoded test pictures to envision the distinction in pixels' qualities circulation between the scrambled and the first picture. The connection coefficients allude to the real connection between two contiguous pixels of a figure, evenly, vertically, and tilted. The proposed calculation utilizes 22 distinct boundaries as encryption keys. It assesses its entropy esteem, mean square blunder, top sign to clamor proportion, level of changed pixels' qualities, and power of this change in the code picture concerning the first picture. The commitment is the increasing speed of the proposed encryption plot in a total equipment arrangement reasonable for continuous IoT imaging applications.

The proposed encryption calculation (Wu, et al., 2019) comprises of seven stages containing Initial credential age, Pseudo-arbitrary succession age, Permutation vector age, Confusion, DNA encoding, Diffusion, and DNA disentangling. The information has plaintext alongside two boundaries. It will produce starter certification. The essential ones create two change vectors. The image uses these vectors. The pseudo arrangement and planning rules, two DNA successions are made. These and planning rules generate the figure.

The invisible layer encryption (Lv, Liu, & Sun, 2019) partitions into four sections. Information assortment and Data move part is answerable for routinely gathering information from camera sensors which circulated in savvy urban communities, and putting away in edge server farm or cloud server farm, as per the necessities of IoT applications. The information pre-handling part is principally liable for the preliminary preparation of the gathered information, and recoveries the acquired arrangement of organizing purposes of the prepared article in our social information base. The center of information encryption calculation is answerable for coordinating with the encoded object. After the coordinating is fruitful, our center calculation progressively produces film and passes the film to the information for security information insurance. The framework and Network Monitoring part offer types of assistance.

The plans (Noura, et al., 2018) can partition into two classes-Stream codes and Block figures. The proposed figure plot incorporates a few commitments that prompted a significant level of productivity and security for IoT gadgets contrasted with the ongoing lightweight square codes, late confusing codes. The aging cycle of the dynamic key and the related sub-enters uses in the code. The mystery key is usual between the imparting elements after the shared confirmation step. A pseudo-arbitrary generator produces this Nonce. At that point, the mystery key is Xored, and it is comparing the yield hash to deliver the dynamic credential. It isolates into four distinctive sub-keys that structure the seeds for the distinct code natives and these portray in the accompanying subsections.

The proposition (Abd El-Latif, et al., 2020) is lightweight picture encryption system utilizing one-walker. The introduced arrangement uses the abilities of nonlinear elements of QWs to produce PRNG groupings and build P-boxes. From the start, the first picture is isolated into blocks every one of size 16×16, and afterward, each square is partitioned into two subblocks: right subblock and left subblock. Each subblock previously recombination is permutated and subbed with its own P-box and PRNG that starts from the likelihood appropriation of following up on e-walker on a circle. The encoded blocks are joined together and afterward XORed with another PRNG arrangement to develop the code picture. NIST SP 800-22 tests are applied to research the haphazardness conduct code picture. They comprise of 15 tests on a 106 piece succession.

The SSIR plot (Yan, Chen, & Jia, 2019) empowers the asset compelled customers to move the cycle of preprocessing pictures to cloud cut off and perform looking in cloud workers. It will lessen the expense of the customer. It first needs to build a Hessian grid. It contrasts and its 26 neighbors in the picture space. On the off chance that it is bigger or littler than its neighbors, this point will choose as an intriguing point. The harr wavelet checked in its round neighborhood. That is, in the roundabout neighborhood of the element focuses, the entirety of the level and vertical harr wavelet. The fan shape is pivoted at timespans radians and rehashes this cycle. It has three members. The picture proprietor creates two sets of keys: a public encryption key pair and a mark key pair. The public encryption key uses to scramble the pictures and the element vectors. The mark key uses to approve the customers to play out the picture search over the picture set. Next, through far off verification and neighborhood confirmation, the mystery key of the picture proprietor is moved to the inquiry enclave. The pursuit enclave decodes the encoded inquiry picture, separates the component vectors of the question picture, and runs the hunt calculation on the plaintext. At last, it restores the outcome to the customer.

The gathered data undergoes hashing (Khan & Byun, 2020). Hashing is making a unique mark. If there is a slight change in the data, the entire distinct one will be changed. In the picture encryption measure, a picture modifies into an arrangement of bytes with the goal. It is a helpful procedure to ensure the substance of advanced figures. Diverse cryptographic calculations play out the encryption cycle. Encoded bytes would then be able to be moved to another framework, where it alters to acquire unique qualities utilizing the decoding cycle. For both encryption and decoding measures, we use calculations dependent on some key. The administrator can arrange endorser and non-endorser peers. Since the sensor hubs don't have many force assets to run the mining calculation, a few devices go about as validator hubs. These hubs agree to add another square to the chain. It is an organization that must continue the imitation of a blockchain. It is likewise answerable for preparing the exchange. In an IIoT organization, hubs are battery-or power controlled gadgets perform correspondence and information assortment. The device in the blockchain fuses various squares, state information bases, strategies, and a keen agreement. The condition of the record at given factors and times is spoken to and put away in the state information base.

3. Background

a. **Merkle root -** A Merkle root is a straightforward numerical approach to check the information on a Merkle tree. They are utilized in digital money to ensure information squares went between peers on a shared system. They are key to the calculation required to keep up cryptographic forms of money like bitcoin and ether. A hash tree encodes the blockchain information in a productive and secure way. It empowers by brisk checking of the blockchain information on the distributed organize. Each exchange happening on the blockchain arrange has a hash related with it. These hashes are inserted as a treelike structure with the end goal that each hash is connected to its parent following a parent-kid treelike connection.

Assume that two text messages are hashed at level 1. Let the text be $Text_1$ and $Text_2$. Let the resultant hash value H_1 be derived from hashing of $Text_1$. This is represented in notation (1). Let the resultant hash value H_2 be derived by hashing the text $Text_2$. The same is represented in the notation (2).

$$H_1 \rightarrow hash(Text_1) \tag{1}$$

$$H_2 \rightarrow hash(Text_2) \tag{2}$$

The parent of these two hash values is represented by H_{12}. The same is obtained by hashing both the texts $Text_1$ and $Text_2$. The same is represented in the notation (3).

$$H_{12} \rightarrow hash(Text_1 + Text_2) \tag{3}$$

Table 1. Notations used in the proposal

Notations used in the proposal	Description
D_i	i[th] device of the network
Hello	Hello packets
Ack	Acknowledgement
V_i	Validating node/auxiliary node
D_{id}	Device identification
I_d	dimension of the image
R_i	resolution of the image
B_d	bit depth of the image
I_s	Size of the image
T_i	Considered Time

4. PROPOSED WORK

a. Notations Used in the Work

b. Assumptions Made in the Work

- The devices encompass intelligent sensors capable of handling routine. They are liable to get hacked.
- The work uses two kinds of gadgets –
  - To sense the environment, process, and forward them to the pre-programmed destination. The loading contains a hashing algorithm (blockchain technology) along with other credentials.
  - Auxiliary devices/validating devices that can endorse the transmitted data. These devices are capable of building a hash tree using the Merkle root. Only the validating devices are capable of generating the Merkle root tree using the hash algorithm.

c. Methodology Used in the Proposal

i.   i. *Deployment of the devices* – The deployed devices occupy various locations in the industrial setup. The devices communicate with each other creating a topology. In equation (4), the gadget Di is sending Hello-packet to the device Dj. After receiving the message from the device, Dj sends an acknowledgment to Di. Equation (5) contains the same representation.

$$D_i \rightarrow D_j : \text{Hello} \tag{4}$$

$$D_j \rightarrow D_i : \text{Ack} \tag{5}$$

ii.   ii. *Registrations with the auxiliary node/validating node – The devices get* registered at the auxiliary node by providing their identification. In the equation (6) the device D_i is transmitting its identity D_{id} to the validating node V_i.

$$D_i \rightarrow V_i : D_{id} \tag{6}$$

iii.   iii.   *Deriving the hash value using the blockchain* –The device capturing image calculates the hash value using the blockchain methodology. The following parameters used to derive the hash value – dimension of the image, resolution of the image, bit depth, and size. The corresponding device calculates the hash value using these units and transmits it along with the encrypted data to the respective validation device. In equation (7), the gadget D_i calculates the hash value using the dimension of the image I_d, resolution of the image R_i, bit depth B_d, its size I_s and dispatches it along with encrypted data Data$_i$ to the auxiliary node V_i.

$$D_i \rightarrow V_i : hash\left(I_d, R_i, B_d, I_s\right) \| E_x(Data_i) \tag{7}$$

iv.   iv.   *Deriving the endorsement key for a session* – The auxiliary node uses its and device identification to derive the endorsement key. The construction of the Merkle root uses the identity of the gadget and validating device. Hash$_M$ is the algorithm used to generate the Merkle root tree. In the equation, the device identification D$_{id}$ and validating device identification V$_{id}$ is concatenated. The hash value generation uses the Merkle root tree concept. The device transmits the data to the validating node for endorsement. Equation (8) represents the same. This value is attached to the received message and sent to the destination.

$$V_i \rightarrow hash_M\left(D_{id} \| V_{id}\right) \tag{8}$$

5. Analysis of the Work

The proposal is the improvement of the previous contribution. (Khan & Byun, 2020), is an encryption plot for an IIoT-arranged system processing framework is introduced that depends on a blockchain. The procedure begins with the introduction of the web administration of the blockchain for hubs of the system. There are many picture catching gadgets, and every gadget goes about as a hub. At the point when a hub catches the picture and sends it to the chain for preparing, the proposed calculation will perform introductory checks. It will check that the present time is not as much as that of the message circulation stage and whether the hub is enlisted or not enrolled. The Certificate Authority (CA) allocates a computerized personality to each hub of the system. If the hub has a cryptographically approved advanced testament, mapped by the CA, at that point, it can take an interest in the framework. If the mentioned exchange is as of now prepared, at that point, it is overlooked. After beginning checks, it will begin the encryption procedure for the picture. This picture is prepared, and a hashed exchange ID will be distributed for each picture, which is the key to the whole plan.

The contribution uses the Merkle root method to generate endorsement keys. The devices register themselves with the auxiliary devices by sharing their credentials. It transmits the encrypted data and the hash value (by using blockchain) to the respective validating node. The endorsement keys calculated by auxiliary devices are attached to the received data before transmitting them. The endorsement keys are derived using the identity of the transmitted device and validating node. Hence the reliability is increased by 2.58% compared to previous work. Figure 1 is used to represent the same.

The work is simulated in NS2. Table 2. Contains the parameters used the work for simulation.

6. FUTURE WORK

The contribution uses the Merkle root method to generate endorsement keys. The devices register themselves with the auxiliary devices by sharing their credentials. It transmits the encrypted data and the hash value (by using blockchain) to the respective validating node. The endorsement keys calculated by auxiliary devices are attached to the received data before transmitting them. The endorsement keys are derived using the identity of the transmitted device and validating node. Hence the reliability is increased

Table 2. Parameters used during simulation

Parameters used	Description
Number of gadgets installed	4
Number of validating or auxiliary device employed	1
Length of the identity (validating or sensing device)	16 bits
Length of the Hash value obtained (endorsement key)	8 bits
Length of dimension of the image	32 bits
Length of resolution of the image	16 bits
Length of bit depth of the image	12 bits
Length of image size	16 bits
Length of hash value derived (blockchain)	11 bits
Length of data bits	256 bits
Simulation time	60 ms

by 2.58% compared to previous work. Figure 1 is used to represent the same. As the amount of data transmission increases, the energy in these devices decreases. So, suggestions for Security-centric and energy-centric algorithms are essential in the future.

Figure 1.

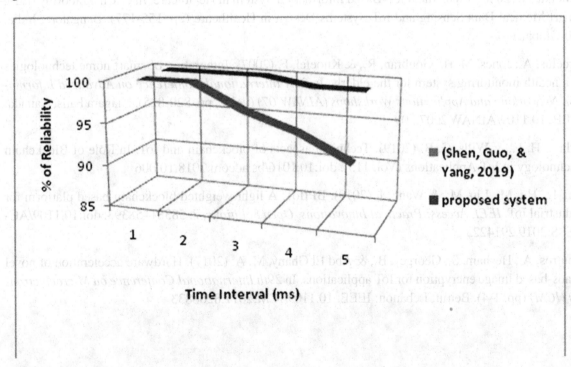

7. CONCLUSION

IoT is used in Industrial setup to increase security and provide ease to the user. The manual efforts decrease in this environment. The previous work concentrates on capturing images and transmitting the encrypted image. It uses the Merkle root and blockchain to make the transmission reliable. The suggestion increases reliability to the previous work. The system uses the Merkle root to endorse the key to the transmitting devices. The usage of the identity of the validating node and the sensing device is made. The work increases reliability by 2.58% compared to the previous contribution.

REFERENCES

A, B., & K, M. V. (2016). Blockchain platform for industrial internet of things. *Journal of software Engineering and Applications, 9*(10), 533.

Abd El-Latif, A., Abd-El-Atty, B., Venegas-Andraca, S., Elwahsh, H., Piran, M., Bashir, A., ... Mazurczyk, W. (2020). Providing End-to-End Security Using Quantum Walks in IoT Networks. *IEEE Access: Practical Innovations, Open Solutions*, 8, 92687–92696. doi:10.1109/ACCESS.2020.2992820

Ahmad, J., Larijani, H., Emmanuel, R., & Mannion, M. (2018). *Secure occupancy monitoring system for iot using lightweight intertwining logistic map. In 10th Computer Science and Electronic Engineering (CEEC)*. IEEE.

Ambika, N. (2020). Encryption of Data in Cloud-Based Industrial IoT Devices. In S. Pal & V. G. Díaz (Eds.), *IoT: Security and Privacy Paradigm* (pp. 111–129). CRC press, Taylor & Francis Group.

Ambika, N. (2020). Methodical IoT-Based Information System in Healthcare. In C. Chakraborthy (Ed.), Smart Medical Data Sensing and IoT Systems Design in Healthcare (pp. 155-177). Bangalore, India: IGI Global.

Arcelus, A., Jones, M. H., Goubran, R., & Knoefel, F. (2007). Integration of smart home technologies in a health monitoring system for the elderly. In *21st International Conference on Advanced Information Networking and Applications Workshops (AINAW'07)* (*vol. 2*, pp. 820-825). Niagara Falls, Canada: IEEE. 10.1109/AINAW.2007.209

Atlam, H. F., & Wills, G. B. (2019). Technical aspects of blockchain and IoT. In Role of Blockchain Technology in IoT Applications (Vol. 115). doi:10.1016/bs.adcom.2018.10.006

Bai, L., Hu, M., Liu, M., & Wang, J. (2019). BPIIoT: A light-weighted blockchain-based platform for Industrial IoT. *IEEE Access: Practical Innovations, Open Solutions*, 7, 58381–58393. doi:10.1109/ACCESS.2019.2914223

Boutros, A., Hesham, S., Georgey, B., & Abd El Ghany, M. A. (2017). Hardware acceleration of novel chaos-based image encryption for IoT applications. In *29th International Conference on Microelectronics (ICM)* (pp. 1-4). Beirut, Lebanon: IEEE. 10.1109/ICM.2017.8268833

Chandel, V., Sinharay, A., Ahmed, N., & Ghose, A. (2016). Exploiting IMU Sensors for IOT Enabled Health Monitoring. In *First Workshop on IoT-enabled Healthcare and Wellness Technologies and Systems* (pp. 21-22). Singapore: ACM. 10.1145/2933566.2933569

Chen, B., Wu, L., Kumar, N., Choo, K. K., & He, D. (2019). Lightweight searchable public-key encryption with forward privacy over IIoT outsourced data. *IEEE Transactions on Emerging Topics in Computing*, 1–1. doi:10.1109/TETC.2019.2921113

Chen, W., Zhang, Z., Hong, Z., Chen, C., Wu, J., Maharjan, S., Zheng, Z., & Zhang, Y. (2019). Cooperative and distributed computation offloading for blockchain-empowered industrial Internet of Things. *Internet of Things Journal*, 6(5), 8433–8446. doi:10.1109/JIOT.2019.2918296

Elhoseny, M., Ramírez-González, G., Abu-Elnasr, O. M., Shawkat, S. A., Arunkumar, N., & Farouk, A. (2018). Secure medical data transmission model for IoT-based healthcare systems. *IEEE Access: Practical Innovations, Open Solutions*, 6, 20596–20608. doi:10.1109/ACCESS.2018.2817615

Hossain, M., & Muhammad, G. (2016). Cloud-assisted industrial internet of things (iiot)–enabled framework for health monitoring. *Computer Networks*, 101, 192–202. doi:10.1016/j.comnet.2016.01.009

Huang, J., Kong, L., Chen, G., Wu, M. Y., Liu, X., & Zeng, P. (2019). Towards secure industrial IoT: Blockchain system with credit-based consensus mechanism. *IEEE Transactions on Industrial Informatics*, 15(6), 3680–3689. doi:10.1109/TII.2019.2903342

Khan, J., Li, J. P., Ahamad, B., Parveen, S., Haq, A. U., Khan, G. A., & Sangaiah, A. K. (2020). SMSH: Secure Surveillance Mechanism on Smart Healthcare IoT System With Probabilistic Image Encryption. *IEEE Access: Practical Innovations, Open Solutions*, 8, 15747–15767. doi:10.1109/ACCESS.2020.2966656

Khan, P. W., & Byun, Y. (2020). A Blockchain-Based Secure Image Encryption Scheme for the Industrial Internet of Things. *Entropy (Basel, Switzerland)*, 22(175), 1–26. doi:10.3390/e22020175 PMID:33285950

Khan, P. W., & Byun, Y. (2020). A Blockchain-Based Secure Image Encryption Scheme for the Industrial Internet of Things. *Entropy (Basel, Switzerland)*, 22(2), 175. doi:10.3390/e22020175 PMID:33285950

Li, Z., Kang, J., Yu, R., Ye, D., Deng, Q., & Zhang, Y. (2017). Consortium blockchain for secure energy trading in industrial internet of things. *IEEE Transactions on Industrial Informatics*, 14(8), 3690–3700. doi:10.1109/TII.2017.2786307

Liu, D., Alahmadi, A., Ni, J., Lin, X., & Shen, X. (2019). Anonymous reputation system for IIoT-enabled retail marketing atop PoS blockchain. *IEEE Transactions on Industrial Informatics*, 15(6), 3527–3537. doi:10.1109/TII.2019.2898900

Liu, M., Yu, F. R., Teng, Y., Leung, V. C., & Song, M. (2019). Performance optimization for blockchain-enabled industrial Internet of Things (IIoT) systems: A deep reinforcement learning approach. *IEEE Transactions on Industrial Informatics*, 15(6), 3559–3570. doi:10.1109/TII.2019.2897805

Liu, Y., Wang, K., Lin, Y., & Xu, W. (2019). A Lightweight Blockchain System for Industrial Internet of Things. *IEEE Transactions on Industrial Informatics*, 15(6), 3571–3581. doi:10.1109/TII.2019.2904049

Lu, Y., Li, J., & Zhang, Y. (2019). Privacy-Preserving and Pairing-Free Multirecipient Certificateless Encryption With Keyword Search for Cloud-Assisted IIoT. *IEEE Internet of Things Journal*, 7(4), 2553–2562. doi:10.1109/JIOT.2019.2943379

Lv, S., Liu, Y., & Sun, J. (2019). IMES: An Automatically Scalable Invisible Membrane Image Encryption for Privacy Protection on IoT Sensors. In *International Symposium on Cyberspace Safety and Security* (pp. 265-273). Guangzhou, China: Springer.

Ma, M., He, D., Kumar, N., Choo, K. K., & Chen, J. (2017). Certificateless searchable public key encryption scheme for industrial internet of things. *IEEE Transactions on Industrial Informatics*, 14(2), 759–767.

Muhammad, K., Hamza, R., Ahmad, J., Lloret, J., Wang, H., & Baik, S. W. (2018). Secure surveillance framework for IoT systems using probabilistic image encryption. *IEEE Transactions on Industrial Informatics*, 14(8), 3679–3689. doi:10.1109/TII.2018.2791944

Noura, H., Chehab, A., Sleem, L., Noura, M., Couturier, R., & Mansour, M. M. (2018). One round cipher algorithm for multimedia IoT devices. *Multimedia Tools and Applications*, 77(14), 18383–18413. doi:10.100711042-018-5660-y

Seitz, A., Henze, D., Miehle, D., Bruegge, B., Nickles, J., & Sauer, M. (2018). Fog computing as enabler for blockchain-based IIoT app marketplaces-A case study. In *Fifth international conference on internet of things: systems, management and security* (pp. 182-188). Valencia, Spain: IEEE.

Seok, B., Park, J., & Park, J. H. (2019). A lightweight hash-based blockchain architecture for industrial IoT. *Applied Sciences (Basel, Switzerland)*, 9(18), 1–17. doi:10.3390/app9183740

Wan, J., Li, J., Imran, M., Li, D., & Fazal-e-Amin. (2019). A blockchain-based solution for enhancing security and privacy in smart factory. *IEEE Transactions on Industrial Informatics*, 15(6), 3652–3660. doi:10.1109/TII.2019.2894573

Wang, E. K., Liang, Z., Chen, C. M., Kumari, S., & Khan, M. K. (2020). PoRX: A reputation incentive scheme for blockchain consensus of IIoT. *Future Generation Computer Systems*, 102, 140–151. doi:10.1016/j.future.2019.08.005

Wu, T.-Y., Chen, C.-M., Wang, K.-H., & Wu, J. M.-T. (2019). Security Analysis and Enhancement of a Certificateless Searchable Public Key Encryption Scheme for IIoT Environments. *IEEE Access: Practical Innovations, Open Solutions*, 7, 49232–49239. doi:10.1109/ACCESS.2019.2909040

Wu, T. Y., Fan, X., Wang, K. H., Lai, C. F., Xiong, N., & Wu, J. M. (2019). A DNA Computation-Based Image Encryption Scheme for Cloud CCTV Systems. *IEEE Access: Practical Innovations, Open Solutions*, 7, 181434–181443. doi:10.1109/ACCESS.2019.2946890

Xu, Y., Ren, J., Wang, G., Zhang, C., Yang, J., & Zhang, Y. (2019). A blockchain-based nonrepudiation network computing service scheme for industrial IoT. *IEEE Transactions on Industrial Informatics*, 15(6), 3632–3641. doi:10.1109/TII.2019.2897133

Yan, H., Chen, Z., & Jia, C. (2019). SSIR: Secure similarity image retrieval in IoT. *Information Sciences*, 479, 153–163. doi:10.1016/j.ins.2018.11.046

Yu, Y., Chen, R., Li, H., Li, Y., & Tian, A. (2019). Toward data security in edge intelligent IIoT. *IEEE Network*, *33*(5), 20–26. doi:10.1109/MNET.001.1800507

Zhang, K., Zhu, Y., Maharjan, S., & Zhang, Y. (2019). Edge intelligence and blockchain empowered 5G beyond for the industrial Internet of Things. *IEEE Network*, *33*(5), 12–19. doi:10.1109/MNET.001.1800526

Zhao, S., Li, S., & Yao, Y. (2019). Blockchain enabled industrial Internet of Things technology. *IEEE Transactions on Computational Social Systems*, *6*(6), 1442–1453. doi:10.1109/TCSS.2019.2924054

Zhou, R., Zhang, X., Du, X., Wang, X., Yang, G., & Guizani, M. (2018). File-centric multi-key aggregate keyword searchable encryption for industrial internet of things. *IEEE Transactions on Industrial Informatics*, *14*(8), 3648–3658. doi:10.1109/TII.2018.2794442

Chapter 7
Current Trends in Integrating the Blockchain With Cloud–Based Internet of Things

Anchitaalagammai J. V.
Velammal College of Engineering and Technology, India

Kavitha S.
Velammal College of Engineering and Technology, India

Murali S.
Velammal College of Engineering and Technology, India

Hemalatha P. R.
Velammal College of Engineering and Technology, India

Subanachiar T.
Velammal College of Engineering and Technology, India

ABSTRACT

Blockchains are shared, immutable ledgers for recording the history of transactions. They substitute a new generation of transactional applications that establish trust, accountability, and transparency. It enables contract partners to secure a deal without involving a trusted third party. The internet of things (IoT) is rapidly changing our society to a world where every "thing" is connected to the internet, making computing pervasive like never before. It is increasingly becoming a ubiquitous computing service, requiring huge volumes of data storage and processing. The stable growth of the internet of things (IoT) and the blockchain technology popularized by cryptocurrencies has led to efforts to change the centralized nature of the IoT. Adapting the blockchain technology for use in the IoT is one such efforts. This chapter focuses on blockchain-IoT research directions and to provide an overview of the importance of blockchain-based solutions for cloud data manipulation in IoT.

DOI: 10.4018/978-1-7998-6694-7.ch007

I INTRODUCTION

IoT is a network system in both wired and wireless connection that consists of many software and hardware entities such as manufacturing management, energy management, agriculture irrigation, electronic commerce, logistic management, medical and healthcare system, aerospace survey, building and home automation, infrastructure management, large scale deployments and transportation.

There is a need of an advanced prototype for security, which considers the security issues from a holistic perspective comprising the advanced users and their intercommunication with this technology. Internet is primary of IoT hence there can be security loophole. Intercommunication paradigms are developed based on sensing programming for IoT applications, evolving an intercommunication stack to develop the required efficiency and reliability. Securing intercommunication is a crucial issue for all the paradigms that are developing based on sensing programming for IoT applications (Choudhury et al., 2017). Data generated by the IoT devices is massive and therefore, traditional data collection, storage, and processing techniques may not work at this scale. Furthermore, the sheer amount of data can also be used for patterns, behaviors, predictions, and assessment. Additionally, the heterogeneity of the data generated by IoT creates another front for the current data processing mechanisms. Therefore, to harness the value of the IoT-generated data, new mechanisms are needed. If we provide good solution which insures about security of the cloud storage system and communication between IoT device and cloud, then there is no problem to accept cloud storage to store IoT data.

Figure 1. Illustration of Cloud based IoT

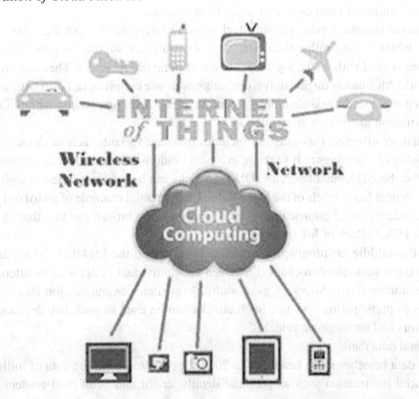

Blockchains, or distributed ledgers for recording transactions, are showing potential for changing how the IoT operates. With the emergence and rapid popularization of the blockchain technology, mainly because of the hype around cryptocurrencies such as Bitcoin (Hussain et al., 2018), people started looking at blockchains as a possible alternative to the centralized solutions. An implicit immutability and decentralization are properties highly desirable in particular IoT scenarios. However, due to certain limitations of blockchains, such as limited scalability, or high computational cost of operating blockchain networks, blockchains are not originally suitable for work with IoT devices. Naturally, research of adapting blockchains for use in the IoT ecosystem has quickly evolved. The chapter the reader to navigate through the blockchain-IoT research directions and to provide an overview of the existing approaches and solutions.

II POTENTIAL ATTACKS IN IOT

A handful of IoT-related attacks seem to receive the most attention in the popular press which few of them are as follows.

1. **Denial of Service (DoS) attacks**: A denial-of-service (DoS) attack deliberately tries to cause a capacity overload in the target system by sending multiple requests. Unlike phishing and brute-force attacks, attackers who implement denial-of-service don't aim to steal critical data. However, DoS can be used to slow down or disable a service to hurt the reputation of a business. For instance, an airline that is attacked using denial-of-service will be unable to process requests for booking a new ticket, checking flight status, and canceling a ticket. In such instances, customers may switch to other airlines for air travel. Similarly, IoT security threats such as denial-of-service attacks can ruin the reputation of businesses and affect their revenue.

2. **Side-channel attack:** A side-channel attack is the IT equivalent to spotting a liar by their nervous behavior while fibbing rather than what they say. In other words, the attacker can infer which encryption is used without having access to either plain or ciphertext. There are myriad ways this might work. An attacker might study a device's power use or optical or radio emanations. A hacker could even observe the sounds coming from the electronic components within a device and use that information to crack its encryption key.

3. **Pure software attacks:** This category includes malware variants such as viruses and trojans and worms. Also in this category is fuzzing, in which random data is thrown at software to see how it reacts. Distributed Denial of Service (DDoS) attacks can be software-based as well, although they can also occur at lower levels of the OSI Model. One potential example of an IoT-related DDoS risk would be safety-critical information such as warnings of a broken gas line that can go unnoticed through a DDoS attack of IoT sensor networks.

4. **Man-in-the-middle cryptographic attacks:** In a Man-in-the-Middle (MiTM) attack, a hacker breaches the communication channel between two individual systems in an attempt to intercept messages among them. Attackers gain control over their communication and send illegitimate messages to participating systems. Such attacks can be used to hack IoT devices such as smart refrigerators and autonomous vehicles.

5. Identity and data theft

6. Multiple data breaches made headlines in 2018 for compromising the data of millions of people. Confidential information such as personal details, credit and debit card credentials, and email

addresses were stolen in these data breaches. Hackers can now attack IoT devices such as smart watches, smart meters, and smart home devices to gain additional data about several users and organizations. By collecting such data, attackers can execute more sophisticated and detailed identity theft.

7. Attackers can also exploit vulnerabilities in IoT devices that are connected to other devices and enterprise systems. For instance, hackers can attack a vulnerable IoT sensor in an organization and gain access to their business network. In this manner, attackers can infiltrate multiple enterprise systems and obtain sensitive business data. Hence, IoT security threats can give rise to data breaches in multiple businesses.

8. **Inside-job:** Here person, employee or staffs who have the knowledge of system can attack the cloud system.

III OVERVIEW OF BLOCKCHAIN

Blockchain is a distributed database that maintains a continuously growing list of records, called blocks, secured from tampering and revision (Nakamoto, 2009). Blockchain was first used to support the digital currency BitCoin (Swan, 2015). It was later adopted by other digital currencies and was the subject of highly publicized successes and failures. At the core of the blockchain technology is a distributed ledger with two types of transactions. A single genesis transaction which creates value and a transfer transaction that transfers value from one party to another. Each transaction is digitally signed by the issuer and posted to the global ledger. A group of transactions are then collected into a block, the block is validated by a third party (a miner) and is locked. This mechanism represents the strength of the blockchain technology. Each block in the chain is immutable since it is linked to its predecessor and any change to any of the blocks invalidates all the blocks downstream in the chain. Each participant in the global network keeps a copy of the ledger and every time a new block is created, it is broadcasted to all the participants that add it to their local copy of the ledger.

Blockchain Types

Blockchains splits into two main categories: public, private and hybrid.

Public blockchains are open blockchains that anyone can join, contribute to, and see its contents. They represent true decentralization and transparency. However, they are generally slower and more expensive to maintain and operate as more difficult consensus mechanisms to prevent Sybil attacks need to be employed.

Private blockchains are valuable for enterprises who want to collaborate and share data, but don't want their sensitive business data visible on a public blockchain. These chains, by their nature, are more centralized; the entities running the chain have significant control over participants and governance structures.

In between the two models stands the hybrid model that combines both the public and private blockchain. For example, selected transactions can be submitted from the private to the public blockchain for open access and secure data provenance.

IV CHALLENGES OF BLOCKCHAIN-IOT INTEGRATION

Blockchain was originally not designed for use in the environment of resource-restricted devices. Certain drawbacks need to be thus first resolved in order to take a full advantage of it.

Throughput and Latency

Compared to centralized solutions, blockchains generally offer lower transaction processing throughput and higher latencies (caused mainly by the blockchain verification process).

Blockchain Size

Depending on the design of the blockchain, all participating nodes need to store some section of the blockchain, if not the whole chain, locally, in order to participate in the validation of blocks. With ever-growing number of participating devices and transactions, the blockchain car reach sizes problematic even for regular computers. For example, the current size of the Bitcoin blockchain is larger than 180GB. For resource-restricted devices, some ways of reducing the blockchain size need to be applied, such as pruning the chain or storing it remotely.

Storage Capacity and Scalability

IoT devices generate lots of data at fast pace. Centralized cloud solutions are usually designed for coping with high storage requirements and can increase their scalability if needed. Availability of data is another important factor of why a centralized cloud is used (for real-time systems, manufactures, etc). Such properties, if not better, need to be ensured in blockchain solutions, as well.

Privacy and Transactional Confidentiality

The drawback of a shared open ledger of transactions is the possibility of corrupted users taking advantage of the available transaction data. Transactions happen in the open and so patterns and connections between nodes can be extracted and used against the users. Also, the content of every transaction is exposed to every node, so private data need to be encrypted or hidden in some other way

Computational Resources

Consensus algorithms are time and resource expensive. Blockchain was designed for an Internet scenario with powerful computers, and this is far from the IoT reality. Blockchain transactions are digitally signed, and therefore devices capable of operating with the currency must be equipped with this functionality. There are several possible solutions to this, e.g., new alternative consensus algorithms could be used, or the signing responsibility could be delegated to an entity capable of such computations. Also, energy efficiency goes hand in hand with resource costliness and the need of nodes to be up and running.

V DIFFERENT CONSENSUS MODELS

Three predominant mechanisms provide consensus in a blockchain:

Byzantine Fault Tolerance (BFT) Algorithms are designed to avoid attacks and software errors that cause faulty nodes to exhibit arbitrary behavior (Byzantine faults). BFT (Lamport et al., 1982) provides consensus despite participation of maliciously misbehaving (Byzantine) nodes. A drawback of this approach, however, is the scalability limit in terms of number of nodes that form the blockchain network (Castro & Liskov, 2002). Alternative approaches to BFT have been proposed, including Practical Byzantine Fault Tolerance (PBFT) (Castro & Liskov, 2002). Examples of blockchain implementations currently exploiting PBFT are Linux Foundation Hyperledger fabric (0.6) and Ripple.

Proof-of-Work (POW), used by Bitcoin and Ethereum, is the widely known mechanism for establishing consensus. In POW, a single node can provide its conclusions to others nodes, which can be in turn validated by the other nodes in the network. A node submitting a generated block, in order to have the consensus reached, must also provide proof of the work it performed, which is a computationally difficult task (a "cryptographically hard puzzle" based on hash functions). POW provides great network stability (Nakamoto, 2008). However, POW is particularly costly because of the computational resources expended. "Miners" are incentivized to participate to earn a cryptomonetary reward, which is granted in return for a successful block generation.

Figure 2. POW consensus mechanism

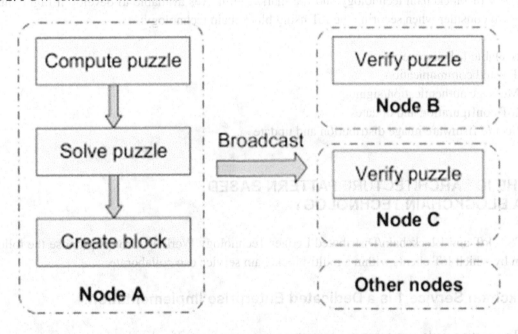

Proof-of-Stake (POS) is similar to POW: nodes are rewarded upon generating a block. However, only a few nodes can participate in this phase (Vasin, 2014). Indeed, the next generator node is picked up deterministically based on the accumulated wealth (i.e., the "Stake"). The mining process for a blockchain based on POS is usually referred to as "forgery" or "minting". The technology that launched PoS was PeerCoin.

VI SELECTION OF BLOCKCHAIN TECHNOLOGY FOR IOT SECURITY

Blockchain technology can help secure IoT devices. IoT devices can be configured either to make use of public blockchain services or to communicate with private blockchain nodes in the cloud over a secure API. Incorporating blockchain technology into the security framework of an IoT system allows IoT devices to securely discover each other, encrypt machine-to-machine transactions using distributed key management techniques, and validate the integrity and authenticity of software image updates, as well as policy updates.

Based on the potential architectural patterns detailed in this report, an IoT device will communicate with a blockchain transaction node via an API, allowing even constrained devices to participate in the blockchain service.

To ensure security, care should be taken during the bootstrapping of an IoT device onto a particular blockchain service. Below is a use case for IoT discovery that supports the enrollment of an IoT device into a transaction node. The IoT device must first be provisioned with credentials that can be used to prove authorization in order to be added to a transaction node. This credential provisioning must be done in a secured environment that safeguards against threats of a particular IoT device ecosystem.

Review of blockchain technology and the market initiatives available to develop it highlights five features to consider when securing the IoT using blockchain technology:

1. Scalable IoT discovery
2. Trusted communication
3. Message authentication/signing
4. IoT configuration and updates
5. Secure firmware image distribution and update

VII THE IOT ARCHITECTURE PATTERN BASED ON A BLOCKCHAIN TECHNOLOGY

The CSA IoT and Blockchain/Distributed Ledger Technology Working Groups propose the following system by which IoT clients within a multi-blockchain service can collaborate.

Blockchain Service 1 is a Dedicated Enterprise Implementation:

- Transaction nodes are corporate computers or servers hosted in the cloud.
- IoT blockchain clients are sensors and smart devices deployed within the enterprise area.

    Blockchain Service 2 is a Consumer Smart Home:

- Transaction nodes are personal computers and other devices or cloud subscriptions.

Figure 3. A graphic explanation of how a blockchain works in IoT

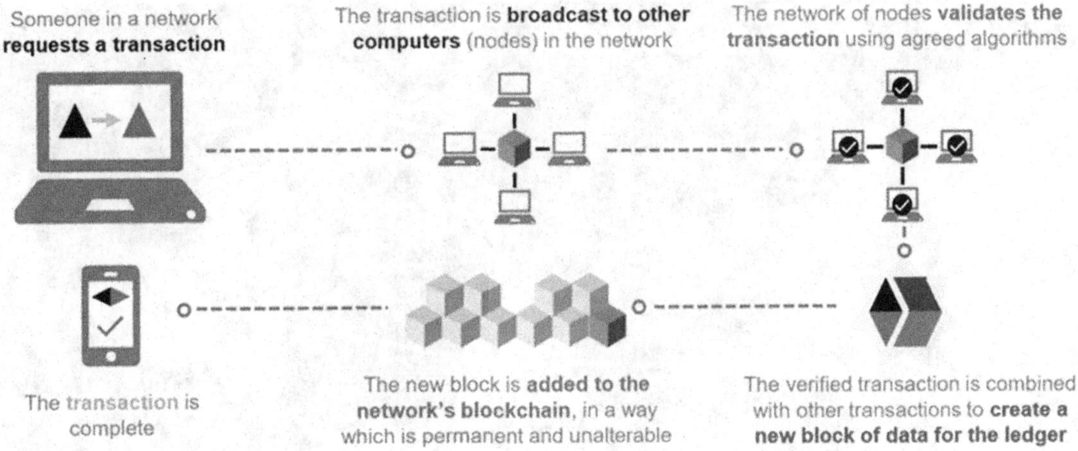

- IoT blockchain clients are smart devices, such as refrigerators, temperature sensors and security cameras.

The architecture in which IoT devices are clients of a blockchain service is primarily adopted by current industry efforts for implementing blockchain technology.

Examples of Blockchain Based IoT Projects

There are some examples of companies and projects that are working on blockchain solutions for IoT and supply chains. Below follows a few examples that shows relevant prospects. Table 1 shows some different blockchain technology capabilities with IoT and Blockchain.

A company that has delivered solutions for supply chains involving both blockchain and IoT are Chronicled. This company offers a solution where partners in a supply chain network can cooperate on a blockchain where sensitive information is kept safe. All partners can register events in the supply chain, like data and IoT devices into the Ethereum blockchain ledger. Smart contracts can act as a complement that can supplement traditional business contracts. Trusted parties have access to a shared system with records on an immutable ledger. IoT devices are used for tracking, custody events, money flows and environmental conditions.

Hyperledger Fabric is a project within the Hyperledger framework, originally contributed by IBM. In early 2018, Maersk and IBM announced that they are launching a digital joint venture that is applying this blockchain technology in order to improve global trade and digitalise supply chains. The goal is to offer a platform built on open standards where parts of that platform will use the blockchain ledger. All parties in the supply chain will have access to the platform where they can participate and exchange value. This platform should hopefully address current problems with visibility and documentation.

IOTA is a variant of a public blockchain targeting IoT that uses an invention called "Tangle" at its core, which is a new data structure. Tangle has no blocks, no chain and no miners as a blockchain usually has. Since there are no miners, IOTA needs to achieve consensus in another way and does this by making sure that every participant that wants to make a transaction needs to participate in the consensus

Figure 4. IoT Architecture Pattern Based on a Blockchain Technology

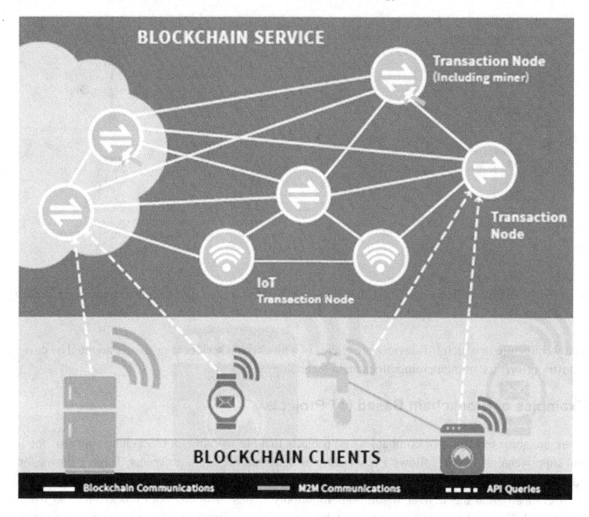

by approving the two past transactions. This new architecture means that IOTA has two benefits that are scalability and no transaction fees.

Explanation of Terminologies Used in Table 1:

- Cryptocurrency: the electronic currency used by different blockchains.
- Transaction fee: an extra fee (usually very small) for transacting cryptocurrency via blockchains.
- Private/Public: different types of blockchains.
- Anonymity: different blockchains includes anonymity when being a part of the network.
- Network access: if nodes need permission to join the network or if everyone can join (permissionless).
- Decentralised applications: if the blockchain supports applications to be run on the platform (for example smart contracts).
- Consensus algorithm: how trust is created.
- Suitable for IoT: if the particular blockchain is suitable for being used in IoT systems

Table 1. Showing essential characteristics for possible Blockchains that might fit for usage within IoT systems

	Bitcoin	**Ethereum**	**IOTA**	**Hyperledger Fabric**
Cryptocurrency	Yes	Yes	Yes	No
Transaction fee	Yes	Yes	No	No
Private/Public	Public	Public (can be Private)	Public	Private
Anonymity	Yes	Yes	Optional	No
Network access	Permissionless	Permissionless	Optional	Permissioned
Decentralised applications	Very limited	Yes, Solidity	Very limited	Yes, Go and Java
Consensus algorithm	PoW	PoW (soon PoS)	Tangle	PBFT
Suitable for IoT	No	Yes (with constraints)	Yes	Yes

VI CONCUSION

IoT security and privacy are very importance and play a vital role in the commercialization of the IoT technology. Traditional security and privacy solutions suffer from a number of issues that are related to the dynamic nature of the IoT networks.

Blockchain technology promises to play a major role in addressing these challenges. Throughout this chapter, we have highlighted features to consider when attempting to secure connected devices using blockchain technology. Yet, due to hardware limitations of IoT, we conclude that in a context of several hundred thousand or more IoT devices many of these devices could not serve as transaction nodes (generating transactions, providing consensus, etc.), and thus would fall outside the secure blockchain.

Many devices will benefit from the security and other features offered by blockchain services through APIs from upstream transaction nodes of networks or by specialized intermediaries. Those upstream capabilities can be used to secure IoT devices (configuration and update control, secure firmware update) and communications (IoT discovery, trusted communication, message authentication/signing). We hope this chapter inspires many readers embracing the blockchain opportunity to extend the capabilities of this technology to secure the Internet of Things.

REFERENCES

Castro, M., & Liskov, B. (2002, November). Practical Byzantine fault tolerance and proactive recovery. *ACM Transactions on Computer Systems*, *20*(4), 398–461. doi:10.1145/571637.571640

Choudhury, T., Gupta, A., Pradhan, S., Kumar, P., & Rathore, Y. S. (2017). Privacy and Security of Cloud-Based Internet of Things (IoT). *International Conference on Computational Intelligence and Networks*, 41-45. 10.1109/CINE.2017.28

Hussain, F., Hussain, R., Hassan, S. A., & Hossain, E. (2018). Machine Learning in IoT Security: Current Solutions and Future Challenges. Academic Press.

Lamport, L., Shostak, R., & Pease, M. (1982, July). The Byzantine Generals problem. *ACM Transactions on Programming Languages and Systems*, *4*(3), 382–401. doi:10.1145/357172.357176

Nakamoto. (2009). *Bitcoin: A peer-to-peer electronic cash system.* url:http://www.bitcoin.org/bitcoin.pdf

Nakamoto, S. (2008). *Bitcoin: A peer-to-peer electronic cash system.* https://bitcoin.org/bitcoin.pdf

Nian, L. P., & Chuen, D. (2015). *Introduction to bitcoin, Handbook of Digital Currency: Bitcoin.* Innovation, Financial Instruments, and Big Data.

Swan, M. (2015). *Blockchain: Blueprint for a new economy.* O'Reilly Media, Inc.

Vasin, P. (2014). *Blackcoin's proof-of-stake protocol v2.* https://blackcoin.co/blackcoin-pos-protocol-v2- whitepaper.pdf

Chapter 8
Blockchain:
Emerging Digital Currency and Need of the Modern Industrialization

Aprajita Shriwastawa
Galgotias University, India

Nitya Singhal
Galgotias University, India

S. Prakash
Galgotias University, India

ABSTRACT

Blockchain is an emerging technology of the new generation. Safety and protection of the data have been the prime concern of people. Digitalization has paved the way for the generation of trillions of data every second. With these developing lives of people, blockchain is the solution. The authors discuss the applications of blockchain in various aspects of life along with the introduction of digital currency. The means and norms are considered for digital money transfer and generation of end-to-end encrypted code for the sake of high-end security. They discuss the framework that can be used by the organizations to develop a new form of the internal network. Finally, the suggestion for future work and development along with all the cons is shown.

1 INTRODUCTION

1.1 Blockchain

Blockchain in literal ways is the chain of blocks, where block represents the information storage and chain is the public database to hold blocks. Blocks stores information about transactions. Blockchain is a distributed ledger where we store information, and each node is allowed to copy the information of ledger to reduce the chances of failure. It is secured where all copies are updated and verified simultane-

DOI: 10.4018/978-1-7998-6694-7.ch008

ously (Stephan et al., 2019). It allows making transactions of bitcoin in cryptographic form. Data stored in the blockchain is immutable. Blockchain can be easily understood if you know about cryptography, distributed computing, and game theory. blockchain is an opportunity to make the market fair for every individual. Some say it is one of the very best ways to decentralize the system of the market where all the rights are distributed among each member. Blockchain is the technology that is expected to grow very vastly shortly (Lin & Liao, 2017). Soon there will be the change of era and adaptability of blockchain in the market will lead us to a very new way of thinking and development. There will be a decentralized organization where there will be no boss to measure your work but you will be measuring your day's work and help you by improving yourself. This is all about making everything secure and reliable for everyone. A place where dependency will be minimal and we can expect higher results. Blockchain works on peer to peer network.

Blockchain works in 4 easy steps: For adding a new block,

- A transaction must take place.
- Then that transaction must get verified.
- The details of the transaction are added into a block
- Hash is generated for that block data.
- Now for adding that block into chain previous block hash is also added in the new block (Holotescu, 2018).

Apart from this, blockchain is well known for the feature of distributed or peer-to-peer computing. Distributed computing is the network of many independent nodes. These nodes can communicate with each other in such a programmed way that they are failure-prone. All the nodes in distributed computing are capable of sending and receiving data to any nodes in the network. This enables transparency and scalability over the network. The decentralization process uses TCP/IP protocol to manage the connection from peer-to-peer (P2P). There is no central authority in this network architecture. Simply it's just are some computers which are connected to each other via the internet. This data can directly be shared on networks without any central server. Each computer in the P2P network becomes a file server. Some features of distributed computing are:

1. It is easily configurable and installed.
2. If any node gets down, it doesn't affect the whole system.
3. It is cost-effective.

1.2 Basic Terminologies in Blockchain

· **Node**: Blockchain applies on nodes only. Nodes can be any device (computer, phones) with a large amount of stored data. Node is the infrastructure of blockchain. Nodes store, secure and spread data of blockchain. Nodes copy the full transaction history of blockchain to secure it. Nodes can be online and offline (Swan, 2015). Nodes also verify the block whether to accept or reject it. So basically, nodes do:

- Preserving the data from getting hacked.
- Stores the data of Blockchain.
- Verifies the blocks.

- Broadcast the transaction history to another node to create a chain

· **Miner**: Miner always tries to create new blocks of transactions in the blockchain. Miner is somehow similar to the node but not exactly the same. Miner always runs a full node to select valid transactions. The miner needs huge computing power to run i.e. a large number of CPUs and GPUs. The miner does not have permission to access the full transaction history. There is also an incentive side as well, every time you mine a new block you earn some sort of reward or transaction fee.

· **Ledger**: the ledger is basically the database of blockchain. In the ledger, we store journals of transaction, but we don't note every minor detail of transaction in ledger rather than that we actually store facts about objects and history of the transaction (Holotescu, 2018)[5].

· **Hyperledger**: It is an open-source community that focus on developing suit of stable frameworks, tools, and libraries for enterprise-grade blockchain deployment. It is a partnership hold by Linux Foundation that includes banking, manufacturing and technology, the leader in finance, internet of things, supply chains.

Proof of work: It is a piece of data that is difficult to produce but easy for others to verify and which satisfies certain requirements (Swan, 2015)[5]. Making a proof of work can be in short probability so that an average trial and error is required before a valid evidence of work is produced.

Consensus: it is a powerful way of approaching concurrence in a group. A way of getting the legal agreement of every node in the group to create affairs and legal society. Consensus can be defined as agreement seeking, collaborative, cooperative, egalitarian, inclusive, and participatory.

Cryptocurrency: Cryptocurrency is a means of exchange but a digital one. We can also say a digital currency that is encrypted in such form that from generation to verification is it secured at another level (Narayanan et al., 2016)[5].

Bitcoin: it a type of cryptocurrency (electronic cash) for which there is no central authority for keeping the track of it. We need a wallet to send or receive bitcoin. It can be controlled by anyone who is in-network. It can send from user to user without any intermediary interruption.

Ethereum: it is a community which decentralized to create and run the decentralised application over the internet. We need Ethereum virtual machine to run applications on the Ethereum world. Cryptocurrency we used in Ethereum is ether. It also enables the creation of smart contracts (Blockchain Terminology, n.d.)[5].

Immutability: Things which can't be changed by anyone in any node or block without the permission of every single entity in the chain.

Decentralization: It is a process of giving out and spread power away from a central authority. It means there is no single authority to give orders. Here everybody works own on their own departments.

Digital signature: it is a detail of electronic information that is used to identify the person to whom it belongs. It is used to provide authentication in the blockchain network. Let's say node B received a message claiming that it is sent from node A, but how can B be sure that node A sent the message, so to solve such problem of authentication, we started to sign the after writing a message that signature is termed as a digital signature in a digital world (Xu et al., 2019)[6]. Digital signature works in the following steps:

Let's say a node A sends a message to node B then,

1. After writing the message node A will encrypt the message using A's private key.
2. After that, A will again encrypt the encrypted message using B's public key.

3. After double, the message is received by node B.
4. Now he will first decrypt the message with B's private key.
5. Then he will again decrypt the message with A's public key. In this way, digital signature works and provides both authentication and confidentiality to algorithm.

Hashing: hashing is the process of creating a hash function. A hash function takes an arbitrary length of input and converts them into a ciphertext of fixed length. So, we can say in the hash function the length of the output is fixed always. There are many algorithms to create a hash function such as digest algorithm or SHA. it is used to provide integrity (Xu et al., 2019). For same input, you will get same hash value every time and small change input will change the hash completely. Hashing is irreversible i.e. you can create a hash of a message but you can't get same message back from hash. Let's understand hashing from example: let's say we want download some software from google and you get to know its paid, so instead of paying, you will search for same software on other sites which is free. But how can you check the software which is available free is not malicious that's where hash value comes in work. The paid site will show the hash value of real software and you can create the hash value of data available on the free site and you can compare both hashes if both are the same as the software is not malicious.

GAME THEORY IN BLOCKCHAIN:

- It is a competitive environment. In this one company tries to take the competitive advantages of its opponent. In other words, one gets advantages while others get disadvantages (Blockchain Terminology, n.d.).
- Game theory in cryptocurrency: - By game theory in cryptocurrency we can see two different main effects occur on cryptocurrency in both internal and external.
- Internal game theory: - Game theory in cryptocurrency has to do with inducement with system both good or bad. If we break the rule with the algorithm's system, there has to be a consequence that far outweighs the benefit. This is an asymmetrical design.
- External game theory: - In external game theory user takes advantage of the attackers who attack him to take his bitcoins.

1.3 ARCHITECTURE OF BLOCKCHAIN

Blockchain consists of a chain of blocks containing information in it (Narayanan et al., 2016). A block consists of the following field:

Figure 1. Architecture of Blockchain

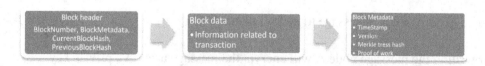

Block header, Block data, Block metadata

A transaction which get stored as block data consists of following fields:

- Header
- Signature
- Response
- Endorsement
- Proposal

1.4 IMPORTANCE OF CRYPTOCURRENCY

As we all know digital currency is based on Blockchain technology, Blockchain technology is much simpler, cheaper, and transparent as compared to our traditional financial transactions (Blockchain Terminology, n.d.). But most importantly cryptocurrency cannot be counterfeited. The cryptocurrency revolution is spreading everywhere in the world today, in 2009 when bitcoin first gained momentum because of a tremendous spike in it's worth and gained great trust among the investors. Today many major technology companies have invested in cryptocurrency. There are countless reasons for investing in cryptocurrency like-

1. It's easy to access since there are more people with access to the internet,
2. It supports instant settlement; ease of use is the reason why the cryptocurrency is in high demand. All you need is an internet connection.
3. It is more secure since there are no chances of fraud or identity theft.
4. The benefits of cryptocurrency in today's economy could appear to be outstanding, breaking down geographical barriers. It cannot be denied that it is the future.
5. All transactions should be made over the internet.
6. No personal identity got revealed, you are recognized by your virtual identity.
7. A single user can have many virtual identities.
    1. SEND AND RECEIVE MONEY THROUGH BLOCKCHAIN? (Narayanan et al., 2016)
    2. Let's say node A wants to send a bitcoin to node B:
        1. He needs his bitcoin wallet.
        2. He needs to copy B's address and fill the amount and the fees
        3. And he clicks on sends now his work done machine starts its mechanism.
        4. Wallet signs the transaction using A's private key.
        5. The transaction is propagated and validated by the network node
        6. Mining gets starts. Miners include the transaction in the next block to be mined.
        7. The miner who solves the proof of work propagates the new block in network.
        8. The node verifies the result and propagates the block.
        9. B receives the notification of receiving bitcoin.

1.5 CRYPTOGRAPHY IN BLOCKCHAIN

It is a science of converting the original text into coded language. It means that the text has been changed by the process of cryptography can only be understood by the sender and receiver (Casino et al., 2019). It protects the data by the threat of alteration and provides user authentication or verification. It also provides: -

1. Confidentiality: - The data stored in the block or node cannot be understood by anyone or others.
2. Integrity: - The data cannot be changed by anybody except the sender.
3. Non- repudiation: - The sender cannot refuse that his/her sent or sender cannot refuse the intension of the data which he/she sent.
4. Authentication: - It confirms to the sender and receiver or it gives user verification.

There are two types of cryptography.

*   Symmetric key cryptography: In this sender and receiver uses only one key. It means to encrypt and decrypt for both there is only one key. It means the sender uses this key to encrypt the original text to ciphertext and send it to the receiver. On the other hand, the same key is used by the receiver to decrypt the ciphertext to the original text (Ostern, 2020).
*   Asymmetric key cryptography: In these two keys are used. It means there is a separate key for encrypting the text and separate key for decrypt the text. It is highly secured. There is no chance to alternate or hack the data of the block or node. We usually use Asymmetric cryptography in the blockchain.

1.6 NEED OF CRYPTOGRAPHY IN BLOCKCHAIN

Cryptography helps us to make our data secure and theft proof; it minimizes chances of unauthorised access or any data alteration (Ostern, 2020)[10]. Cryptography is the practice of developing protocols that prevent third parties from viewing private data. Cryptography is an integral part of the inner-workings of blockchain technology. Public-key encryption serves as the basis for blockchain wallets and transactions.

It plays huge role from the creation of cryptocurrency to its transfer, when cryptocurrency is created, all confirmed transactions are stored in a public ledger. All identities of coin owners are encrypted to a new format that cannot be read without decryption to ensure the legitimacy of record keeping (Dannen, 2017). The ledger ensures that all transactions between "digital wallets" can calculate an accurate balance. All transactions are checked to make sure that the coins used are owned by the current spender. This public ledger is also referred to as a "transaction blockchain".

Blockchain technology ensures secure digital transactions through encryption and "smart contracts" that make the entity virtually unalterable and void of fraud. All data is stored and transferred in a new format called hash values which unreadable without a key, that's how cryptography ensures and strengthens security.

2 LITERATURE SURVEY

As suggested by NITI Aayog the Blockchain technology is the new emerging root of a revolution between the governments, businesses, and citizens. It is expected to grow as a new generation of technology in the coming era. It is expected that the business will be made easy to carry due to the decentralization nature and efficiency provided by blockchain (Blockchain: The India Strategy, n.d.). While doing any sort of transactions or for data storage we always have 'trust' issues. We do not trust people or third-party involved until they are verified. Here in India, we generally trust banks as a third-party for the transactions because they are made relevant for use over time by the government of India. For online transactions, we transfer our money digitally and then there is a bank involved who deducts the amount from the sender's account and adds to the receiver. Blockchain is the technology where trust is no more the problem. The decentralized nature of the blockchain technology makes it free from third-party involvement (Blockchain: The India Strategy, n.d.)[12]. The confidentiality of the data can be maintained due to its immutable nature of the blocks. The security can be confirmed by the algorithms and math which has been used to implement the structure. The peer-to-peer connectivity ensures that the two parties are directly connected and there is no third-party involvement. Every transaction made in a blockchain is digitally signed by the sender so there is no chance of identity fraud. Cryptography on the other hand compliments the technology with its highly efficient mathematical implementations which can be written as a source code. According to McKinsey's study, it has been established that due to a reduced number of records which are being kept and the administrative power which is being utilized to maintain the same will directly lead to the cost cut of many values (Blockchain: The India Strategy, n.d.)[13]. Resolving the issues of the intermediates involved will directly hit the cost of the product in a positive way. Later complimentary benefits can be seen in revenue growth and capital formation. While reading through multiple use-cases the very revolutionary development was fund in the agriculture sector. The benefits which are ought to be used by the farmers is delivered to them. While the country is growing digitally the requirement of the decentralized system will be a boon. Blockchain cannot exactly eliminate all he intermediaries but the main aim behind is to reduce the number so that money in between is saved. For a farmer producing goods, we can make deliver the products directly to the mandi for selling. In between, from collecting the goods to transferring in the market, the middle man cuts off a lot of amounts which directly affects the pocket of the consumer. To avoid the same, we can design the system where there is no middle man in between the farmers and the mandi dealers (Swan, 2014). Similarly, in fertilizer subsidy supply chain. Blockchain and its applications are useful where the transactions are saved as records. While the transaction happening as a physical entity cannot be made in blocks and so is not valid to apply blockchain. So again, coming upon fertilizers, the GNFC (Gujarat Narmada Valley Fertilisers and Chemicals) business flow comprises of the manufacturer, warehouse, certifying agency, retailer, chartered accountant, and department of fertilizers. Earlier days went on like: The manufacturers manufactured the goods and it was shipped. The warehouse, after receiving the shipment sent the challan to manufacturers, then after the fertilizers were sent to the retailers. The certifying agency in the other hand took the goods and certifies on B1 and B2 levels. After which the retailer receives the product. The retailer using the UIDAI and POS machines subsidized the price and later on send the invoice to the manufacturer and dept of fertilizer. Chartered Accountant reads the documents and claims and then it was sent to the dept of fertilizers. It reads all the claims and sends the payment. With the blockchain model of business let us study the transformed version of the same scenario (Nakamoto, 2008).

- Manufacturer: As soon as the order ships one clicks of a button will send the data in the network, the warehouse will become alert about the shipment and with the help of IoT sensors the fertilizers will be tracked.
- Warehouse: Warehouse will have real-time information about the shipments and if delayed or lost then it will be updated immediately.
- Retailer: The quality assurance can be made by tracing back from the manufacturing source and likewise B2 certificate can be generated.
- Government: The need for data tracing and validity is transparent and can be accounted for very easily. It reduces the need for a chartered accountant to study claims.

3 SUGGESTED FRAMEWORK FOR BUSINESS DEVELOPMENT

As we discussed in previous sections blockchain could be very complex to implement and also can be useful if used with correct planning and strategy (Sabah et al., 2019). Implementing blockchain in a business firm could be challenging because we have read many of the case studies where due to the immutable nature of the blockchain the company's architecture has been compromised and thus lead to a complete shutdown. Here we will discuss a scenario in which we will try to study the private blockchain inside a company's network. There are three types of blockchain.

Private blockchain: It is a single entity network. In this, only those who can work those are assigned by that single entity (Notheisen et al., 2017). It allows the organisation to pay distributed ledger technology without making the data public. There are two types of the private blockchain.

- Permissioned blockchain: Permissioned blockchains are blockchain networks that require access to be part of. It is a faster private membership. It is legal and managed by a group of nodes that are pre-defined. It is partially decentralisation and cost are effective. It is less secured.
- Permissionless blockchain: It is slower in speed compared to permission Blockchain's speed. Its privacy is transparent and open (anyone can become a member). It is illegal in legitimacy. Its ownership is public (no one owns the network). It is truly decentralised. It's not so cost-effective and highly secured as compared to permission Blockchain (Blockchain and Emerging Digital Technologies, n.d.).

Public blockchain: It is an open network. In this everyone can be a part of the network. Everybody can read, write, and download the protocol. In this transaction are filed as blocks or nodes and all these are linked together to make a chain.

Hybrid blockchain: It sums up the all benefits of public and private Blockchain. An application can behold on an independent permissioned Blockchain while purchasing a public Blockchain for security and settlements.

USECASE-1

Now, taking the perspective of an Organisation we can surely say that private blockchains are good to be implemented (Birch, 2020). For implementing a private blockchain network the first we will have to fix is the network administrator. While you wish to implement such a complex functionality you have to have a large amount of power and gadgets. Here unlike public blockchain, every activity will be monitored by the admin and each node being added and subtracted will be in control. Blockchain is immutable and if once the blocks are updated, they can't be removed or altered so having a blueprint ready is mandatory. Firstly, decide all the entities of the organisation and the possible additional value should be added and left empty for future reference. We can understand this by taking an example of a periodic table. A table including every block is already present and the blocks which have been left empty are hoped to be filled in future. As soon as a new element is discovered it has a place in the periodic table. After deciding all the entities, we need to think about who is going to be part of this private network. Different branches of the same organisation may stay connected via a centralised system (Blockchain: Powering the Value of Internet, 2020). Salary generation and payment confirmation will be easier. Transporting every need from one branch to the other will be seconds and finally, while you wish to collaborate with your new partner it becomes easier to keep the data secret between both, robust and secure.

For implementation in the basic structure say for the period between (3-12 months) the internal blueprint should be studied well. The opportunities which may strengthen the organisation and innovation should be backed-up. Research work should be continued about the changes happening within the same type of business. The working employees and authorities should be well aware of the technology and threats. Regular workshops should be conducted and tests of the technology implementation should be started (Burchardi et al., 2020).

Implementing the same on a long-term basis say 1-5 years:

Become an exchanger of the cryptocurrency just like Ripple. Make an understanding with the customer and the employees within the organisation. Offering a good deal with discounts to valuable customers may lead to the rise of the organisation. Remove all the intermediaries and processing steps for clearing settlement. Start making partnerships.

Cryptographic algorithms used in the blockchain to make it secure and reliable are:

Figure 2. Organisation Collaboration Model

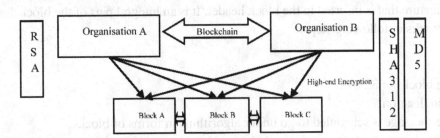

RSA: It is used to provide confidentiality in blockchain. It is an asymmetric Cryptography. It is an authorised public- key encryption and used to secure the important data. It is an exponential functioned algorithm over finite integers including prime numbers. It is used to share the data over an insecure network. It is the most secure way encryption (Deloitte, 2020).

RSA works in: -

1. 1 -Node A sends its public key to the server and requests some confidential data.
2. 2-Node B encrypts the data using the user's public key and sends back the encrypted data.
3. 3-Node C receives the data and decrypts it using their private key.
4. RSA applies to cryptocurrency: -
    1. A's public address will be used to receive cryptocurrencies and consult his/her balance on the Blockchain.
    2. B's private key will be used in correlation to this public key to access and spend his/her cryptocurrency.

MD5: Message digest version 5 is knowns as MD5, this is the type of hashing algorithm. It takes the 512 bits plain text blocks which is then divided into 16 32bit blocks and produces 128-bit message digest which is set of 4 blocks of 32 bits. The main goal of md5 is that it takes an input of any bits and produces an output of fixed length i.e. 128 bits.

It follows two main features that no two messages can form the same hash function and same hash value (CIO's Guide to Blockchain, 2020).

MD5 works in 5 steps:

1. Padding in which adding bits to make the length of message 64 less than multiple of 512.
2. Append length i.e. to add a bit in resulting length which becomes multiple of 512
3. Initialise MFD buffering
4. Processing message block in 16-word block
5. Auxiliary buffering to make bits operational.

SHA256: Secure hash function version 2 256 bits are also known as sha 256. This algorithm is used to take input of any bits but output has constant 256 bits. This is the most secure hashing algorithm until now. As this function is irreversible and collision resistance it makes it more reliable to use in most secured platform i.e. blockchain (Konstantinidis et al., 2018). SHA used in two main ways in the blockchain that are mining and creation of block addresses. SHA 256 is also used to create a Merkle tree which is an important feature that is inserted in the block header. It is an integral part of the blockchain protocol.

SHA 256 works in following steps:

1. Padding
2. Creating blocks of 32 bits
3. Hash initialisation.
4. Then the message is scheduled to go under algorithms in forms of blocks.
5. Big shuffle happens which we also called round key generator.
6. Implementation of signatures.

USE CASE-2

The above explained algorithms complements the centralised ledger format of an organisation. The second model is the contracts. The business of property dealing is the most sensitive business to handle. Here trust and confidentiality play a very important role. As per the survey by NITI Aayog, it as been found that Indian GDP and gross revenue can be altered if all the property dealing takes place in a legal way (Avital, 2018). The government employees waste a lot of time and money handling the database of the land and the owner of the same. The Enormous amount of black money is converted in white and many illegal ways are followed which weakens the GDP. One of the applications or use cases can be made in the field of blockchain. Here one-time uploading of all the data and records can be maintained in the form of blocks and later on crosscheck and verification can be automated. Like we understood the example of the manufacturer and department of fertilisers in the literature survey. We can keep track of all the events taking place and if the form is rejected by the court one can file a case against any mishappening. Apart from all the data transparency the one thing that is achieved is no more keeping ledgers and spending on human resources. The role of middle man will be minimised and it will be just seller and the buyer (Beck et al., 2017). As the data is immutable any alteration won't be possible and thus, we will achieve what desired. It will have three benefits:

1. Person willing to buy and the person willing to sell will directly be contacted to each other like any anonymous person in the network. While all the transactions will be in the public ledger. So, there is no risk of integrity.
2. It will be a written code so if any unwelcomed event arouses such as fall of the price of property or rise in the price of land will automatically be updated by making required calculations.
3. Anybody willing to have a track of the market or willing to study the functioning of the same can access the public chain and take part in the network to view the same.

4 PROS AND CONS OF BLOCKCHAIN

Advantages:
Merits of blockchain due to which variety of sectors use it (Zheng et al., 2017):

1. It is the faster way to conduct the transaction as compared to the other ways of conducting transactions
2. It is more secured compared to others. It's impossible to hack into a specific block, while big banks are very easy to hack or hacking attacks.
3. It has the high-level reliability compared to others
4. It finishes the ability of cheating
5. It increases the transparency rate.
6. It removes the intermediary fees
7. It increases the frequency and efficiency of trades
8. It increases access for population and location
9. It allows more peoples and businesses to trade (Deshpande et al., 2017)
10. It has greater ability to customise
11. It's network can be public, private and open with restricted membership

Disadvantages:
Limitation in blockchain:

1. There is a problem in speed and scalability in a blockchain there are only 7-15 transactions per second in bitcoin and Ethereum.
2. Problem of privacy arises mostly. i.e. Need for business confidentiality vs. transparency
3. There is too much power consumption in the blockchain. Bitcoin consumes 343 megawatts
4. There is unknown security. Peoples does not understand its low and immature technology of cryptography (Tama et al., 2017).
5. Evolving the codes is a bit issue in the blockchain. Due to a low understanding of this technology, a question arises "Who updates the software to address bugs and changes in the operating environment?".

5 FUTURE APPLICATIONS OF BLOCKCHAIN

Nowadays, blockchain is not limited to just cryptocurrency and bitcoin. There are a variety of sectors in which we can use blockchain in different ways. Blockchain is a trending technology nowadays, every IT firm is introducing a new invention using blockchain (Crosby et al., 2016). Not only this, in the medical sector blockchain is growing adversely. Below mentioned are the sectors in which we can use blockchain:

- Agriculture: Connecting farmers and mandi dealers.
- Arts and recreation: Copy formatting detection.
- Automotive and utilities
- Healthcare: Maintaining electronic registers of the patients.
- Financial service and insurance: Guarantee of integrity.
- Mining and manufacturing: tracking of products and reducing intermediaries.
- Property: Smart contracts.
- Public sector and retail: Coded successfully to keep track of market trends.
- Transport and logistic: Sensors monitoring.
- Technology, media, and telecommunication

Below mentioned is some use cases of blockchain (The Future of Blockchain, 2020):

- Security of sharing data's
- Tracking of musical royalties
- Online payments
- Operating systems of real-time lot
- Security of personal identity
- Laundering the tracking system of anti-money
- Voting mechanics
- Advertisement insight
- Creating original contents
- Exchange Cryptocurrency
- Platform of real state processing

Figure 3. Investment in Blockchain
(ref:https://www2.deloitte.com/content/dam/Deloitte/ie/Documents/Consulting/Blockchain-Trends-2020-report.pdf) Deloitte Report.

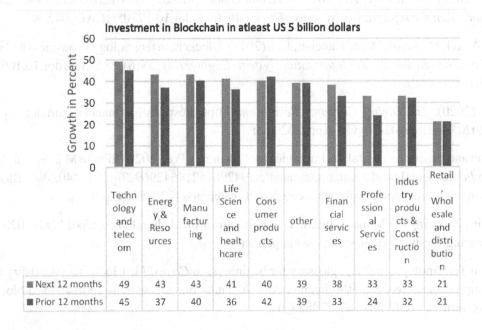

	Techn ology and telec om	Energ y & Reso urces	Manu factur ing	Life Scien ce and healt hcare	Cons umer produ cts	other	Finan cial servic es	Profe ssion al Servic es	Indus try produ cts & Const ructio n	Retail , Whol esale and distri butio n
■ Next 12 months	49	43	43	41	40	39	38	33	33	21
■ Prior 12 months	45	37	40	36	42	39	33	24	32	21

6 CONCLUSION AND SCOPE

In this paper, we tried explaining all the basic elements of Blockchain which included every small detail about understanding and generation of blockchain. We discussed cryptocurrency and cryptography with their different terminologies. By taking the viewpoint from NITI Aayog of the government of India we understood the working of the fertilizer subsidy under blockchain implementation. Taking forward the work, two use cases were explained. Firstly, the collaboration of two industries was explained and the dilemma for making the events occur. The algorithms that come together to secure the private blockchain and their principles were briefly described. Secondly, we tried elaborating on the concept of smart-contracts and its use cases in shaping the current structure of revenue and GDP. The investment ratio in the graphical structure represents the scenario within the two consecutive years (i.e. 2019 & 2020). The advantages and disadvantages along with the future applications on the blockchain summarize the paper. As for future parts of the study, we can suggest the implementation of blockchain in climate markets which can be very useful in future perspectives. Assumptions based on the study will be very helpful to build a pipeline of information.

REFERENCES

Avital, M. (2018). Peer review: Toward a blockchain-enabled market-based ecosystem. *Communications of the Association for Information Systems*, *42*(1), 646–653. doi:10.17705/1CAIS.04228

Beck, R., Avital, M., Rossi, M., & Thatcher, J. B. (2017). Blockchain technology in business and information systems research. *Business & Information Systems Engineering*, *59*(6), 381–384. doi:10.100712599-017-0505-1

Birch, D. (2020). *The Digital Currency Revolution*. https://responsiblefinanceforum.org/wp-content/uploads/2020/04/Birch_02-20_v81-April2020.pdf

Blockchain and Emerging Digital Technologies for Enhancing Post-2020 Climate Markets. (n.d.). *World Bank*. http://documents1.worldbank.org/curated/en/942981521464296927/pdf/124402-WP-Blockchain-andemergingdigitaltechnologiesforenhancingpostclimatemarkets-PUBLIC.pdf

Blockchain: Powering the Value of Internet. (2020). https://blockchainlab.com/pdf/bank-2020---blockchain-powering-the-internet-of-value---whitepaper.pdf

Blockchain Terminology. (n.d.). A glossary for beginners. In *CompTIA*. Blockchain Advisory Council. https://comptiacdn.azureedge.net/webcontent/docs/default-source/research-reports/07576-blockchain-glossary-of-terms-r3.pdf?sfvrsn=7df7462a_0

Blockchain: The India Strategy. (n.d.). https://niti.gov.in/sites/default/files/2020-01/Blockchain_The_India_Strategy_Part_I.pdf

Burchardi, K., Mikhalev, I., Song, B., & Alexander Kok, S. (2020). Get ready for the future of money. *BCG*. https://www.bcg.com/publications/2020/get-ready-for-the-future-of-money.aspx

Casino, F., Dasaklis, K. T., & Patsakis, C. (2019). A systematic literature review of blockchain-based applications: Current status, classification and open issues. *Telematics and Informatics, 36*, 55-81. doi:10.1016/j.tele.2018.11.006

CIO's Guide to Blockchain. (2020). https://www.gartner.com/smarterwithgartner/the-cios-guide-to-blockchain/#:~:text=Gartner%20estimates%20blockchain%20will%20generate,be%20exploring%20the%20technology%20now

Crosby, M., Nachiappan, P., Verma, S., & Kalyanaraman, V. (2016). Blockchain beyond bitcoin. Applied Innovation Review, (2).

Dannen, C. (2017). *Introducing Ethereum and Solidity: Foundations of Cryptocurrency and Blockchain Programming for Beginners* (1st ed.). Apress., doi:10.1007/978-1-4842-2535-6

Deloitte. (2020). *5 Blockchain Trends for 2020*. CS suits briefing. https://www2.deloitte.com/content/dam/Deloitte/ie/Documents/Consulting/Blockchain-Trends-2020-report.pdf

Deshpande, A., Stewart, K., Lepetit, L., & Gunashekar, S. (2017). *Distributed Ledger Technologies/Blockchain: Challenges, Opportunities and the Prospects for Standards*. Technical report, The British Standards Institution (BSI). Available online at: https://bit.ly/32QxvKp

Holotescu, C. (2018). Understanding blockchain technology and how to get involved. The 14th International Scientific Conference eLearning and Software for Education, 19-20.

Konstantinidis, I., Siaminos, G., Timplalexis, C., Zervas, P., Peristeras, V., & Decker, S. (2018). *Blockchain for Business Applications: A Systematic Literature Review*. . doi:10.1007/978-3-319-93931-5_28

Lin, I.-C., & Liao, T.-C. (2017). A survey of blockchain security issues and challenges. *International Journal of Network Security, 19*, 653–659. doi:10.6633/IJNS.201709.19(5).01

Nakamoto. (2008). *Bitcoin: A peer-to-peer electronic cash system*. Academic Press.

Narayanan, A., Bonneau, J., Felten, E., Miller, A., & Goldfeder, S. (2016). *Bitcoin and Cryptocurrency Technologies*. Princeton University Press.

Notheisen, B., Hawlitschek, F., & Weinhardt, C. (2017). Breaking down the blockchain hype – Towards a blockchain market engineering approach. In *Proceedings of the 25th European Conference on Information Systems (ECIS)* (pp. 1062-1080). https://aisel.aisnet.org/ecis2017_rp/69

Ostern, N. (2020). Blockchain in the IS research discipline: A discussion of terminology and concepts. *Electronic Markets, 30*(2), 195–210. doi:10.100712525-019-00387-2

Sabah, S., Mahdi, N., & Majeed, I. (2019). *The road to the blockchain technology: Concept and types*. Academic Press.

Stephan, L., Steffen, S., Moritz, S., & Bela, G. (2019). A Review on Blockchain Technology and Blockchain Projects Fostering Open Science. *Frontiers in Blockchain, 2*, 16. doi:10.3389/fbloc.2019.00016

Swan. (2015). *Blockchain: Blueprint for a New Economy* (1st ed.). O'Reilly Media, Inc.

Swan, M. (2014). Blockchain-Enforced Friendly AI. In *Crypto Money Expo*. http://cryptomoneyexpo.com/expos/inv2/#schedule

Tama, B. A., Kweka, B. J., Park, Y., & Rhee, K. H. (2017). A Critical Review of Blockchain and Its Current Applications. *International Conference on Electrical Engineering and Computer Science*, 109–113. 10.1109/ICECOS.2017.8167115

The Future of Blockchain. (2020). https://www.finextra.com/researcharticle/136/the-future-of-blockchain-2020

Xu, M., Chen, X., & Kou, G. (2019). A systematic review of blockchain. Financ Innov, 5, 27. doi:10.118640854-019-0147-z

Zheng, Z., Xie, S., Dai, H., Chen, X., & Wang, H. (2017). An Overview of Blockchain Technology: Architecture, Consensus, and Future Trends. *IEEE 6th International Congress on Big Data*, 557–564. 10.1109/BigDataCongress.2017.85

Chapter 9
Blockchain in a Nutshell:
State-of-the-Art Applications and Future Research Directions

A. K. M. Bahalul Haque
North South University, Bangladesh

Bharat Bhushan
iD https://orcid.org/0000-0002-9345-4786
Sharda University, India

ABSTRACT

Blockchain gets its name from being a series of blocks that are linked together to form a chain. Once the information has been added to the chain, it cannot be changed. There are several consensus protocols, and each of them is chosen based on the type of blockchain and the system requirements. With the rapid urbanization of the world, several economic, social, and environment-related issues have been raised. Smart cities are an emerging concept that holds the solution to these urban problems. Blockchain is such an innovation that can promote the development of smart cities. Along with its application in the internet of things, smart cities, and logistics, blockchain truly is state-of-the-art technology. Here, the authors aim to provide an in-depth look into this relatively new technology, beginning with blockchain's fundamentals and then covering the applications, issues, and future scope.

INTRODUCTION

Blockchain (Wright, 2019)is a prominent and trending technology in distributed ledger technology (DLT) (Sakız & Gencer, 2019). This technology holds the characteristics of an immutable, decentralized, and sharable database. It is an innovation that hits a breakthrough in secure computing, making all the transactions decentralized. Blockchain enables users to communicate and make transactions among themselves without any third party making it more secure. It is the building block of Bitcoin. Both of them were invented in 2008 by Satoshi Nakamoto and implemented in 2009 for open source after releasing the code. Owing to blockchain technology's several benefits, it is in high demand(Gupta et al., 2020; et al., 2018).

DOI: 10.4018/978-1-7998-6694-7.ch009

Blockchain spread across various application domains included the financial sector, traffic management, risk management, healthcare, and other social services(Pilkington, 2016; Xu et al., 2019) . It also can be used in digital assets, remittance and online payment, smart contracts, public services, hyperledger, insurance, supply chain management, reputation systems, and security services(Labazova et al., 2019). Blockchain technology uses particular consensus algorithms for creating a balanced distributed ledger inside the network. The transaction information is stored chronologically inside the blocks which are interlinked in a chain. The entire ledger or database is stored as multiple copies across all the nodes of the peer-to-peer network. Blockchain can be public or private, with private ones requiring permission from the owner for someone to join(Tasca & Tessone, 2017).

There are mainly two types of blockchain: the public or permissionless blockchain and the private or permissioned blockchain. Examples of public Blockchain include the Bitcoin or Ethereum platform, which allows anyone to join in on the network(Vujičić et al., 2018). Private Blockchain pre-verifies its participants within the network. Usually, they are known to each other. A hybrid kind is a mixture of both that utilizes the advantageous characteristics of each type of blockchain. The applicability of various blockchain types depends on the nature of the application(Hao et al., 2018; Ismail & Shehab, 2019) . This paper facilitates potential readers with the following –

- Latest pieces of literature and their contribution related to blockchain survey
- A detailed overview of blockchain fundamentals
- A precise description fo consensus algorithms used in the blockchain network
- Explanation of state-of-the-art applications related to blockchain
- A Categorical representation of blockchain's future research direction.

The rest of the paper is organized as section 2 contains the blockchain fundamentals. This part includes blockchain characteristics, block structure, blockchain architecture, and a comparative overview of various blockchain types. Section 3 includes a brief description of various consensus algorithm principles used in blockchain. Section 4 consists of the application related to blockchain in various sectors. Section 5 consists of a well-defined categorical representation of future research direction, and section 6 concludes the paper.

LITERATURE SURVEY

Since the inception of blockchain technology, several surveys have been conducted. Those surveys focused on specific attributes of blockchain technology. The surveys and their contributions are given below in Table 1 –

From the above table, it is observed that there is a lack of a comprehensive survey of blockchain technology that will cover the principles, applications, and future research challenges to the best of our knowledge

Table 1. Recent surveys and their contributions related to Blockchain

Reference	Contribution
(X. Li et al., 2020)	Security issues, vulnerabilities and future research direction of blockchain
(Panarello et al., 2018)	Blockchain and IoT Integration, data management including future challenges
(Salman et al., 2019)	Resolving security issues with blockchain including the issues and challenges faced
(Fernández-Caramés & Fraga-Lamas, 2018)	Principles of blockchain, BIoT applications, challenges and optimization of blockchain for IoT
(Shen & Pena-Mora, 2018)	Survey of application of blockchain in urban areas
(Feng et al., 2019)	Privacy issues and the defense mechanism of blockchain
(Nguyen & Kim, 2018)	Detail analysis of consensus algorithm in blockchain
(Lu, 2018)	Principles, applications, and issues of blockchain
(Bernal Bernabe et al., 2019)	Privacy issues and solutions of various blockchain-based applications
(Xie et al., 2019)	Blockchain for smart city perspective including issues and implications
(Wu et al., 2019)	Analysis of blockchain and IoT integration in the layered approach
(Dai et al., 2019)	The proposed architecture of Blockchain for IoT including issues and industrial application
(Dasgupta et al., 2019)	Blockchain security vulnerabilities, solutions, and prospects
(Mazlan et al., 2020)	Survey of scalability issues, solutions, and limitations of blockchain for healthcare
(Fernandez-Carames & Fraga-Lamas, 2019)	Securing industrial applications with blockchain for Industry 4.0
(Al-Jaroodi & Mohamed, 2019)	Survey of opportunities and threats of blockchain usage for Industry
(Abou Jaoude & George Saade, 2019)	Detailed description of Blockchain applications in diverse sectors
(W. Wang et al., 2019)	wholistic survey of consensus, mining, and application of blockchain
(Saad et al., 2020)	Survey of security and privacy attacks on blockchain
(Hafid et al., 2020)	scalability issues and performance analysis of the current solutions of blockchain technology

BLOCKCHAIN FUNDAMENTALS

Blockchain is made up of blocks, with each block linking to its predecessor to form a chain. Information that has been added to the chain is immutable. Block addition needs some transactions also. These are the fundamentals of blockchain and elaborated upon below.

Characteristics

Blockchain has several exciting and unique attributes. These attributes have made technology efficient. These are discussed as follows(Zheng et al., 2017) -

- Decentralized: Transaction is validated without any centralized authority. The work is done collectively, and all miners have a copy of the ledger and can validate transactions to add them to the chain. Decentralized networks involve peer-to-peer (P2P) transmissions.
- Immutability: Transactions cannot be tampered with. Every block includes has of the previous (Islam et al., 2020). Moreover, blocks store the timestamp also.

- Public Key Cryptography (PKC): Transactions are signed and verified with the cryptographic keys. In this case, a private key is used for signing. Nowadays, private keys are longer and kept secret. Public keys are derived from private keys and used to ensure that signatures have not been forged.
- Data validation: Several nodes have to validate each block before it is appended to the chain. It is done through the use of one of the many available consensus algorithms. Miners are often incentivized by financial means.

The Block Structure

User data and transaction data is stored inside a block. The block structure shows various elements that are saved. A brief description of various elements that exist inside a block are shown below (Gobel & Krzesinski, 2017)-

- Data: The data stored in each block differs from application to application. This data may be transaction data as in cryptocurrency, or a distributed database's information, or files that are part of a P2P file system, etc.
- Parent block hash: The hash value of the previous block is used as a parameter to compute the block hash. The 256-bit output will be unique and based on the input. Any small change in the input provides a drastically different result. This hash value is used to confirm that data has not been tampered with anywhere along with the blockchain.
- Merkle tree root hash: The data structure is used because it allows large amounts of data to be stored securely and efficiently. Using the root hash, a specific transaction can be verified without having to download the entire blockchain.
- Timestamp: Each block has an attached timestamp of when it was created. This property is useful to track when a particular document stored in the block was created or modified. It is also useful in the business and legal world. It is a reliable way to determine whether a document was available to a specific party at a particular date or time.
- Nonce: A 4-byte long value that is incremented starting from 0 for every hash calculation. The Merkle tree root hash is combined with the nonce, the previous block's hash, and some other information to create the block's overall hash.
- nBits: The value represented by the nBits is the target threshold for miners who are trying to produce a valid block hash. If the hash produced by a miner is lower than or equal to the nBits value, then the block is valid. The lower the nBits value, the more difficult it is to produce a valid hash.
- Other information stored in the block is digital signatures, block version, and a few different user-defined values. Digital signatures involve both the public and private keys of a user.

Blockchain Classification

A few different types of blockchain are classified according to the access rights of nodes in the network. These are:

Public blockchain or Permissionless Blockchain: Networks using public blockchain have the most anonymity and decentralization. Any person can join the network. All nodes can carry out transactions and contracts. There is complete transparency, as everyone can see all the information in the blockchain.

These types of networks are self-sustainable and thus have much lower management costs (Casino et al., 2019).

Private Blockchain or Permissioned Blockchain: Blockchain networks often have a centralized administrator, although it is still stored in a distributed manner. Here, access to the data in the blockchain is strictly managed and monitored by the central authority. Only certain users have permission to carry out network operations. Mining is usually carried out solely by the authority, thus making it faster. However, this does remove some of the security that decentralization provides.

Consortium blockchain: It is also known as federated blockchain or permissioned public blockchain. It has the efficiency and privacy associated with a private blockchain, but instead of one entity to verify transactions, there is a set of leader nodes assigned to the task. Leader nodes can give other users permission for network operations. This type of blockchain would be useful when several companies are collaborating.

Table 2. Comparative analysis of various kinds of Blockchain

Class	Consensus determination	Node access	Benefits	Applications
Public (Casino et al., 2019)	Anyone can mine	Read/write access given to all	Low infrastructure costs	Cryptocurrency
Consortium (Zheng et al., 2017)	Set of leader nodes mine	Read access given to all, write access granted by leader nodes	Fast speed of transaction, light PoW	Banking and industry sectors
Private (Islam et al., 2020)	Centralized organization mines	Read/write access granted by a centralized organization	High level of privacy and security	Database management, auditing

Blockchain Architecture

Although the number of layers in blockchain technology is not fixed, there are mainly six that most experts agree upon (Yassein et al., 2019). This number may vary according to individual applications.

- Data layer: As the lowest layer, the data layer encapsulates several different mechanisms. These are the hash function, asymmetric encryption, timestamp, chain structure, Merkel tree, and data block. In this layer, new blocks are created, and information about each block like the timestamp, is stored. The node which wins according to the consensus algorithm will be allowed to add its block to the chain.
- Network layer: This layer's mechanisms include data propagation, data verification, distributed networking, data authentication, data dissemination, and data forwarding. The purpose of this layer is to ensure the validity of the transactions that have been generated. Invalid transactions are discarded in this layer.
- Consensus layer: This layer consists of one of the many different consensus algorithms used to determine between different nodes. Consensus algorithms are further elaborated in the next section.

- Incentive layer: This layer is to do with how the winning node will be rewarded for its work. This layer deals with economic incentive issuance, distribution mechanisms, and allocation mechanisms.
- Contract layer: This layer is where programmable features of blockchain are implemented. The most common example is smart contracts.
- Application layer: This is unique to each blockchain application and depends on its applications such as smart cities, IoT, intellectual property, etc.

CONSENSUS ALGORITHM

Consensus algorithms are a strategy that a computer group used to agree with each other on what is right. This algorithm helps a decentralized network decide unanimously whenever required (Ferdous et al., 2020). The consensus algorithm helps achieve synchronization, verifiability, and authentication (Bhushan et al., 2020; Lamport et al., 2008). There are several consensus mechanisms, and each is suited for different kinds of platforms. Some of the common ones are presented as follows.

Proof of Work (PoW)

This is a proof-based protocol. A new block can be added if a node mines a block with sufficient proof of its effort (W. Wang et al., 2019). If any node adds a new block to the blockchain without any verified process, it will create an authenticity issue for the whole blockchain network. That is why the consensus is introduced. In this case, the nodes need to solve a complex puzzle for attaching new blocks. The participating mining nodes continually compute the hash value. The nonce value helps in this case. Once the value is found, the miner broadcasts it. All the other miners check it and approve it. After that, the block is added to the blockchain. Sometimes this process leads to forking, where valid blocks get generated simultaneously. Proof of Work uses the most extended chain rule to solve this issue, and so branches might form. The implementation of the algorithm was seen in Bitcoin (Judmayer et al., 2017). As the algorithm requires substantial computational resources and can have only one successful miner, it is not sustainable.

Proof of Stake (PoS)

This one is an energy-efficient algorithm used as a substitute for PoW and is more effective. In this mechanism, the miners need to own an ample amount of currencies to get chosen. A particular node acts as a validator. It is selected considering its stake (amount of money) that exists currently in the network. Once the block has been accepted, the validators receive the fees. Sometimes the combination of stake size and nodes age in the network is used as a parameter for finding miners. For example, Peercoin leans towards older and larger sets of coin holders (King & Nadal, 2012). It is more vulnerable to different kinds of attacks. This is why many blockchain-based networks begin with Proof of Work and then gradually transmute to Proof of Stake algorithm.

Delegated Proof of Stake (DPoS)

Apart from the other similar characteristics of PoS, in DPoS, the stakeholders are required to vote and elect a delegate to generate blocks. As such, the number of participants is fewer, and they can get block generation and transaction verification done much easier and faster. *Bitshare* was implemented using this consensus algorithm (*BITSHARES: THE FIRST DECENTRALISED EXCHANGE*, n.d.). DPoS is more productive than PoS, but it tends to centralize because the participants can vote themselves and manipulate others into voting.

Proof of Elapsed Time (PoET)

Intel first came up with the consensus algorithm, namely, Proof of Elapsed Time, to create a blockchain-based computing platform, Software Guard Extensions (SGX) (*Sawtooth (Hyperledger)*, n.d.). The workflow includes the calculation of a randomly generated number. Here the waiting time between two block creation is also considered. The waiting time is associated with the random number of each node. Here, one single node is selected for creating a new block in the blockchain. The chosen node is chosen based on its time remaining in the network. The least expiry time gets the priority in case of selecting the node (Chen et al., 2017).

Practical Byzantine Fault Tolerance (PBFT)

This is a replication algorithm where two communicating nodes over a distributed network can reach consensus, even if a few misbehaving nodes are present (X. Wang et al., 2018). This protocol can handle up to $1/3^{rd}$ of the malfunctioning byzantine replicas. Here, a group of a node is lead by a single node known as the leader. The group of nodes acts as a backup node. The leader generally receives a new request. After that, it is transferred to the helper nodes for checking the integrity and originality of the request. The leader can move forward to the next phase of the 3 phases PBFT if it receives majority votes. Considering these factors, the algorithm is efficient and sustainable; even it faces a few infected nodes. Hyperledger Fabric is an application of the PBFTprotocol (*Hyperledger* Fabric). However, work needs to be done on its scalability aspect.

Proof of Authority (PoA)

It has been specifically designed for use in private blockchains. In Proof of Work, the resource consumption and dependencies were too high. These problems are solved in the Proof of Authority mechanism. PoA considers a few aspects here, such as the majority of the nodes, shall be honest. The authoritative nodes that execute the consensus are selected based on their financial capability in the network. For an efficient and optimized block distribution purpose, "mining rotation schema" acts as a principle of PoAs (De Angelis et al., 2018). Aura (*Parity-Ethereum (Aura)*, n.d.) and Clique(*Clique PoA Protocol & Rinkeby PoA Testnet*, n.d.) have used the Proof of Authority to implement their systems. The only limitation of this protocol is that it is not scalable.

Raft

Raft is an election-based consensus protocol. It can also be seen as a real-life implementation of Paxos. Selecting leader and log management are the two most crucial tasks of Raft. The leader is responsible for managing the transactions. In the replicating log phase, the leader takes into account the log entries from clients and displays them (Ongaro & Ousterhout, 2019). Quorum and Corda have implemented their blockchain-based systems using this consensus protocol. Usually, Raft has less latency and excellent throughput, but its overall performance relies on the dominant leader (Kwon, 2014).

Application of Blockchain

Various applications of blockchain have been proposed over the years. In this section, the application of blockchain technology in different areas is discussed.

Blockchain for Financial Service

The financial services industry can optimize its business effectively with blockchain technology. Blockchain is a new and exciting option in contrast to conventional financing, banking, and exchange strategies. Blockchain can potentially change the traditional currency transaction techniques. It is essentially a disseminated record that keeps up a persistently developing rundown of each exchange that is circulated into countless PCs. This makes it practically impossible to hack, changing how banking is done in the current world. The vast majority know the expression 'blockchain' corresponding to the cryptographic money Bitcoin (Tomov, 2019). Blockchain technology uses any particular consensus algorithm to create a distributed ledger that is stored across all the nodes of the network.

When a trade occurs, it is immediately added to each copy of the record. It ensures an exact record of transactions. Since there are various copies of the record, blockchain is perpetual and secured in every practical sense. Blockchain encourages sheltered, simple exchanges, and constructs trust between exchanging accomplices. It can also be utilized to recognize people through computerized IDs rapidly. Banks and other money-related organizations are now using blockchain to improve their administration, curtailed extortion, and decrease clients' expenses. Blockchain is also used in Cross-border exchanges(Gebrekiros & Doorman, 2014), Trade account stages(Tanwar et al., 2020), clearing and settlements, and digital identity confirmation.

Blockchain for Healthcare

Healthcare industry consists of many sectors such as patients, hospitals, doctors, researchers, pharmacies, medical staff, diagnostic centers, etc. All of these create a massive amount of data. Blockchain, with its efficient data structure and algorithm, can process big data in an extensive network. Storage and sharing of patient's data are susceptible and thus should be given access to appropriate authorities. For this purpose, Electronic health records (EHR) utilize the improvement of the medical care system. More sharing of EHR means an improvement in the quality of medical care (Tama, 2015). EHR also enhances the recommendation for doctors(Tama & Rhee, 2019) . Nowadays, storing and analyzing healthcare data securely is a big challenge for healthcare data holders. The blockchain storage platform named healthcare data gateway (HDG) is the best way to overcome this issue.

A smartphone application can be used to monitor data sharing. This system ensures the privacy of a patient's data. An immutable blockchain storage system makes sure that the data is not altered. Even the patients, doctors, and nurses are not permitted to do that. Gem, a start-up company, developed an application implementing this as a universal healthcare data infrastructure(*Bitcoin Magazine,*). Proper management of healthcare information can help analyze patients' conditions, medical discoveries, and comprehensive research. It will enable the working procedure to be conducted securely and anonymously(Benchoufi & Ravaud, 2017). Smart contracts are useful for access control automation and adding new records to the chain (Azaria et al., 2016). The system is called MedRec. The authors (Zhang et al., 2016) proposed healthcare based on a pervasive social media network (PSN). Data is collected through medical sensors. Blockchain is used for sharing data with a smartphone and healthcare providers when needed.

Smart Grid

Blockchain can also be a great solution in the management of power and energy. The majority of the energy resources in the world we use today are limited and are not renewable. Moreover, using these resources hamper our environment. Blockchain can be utilized to use these resources in a limited, economical way. The peer-to-peer network can be a powerful aspect of energy trading. A token-based framework enabling peer-to-peer network can implement a multi-signature approach (Aitzhan & Svetinovic, 2018). It introduces a secure and decentralized energy system. A trusted environment among the participants is also preferable for a third-party meter reading. EnergyChain is a great example. It uses 100 residential households to execute proof-of-concept on the Ethereum platform. An operational auction mechanism is proposed to conduct payment using smart contracts. It can quickly meet demand and supply (Mengelkamp, Notheisen, et al., 2018).

PETra (Laszka et al., 2017) and Helios (Kounelis et al., 2017) are two examples of blockchain integrated energy management models. A microgrid of 130 buildings in Brooklyn, NY utilizes blockchain (Mengelkamp, Gärttner, et al., 2018). They buy and sell power amongst themselves without intermediaries. Energy losses can be tracked, including cost minimization (Sanseverino et al., 2018). It can be scaled up to smart grids, allowing for secure monitoring of energy consumption and trading within the city without a central authority (Aitzhan & Svetinovic, 2018).

Smart Transportation

Self-driving cars using artificial intelligence and machine learning have opened a new transportation system window. For this self-driving car concept and other vehicles, comfort, security, travel efficiency, road safety, and drivers and passenger-communication are some aspects that need to be modernized too. A smart vehicle is embedded with different interfaces such as WiFi, WiMAX, Bluetooth, DSRC, etc. to communicate with other vehicles and maintain traffic rules. The vehicles continuously exchange data among vehicles as well as persons. Blockchain can architect this kind of system with a decentralized, secured, and trusted environment. The vehicles can transmit information easily and quickly (Sharma et al., 2018).

Electric Vehicles (EVs) use environment-friendly batteries that can be charged at charging stations. The process can be implemented with blockchain architecture (Knirsch et al., 2018). At First, EV requests the required energy. Then, the nearby station sends bids against the energy needed. An appropriate station is then chosen and the EV can charge and confirm the transaction over a certain period. An incentive-based vehicular network called CreditCoin proposed a way to inspire all the vehicles to participate (L. Li et al., 2018). Eco-Announcement is a protocol designed to gather messages in exchange for transactions made through Coin. The most advanced technology in this smart transportation system is Vehicular AdHoc Networks (VANETs) (Leiding et al., 2016). This model ensures transmitting messages between the vehicles and the Road Side Units (RSU).

A rating-based decentralized system is proposed to manage these messages (Yang et al., 2019). Each vehicle gets the chance to rate the neighboring vehicle and upload this rating to Roadside Unit(RSU). All the RSUs, in combined order, upload the data to a network using PoW and PoS. Dirichlet method protects the location privacy of the VANET. The idea is to facilitate communication links between the trusted vehicles using a publicly available block using smart contracts (Luo et al., 2020). It still needs much work on managing appropriate vehicles for blind and physically challenged people. Vehicles working under private organizations, businesses, and the government can be efficiently monitored by blockchain.

Supply Chain Management

It has gained traction in the last few years (Cooper et al., 1997). Transportation, customer management, marketing, distribution, or manufacturing, and more industries have explored supply chain management (Ross, 1998). Transportation organizations, retailer merchants, wholesalers, product assemblers, component producers, the raw material are essentially its core segments (La Londe & Masters, 1994). Supply chain management is a set of networks of different organizations that maintain any product's ecosystem through upstream and downstream linkages(Christopher & Ryals, 1999; Mentzer et al., 2001). Billions of products are manufactured, designed, and delivered through complex, digital and global supply chains in a single day(Prockl et al., 2017). Blockchain can ensure security and trust among suppliers, distributors, retailers, transporters (., 2016; Milani et al., 2016). Blockchain reduces corruption and fraud, generating a manual process to automate and control all over authentication issues (Madaan et al., 2021; Saxena et al., 2020).

Blockchain technology gives each entity a granular view of the complete supply chain. Hashing and timestamp methods keep a record of the life cycle of a product. It can track manufacturing issues involving multiple organizations as blockchain stores information about each stage of manufacturing and distribution. RFID technology collects, circulates, and shares data agri-food supply chains. Blockchain guarantees the authenticity and reliability of the shared information about the production, processing, warehousing, distribution, and sales links(Nakasumi, 2017; *Ownest* ; Tian, 2016). Several startups have launched applying blockchain to this industry. Examples are Provenance (Steiner & Baker, 2015), which connects producers and consumers, and Hijro (*Hijro*, n.d.), which connects clients globally to help supply chain management across countries.

Smart Education

Digital education system uses various digital tools such as smartphones, tablets, projectors, laptops, digital textbooks, etc. A student can attend classes online without needing to go to school physically. They can pay their tuition fees via a smart payment system (Zhu et al., 2016). Smart education allows the students to maintain their learning progress at their own pace. It also allows students to learn at the place of their own choice. Blockchain ensures the authenticity of academic diplomas. The hashes of academic certificates are preserved on the blockchain. Validation of integrity and non-repudiation of academic certificates are managed by the digital signature and chain-based block structure (Bond et al., 2015). Thus, fake or fraudulent student information is detected quickly. EduCTX is a blockchain-based global higher education credit platform. It provides a decentralized system to store, manage, and process the course record (Turkanović et al., 2018).

Smart Business

Electronic business has become quite popular because of the decentralized marketplace, anonymous user identification, sharing of possible information, and secure data storage is the advantages of the blockchain-based business. The trust issue is one of the most challenging issues in the business sector. Hence, blockchain ensures that the element of trust is strengthened using its attributes. It utilizes the perfect immutability of records and shows every party the previous ownership record, making it nearly impossible to fraud. The P2P reputation system is essential in the blockchain because every participant can increase business activity (Dennis & Owen, 2016; Weber et al., 2016).

Smart Government

A blockchain-based smart government system includes secure document management, a service-based attitude, promoting the integration of resources, and so on (Hou, 2017). The government gathers information through interconnected IoT devices, smart surveillance systems, applications used by the residents, and various institutions and processes to ensure a better service. Another application is the electronic voting system. It utilizes authenticity and integrity (Koç et al., 2018; Sethi et al., 2021) . The Ethereum platform can be used to store voting information. Smart contracts are used to count and check each vote's validation afterward to ensure the process's legitimacy.

Blockchain for Real Estate

Blockchain can be utilized to create a transparent trading system for real estate. Sales agreements, lease, and payment processes can be implemented using smart contracts. Blockchain-based digital IDs will help verify the background of each party. So, the process will be free of fraud. The public ledger system lets every buyer and seller know the previous history of property ownership. Since the data stored there is immutable, ownership information is legitimate. This system is decentralized, and the public ledger increases the trust between the trading parties for the transaction to occur. This system eliminates third parties, lawyers, and banks. As a result, low intermediaries reduce the cost of the whole contract management process.

Blockchain for Electronic Voting System

The traditional voting system with ballot papers that required voters' physical presence is quite outdated. There is no strict verification system to check whether a vote is cast or not. Blockchain technology-based electronic voting systems can bring a drastic change here. Since each voter has their ID, they can cast only one vote. The ballot box is virtual, and all data are shown in a public ledger and are immutable. Everyone can see the voting status and the result in the ledger involved in the voting process. Blockchain verifies all voters' identity to ensure the maximum legitimacy of the results. As the registered members with valid IDs can cast their votes, the system is free of third-party attacks. It is ensured that each voter casts their ballot at a specified time.

FUTURE RESEARCH DIRECTIONS

Blockchain technology has an extraordinary future, and a great extent of it has been seen in the money related field. The budgetary associations could not adequately deal with the substantial remaining burden after demonetization. So, they elicited the issues of having an incorporated expert for taking care of the monetary exchanges (A. K. M. B. Haque & Rahman, 2020; et al., 2018). Consolidating blockchain with monetary exchanges gives stunning advantages. Like, saving time and cash, remembering a radical decrease in the time required for handling and approving exchanges. The blockchain capacities on a dispersed information base make the activities easy, guaranteeing tight security and safety from digital assaults. Let us view the further scope of Blockchain innovation:

Blockchain in Digital Advertising

Presently, advanced promotion faces many difficulties like area extortion, bot traffic, absence of straightforwardness, etc. Blockchain conveys straightforwardness to the flexible chain as it imparts trust in any situation and permits the rightful organizations to succeed by reducing the awful parts in the flexible chain. Blockchain innovation is still in its early stage, yet all promotion organizations see how it will upgrade their business.

Blockchain in Cyber Security

Although the blockchain is a public record, it is checked and scrambled utilizing creative cryptography innovation. As such, the data or information is more averse to be assaulted or modified without approval (Madaan et al., 2021) [99]. Blockchain provides data integrity since data inside a block cannot be changed once it is added within a chain. Besides, blockchain being a decentralized architecture, targeting a single node will not destroy the data and infrastructure since other nodes of the network have an identical copy of data. In recent days blockchain is also a very effective technology for providing IoT security and privacy (A. B. Haque et al., 2021).

Remove the Third Party's Requirement

The traditional financial system raises the need for confiding in an outsider during exchanges. SWIFT and the Depository Trust Cleaning Company work likewise. Corporate chances thrive for organizations that can apply Blockchain advancements focusing on specific tradeoffs, similar to the home loan industry. The current home loans require a convoluted trap of title look, protection, and uncountable minor exchange expenses that keep the framework running. Blockchain innovation addresses each of these worries. A specific property's record comprises an evident and approved exchange history, including the need for establishments down for hazard adjustment and trust administrations.

Supply Chain Management

With blockchain's assistance, reporting the exchange in a never-ending appropriated record and administering the exchanges all the more sturdily and straightforwardly is quite feasible. It also limits human blunders and time delays. Likewise, it is utilized for screen costs, work, and deliveries at each purpose of the graceful chain. In any circumstance, this has a severe impact on comprehension and environmental elements. Not just this, the decentralized record can be used to check the authenticity or reasonable exchange status of items by tailing them to structure their source.

Testing Different Types of Blockchain

Blockchain is a technology used in different platforms for its different approaches. So, there has to be a testing policy if the system is suited to a specific purpose. This testing procedure can be divided into two steps: standardization and testing. First, blockchain must satisfy every criterion that the system requires. Standardization will ensure reliable performance by blockchain. Then, for every criterion, blockchain needs to test. For instance, to implement the blockchain system in healthcare networks, a proper storage system and security are mandated. Thus the capacity, consensus procedure, formation, etc. are to be tested.

CONCLUSION

Blockchain technology is one of the most popular emerging technologies. Widespread adoption and implementation of blockchain have been possible due to the facilities it provides when implemented. The application of blockchain ranges from individual to industry level. Several implementation issues exist due to the lack of efficient framework generation and efficient human resources suitable for applying blockchain technology. Privacy and security issues also hamper performance. Apart from the issues involved, the technology keeps on evolving, addressing the challenges.

REFERENCES

Abou Jaoude, J., & George Saade, R. (2019). Blockchain applications - Usage in different domains. *IEEE Access: Practical Innovations, Open Solutions*, 7, 45360–45381. https://doi.org/10.1109/ACCESS.2019.2902501

Aitzhan, N. Z., & Svetinovic, D. (2018). Security and Privacy in Decentralized Energy Trading Through Multi-Signatures, Blockchain and Anonymous Messaging Streams. *IEEE Transactions on Dependable and Secure Computing*, 15(5), 840–852. https://doi.org/10.1109/TDSC.2016.2616861

Al-Jaroodi, J., & Mohamed, N. (2019). Blockchain in Industries: A Survey. *IEEE Access: Practical Innovations, Open Solutions*, 7, 36500–36515. https://doi.org/10.1109/ACCESS.2019.2903554

Azaria, A., Ekblaw, A., Vieira, T., & Lippman, A. (2016). MedRec: Using blockchain for medical data access and permission management. *Proceedings - 2016 2nd International Conference on Open and Big Data, OBD 2016*, 25–30. doi:10.1109/OBD.2016.11

Benchoufi, M., & Ravaud, P. (2017). Blockchain technology for improving clinical research quality. *Trials, 18*(1), 335.

Bernal Bernabe, J., Canovas, J. L., Hernandez-Ramos, J. L., Torres Moreno, R., & Skarmeta, A. (2019). Privacy-Preserving Solutions for Blockchain: Review and Challenges. *IEEE Access: Practical Innovations, Open Solutions, 7*, 164908–164940.

Bhushan, B., Khamparia, A., Sagayam, K. M., Sharma, S. K., Ahad, M. A., & Debnath, N. C. (2020). Blockchain for smart cities: A review of architectures, integration trends and future research directions. *Sustainable Cities and Society, 61*. doi:10.1016/j.scs.2020.102360

Bond, F., Amati, F., & Blousson, G. (2015). *Blockchain, academic verification use case.* https://s3.amazonaws.com/signatura-usercontent/blockchain_academic_verification_use_case.pdf

Casino, F., Dasaklis, T. K., & Patsakis, C. (2019). A systematic literature review of blockchain-based applications: Current status, classification and open issues. *Telematics and Informatics, 36*, 55–81.

Chen, L., Xu, L., Shah, N., Gao, Z., Lu, Y., & Shi, W. (2017). On security analysis of proof-of-elapsed-time (PoET). *Lecture Notes in Computer Science (Including Subseries Lecture Notes in Artificial Intelligence and Lecture Notes in Bioinformatics), 10616 LNCS*, 282–297. doi:10.1007/978-3-319-69084-1_19

Christopher, M., & Ryals, L. (1999). Supply Chain Strategy: Its Impact on Shareholder Value. *International Journal of Logistics Management, 10*(1), 1–10. https://doi.org/10.1108/09574099910805897

Cooper, M. C., Lambert, D. M., & Pagh, J. D. (1997). Supply Chain Management: More Than a New Name for Logistics. *International Journal of Logistics Management, 8*(1), 1–14. https://doi.org/10.1108/09574099710805556

Dai, H. N., Zheng, Z., & Zhang, Y. (2019). Blockchain for Internet of Things: A Survey. *IEEE Internet of Things Journal, 6*(5), 8076–8094. doi:10.1109/JIOT.2019.2920987

Dasgupta, D., Shrein, J. M., & Gupta, K. D. (2019). A survey of blockchain from security perspective. *Journal of Banking and Financial Technology, 3*(1), 1–17. https://doi.org/10.1007/s42786-018-00002-6

De Angelis, S., Aniello, L., Baldoni, R., Lombardi, F., Margheri, A., & Sassone, V. (2018). PBFT vs proof-of-authority: Applying the CAP theorem to permissioned blockchain. *CEUR Workshop Proceedings*, 2058.

Dennis, R., & Owen, G. (2016). Rep on the block: A next generation reputation system based on the blockchain. *2015 10th International Conference for Internet Technology and Secured Transactions, ICITST 2015*, 131–138. doi:10.1109/ICITST.2015.7412073

Feng, Q., He, D., Zeadally, S., Khan, M. K., & Kumar, N. (2019). A survey on privacy protection in blockchain system. *Journal of Network and Computer Applications, 126*, 45–58.

Ferdous, M. S., Chowdhury, M. J. M., Hoque, M. A., & Colman, A. (2020). *Blockchain consensus algorithms: a survey.* ArXiv.

Fernández-Caramés, T. M., & Fraga-Lamas, P. (2018). A Review on the Use of Blockchain for the Internet of Things. *IEEE Access: Practical Innovations, Open Solutions, 6*, 32979–33001.

Fernandez-Carames, T. M., & Fraga-Lamas, P. (2019). A Review on the Application of Blockchain to the Next Generation of Cybersecure Industry 4.0 Smart Factories. *IEEE Access: Practical Innovations, Open Solutions, 7*, 45201–45218. https://doi.org/10.1109/ACCESS.2019.2908780

Gebrekiros, Y., & Doorman, G. (2014, February 10). Optimal transmission capacity allocation for cross-border exchange of Frequency Restoration Reserves (FRR). *Proceedings - 2014 Power Systems Computation Conference, PSCC 2014*. doi:10.1109/PSCC.2014.7038426

Gobel, J., & Krzesinski, A. E. (2017). Increased block size and Bitcoin blockchain dynamics. *2017 27th International Telecommunication Networks and Applications Conference, ITNAC 2017*, 1–6. doi:10.1109/ATNAC.2017.8215367

Gupta, S., Sinha, S., & Bhushan, B. (2020). Emergence of Blockchain Technology: Fundamentals, Working and its Various Implementations. *SSRN Electronic Journal*. doi:10.2139srn.3569577

Hafid, A., Hafid, A. S., & Samih, M. (2020). Scaling Blockchains: A Comprehensive Survey. *IEEE Access: Practical Innovations, Open Solutions, 8*, 125244–125262. https://doi.org/10.1109/ACCESS.2020.3007251

Hao, Y., Li, Y., Dong, X., Fang, L., & Chen, P. (2018). Performance Analysis of Consensus Algorithm in Private Blockchain. *IEEE Intelligent Vehicles Symposium, Proceedings*, 280–285. doi:10.1109/IVS.2018.8500557

Haque, A. B., Najmul Islam, A. K. M., Hyrynsalmi, S., Naqvi, B., & Smolander, K. (2021). GDPR Compliant Blockchains – A Systematic Literature Review. *IEEE Access*, 1–1. doi:10.1109/ACCESS.2021.3069877

Haque, A. K. M. B., & Rahman, M. (2020). Blockchain Technology : Methodology, Application and Security Issues. *International Journal of Computer Science and Network Security, 20*(2), 21–30. https://www.researchgate.net/publication/339973150_Blockchain_Technology_Methodology_Application_and_Security_Issues/citations

Hijro. (n.d.). Retrieved April 1, 2021, from https://hijro.com/

Hou, H. (2017, September 14). The application of blockchain technology in E-government in China. *2017 26th International Conference on Computer Communications and Networks, ICCCN 2017*. doi:10.1109/ICCCN.2017.8038519

Hyperledger. (2019). *Hyperledger – Open Source Blockchain Technologies*. Hyperledger. https://www.hyperledger.org/

Islam, I., Munim, K. M., Oishwee, S. J., Islam, A. K. M. N., & Islam, M. N. (2020). A Critical Review of Concepts, Benefits, and Pitfalls of Blockchain Technology Using Concept Map. *IEEE Access: Practical Innovations, Open Solutions, 8*, 68333–68341. https://doi.org/10.1109/ACCESS.2020.2985647

Ismail, A., & Shehab, A. (2019). Security in Smart Cities: Models, Applications, and Challenges.). *Future Generation Computer Systems, 9*(November).

Judmayer, A., Stifter, N., Krombholz, K., & Weippl, E. (2017). Blocks and Chains: Introduction to Bitcoin, Cryptocurrencies, and Their Consensus Mechanisms. *Synthesis Lectures on Information Security, Privacy, and Trust, 9*(1), 1–123. doi:10.220000773ed1v01y201704spt020

King, S., & Nadal, S. (2012). *PPCoin: Peer-to-Peer Crypto-Currency with Proof-of-Stake*. Academic Press.

Knirsch, F., Unterweger, A., & Engel, D. (2018). Privacy-preserving blockchain-based electric vehicle charging with dynamic tariff decisions. *Computer Science -. Research for Development, 33*(1–2), 71–79. https://doi.org/10.1007/s00450-017-0348-5

Koç, A. K., Yavuz, E., Çabuk, U. C., & Dalkiliç, G. (2018). Towards secure e-voting using ethereum blockchain. *6th International Symposium on Digital Forensic and Security, ISDFS 2018 - Proceeding*, 1–6. doi:10.1109/ISDFS.2018.8355340

Kounelis, I., Steri, G., Giuliani, R., Geneiatakis, D., Neisse, R., & Nai-Fovino, I. (2017, August 23). Fostering consumers' energy market through smart contracts. *Energy and Sustainability in Small Developing Economies, ES2DE 2017 - Proceedings*. doi:10.1109/ES2DE.2017.8015343

Kwon, J. (2014). TenderMint : Consensus without Mining. In *The-Blockchain.Com* (Vol. 6). tendermint. com/docs/tendermint.pdf

La Londe, B. J., & Masters, J. M. (1994). Emerging Logistics Strategies: Blueprints for the Next Century. *International Journal of Physical Distribution & Logistics Management, 24*(7), 35–47. https://doi. org/10.1108/09600039410070975

Labazova, O., Dehling, T., & Sunyaev, A. (2019). From Hype to Reality: A Taxonomy of Blockchain Applications. *Proceedings of the 52nd Hawaii International Conference on System Sciences*. doi:10.24251/ hicss.2019.552

Lamport, L., Shostak, R., & Pease, M. (2008). The byzantine generals problem. *Dr. Dobb's Journal, 33*(4), 30–36. https://doi.org/10.1145/3335772.3335936

Laszka, A., Dubey, A., Walker, M., & Schmidt, D. (2017). Providing privacy, safety, and security in IoT-based transactive energy systems using distributed ledgers. *ACM International Conference Proceeding Series*, 1–8. doi:10.1145/3131542.3131562

Leiding, B., Memarmoshrefi, P., & Hogrefe, D. (2016). Self-managed and blockchain-based vehicular ad-hoc networks. *UbiComp 2016 Adjunct - Proceedings of the 2016 ACM International Joint Conference on Pervasive and Ubiquitous Computing*, 137–140. doi:10.1145/2968219.2971409

Li, L., Liu, J., Cheng, L., Qiu, S., Wang, W., Zhang, X., & Zhang, Z. (2018). CreditCoin: A Privacy-Preserving Blockchain-Based Incentive Announcement Network for Communications of Smart Vehicles. *IEEE Transactions on Intelligent Transportation Systems, 19*(7), 2204–2220. https://doi.org/10.1109/ TITS.2017.2777990

Li, X., Jiang, P., Chen, T., Luo, X., & Wen, Q. (2020). A survey on the security of blockchain systems. *Future Generation Computer Systems, 107*, 841–853. https://doi.org/10.1016/j.future.2017.08.020

Lu, Y. (2018). Blockchain: A Survey on Functions, Applications and Open Issues. *Journal of Industrial Integration and Management, 03*(04), 1850015. https://doi.org/10.1142/s242486221850015x

Luo, B., Li, X., Weng, J., Guo, J., & Ma, J. (2020). Blockchain Enabled Trust-Based Location Privacy Protection Scheme in VANET. *IEEE Transactions on Vehicular Technology, 69*(2), 2034–2048. https:// doi.org/10.1109/TVT.2019.2957744

Madaan, G., Bhushan, B., & Kumar, R. (2021). Blockchain-Based Cyberthreat Mitigation Systems for Smart Vehicles and Industrial Automation. Springer. https://doi.org/10.1007/978-981-15-7965-3_2.

Mazlan, A. A., Daud, S. M., Sam, S. M., Abas, H., Rasid, S. Z. A., & Yusof, M. F. (2020). Scalability Challenges in Healthcare Blockchain System-A Systematic Review. *IEEE Access: Practical Innovations, Open Solutions, 8,* 23663–23673.

Mengelkamp, E., Gärttner, J., Rock, K., Kessler, S., Orsini, L., & Weinhardt, C. (2018). Designing microgrid energy markets: A case study: The Brooklyn Microgrid. *Applied Energy, 210,* 870–880. https://doi.org/10.1016/j.apenergy.2017.06.054

Mengelkamp, E., Notheisen, B., Beer, C., Dauer, D., & Weinhardt, C. (2018). A blockchain-based smart grid: Towards sustainable local energy markets. *Computer Science -. Research for Development, 33*(1–2), 207–214. https://doi.org/10.1007/s00450-017-0360-9

Mentzer, J. T., DeWitt, W., Keebler, J. S., Min, S., Nix, N. W., Smith, C. D., & Zacharia, Z. G. (2001). Defining Supply Chain Management. *Journal of Business Logistics, 22*(2), 1–25. https://doi.org/10.1002/j.2158-1592.2001.tb00001.x

Milani, F., García-Bañuelos, L., & Dumas, M. (2016). *Blockchain and Business Process Improvement.* BPTrends. www.bptrends.com

Nakasumi, M. (2017). Information sharing for supply chain management based on block chain technology. *Proceedings - 2017 IEEE 19th Conference on Business Informatics, CBI 2017, 1,* 140–149. doi:10.1109/CBI.2017.56

Nguyen, G. T., & Kim, K. (2018). A survey about consensus algorithms used in Blockchain. *Journal of Information Processing Systems, 14*(1), 101–128. https://doi.org/10.3745/JIPS.01.0024

Ongaro, D., & Ousterhout, J. (2019). In search of an understandable consensus algorithm. *Proceedings of the 2014 USENIX Annual Technical Conference, USENIX ATC 2014.*

Ownest. (n.d.). Retrieved April 1, 2021, from https://ownest.io/

Panarello, A., Tapas, N., Merlino, G., Longo, F., & Puliafito, A. (2018). Blockchain and iot integration: A systematic survey. *Sensors (Switzerland), 18*(8), 2575. doi:10.339018082575

Pilkington, M. (2016). Blockchain technology: Principles and applications. In Research Handbooks on Digital Transformations (pp. 225–253). Edward Elgar Publishing Ltd. https://doi.org/10.4337/9781784717766.00019.

Prashanth Joshi, A., Han, M., & Wang, Y. (2018). A survey on security and privacy issues of blockchain technology. *Mathematical Foundations of Computing, 1*(2), 121–147. doi:10.3934/mfc.2018007

Prockl, G., Bhakoo, V., & Wong, C. (2017). Supply chains and electronic markets - impulses for value co-creation across the disciplines. *Electronic Markets, 27*(2), 135–140. https://doi.org/10.1007/s12525-017-0253-6

Quentson, A. (2016). *Bitcoin Magazine.* https://bitcoinmagazine.com/%0Aarticles/how-bitcoin-and-blockchain-can-avert-systemic-bank-collapses-1461170796/

Ross, D. F. (1998). Competing Through Supply Chain Management. In *Competing Through Supply Chain Management*. Springer US. doi:10.1007/978-1-4757-4816-1

S. A. A. (2016). Blockchain Ready Manufacturing Supply Chain Using Distributed Ledger. *International Journal of Research in Engineering and Technology*, *05*(09).

Saad, M., Spaulding, J., Njilla, L., Kamhoua, C., Shetty, S., Nyang, D. H., & Mohaisen, D. (2020). Exploring the Attack Surface of Blockchain: A Comprehensive Survey. *IEEE Communications Surveys and Tutorials*, *22*(3), 1977–2008. https://doi.org/10.1109/COMST.2020.2975999

Sakız, B., & Gencer, A. H. (2019). Blockchain Technology and its Impact on the Global Economy. *International Conference on Eurasian Economies 2019*. doi:10.36880/c11.02258

Salman, T., Zolanvari, M., Erbad, A., Jain, R., & Samaka, M. (2019). Security services using blockchains: A state of the art survey. *IEEE Communications Surveys and Tutorials*, *21*(1), 858–880. https://doi.org/10.1109/COMST.2018.2863956

Sanseverino, E. R., Di Silvestre, M. L., Gallo, P., Zizzo, G., & Ippolito, M. (2018). The blockchain in microgrids for transacting energy and attributing losses. *Proceedings - 2017 IEEE International Conference on Internet of Things, IEEE Green Computing and Communications, IEEE Cyber, Physical and Social Computing, IEEE Smart Data, IThings-GreenCom-CPSCom-SmartData 2017*, 925–930. doi:10.1109/iThings-GreenCom-CPSCom-SmartData.2017.142

Saxena, S., Bhushan, B., & Yadav, D. (2020). Blockchain-powered Social Media Analytics in Supply Chain Management. *SSRN Electronic Journal*. doi:10.2139srn.3598906

Sethi, R., Bhushan, B., Sharma, N., Kumar, R., & Kaushik, I. (2021). Applicability of Industrial IoT in Diversified Sectors: Evolution, Applications and Challenges. Springer. https://doi.org/10.1007/978-981-15-7965-3_4

Sharma, P. K., Chen, M. Y., & Park, J. H. (2018). A Software Defined Fog Node Based Distributed Blockchain Cloud Architecture for IoT. *IEEE Access: Practical Innovations, Open Solutions*, *6*, 115–124. https://doi.org/10.1109/ACCESS.2017.2757955

Shen, C., & Pena-Mora, F. (2018). Blockchain for Cities - A Systematic Literature Review. *IEEE Access: Practical Innovations, Open Solutions*, *6*, 76787–76819. https://doi.org/10.1109/ACCESS.2018.2880744

Steiner, J., & Baker, J. (2015). *Blockchain: the solution for supply chain transparency*. Provenance. https://www.provenance.org/whitepaper

Szilágyi, P. (2017). *Clique PoA protocol & Rinkeby PoA testnet · Issue #225 · ethereum/EIPs*. https://github.com/ethereum/EIPs/issues/225

Tama, B. A. (2015). Learning to Prevent Inactive Student of Indonesia Open University. *Journal of Information Processing Systems*, *11*(2), 165–172. https://doi.org/10.3745/JIPS.04.0015

Tama, B. A., & Rhee, K. H. (2019). Tree-based classifier ensembles for early detection method of diabetes: An exploratory study. *Artificial Intelligence Review*, *51*(3), 355–370. https://doi.org/10.1007/s10462-017-9565-3

Tanwar, S., Parekh, K., & Evans, R. (2020). Blockchain-based electronic healthcare record system for healthcare 4.0 applications. *Journal of Information Security and Applications, 50,* 102407. https://doi.org/10.1016/j.jisa.2019.102407

Tasca, P., & Tessone, C. J. (2017). *Taxonomy of blockchain technologies. Principles of identification and classification.* doi:10.5195/ledger.2019.140

Tian, F. (2016, August 9). An agri-food supply chain traceability system for China based on RFID & blockchain technology. *2016 13th International Conference on Service Systems and Service Management, ICSSSM 2016.* doi:10.1109/ICSSSM.2016.7538424

Tomov, Y. K. (2019, September 1). Bitcoin: Evolution of blockchain technology. *2019 28th International Scientific Conference Electronics, ET 2019 - Proceedings.* doi:10.1109/ET.2019.8878322

Turkanović, M., Hölbl, M., Košič, K., Heričko, M., & Kamišalić, A. (2018). EduCTX: A blockchain-based higher education credit platform. *IEEE Access: Practical Innovations, Open Solutions, 6,* 5112–5127. https://doi.org/10.1109/ACCESS.2018.2789929

Vujičić, D., Jagodić, D., & Randić, S. (2018). Blockchain technology, bitcoin, and Ethereum: A brief overview. *2018 17th International Symposium on INFOTEH-JAHORINA, INFOTEH 2018 - Proceedings,* 1–6. doi:10.1109/INFOTEH.2018.8345547

Wang, W., Hoang, D. T., Hu, P., Xiong, Z., Niyato, D., Wang, P., Wen, Y., & Kim, D. I. (2019). A Survey on Consensus Mechanisms and Mining Strategy Management in Blockchain Networks. *IEEE Access: Practical Innovations, Open Solutions, 7,* 22328–22370. https://doi.org/10.1109/ACCESS.2019.2896108

Wang, X., Weili, J., & Chai, J. (2018). The Research on the Incentive Method of Consortium Blockchain Based on Practical Byzantine Fault Tolerant. *Proceedings - 2018 11th International Symposium on Computational Intelligence and Design, ISCID 2018, 2,* 154–156. doi:10.1109/ISCID.2018.10136

Weber, I., Xu, X., Riveret, R., Governatori, G., Ponomarev, A., & Mendling, J. (2016). Untrusted business process monitoring and execution using blockchain. *Lecture Notes in Computer Science (Including Subseries Lecture Notes in Artificial Intelligence and Lecture Notes in Bioinformatics), 9850 LNCS,* 329–347. doi:10.1007/978-3-319-45348-4_19

Wright, C. S. (2019). Bitcoin: A Peer-to-Peer Electronic Cash System. *SSRN Electronic Journal.* doi:10.2139srn.3440802

Wu, M., Wang, K., Cai, X., Guo, S., Guo, M., & Rong, C. (2019). A Comprehensive Survey of Blockchain: From Theory to IoT Applications and beyond. *IEEE Internet of Things Journal, 6*(5), 8114–8154. doi:10.1109/JIOT.2019.2922538

Xie, J., Tang, H., Huang, T., Yu, F. R., Xie, R., Liu, J., & Liu, Y. (2019). A Survey of Blockchain Technology Applied to Smart Cities: Research Issues and Challenges. *IEEE Communications Surveys and Tutorials, 21*(3), 2794–2830. https://doi.org/10.1109/COMST.2019.2899617

Xu, X., Weber, I., & Staples, M. (2019). Architecture for Blockchain Applications. In *Architecture for Blockchain Applications.* Springer International Publishing. doi:10.1007/978-3-030-03035-3

Yang, Z., Yang, K., Lei, L., Zheng, K., & Leung, V. C. M. (2019). Blockchain-based decentralized trust management in vehicular networks. *IEEE Internet of Things Journal, 6*(2), 1495–1505. doi:10.1109/JIOT.2018.2836144

Yassein, M. B., Shatnawi, F., Rawashdeh, S., & Mardin, W. (2019). Blockchain technology: Characteristics, security and privacy; Issues and solutions. *Proceedings of IEEE/ACS International Conference on Computer Systems and Applications, AICCSA, 2019-November*. doi:10.1109/AICCSA47632.2019.9035216

Zhang, J., Xue, N., & Huang, X. (2016). A Secure System for Pervasive Social Network-Based Healthcare. *IEEE Access: Practical Innovations, Open Solutions, 4*, 9239–9250. https://doi.org/10.1109/ACCESS.2016.2645904

Zheng, Z., Xie, S., Dai, H., Chen, X., & Wang, H. (2017). An Overview of Blockchain Technology: Architecture, Consensus, and Future Trends. *Proceedings - 2017 IEEE 6th International Congress on Big Data, BigData Congress 2017*, 557–564. doi:10.1109/BigDataCongress.2017.85

Zhu, Z. T., Yu, M. H., & Riezebos, P. (2016). A research framework of smart education. *Smart Learning Environments, 3*(1), 4. doi:10.118640561-016-0026-2

Chapter 10
Applications of Secured Blockchain Technology in the Manufacturing Industry

Kamalendu Pal
https://orcid.org/0000-0001-7158-6481
City, University of London, UK

ABSTRACT

The manufacturing industry inclines to worldwide business operations due to the economic advantage of product design and development. In this way, globalized manufacturing supply chains make their management and control more difficult. As a distributed ledger technology that ensures transparency, trust, traceability, and cybersecurity, blockchain technology promises to ease some global manufacturing operation problems. This chapter presents blockchain technology basics and analyses the issues (e.g., traceability, cybersecurity, flexibility, and smart contracts) related to the blockchain-based manufacturing information system. Next, the chapter presents related research work in the manufacturing industry in recent years. It also includes a classification mechanism for manufacturing information systems based on specific properties. It is followed by discussing the critical issues that need to consider in designing industry-specific reference information system architecture. Finally, the chapter discusses the scope of future research.

INTRODUCTION

Manufacturing in the modern economy organizes supply chains, including business processes ranging from product design, product development, and delivery of the final product to customers. In a typical manufacturing supply chain, raw materials purchase from suppliers and products manufactured at one or more production plants. Then the product move to intermediate storage (e.g., warehouse, distribution centres) for packing and shipping to retailers or customers (Pal, 2017; Pal, 2019). In this way, a manufacturing supply chain consists of business partners in the network, and these are the suppliers, transporters, manufacturers, distributors, retailers, and end-customers. Any manufacturing supply chain's

DOI: 10.4018/978-1-7998-6694-7.ch010

ultimate performance depends on the involved stakeholders' business practices and corporate practices (e.g., public policies, business environment) and infrastructures.

In this way, a manufacturing supply chain creates a complex network of business processes. Also, due to globalisation and business process decentralisation, the efficient performance of a manufacturing supply chain requires a high degree of visibility - defines as the capability of sharing on time and accurate data throughout the entire supply chain, and coordination among supply chain partners. In today's global business environment, companies recognise the strategic importance of well-managed manufacturing supply chains.

Technologies provide the impetus in how industrial and manufacturing companies manage their regular business practices and supply chains. With the help of sophisticated automated business process solutions, like real-time monitoring of manufacturing network operations, warehouse daily operation management, and enterprise resource planning (ERP) systems, as well as advanced data capture and wireless networking facilities, many organisations from different sectors (e.g., automotive, apparel) are squeezing more and more efficiency out of their regular business process operations.

Blockchain-based computing is one of the essential technologies for the automation of geographically distributed complex manufacturing information systems. Many academics and practitioners believe that blockchain-based technologies represent the most attractive new paradigm for information systems development in recent decades (Pal, 2020a) (Pal, 2020b). The usage of blockchain-based information systems has already found different applications in manufacturing, real-time control system, electronic commerce, network management, transportation system, medical care, and entertainment business. The increasing success of blockchain-based computing applications in these areas is that the inherent distribution allows for the system's natural decomposition into multiple blocks that interact to attain a target strategic-objective. The blockchain-based computing paradigm can significantly improve the design and analysis of the problem domains under the following three conditions: (i) the problem domain is geographically distributed; (ii) the subsystems exist in a dynamic environment; and (iii) the subsystems need to interact with each other more flexibly.

Figure 1. A diagrammatic representation of a blockchain

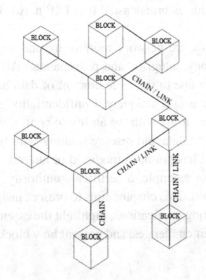
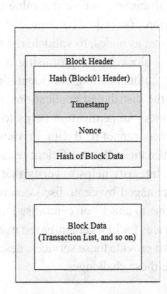

The domain of global manufacturing communication systems is well suited to a blockchain-based approach because of its geographically distributed nature, and it is hybrid information system-based operating characteristics. From an intelligent manufacturing management perspective, blockchain-based systems' most appealing traits are autonomy, collaboration, and reactivity. Blockchain-based systems can work without the direct intervention of humans or others. This feature helps to implement an automated information system in the global manufacturing industry.

The advance of manufacturing technologies relates closely to information technologies. Since a manufacturing system's design and operation need numerous decision-making activities, prompt and effective decisions depend not only on reasoning techniques but also on the quality of information. Therefore, current manufacturing control systems need appropriate security of their data.

Blockchain is a modern information technology intended at implementing secure decentralised distributed information systems. In these systems, transactional data need sharing, stored, and verified by participants of a system using cryptography and consensus mechanisms. First, blockchain technology introduces the industry in 2008, where Satoshi Nakamoto developed it as the technology behind cryptocurrency (Nakamoto, 2008). Blockchain is a peer-to-peer (P2P) distributed ledger technology underpinning cryptocurrency (or bitcoin).

Blockchain technology is considered a strong foundation of research in cryptography, hashing, peer-to-peer (P2P) networks and consensus protocols. The initial excitement about Blockchain technology-enabled P2P transfers of digital currency to anybody in the world, crossing human-created boundaries (such as countries' borders) without intermediaries such as banks. This excitement heightened by realising that P2P ability can be applied to other, non-crypto currency types of transactions. These transactions involve assets such as titles, deeds, music and art, secret codes, contracts between businesses, autonomous driver decisions, and artefacts resulting from many everyday human endeavours. A transaction record may contain other details based on the blockchain protocol and the application. In simple, a transaction in the blockchain is a transferable activity between different business-partners.

A blockchain consists of a set of blocks, as shown in Figure 1, and an individual block encapsulates a hash of the previous block, which is creating a chain of blocks from the first, also called a genesis block the current block, where these blocks consist of transactions. These transactions mean an agreement between two participants, where the value of transfer may be of physical or digital assets, or it could be the completion of a task. The requested transaction is broadcasted to a P2P network consisting of computers, known as nodes, to validate the transfer.

Some of the blockchains' promising applications are network monitoring and security services (e.g., including authentication, confidentiality, privacy, integrity, and provenance). All these services are crucial for the distributed applications, primarily due to the large amount of data being processed over the networks. Authentication helps to identify a user uniquely. Confidentiality guarantees that unauthorised users cannot read data. Privacy provides users with the ability to control who can access their data. Provenance allows efficient tracking of the data and resources along with their ownership and utilisation. Integrity helps to verify that the data has not been modified or altered. These services are currently managed by centralised controllers, for example, a certificate authority. Therefore, the benefits are prone to attacks on centralised information. This chapter aims to present insights on the use of security services for blockchain-based manufacturing applications, highlight the essential techniques currently used to provide these services, describe their challenges, and present how blockchain technology can resolve these challenges.

Below, this chapter introduces first the basic idea of blockchain technology. Next, the chapter presents the use of blockchain technology in the manufacturing industry. This section also analyses the issues (e.g., traceability, security, flexibility, and smart contracts) related to the blockchain-based manufacturing system. The chapter presents related research work in the manufacturing industry in recent years. Then the uses of blockchain-based technology in the manufacturing industry have been discussed. It followed by a discussion regarding the critical issues that need to consider in designing industry-specific reference architecture. It also includes different secure manufacturing problems in business process automation. Finally, the chapter concludes with concluding remarks and lays out future research work.

BACKGROUND OF BLOCKCHAIN TECHNOLOGY

The blockchain technology infrastructure has motivated many innovative applications in manufacturing industries. This technology's ideal blockchain vision is tamper evident and tamper resistant ledgers implemented in a distributed fashion, without a central repository. The central ideas guiding blockchain technology emerged in the late 1980s and early 1990s. A research paper (Lamport, 1998) published with the background knowledge of the Paxos protocol, which provided a consensus method for reaching an agreement resulting in a network of computers. The central concepts of that research were combined and applied to the electronic cash-related research project by Satoshi Nakamoto (Nakamoto, 2008), leading to modern cryptocurrency or bitcoin-based systems.

Distributed Ledger Technology (DLT) Based Blockchain

The blockchain's initial basis is to institute trust in a P2P network bypassing any third managing parties' need. For example, Bitcoin started a P2P financial value exchange mechanism where no third-party (e.g., bank) is needed to provide a value-transfer transaction with anyone else on the blockchain community. Such a community-based trust is the main characteristic of system verifiability using mathematical modelling technique for evidence. The mechanism of this trust provision permits peers of a P2P network to transact with other community-members without necessarily trusting each other. This behaviour is often referred to as the trustless behaviour of a blockchain system. The trustlessness also highlights that a blockchain network-partner interested in transacting with another business-entity on the blockchain does not necessarily need to know the real identity.

It permits users of a public blockchain system to be anonymous. A record of transactions among the peers is stored in a chain of a data structure known as blocks, the name blockchain's primary basis. Each block (or peer) of a blockchain network keeps a copy of this record. Moreover, a consensus, digital voting mechanism to use many network peers, is also decided on the blockchain state that all network stores' nodes. Hence, blockchain is often designed as distributed ledger-based technology. An individual instance of such a DLT, is stored at each node (or peer) of the blockchain network and gets updated simultaneously with no mechanism for retroactive changes in the records. In this way, blockchain transactions cannot be deleted or altered.

Intelligent use of Hashing

Intelligent techniques are used in hashing the blocks encapsulating transaction records together, which makes such records immutable. In other words, blockchain's transactions achieve validity, trust, and finality based on cryptographic proofs and underlying mathematical computation between different trading-peers (or partners), known as a hashing function. Encryption algorithms are used to provide confidentiality for creating hash function. These algorithmic solutions have the essential character that they are reversible in the sense that, with knowledge of the appropriate key, it must be possible to reconstruct the plaintext message from the cryptographic technique. This way hashing mechanism of a piece of data can be used to preserve the blockchain system's integrity. For example, Secure Hash Algorithm 256 (SHA256) is a member of the SHA2 hash functions currently used by many blockchain-based systems such as Bitcoin.

A simplified blockchain is shown in Figure 2. A block consists of four main fields (i.e., block number, previous hash (or prev), hash, data). Block number (e.g., #1, #2, #3) uniquely identify a block. The Prev field contains the previous block's (i.e., the block that comes before it) hash value. It is the way the chain of blocks stays together. The first block in a blockchain is often called the genesis block, is shown by its Prev field initialised to all zeros. The fourth field is the Merkle tree root, a data structure that keeps all the block's transaction-related information. Thus, the block body stores a record of all transactions categorised into input and output. It should be noticed that there is a technical difference between a transaction chain and a blockchain. Every block in a blockchain can contain multiple transaction chains, as shown in Figure 3. In turn, each transaction chain shows the value transferred from one peer of the network to another. Each such transaction chain is sometimes referred to as a digital coin or more usually as a token.

The communication among peer (or user) on blockchain uses a decentralised network in which an individual peer represents a node at which a blockchain client is installed. Once a peer performs a transaction with another peer or receives data from another user, it verifies its authenticity. Afterwards, it broadcasts the validated data to all other relevant nodes for business operation purpose.

Figure 2. Immutable hashing mechanism in blockchain

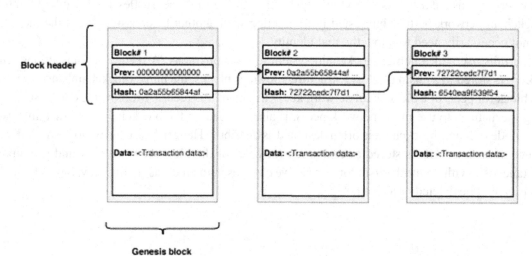

Figure 3. Diagrammatic representation of transaction chain

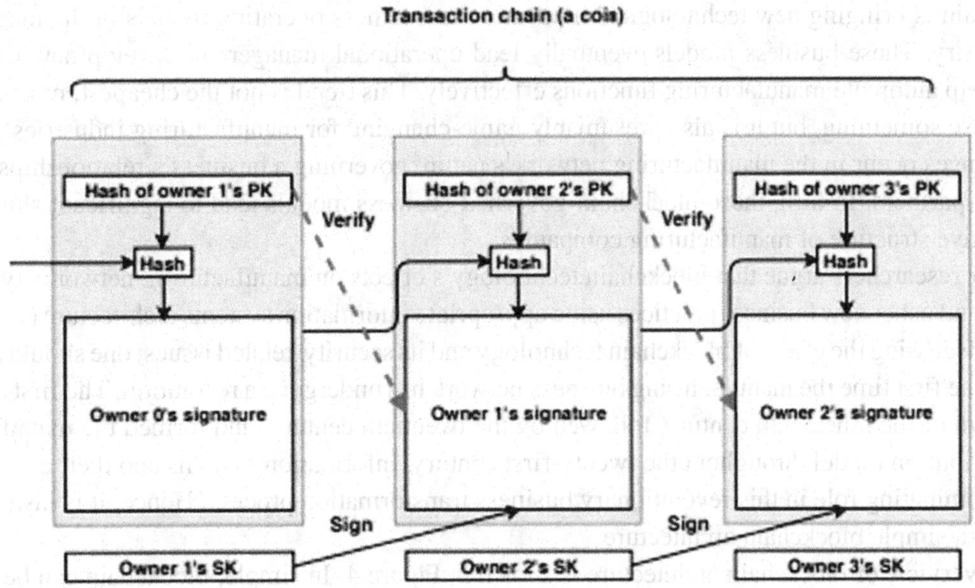

Transaction chain (a coin)

Blockchain systems need acceptance and verification by all the chain peers, and this mechanism is known as a consensus. There are different algorithmic solutions available to cope with the distributed nature of this problem.

Distributed Consensus

These distributed consensus algorithms help the blockchain system users say regarding the overall state of the records preserved (or stored) in the blockchain network blocks. This section briefly introduces four of these algorithms, and they are - (i) Proof-of-Work (PoW), (ii) Proof of Stake (PoS), (iii) Practical Byzantine Fault Tolerance (PBFT), and (iv) Delegated Proof of Stake (DPoS).

The PoW consensus algorithm is widely popularised by Bitcoin and assumes that all users vote with their "computing power" by solving consensus instances and creating the appropriate blocks. The PoS algorithm uses the existing way of achieving consensus in a distributed system. This algorithm needs the user to prove ownership of an amount of currency. It provides more efficient energy consumption in comparison to PoW. The PBFT consensus algorithm uses a state machine replication method to maintain with Byzantine faults. This algorithm uses an effective authentication method based on public-key cryptography. The DPoS uses a democratic technique to validate a block. It can confirm the transaction quickly.

The blockchain technology is proposed for many manufacturing use-cases where business needs data immutability and P2P consensus, and transaction confidentiality. There are different types of blockchain-based architectures available as industry-specific solution platforms.

Blockchain Technology Architecture in Manufacturing Industry

Blockchain is bringing new technological innovation to business operating models in the manufacturing industry. These business models eventually lead operational managers to develop new processes, which help automate manufacturing functions effectively. This trend is not the cheapest, most effective way to use something, but it is also presumably game-changing for manufacturing industries. As a result, changes occur in the manufacturing network's nature governing a business's relationships with its business partners. In turn, these blockchain-governed business models lead to significant shifts in the competitive structure of manufacturing companies.

Many researchers argue that blockchain technology's effects on manufacturing networks typify this process and usher new business practices using appropriate information systems architecture (Pal, 2020). Before discussing the effect of blockchain technology and its security-related issues, one should note that it is not the first time the manufacturing business network has undergone a revolution. The first occurred at the turn of the nineteenth century, followed by the twentieth century, and formed the manufacturing and distribution model throughout the twenty-first century. Information systems and their architectures play a dominating role in this revolutionary business transformation process. Hence, it is instructive to consider a simple blockchain architecture.

An overview of blockchain architecture is shown in Figure 4. In simple, blockchain can be of three different types: (i) public blockchain, (ii) private blockchain, and (iii) hybrid blockchain. A blockchain is permissionless when anyone is free to be involved in the process of authentication, verification and reaching consensus. A blockchain is a permission where its participants are pre-selected. A few different variables could apply to make a permissionless or permission system into some form of hybrid.

Figure 4. An overview of blockchain architecture

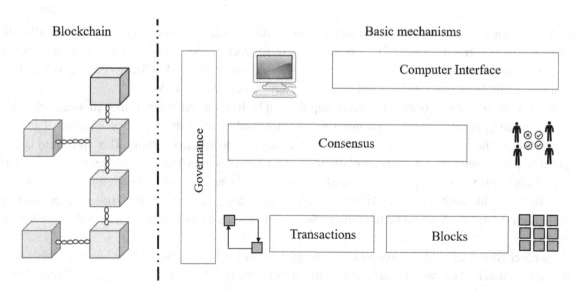

The validation occurs to the next layer of the blockchain infrastructure, consensus, where nodes must agree on which transactions must be kept and validated in the blockchain. There are different security measures used to verify transactions within a blockchain system, the most known approaches to research a consensus today are PoW, PoS, and PBFT. Having a good consensus algorithm means better efficiency, safety, and convenience; nevertheless, which consensus an organisation should choose depends on the use case.

The upper layer, computer interface, allows blockchains to offer more functionality to the system. In this part, blockchain stores information on all the transactions that the users have made. For more advanced applications, one needs to store complex states which are dynamically changing, which means that the state shift from one to another once specific criteria are met in this system. These applications have given rise to smart contracts.

Smart contracts are the most transformative blockchain application, which could dramatically change how organisations work. The smart contracts can automate the transfer of assets when the negotiated conditions are met in this application; for example, when a shipment is delivered and verified, the contract will automatically enforce payments.

The governance layer (as shown in Figure 4) is human centred in blockchain architecture. Blockchain protocols are affected by inputs from different people who integrate new methods, improve the blockchain protocols, and patch the system.

In blockchain systems assets, monetary values are called tokens, and as stated by Nakamoto (Nakamoto, 2008), these are essential building blocks for the technology. The term tokenisation means converting the rights and values of an asset into a digital token. Blockchain technology turns assets into digitally encoded token that can be registered, tracked, and traded with a private key (Francisco & Swanson, 2017). It means that everything of value can be uploaded as a digital object in the blockchain system.

One of the critical aspects of blockchain technology is the decentralisation of its operations. Decentralisation means that each transaction in a blockchain transaction system does not need to be validated through a central trusted agency (e.g., bank or other financial organisations). This new validation technique implies that third parties resulting in higher costs and performance bottlenecks at the central services are no longer needed. It is here consensus algorithms used to maintain data consistency in a distributed network. For an entity to operate in a decentralised network, an organisation would be issued a digital identity that it could use in all business interactions.

In blockchain-based information systems, users are anonymous, but their account identifiers are not. Also, all asset transactions are publicly visible. Since blockchain technology users are unknown, it is essential to create trust in this system architecture. To build trust within a blockchain network enabled by four critical characteristics, as described below:

Ledger: One of the essential characteristics of blockchain-based operation is Distributed Ledger Technology (DLT). It is a decentralised technology to eliminate the need for a central authority or intermediary to process, validate or authenticate transactions. Manufacturing businesses use DLT to process, validate or authenticate transactions or other types of data exchanges.

Secure: Blockchain technology produces a structure of data with inherent security qualities. It is based on principles of cryptography, decentralisation, and consensus, which ensure trust in transactions. Blockchain technology makes sure that the data within the network of blocks is not tampered with, and that the data within the ledger is attestable.

Shared: Blockchain data is shared amongst multiple users of this network of nodes. It gives transparency across the node users in the network.

Distributed: Blockchain technology can be geographically distributed. The decentralisation helps to scale the number of nodes of a blockchain network to ensure it is more resilient to predators' attacks. By increasing the number of nodes, a predator's capability to impact the blockchain network's consensus protocol is minimised.

Also, for blockchain-based system architectures that permit anyone to anonymously create accounts and participate (called *permissionless* blockchain networks), these capabilities produce a level of trust amongst collaborating business partners with no prior knowledge of one another. Blockchain technology provides decentralisation, with the collaborating-partners across a distributed network. This decentralisation means there is no single point of failure, and a single user cannot change the record of transactions.

RELATED RESEARCH WORK

Manufacturing businesses have been leveraging blockchain technology and its built-in capabilities, as an essential component within the software system architecture, to provide more secure and dependable computation capability. However, ill-informed, or incorrect design decisions that relate to the choice and usage of a blockchain and its components are probably the root cause of potential security risks into the system. For example, adversaries can exploit the envisioned design and verification limitations to compromise the system's security. The system becomes vulnerable to malicious attacks from cyberspace (Sturm et al., 2017). Some of the well-known attacks (e.g., Stuxnet, Shamoon, BlackEnergy, WannaCry, and TRITON) (Stouffer, 2020) created significant problems in recent decades.

The distributed manufacturing industry's critical issues are coordinating and controlling secure business information and its operational network. The application of cybersecurity controls in the operating environment demands the most significant attention and effort to ensure that appropriate security and risk mitigation are achieved. For example, manufacturing device spoofing and false authentication in information sharing (Kumar & Mallick, 2018) are significant problems for the industry. Besides, the heterogeneous nature of diversified equipment and the individualised service requirements make it difficult for blockchain-based P2P business operation (Leng et al., 2020).

In blockchain-based manufacturing business applications, trust and confidentiality among corporate partners play crucial roles in day-to-day operations (Ghosh & Tan, 2020). These issues also get compounded with individual products' personalisation requirements across systems, which massively complicates the manufacturing and supply business activities (Mourtzis & Doukas, 2012). The other important issue is related to the manufacturing information system's data storage strategy. The fact is, it is easier to keep data, and other files secure on a decentralised server than on a centralised one. With data stored across many computers in multiple locations, the risk of a single-entry point is mitigated and make fewer data accessible at each end. Decentralised platforms can even avoid holding sensitive information altogether, and it makes a better choice for manufacturing information system (Shen, 2002).

A literature survey shows that the techniques and methods of cybersecurity issues have been applied to the field of modern manufacturing information management systems, including traceability of operations (Mohamed & Al-Jaroodi, 2019), cyber-attacks to the digital thread (Sturm et al., 2017). Advanced virus on control system (e.g., Stuxnet) (12), device spoofing and false authentication in data sharing (Kumar & Mallick, 2018), interoperability among heterogenous equipment (Leng et al., 2020), confidentiality and trust between participants (Debabrata & Albert, 2020), information vulnerability and reliability across systems (Mourtzis & Doukas, 2012), and failure of critical nodes in centralised platforms (Shen, 2002).

All these cybersecurity-related issues may be resolved by existing technologies/tools. For example, service-oriented computing (e.g., RESTFul services) application can mitigate interoperability among heterogeneous equipment (Leng et al., 2020) in the manufacturing industry. Most of the challenges are solvable by using blockchain-based appropriate system architecture (or platforms).

USE OF BLOCKCHAIN TECHNOLOGY IN MANUFACTURING BUSINESS

In the recent decade, Information and Communication Technology (ICT) - in particular, the Internet and embedded systems technologies - is undergoing rapid development, which has given rise to a few novel technologies, such as Cyber-Physical Systems (CPS), Internet of Things (IoT), Service-Oriented Computing (SOC), big data analytics, and Blockchain. The advent of these new technologies enables creating a smart, networked world, in which "things" are endowed with a particular degree of intelligence and is increasingly connected. In the modern manufacturing world, the widespread deployment of sensors and extensive use of blockchain-based software applications in industrial production brings together the physical and virtual worlds.

Blockchain has been hailed as a new secured and shareable computing paradigm. Implementation of Blockchain in the manufacturing industry is usually developed based on the mainstream blockchain platforms' infrastructure shown in Table - 1. Blockchain provides a set of distributed data structures, interaction mechanisms, and computing paradigms, which offers an additional security method to exchange information, service, or product (Al-Jaroodi & Mohamed, 2019).

Classification Categories for Blockchain-Based Manufacturing

In this section, blockchain-based manufacturing systems are analysed based on a classification mechanism. This classification system uses four main categories (i.e., cybersecurity, decision architecture, system performance, trust enhancement). The main types are further classified using the Classification Category (CC) number from CC1 to CC10. A tabular representation of this classification mechanism is shown in Table - 2.

Blockchain is a promising technology that may alleviate the risk of cyberattack directed to a single point, bringing down the entire network. However, a coded intrusion or system vulnerability could allow more negative consequences to the system's security. For example, if successful, an attacker would gain access to the information stored at the point of attack and all data recorded in the ledger. Thus, security issues related to blockchain resilient and robustness are critical in cybersecurity (Andrews et al., 2020). The blockchain links data blocks need to be protected from being tampered with using a cryptographic technique (CC1). The CC1 category helps manufacturing businesses with secure product designs, enhance intellectual property right verification, validation of engineering parts and sub-parts of an artefact, and collaborative design and manufacturing decisions within third-party validation processes. Beside secure design, blockchain technology provides data provenance (CC2) that was conventionally hard to follow, making the ultimate system much more transparent (Lee & Pilkington, 2017).

The automated decision and control system architecture plays a significant role in the manufacturing industry. Blockchain-based decentralised decision architecture is a potential solution (CC3) to making the control complexity in flexible manufacturing operational flows in the context of disturbances (Shah, 2019). Also, blockchain's smart contracts technical facility helps decentralise and collaborate in the

Table 1. List of blockchain platforms

Platforms	Language	Website
Aion	Aion, Solidity	aion.network
ArcBlock	Java, Python, JS	arcblock.io
Ardor	Java	ardorplatform.org
Cardano	Plutus	cardano.org
Croda	Kotlin, Java	corda.net
Enigma	Solidity	enigma.co
EOS	C++, WebAssembly	eos.io
Ethereum	Solidity, LLL	ethereum.org
Hyperledger Fabric	Go, Java	hyperledger.org
Hyperledger Sawtooth	Python, C++, Go, Java, Trust	hyperledger.org
ICON	Python	icon.foundation
IOTA	Rust, Go, JS, Java, C++	iota.org
Komodo	Any	komodoplatform.com
Neblio	JS, C#, Ruby, Python, PHP	nebl.io
NM	Any	nem.io
NEO	C#, VB.Net, Java, Python	neo.org
Nxt	JS	nxtplatform.org
OpenChain	Any	openchain.org
Qtum	Solidity	qtum.org/en
Smilo	Solidity, Java, Python, JS	smilo.io/
Stellar	Go, Java, JS	stellar.org
Straits	C#, .NET	stratisplatform.com
Tezos	Michelson	tezos.com
Wanchain	Solidity	wanchain.org
Waves	RIDE	wavesplatform.com
Zilliqa	Scilla	zilliq.com

distributed manufacturing business. Some other collaborations and coordination challenges are - order delay, damage to products, and multiple data entry are optimisable by using blockchain-based solutions (CC4) (Tijan et al., 2019). Blockchain-based disruptive technology could bring much more coordination and enhanced data sharing facilities in distributed manufacturing networks (CC5) (Zhang et al., 2019).

The performance of a blockchain-based system often attributed to smart contracts, system sustainability, and system resilience. From the manufacturing system performance point of view, the blockchain-based system's transparency improves the ability to secure transactions at lower costs. Manufacturing companies can quickly reduce the cost of managing business-partner relations and make outsourcing decisions more effective using smart contracts (CC6) (Zheng et al., 2020). Besides, the transparency furnishes the reputation and competitiveness of manufacturing companies, and in this way - it makes sure the system sustainability of modern manufacturing (CC7) (Pan et al., 2020). The blockchain-based

Table 2. Blockchain-based manufacturing system classification categories

Category (C)	Classification Category (CC)	Notes
C1: Cybersecurity	CC1: Data tamper-resisting	Chain structure links data blocks sequentially (Andrews, 2020)
	CC2: Data province	Make the manufacturing more immutable (20)
C2: Decision architecture	CC3: Decentralised decision	Use shared ledger that is free from intermediaries (Shah, 2019)
	CC4: Collaborative optimisation	Minimise order delay, damage to products, and data entry (Tijan et al., 2019)
	CC5: System flexibility	Realise broader and more flexible collaboration (Zhang et al., 2019)
C3: System performance	CC6: Cost saving	Manage integration relations quickly via smart contracts (Zheng et al., 2020)
	CC7: System sustainability	Improve profitability and competitiveness (Pan et al., 2020)
	CC8: System resilience	Enhance system resilience under risks and attacks (26, 27)(Min, 2019) (Ivanov et al., 2019)
C4: Trust enhancement	CC9:Network transparency	Provide traceability, visibility, and disintermediation (Tonnissen & Frank, 2020)
	CC10: Reputation enhancement	Make their systems' data accessible to other partners (Leng et al., 2019)

system can improve the manufacturing network's resilience under risks and uncertainty (CC8) (Min, 2019). Manufacturing business risk can be mitigated through appropriate inventory management, control of buffer, and a backup plan. It needs to reflect on the operational contingency strategy, and it includes a record of activities and appropriate resources to overcome the problems. Blockchain solution can reduce these kinds of issues based on algorithmic solutions in decentralised decision-making processes (Ivanov et al., 2019). In this way, algorithmic decision-making processes can be translated into smart contracts. Therefore, the flexibility and robustness for managing disturbances (Nejad et al., 2011) make smart contract-based solutions very appropriate to automate the modern manufacturing industry.

A properly written smart contract should describe all possible outcomes of the contract. A smart contract is deterministic by nature; the same input will always produce the same output. If one writes a non-deterministic contract, it will execute on every node on the blockchain network when it is triggered. It may return different random results, thus preventing the network from reaching a consensus on its execution result. In a properly built blockchain platform, writing non-deterministic smart contracts is either impossible (by forcing the contract developers to use a programming language that does not have any non-deterministic constructs), or it is possible. However, an attempt to deploy such a contract on the network will be rejected.

A smart contract resides on the blockchain, and every network participant can inspect such its instructions. Since all the interactions with a contract happen through signed messages on the blockchain, all the network participants get a cryptographically verified trace of the contract's operations. A blockchain that supports transactions enables asset transfers between counterparties that do not trust each other. However, a blockchain that supports smart contracts takes this further and allows for multi-step processes (or, more generally: *interactions*) to occur between mutually distrustful counterparties. The transacting entities get to (i) inspect the instruction and identify its outcomes before deciding to engage with the contract, (ii) have certainty of execution since the code is already deployed on a network that neither of them controls fully, and (iii) have verifiability over the process since all the interactions are digitally signed. The possibility of a dispute is eliminated (when all possible outcomes are accounted for) since the participants cannot disagree over the result of this verifiable process, they engaged in. Smart contracts operate as autonomous actors whose behaviour is entirely anticipated. For example, they can be trusted to drive forward any on-chain logic that can be expressed as a function of on-chain data inputs, provided that the data they need to manage is within their reach.

As described in (Ethereum, 2020), the simplest example is a smart contract that calls another deal by address to perform its primary operation. This address resides in the mutable area of the contract's internal database. The agreement also carries a list of members, addresses (public keys) that get to vote on its behaviour. A rule can be used in the contract. Suppose many of those voters vote in a certain way. In that case, the contract will modify its behaviour by calling the address that received most of the votes to execute its primary function. Therefore, trust plays a crucial role in manufacturing blockchain-based applications.

Trust across multiple manufacturers is one of the dominating factors that offer enhanced disintermediation, visibility, and traceability (CC9) (Tonnissen & Frank, 2020). The transparency achieved by the blockchain system is a crucial factor to address the trust issues in the decentralised manufacturing network and its supply chain (Lu, 2018). Blockchain can record all design, manufacturing, maintenance, logistics, capital, and other information to facilitate supervision and resolve liability disputes. Manufacturing business operations can be synchronised and shared across a community, and the data stored on the blockchain is immutable. Manufacturers can make their organisation's data accessible to other nodes on the network to establish the reputation and hence, partially generate trust (CC10) (Leng et al., 2019). With smart contracts, blockchain can provide personalised manufacturing services (Ren et al., 2018).

SMART MANUFACTURING REFERENCE ARCHITECTURE

Modernising manufacturing is vitally important, and rapidly advancing technologies provide the means for manufacturing companies to achieve highly efficient, real-time synchronised production as a holistic enterprise rather than a collection of functional silos. It is driving the integration of supply chain, operations, automation, customer service, and logistics.

A critical success factor in sustaining a competitive advantage is evaluating and using the best new technological solutions for the application to manufacture. Business processes intercommunication is an enabling factor in this process and links real-time business systems with production data from the sensor to manufacturing enterprise systems.

In the past, manufacturing businesses control and automation are done by programmable logic controllers, and the edge and embedded computing are replacing this control system and other dedicated controllers. This new generation information system uses Big Data Analytics (BDA) in the advance control incorporated into edge computers and smart sensors usher more efficient and responsive business operations.

Blockchain technologies benefit the manufacturing operation as it builds trust between the supplier, manufacturer, and customers, enhancing business loyalty. Also, edge computing opening new opportunities for the manufacturing industry. Edge computing is a distributed computing paradigm that brings

Figure 5. Reference architecture of the blockchain-secured smart manufacturing system

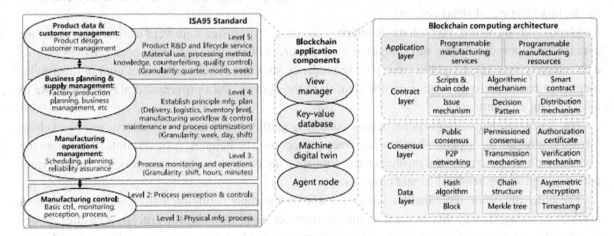

industrial computation and data storage closer to the location needed to improve response times. In this way, if problems are identified at an early stage of the production process, they can be mitigated before they hit the shelves.

Recent advances in edge computing and the Internet of Things (IoT) provide a new impetus to reforming manufacturing businesses' operational functionalities. Adoption of blockchain-based systems in this edge and IoT operated infrastructure enhance manufacturing information systems efficiency. This new generation hybrid (e.g., edge, IoT, and blockchain) information infrastructure could effectively prevent the whole network from a rash when hackers breach any single node or transmission channel in the system. Since the data captured by blockchain is immutable, securing the manufacturing data provenance, which was tricky in a legacy system, now can be realised.

The International Society of Automation (i.e., ISA - www.isa.org) came up with an integration of enterprise and control systems architecture, as shown in Figure 5 - the reference architecture made-up of multiple layers. The blockchain component of this architecture consists of four different subparts: (i) agent node, (ii) machine digital twin, (iii) key-value database, and (iv) view manager.

At the level of process perception and controls (Level 2), the time-critical and data-intensive computations are integrated with the physical manufacturing process on system automation's edge processes. The captured manufacturing data from the sensors/controllers are used as the blockchain system's original data source. At the level of process monitoring and operations (Level 3), the system-level operations are mapped into the smart contracts layer that implements and executes a blockchain to flatten the hierarchy automation pyramid. Using intelligent contract-enabled services, edge computing on devices can synchronise their state, publish locally scoped information that needs to be aggregated on a global scope, make local decisions, and achieve the smart's flexibility and resilience manufacturing system. The distributed machine tools and machining centres in the workshop are dynamically organised using smart contracts to finish the manufacturing tasks. At Level 4, the decentralised applications (DApps) are integrated with smart contracts for formulating manufacturing plans. At Level 5, advanced artificial intelligence algorithms are encapsulated into the DApps for assisting the upper-level decision making in product data management, and social manufacturing is critical. Data security in a distributed smart manufacturing environment can be categorised into integrity, confidentiality, and availability, enhanced by the blockchain and smart contract.

Manufacturing world, blockchain developers are using group signature verification algorithms for data integrity purpose. In this way, the smart manufacturing blockchain platforms preserve the system's data integrity by using a highly isomorphic redundancy structure. The most crucial goal of this implementation technique is to control digital identity in the system. Data provenance plays a vital role to achieve data accountability.

For data confidentiality purpose, access control is getting importance. Manufacturing blockchain infrastructures are using public-key based privacy preservation techniques. A smart contract can store the updated ciphertext, express the business logic for capturing control preservation policies, and interpret authorisation semantics for different contexts.

The other important issue that the smart manufacturing implementation team is looking for is data availability. Also, data quality in the dynamic manufacturing environment is crucial; it ensures proper synchronisation of transaction information. A secure, searchable data service is another essential characteristic in a distributed manufacturing system. In this way, the data owner can upload their data in an encrypted format, allowing other legitimate users to search this data.

CONCLUSION

Manufacturers are facing changes in many industry-specific challenges. Advanced manufacturing - in the form of smart factories, automated machines, and other operational technologies - is ushering in a new modern production age. Simultaneously, increased secure connectivity and ever more sophisticated data-gathering and analytics capabilities enabled by blockchain technology have led to a shift towards a better information-based global manufacturing operation.

This chapter analyses different technological issues in the modern manufacturing business and tries to relate those issues in a systematic literature review. The research results demonstrate the potential of using hybrid information system architecture to improve the manufacturing industry's performance. Based on insights gathered from the study of research issues, technical challenges are highlighted in the manufacturing industry. Then the chapter presents a standard manufacturing information system's architecture proposed by the international society of automation. Future research will look for blockchain-secured smart manufacturing. It will include middleware for integrating blockchain-based manufacturing operational services, highly efficient consensus algorithms and smart contacts, blockchain-based data mining, and appropriate privacy and security related issues.

REFERENCES

Abeyratne, S. A., & Monfared, R. P. (2016). Blockchain ready manufacturing supply chain using distributed ledger. *Int. J. Res. Eng. Technol.*, *5*(9), 1–10.

Ahram, T., Sargolzaei, A., Sargolzaei, S., Daniels, J., & Amaba, B. (2017). Blockchain technology innovations. *Proc. IEEE Technol. Eng. Manag. Conf.*, 1-6.

Al-Jaroodi, J., & Mohamed, N. (2019). Blockchain in Industries: A survey. *IEEE Access: Practical Innovations, Open Solutions, 7,* 36500–36515.

Andrews, C., Broby, D., Paul, G., & Whitfield, I. (2020). *Utilising Financial Blockchain Technologies in Advanced Manufacturing.* Available: https://strathprints.strath.ac.uk/ 61982/

Ethereum. (2016). *White Paper - Ethereum/WiKi.* Available: https:github.com/Ethereum/wiki/wiki/White-Paper

Fraga-Lamas, P., & Fernández-Caramés, T. M. (2019). A review on blockchain technologies for an advanced and cyber-resilient automotive industry. *IEEE Access: Practical Innovations, Open Solutions, 7,* 17578–17598.

Francisco, K. & Swanson, D. (2018). The Supply Chain Has No Clothes: Technology Adoption of Blockchain for Supply Chain Transparency. *Digital Logistics,* 1-13.

Ghosh, D., & Tan, A. (2020). *A Framework for Implementing Blockchain Technologies to Improve Supply Chain Performance.* Available: https://dspace.mit.edu/handle/1721.1/113244

Grieves, M. (2020). *Digital Twin: Manufacturing Excellence Through Virtual Factory Replication.* Available: http://www.apriso.com

Ivanov, D., Dolgui, A., & Sokolov, B. (2019). The impact of digital technology and industry 4.0 on the ripple effect and supply chain risk analytics. *International Journal of Production Research, 57*(3), 829–846.

Kobzan, T., Biendarra, A., Schriegel, S., Herbst, T., Müeller, T., & Jasperneite, J. (2018). Utilising blockchain technology in industrial manufacturing with the help of network simulation. *Proc. 16th Int. Conf. Ind. Informat.,* 152-159.

Kumar, N. M., & Mallick, P. K. (2018, January). Blockchain technology for security issues and challenges in IoT. *Procedia Computer Science, 132,* 1815–1823.

Laabs, M., & Dukanovic, S. (2018). "Blockchain in industrie 4.0: Beyond' cryptocurrency. *IT-Inf. Technol., 60*(3), 143–153.

Lamport, L. (1998). The Part-Time Parliament. *ACM Transactions on Computer Systems, 16*(2), 133–169.

Lee, J., Azamfar, M. & Singh, J. (2019). A blockchain-enabled cyber-physical system architecture for industry 4.0 manufacturing systems. *Manuf. Lett., 20,* 34-39.

Lee, J., & Pilkington, M. (2017, July). How the blockchain revolution will reshape the consumer electronics industry. *IEEE Consum. Electron. Mag., 6*(3), 19–23.

Leng, J. (2020, January). ManuChain: Combining permissioned blockchain with a holistic optimisation model as bi-level intelligence for smart manufacturing. *IEEE Transactions on Systems, Man, and Cybernetics. Systems, 50*(1), 182–192.

Leng, J, Zhang, H., Yan, D., Liu, Q., Chen, X. & Zhang, D. (2019). Digital twin-driven manufacturing cyber-physical system for parallel controlling of smart workshop. *J. Ambient Intell. Hum. Computer., 10,* 1155-1166.

Lödding, H., Yu, K. W., & Wiendahl, H. P. (2003). Decentralised WIPoriented manufacturing control (DEWIP). *Production Planning and Control, 14*(1), 42–54.

Lu, Y. (2018). Blockchain and the related issues: A review of current research topics. *J. Manag. Anal., 5*(4), 231–255.

Min, H. (2019). Blockchain technology for enhancing supply chain resilience. *Business Horizons, 62*(1), 35–45.

Moghaddam, M., Cadavid, M. N., Kenley, C. R., & Deshmukh, A. V. (2018). Reference architectures for smart manufacturing: A critical review. *Journal of Manufacturing Systems, 49*, 215–225.

Mohamed, N., & Al-Jaroodi, J. (2019). Applying blockchain in industry 4.0 applications. *Proc. IEEE 9th Annu. Comput. Commun. Workshop Conf.*, 852-858.

Mourtzis, D., & Doukas, M. (2012, September). Decentralised manufacturing systems review: Challenges and outlook. *Logist. Res., 5*, 113–121.

Nakamoto, S. (2008). *Bitcoin: A peer-to-peer Electronic Cash System*. https://bitcoin.org/bitcoin.pdf

Nejad, H. T. N., Nobuhiro, S., & Iwamura, K. (2011). Agent-based dynamic integrated process planning and scheduling in flexible manufacturing systems. *International Journal of Production Research, 49*(5), 1373–1389.

Pal, K. (2017). A Semantic Web Service Architecture for Supply Chain Management, In the Proceeding of the 8th International Conference on Ambient Systems, Networks and Technologies (ANT 2017), Portugal, Procedia Computer Science, 999-1004.

Pal, K. (2019). Algorithmic Solutions for RFID Tag Anti-Collision Problem in Supply Cain Management, In the proceeding of 9th International Symposium on Frontier in Ambient and Mobile Systems (FAMS), 29 April – 2 May 2019, Leuven, Belgium, Procedia Computer Science, 929-934.

Pal, K. (2020a). Internet of Things and blockchain technology in apparel manufacturing supply chain data management. *Procedia Computer Science, 170*, 450–457.

Pal, K. (2020b). *Information sharing for manufacturing supply chain management based on blockchain technology*. In I. Williams (Ed.), *Cross-Industry Use of Blockchain Technology and Opportunities for the Future* (pp. 1–17). IGI Global.

Pan, X., Pan, X., Song, M., Ai, B. & Ming, Y. (2020). Blockchain technology and enterprise operational capabilities: An empirical test. *Int. J. Inf. Manag., 52*.

Panetto, H., Iung, B., Ivanov, D., Weichhart, G., & Wang, X. (2019). Challenges for the cyber-physical manufacturing enterprises of the future. *Annual Reviews in Control, 47*, 200–213.

Ren, L., Zheng, S., & Zhang, L. (2018). A blockchain model for industrial Internet. *Proc. IEEE Int. Conf. Internet Things (iThings) Green Comput. Commun. (GreenCom) Cyber Phys. Soc. Comput. (CPSC) Smart Data (SmartData) iThings/GreenCom/CPSCom/SmartData*, 791-794.

Shah, A. (2019). *The chain gang. In Mechanical Engineering*. Springer.

Shen, W. (2002, January/February). Distributed manufacturing scheduling using intelligent agents. *IEEE Intelligent Systems, 17*(1), 88–94.

Stouffer, K. A., Zimmerman, T., Tang, C., McCarthy, J., & Cichonski, J. (2020). *Cybersecurity for Smart Manufacturing Systems.* Available: nist.gov/programs-projects/cybersecuritysmart-manufacturing-systems

Sturm, L. D., Williams, C. B., Camelio, J. A., White, J., & Parker, R. (2017, July). Cyber-physical vulnerabilities in additive manufacturing systems: A case study attack on the. STL file with human subjects. *Journal of Manufacturing Systems, 44,* 154–164.

Tijan, E., Aksentijevic, A., Ivani, K., & Jardas, M. (2019). Blockchain tech-ontology implementation in logistics. *Sustainability (Basel), 11*(4), 1185.

Tönnissen, S., & Frank, T. (2020). Analysing the impact of blockchain technology for operations and supply chain management: An explanatory model drawn from multiple case studies. *International Journal of Information Management, 52*(June), 2020.

Yuan, Y., & Wang, F. (2018, September). Blockchain and cryptocurrencies: Model, techniques, and applications. *IEEE Transactions on Systems, Man, and Cybernetics. Systems, 48*(9), 1421–1428.

Zarreh, A., Wan, H., Lee, Y., Saygin, C., & Janahi, R. A. (2020, February). Risk assessment for cybersecurity of manufacturing systems: A game theory approach. *Procedia Manufacturing, 38,* 605–612.

Zhang, Y., Xu, X., Liu, A., Lu, Q., Xu, L., & Tao, F. (2019, December). Blockchain-based trust mechanism for IoT-based smart manufacturing system. *IEEE Trans. Comput. Soc. Syst., 6*(6), 1386–1394.

Zheng, Z. (2020, April). An overview on smart contracts: Challenges, advances and platforms. *Future Generation Computer Systems, 105,* 475–491.

KEY TERMS AND DEFINITIONS

Address: An alphanumeric string constituting a participant's public key for encryption of messages.

Block: A message sent by a participant in a blockchain system that has been authenticated and verified by that system and consensus reached on it, and which has been added (as a block) to the previous block in this chain of blocks. Blocks typically record transactions or the change in the status of something.

Block Header: A message or messages relating to a transaction are bundled together in a block and given title known as a block header. The block header is dependent on the combination of messages in the block. A block header lists the transaction(s), the time at which the list was made (that is, a timestamp), and a reference back to the most recent block.

Blockchain: A distributed ledger taking the form of an electronic database that is replicated on numerous nodes spread across an organisation, a country, multiple countries over a diverse geographical area form a blockchain. Each hash for a block depends on the block header for that block. The block header for the block contains a reference to the previous block in the chain. Accordingly, therefore is a continuous chain back in time.

Consensus Protocol: A computer protocol in the form of an algorithm constituting a set of rules for how each participant in a blockchain should process messages (say, a transaction of some sort) and how they should accept the processing done by other participants. The purpose of a consensus protocol is to achieve consensus between participants as to what a blockchain should contain at a given time (including new blocks). Terms used to describe consensus protocols in the context of blockchain technologies include "proof of work" or "proof of stake".

Distributed Ledger: A collection of data (making up a database), an identical copy held on numerous computers across an organisation, a country, multiple countries, or the entire world. A blockchain is a distributed ledger, but not all distributed ledgers are blockchains.

Hashing: The process by which a grouping of digital data is converted into a single number, called a hash. The number is unique (effectively a "digital fingerprint" of the source data), and the source data cannot be reverse-engineered and recovered from it. In the context of blockchain, what is hashed is the block header.

Message: A submission of data (typically a transaction) for processing by nodes with the object having the message authenticated and verified and consensus reached.

Node: A single computer involved in processing a message to reach consensus. Nodes are joined to each other through the computer network.

Peer-to-Peer (P2P): Where participants to a network send information to one another without using intermediaries or central points.

Permissioned: A blockchain is permissioned where its participants are pre-selected or subject to gated entry on the satisfaction of certain requirements or approval by an administrator of the blockchain. A permissioned blockchain may use a consensus protocol to determine a blockchain's state, or it may use an administrator or sub-group of participants to do so.

Permissionless: A blockchain is permissionless when anyone is free to submit messages for processing and/or be involved in the process of reaching consensus. While a permissionless blockchain will typically use a consensus protocol to determine the blockchain's current state, it could equally use some other process (such as using an administrator or sub-group of participants) to do so.

Private Key: An instance of code, privately held, and paired with a public key to initiate text encryption algorithms. A primary key is created as part of public-key cryptography during asymmetric key encryption.

Chapter 11
Blockchain-Based Industrial Internet of Things for the Integration of Industrial Process Automation Systems

Charles Tim Batista Garrocho

https://orcid.org/0000-0001-8245-306X

Federal University of Ouro Preto, Brazil

Célio Márcio Soares Ferreira

Federal University of Ouro Preto, Brazil

Carlos Frederico Marcelo da Cunha Cavalcanti

Federal University of Ouro Preto, Brazil

Ricardo Augusto Rabelo Oliveira

Federal University of Ouro Preto, Brazil

ABSTRACT

The industrial internet of things is expected to attract significant investment to the industry. In this new environment, blockchain presents immediate potential in industrial IoT applications, offering several benefits to industrial cyber-physical systems. However, works in the blockchain literature target environments that do not meet the reality of the factory and do not assess the impact of the blockchain on industrial process requirements. Thus, this chapter presents an investigation of the evolution of industrial process automation systems and blockchain-based applications in the horizontal and vertical integration of the various systems in a supply chain and factories. In addition, through an investigation of experimental work, this work presents issues and challenges to be faced for the application of blockchain in industrial processes. Evaluations and discussions are mainly focused on aspects of real-time systems in machine-to-machine communication of industrial processes.

DOI: 10.4018/978-1-7998-6694-7.ch011

INTRODUCTION

Industry 4.0 refers to the fourth industrial revolution that transforms industrial manufacturing systems into Industrial Cyber-Physical Systems (ICPS), introducing emerging paradigms of information and communication, such as the Internet of Things (Serpanos & Wolf, 2018). By 2025, investments in the Industrial Internet of Things (IIoT) in the world should reach US$ 950 billion (Grand View Research [GVR], 2019). The forecasts are that investment in this market will grow by 30% during the forecast period. All this because the IIoT insertion in the factory brings excellent benefits, such as the possibility of increasing productivity by 30%.

IIoT devices have unique features such as low processing and memory, low bandwidth for data transmission, and limited autonomy (Sisinni, Saifullah, Han, Jennehag, & Gidlund, 2018). With the popularization of these devices and faced with such restrictions, it was necessary to develop new types of communication protocols designed to address these limitations. Generally, the protocols used work with the Publish-Subscribe paradigm, which allows data to be available to multiple consumers. Also, some devices may communicate with each other, either directly or through some intermediary, which is called Machine-to-Machine (M2M) communication (Kshetri, 2017).

M2M communication has shown immediate potential in industrial applications (Bartodziej, 2017). However, M2M communication based on the Publish-Subscribe paradigm uses a communication model through an intermediate node that becomes a point of failure. Also, M2M communication latency can affect the time requirements of real-time systems, compromising deadlines. Intending to establish a decentralized Peer-to-Peer (P2P) network and without the need for a reliable intermediary, several works are introducing blockchain-based smart contracts in various industrial environments. The main benefits pointed out in these works are safe, traceable, and independent communication of processes.

Blockchain-based ICPS can benefit from the vertical integration of Industrial Process Automation Systems (IPAS), creating an IIoT data flow from the production level by sensors/actuators to the short- and long-term decision-making levels by corporate servers/workstations. However, advances in recent blockchain and other technologies (hardware and software) do more harm than good when the ICPS needs to meet tight time constraints. The execution time of an ICPS depends on the context, which leads to uncontrollable variability. In addition, programming languages are generally Turing complete, which makes the runtime undecidable (Lee, 2005). Besides, industrial plant updates with new equipment that are expensive and unrealistic for small and medium industries and will replace that equipment that already work perfectly.

Although it is possible to find much research in the literature on blockchain-based smart contracts in the literature, this technology in the industrial field is still in its early stages. In particular, Lin and Liao (2017) initiate a discussion on blockchain-based smart contract platforms in the industrial environment. Reyna, Martín, Chen, Soler, and Díaz (2018) investigated the possibility of blockchain integration with IIoT and presented issues and challenges. The work of Nawari and Ravindran (2019) discusses the potentials and limitations of the application of smart contracts in the architecture, engineering and construction sectors. Alladi, Chamola, Parizi, and Choo (2019) present challenges and research on blockchain applications for IIoT.

However, most existing research suffers from the following limitations: there is no convergence of blockchain and smart contracts with the horizontal and vertical hierarchy of IPAS; There is no study explicitly discussing blockchain and smart contracts for real-time systems, but this topic is of great importance for the development of industry 4.0. Therefore, although blockchain-based smart contracts can benefit the horizontal and vertical hierarchy of IPAS, there are also several challenges to be faced before potentials can be fully unlocked. Therefore, this book chapter aims to present research on the advances, challenges and open research issues of blockchain-based smart contracts in IPAS.

In view of the previous work, we intend in this chapter of the research book: (i) to provide a conceptual introduction to IPAS, real-time systems, blockchain and smart contracts in Section 2; (ii) present an analysis of the potential for incorporating blockchain in sector 4.0 from IPAS applications, and a survey of the works that carry out the horizontal and vertical integration of IPAS in Section 3; (iii) present and discuss problems and challenges regarding the integration of IPAS from the blockchain in Section 4. Finally, Section 5 presents the final considerations.

BACKGROUND

Today, at the beginning of the fourth industrial revolution, the role of industrial networks is becoming increasingly crucial as they are expected to meet new and more demanding requirements in any new operating contexts (Wollschlaeger, Sauter, & Jasperneite, 2017). A notable example in this regard is the widespread adoption of IIoT, which requires a fast and reliable worldwide connection of industrial equipment. This scenario requires securing connectivity to even the most remote field devices through proper communication systems and interfaces.

IIoT networks are used to monitor conditions, manufacturing processes, predictive maintenance, and decision making. These networks have typical configurations, traffic and performance requirements that make them distinct and different from traditional communication systems generally adopted by general purpose applications in homes and businesses. Thus, IIoT networks are designed to meet the requirements derived from their various fields of application. The most critical requirements are time, reliability and flexibility (Felser, 2005).

IPAS Hierarchy and Synchronicity Requirements

Unlike many network protocols and information systems already widely adopted in homes and businesses, M2M communication protocols and process control systems are designed for specific industry environments. As shown in Figure 1, IPAS are typically based on a five-level hierarchy, widely known in the automation area as the IPAS pyramid (Mehta & Reddy, 2014). These systems are generally adopted by continuous industrial processes such as oil and gas distribution, power generation and management, chemical processing and treatment of glass and minerals.

At the bottom of the IPAS pyramid, the field devices level contains sensors and actuators controlled by process control level that consists of devices such as Programmable Logic Controller (PLC) and Distributed Control System (DCS) that provide an interface for Internet Protocol (IP)-based network communication at the supervision level (Vitturi, Zunino, & Sauter, 2019). At the supervisory level, processes are monitored and executed by shop floor workers through systems like the Supervisory Control and Data Acquisition (SCADA). Finally, in the top of the IPAS pyramid, there is corporate and plant management and sending process-related data to the cloud, trough systems like the Manufacturing Execution System (MES) and Enterprise Resource Planning (ERP).

IPAS comprises many nodes, logically positioned at various hierarchical levels and distributed over large geographic areas (Sharma, 2016). Many servers are used to horizontally integrate the supply chain, and also Human Machine Interface (HMI) computers are used for interaction between man and the level of control. In this context, blockchain can decentralize or support decision making in internal processes of a factory and external processes in a supply chain. This approach can make industrial automation systems fully decentralized and automated.

Real-Time Systems

Real-Time Systems are applications in which the deadline to execute tasks is critical. According to Nilsson, Bernhardsson, and Wittenmark (1998), control systems evolved to a state where they are distributed and controlled using the network. Hence, there is a delay related to network flow. Therefore, an essential challenge in the integration of real-time systems in interconnected environments is the communication aspect.

As presented in Figure 1, at the bottom of the pyramid, the processes are mostly synchronous and real-time critical. The practices presented in the top of the pyramid are goal-oriented and mainly asynchronous. The systems at the bottom of the pyramid are mostly synchronous, with soft or hard real-time constraints. In modern industrial approaches, this brings challenges in communication aspects with the concepts of the ICPS (Jeschke, Brecher, Meisen, Özdemir, & Eschert, 2017) and the IIoT (Tao, Cheng, & Qi, 2017).

Cyber-Physical Systems are the enablers of the new industrial era (Colombo, Karnouskos, Kaynak, Shi, & Yin, 2017). These systems are expected to integrate the processes from shop-floors to the business decisions. Also, they are expected to create a link from the customers to the suppliers. Jeschke et al. (2017) enforce that the industry 4.0 concept is a proposition of a fourth industrial revolution based on Internet connections, allowing the integration and cooperation of manufacturing machines. This scenario represents a challenge as the industrial processes rely on synchronous and real-time driven elements. Real-time processing is a system-level requirement in the novel Internet-connected industrial devices (Pinto, Gomes, Pereira, Cabral, & Tavares, 2017).

Tao et al. (2017) affirm that these modern paradigms represent novel information technologies applied in the industrial manufacturing processes. Nevertheless, they enforce that the interconnection is still a challenge, as the equipment is usually heterogeneous, the deployment is not so quick, and the online service generation still does not have a fixed framework. Finally, it is expected that the latency related to network integration becomes a challenge in novel industrial applications. O'Donovan, Gallagher, Bruton, and O'Sullivan (2018) assert that this aspect creates a natural conflict given the difference from decentralized decision-making processes and reliable real-time control.

Blockchain and Smart Contracts

IIoT devices used in locations that are expected to have a long lifespan need to work on an infrastructure that supports this functionality without exposing them to vulnerabilities. Machines that exchange goods or services need the support of M2M transactions; notably, those dealing with financial or other critical resources, require trust and, to be viable, need to operate risk-free and fault-tolerant (Hill, Al-Aqrabi, Lane, & Aagela, 2019). Some blockchain features make it a potential tool for securing M2M communications as it allows the use of a decentralized and trusted P2P network because network nodes do not need a trusted intermediary to exchange messages with each other or with a central authority (Fernández-Caramés & Fraga-Lamas, 2019).

Figure 1. IPAS hierarchy levels and synchronicity requirements

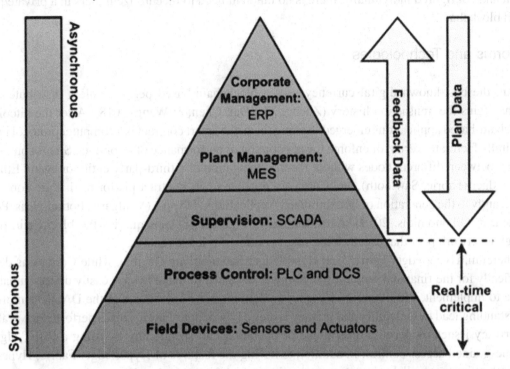

Several works related to the area of security and privacy in M2M communication are introducing concepts of this area in practice in IIoT environment (Zhong et al., 2019). However, classic countermeasures against threats adopted by general-purpose networks (e.g., firewalls, encryption techniques, and intrusion detection systems) can negatively affect the performance of industrial networks. Besides, such countermeasures based on centralized infrastructure requires more significant investment and makes the network prone to failure as all nodes in the network need a reliable central intermediate node to exchange messages with each other.

The blockchain is a decentralized P2P network with no points of failure and has excellent fault tolerance, which transactions on the cannot be deleted or changed. Blockchain is highly scalable, and all transactions are encrypted, making them secure, and auditable. At the heart of this technology, there are the consensus algorithms, which are protocols for obtaining agreements between nodes distributed across the network (Banerjee & Choo, 2018). Consensus algorithms are designed to achieve reliability in a network that involves multiple untrusted nodes. Proof of Work (PoW), Proof of Stake (PoS), Proof of Authority (PoA), and Practical Byzantine Fault Tolerant (PBFT) are the most used algorithms.

Blockchain can be permissionless or permissioned. In permissionless approach, transactions are validated by public nodes. In permissioned blockchain, transactions are validated by a select group of nodes approved by the blockchain's owner. Permissioned systems tend to be more scalable and faster, but are more centralized. Permissionless systems are open for all nodes to participate and thus provide a more decentralized approach where the trade-off is speed and scalability. Generally, on public blockchain networks, to increase network security and stability, consensus algorithms apply a mining process that requires effort from participants in the public network. As for a private network, where all nodes are known and configured individually, there is no inherent need to incentivize miners in a private/permissioned blockchain.

Platforms and Technologies

Bitcoin, the best-known digital currency uses a blockchain-based permissionless distributed ledger that maintains the transaction history (Zheng, Xie, Dai, Chen, & Wang, 2018). After the bitcoin, new blockchain-based applications emerged. Among them, the smart contract is a computer protocol intended to digitally facilitate, verify, or enforce the negotiation or performance of a contract. Smart contracts can transact between different nodes without the intermediation of a third-party entity or agent. Ethereum, Hyperledger (Fabric, Sawtooth), and Corda are popular smart contract platforms that are contributing significantly to the generation of Decentralized Applications (DApps) (Voulgaris, Fotiou, Siris, Polyzos, Jaatinen, & Oikonomidis, 2019). As illustrated in Figure 2, DApps queries the blockchain network through a network peer that executes the smart contract for ledger access.

Ethereum, Hyperledger Fabric, and Hyperledger Sawtooth are flexible, while Corda was designed specifically for the financial sector. Ethereum was designed to make DApps easily understandable and simple to implement. But Ethereum's permissionless mode of operation and the DApps' simplicity of understanding lead to scalability and privacy issues. Hyperledger Fabric solves performance scalability and privacy issues by permissioned mode of operation and specifically by using a PBFT algorithm and fine-grained access control. In addition to having the features of Hyperledger Fabric, Hyperledger Sawtooth relies on parallel transaction processing, which leads to a low latency time for the transaction commit (Dinh, Liu, Zhang, Chen, Ooi, & Wang, 2018).

When defining which platform to use in the industrial environment, the strict time requirements involved in real-time systems must be taken into account. In this context, Hyperledger Fabric and Sawtooth should be adopted for the following reasons: highly modular platform that separates the main system from the application level; supports permissionless and permissioned Infrastructure; allows parallel processing of transactions; compatibility of smart contracts with the public and private network of Ethereum; connectable consensus mechanisms; supports languages such as Rust and C++ for implementing smart contracts, which allows for shorter execution times; and tolerant of Byzantine faults.

Each factory has its private blockchain, where field devices enforce their contracts at a large industrial plant. In a supply chain, one factory can influence the processes of another factory. Thus, smart contracts can define process actions according to external demands. However, smart contracts cannot connect to external data feeds. To address this problem, the Decentralized Oracle Network (DON), a much-needed layer of the trustless future the crypto space, is building. DON, a chain link, connect smart contracts to any external piece of data in a trusted way (Pedro, Levi, & Cuende, 2017). This retrieval of data from the real world is done following the rules of a protocol that incentivizes all nodes, to tell the truth, and punishes them for lying.

CONVERGENCE OF BLOCKCHAIN-BASED IIOT AND IPAS

Blockchain technology is currently in its second stage. As shown in Figure 1, blockchain 1.0 was primarily adopted by Bitcoin to solve issues related to cryptocurrencies and decentralized payments. Blockchain 2.0 has focused on market-wide decentralization and is used to transform assets through smart contracts,

Figure 2. Blockchain-based smart contracts operation overview

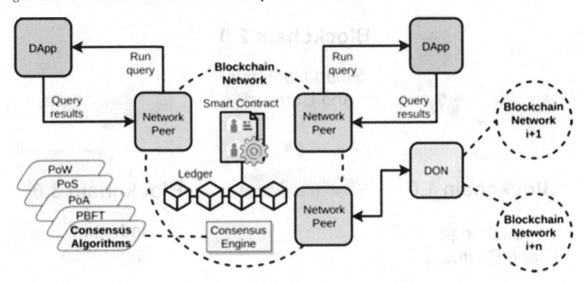

creating value through the emergence of alternatives to Bitcoin. By 2020, blockchain 3.0 is expected to enable real-time transactions, scalability, and unlimited decentralized storage for critical industrial application environments.

Industry 4.0 technologies can benefit from the use of smart contracts, but their application also presents challenges in several ways. Deploying a blockchain today can help cloud-based solutions provide redundancy for storage needs, while at the same time this local blockchain deployment is currently challenging replication on IIoT nodes due to memory and computing constraints. Also, there is a connectivity problem, as field devices (sensors and actuators) use specific networks and protocols like Modbus and ISA100 (Zhao, 2020), while the blockchain network requires an IP-based network.

Therefore, blockchain platforms must be strategically positioned from the IPAS supervisory level, as it is the last layer of IP-based communication, necessary for interaction with the blockchain network. In this way, the levels of corporate management, factory management and supervision now interact in a decentralized way through smart contracts. The blockchain network must act as middleware, in which smart contracts mediate communication between different levels of IPAS, providing an interface for all levels (Garrocho, Ferreira, Junior, Cavalcanti, & Oliveira, 2019).

Most factories currently belong to a supply chain and therefore require communication and negotiation with other factories. No manufacturer is an island, so a digitally connected supply chain is a cornerstone of any industry 4.0 discussion. Working safe and semi-automated with supply chain partners is just a concept, but with smart contracts, this scenario can finally be conceived (Alladi et al., 2019). In this context, analysis and discussion become critical to assess the role and impacts of blockchain-based smart contracts technology in the industrial environment.

Following the Kitchenham (2004) protocol, a survey was carried out covering the terms blockchain and industry. The results of this research were organized into three subsections: in the first subsection, the authors present blockchain-based applications according to the levels of the IPAS hierarchy; finally, in the second subsection, the authors present several works that propose the horizontal and vertical integration of the IPAS hierarchy.

Figure 3. Development of blockchain

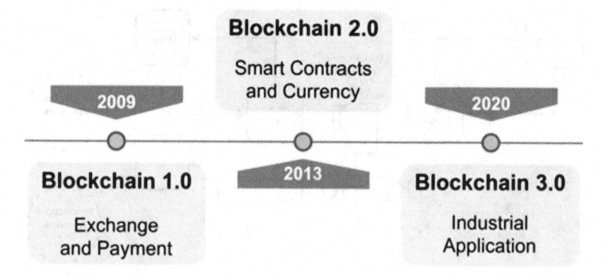

Blockchain-Based Applications in IPAS

Despite the challenges, blockchain-based smart contracts have enormous potential to leverage industry 4.0 scenarios, considering the robustness that M2M communication will add to this new environment (Ferreira, Oliveira, Silva, & Cavalcanti, 2020). This scenario introduces a new era of efficiency, safety, intelligence, and a level playing field for industrial supply chains. In this context, it is possible to identify the following scenarios for the application of blockchain in industry environment:

- **Corporate Management:** is a level of long-term decision making through resource planning. This level can enhance the internal processes through:
  - **Voting system:** In corporate environments of a factory there are moments of choice, in which smart contracts can preserve voters' privacy and increase accessibility, providing transparent, safe and economical voting systems (Dagher, Marella, Milojkovic, & Mohler, 2018).
  - **Online audit:** Through an intelligent audit structure, smart contracts can solve problems of resource sharing difficulties, risks of exposure to privacy, illegal invocation of data and system consistency in the traditional audit mode (Yu, Yan, Yang, & Dong, 2019).
  - **Temporary work contracts:** Smart contracts can guarantee respect for the rights of all actors involved in temporary work in a factory. It guarantees employees fair and legal compensation for job performance and also protection of the employer for inappropriate employee attitudes (Pinna & Ibba, 2018).
  - **Insurance processes**: Different parts of the value chain need to initiate, maintain and close various types of policies in their businesses. In this environment, it is essential that there is a distributed platform based on smart contracts that can execute transactions in insurance processes between the parts of the value chain (Raikwar, Mazumdar, Ruj, Gupta, Chattopadhyay, & Lam, 2018).

- **Plant Management:** is a level of analysis and short-term decision making of processes. At this level, supply chain logistics is an essential process within the industry and requires interaction with other factories. This level can enhance the internal processes through:
  - **Manufacturing on demand**: In the manufacturing services market, users can, through smart contracts, create pre-established machine agreements where they perform standalone requests to other machines directly to take advantage of manufacturing services on an on-demand model (Nguyen & Ali, 2019).
  - **Subscription services**: Consumers can purchase services that require the participation of more than one manufacturer or machine, this subscription governed by a smart contract allows ordering and manufacturing or service to order through transactions between machines (Oktian, Witanto, Kumi, & Lee, 2019).
  - **Stakeholder quality and reputation**: Smart contracts can make machines automatically place orders and trade with other machines, based on reputations on available vendor public quality parameters such as delivery time and ratings provided by other customers (Cha, Chen, Su, & Yeh, 2018).
- **Supervision:** is a level that allows the operator to interact and monitor with field devices (sensors and actuators) through an interface provided by the devices (PLC and DCS) of process control level. This level can enhance the internal processes through:
  - **Autonomy**: Using blockchain, devices can interact with each other without the involvement of any intermediary. It can pave way to develop device-agnostic IIoT applications, like economic autonomous agents (Kapitonov, Lonshakov, Krupenkin, & Berman, 2017).
  - **Machine diagnostics and maintenance**: Intelligent machine diagnostics and self-service can enable monitoring autonomy, enabling preventative and diagnostic actions on issues such as refueling station orders and replacement requests from maintenance service providers (Stodt, Jastremskoj, Reich, Welte, & Sikora, 2019).
  - **Inventory control**: Smart contracts can be responsible for reporting details such as manufacturing date models and other machine identifying data. These details can be read by machines that have smart contracts that coordinate audit or inventory control transactions (Zhu & Kouhizadeh, 2019).
- **Process Control:** this level is made up of automation devices such as PLC and DCS that derive ideal process parameters from the different sensors. This level triggers the actuators as per the processed sensor signals. This level can enhance the internal processes through:
  - **Traceability**: Smart contracts can help track M2M interactions, making the process and asset traceability easier, enabling a complete record of the production process. This traceability would make it easier to identify defective products by analyzing the entire production chain from the history of M2M interactions. In a supply chain application, for example, it is even possible to know who owns the asset and when it is delivered (Shih & Yang, 2019).
  - **Immutable log**: All transactions and states logged in the blockchain are immutable. Blockchain is considered a ledger because it is analogous to the book where the accountant records the inputs and outputs of a company. In a ledger, the sheets and the books themselves are numbered and the releases made there unchanging. One of the goals of a ledger is to record, without the possibility of tampering, the movement of the company, i.e., the log of the input and output records. Blockchains are called ledgers for logging undelete transactions in

a distributed manner and are of fundamental importance in logging M2M messages sent in an industrial environment (Hang & Kim, 2019).

- **Field Devices**: is a level lowest automation hierarchy level and is made up of field devices such as actuators and sensors. The field devices have a core task of transferring machines and processes data to the next level for monitoring and analysis. This level can enhance the internal processes through:
  - ° **Authenticity**: It may be necessary to prove the authenticity of a particular device. Information such as manufacturer, specifications, date of manufacture, expiration date, maintenance dates can be stored in smart contracts on the blockchain, for stock or possession, reducing and even eliminating physical certificates. This ability to verify authenticity can further improve process security and reliability. In this new context, forgery and tampering can be mitigated during the production process and, consequently, in interactions between devices (Rehman, Javaid, Awais, Imran, & Naseer, 2019).
  - ° **Identity**: The use of blockchain allows for better identification of each device. Moreover, it can also provide a trusted means for authentication and authorization of IIoT devices (Hasan, AlHadhrami, AlDhaheri, Salah, & Jayaraman, 2019).

Most blockchain and smart contract technologies today have throughput and latency constraints on their operation, which require some time to reach consensus and for transactions to be carried out effectively. The works of process control level do not take into account the stringent requirements imposed by industrial systems, such as real-time systems (Candell, Kashef, Liu, Lee, & Foufou, 2018). This scenario points to a significant problem for many applications in the IPAS hierarchy that need to react in real-time or near real-time to data and events collected from field devices. This scenario may justify the few works at lower levels of the IPAS hierarchy.

Blockchain-Based Integration in IPAS

One of the concepts of industry 4.0 is to have greater integration between processes and sectors in factories exchanging information in a faster and more efficient way for faster decision making in order to increase productivity, decrease losses, optimize resources and lead to digital transformation into the industries. Therefore, systems integration is one of the pillars of industry 4.0 and aims to connect the different areas of an industry, in order to extract data and information that will be used to make continuous improvements throughout the production process and related support areas (Xu, Xu, & Li, 2018).

Each process of the factory dynamics generates and is supplied with data. In an environment without integration, there is the job of capturing all the information generated by one stage of the manufacturing process and supplying the next, this is often done manually, inefficiently and analogically. The lack of integrated systems also means that management levels have a much greater job of analyzing whether what is being manufactured really matches the demand received and whether suppliers and distributors are aligned with this production (Pérez-Lara, Saucedo-Martínez, Marmolejo-Saucedo, Salais-Fierro, & Vasant, 2018).

As the processes are diverse and involve different agents in a factory, the concept of integration aligned to industry 4.0 was divided into horizontal and vertical integration. As shown in Figure 4, horizontal integration concerns the entire production chain: from suppliers to customers, while vertical integration integrates the functions to be developed within the factory. To achieve the best results, there must still

Figure 4. Horizontal and vertical integration of industry

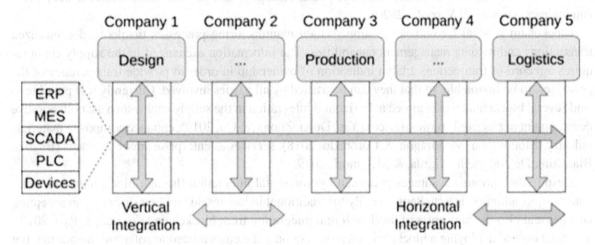

be an interaction between vertical and horizontal integrations to unite processes and optimize production as a whole.

Horizontal Integration

For the factory, horizontal integration represents synchrony, loss reduction, consequently a saving of resources as the demand of suppliers is adjusted to the demand of customers, without waste during the process. Besides, the higher quality of the products represents a lower level of return and increases the consumer confidence index towards the factory, which generates customer loyalty. Also, with delivery control and distribution monitoring, it is possible to be sure that deadlines are met and also to generate data to predict more accurate deliveries.

Traditionally, horizontal integration occurs through manufacturing execution systems, product life cycle management and company resource planning. However, the aforementioned platforms cannot allow connection with other partners or customers in the industry (thus requiring additional integrations, which are generally very expensive and use ad-hoc protocols). Besides, there is a complex relationship between the strategic and operational goals of the different levels of manufacturing systems that inhibit the realization of an intelligent manufacturing system.

A factory needs to deploy networks to connect smart production systems horizontally. Market analysis, supplier management, even production, logistics and distribution, horizontal integration helps sectors to work with more harmony and synchronization, optimizing resources while also integrating market analysis into the manufacturing process (Pérez-Lara et al., 2018). Therefore, industry 4.0 requires higher levels of integration, essential to automate data exchange in factories, communication with suppliers and customers and, finally, their field devices.

When automation is inserted in the connectivity of the horizontal integration, the information can be collected and sent automatically from the various systems implanted in a factory to any of the relevant parts of the value chain. This automation reduces the time for decision making and also reduces the number of intermediate elements (such as employees) and bureaucracy (documents and physical contracts). In this context, blockchain-based smart contracts can help with horizontal integration, providing common and reliable data or money exchange points through which various smart entities in the factory can interact (Di Vaio & Varriale, 2020).

Blockchain is ideal for enhancing supply chain manufacturing processes thanks to decentralized transactions and its data management capabilities. The information exchanged in the supply chain requires a record of transactions and an indication of ownership in order to provide transparency of the processes, to be inviolable, so that they can be trusted by all parties involved. Currently it is possible to find several blockchain works aimed at horizontal integration in the supply chain, such as: collaborative development of electronic power devices (Yan, Duan, Zhong, & Qu, 2017), enhance composite materials industry (Mondragon, Mondragon, & Coronado, 2018), services as enterprise smart contracts (Bagozi, Bianchini, De Antonellis, Garda, & Melchiori, 2019),

Despite the various advantages presented by horizontal integration through blockchain and smart contracts, its adoption is a challenge mainly for traditional industries due to their difficulty in accepting changes and also the high costs of this horizontal integration from blockchain (Ko, Lee, & Ryu, 2018). The final cost of deploying a blockchain includes not only the costs related to software integration, but also the cost of the time required to understand the underlying business processes and define accurate and flexible smart contracts.

Vertical Integration

The vertical integration provides for the connection of the specific systems used at each of the IPAS levels, connecting the data, making the influence flow between all hierarchical levels more quickly and efficiently, reducing the time for decision making and improving the management process industrial. Therefore, vertical integration is in place when inside the factory the employees, computers, manufacturing machines are linked with each other, communicate automatically with each other, and their interaction exists not only in the real world but also in virtual reality, in the model of the entire system.

Vertical integration makes the traditional IPAS pyramid view disappear. The same goes for several systems and applications across these various levels. Other systems such as ERP, MES, and SCADA will dramatically change while still others will be replaced by rapidly emerging applications in the scope of Industrial IoT platforms (Frank, Dalenogare, & Ayala, 2019). In this context of automation and systems integration, the vertically integrated company in Industry 4.0 gains a crucial competitive advantage by being able to respond appropriately and quickly to changes in market signals and new opportunities.

Industry 4.0 aims for a highly flexible and digitized industrial production model that is smarter and more reliable than today's possibilities. This requires vertical integration of different operations in one manufacturing to promote a reconfigurable intelligent factory. Using raw data as an asset from which value can be created to support business and manufacturing decisions has motivated many scientists to explore the challenges of how to exploit that value. In this context, works like (Pal, Vain, Srinivasan, & Ramaswamy, 2017) introduce optimization models to schedule maintenance operations using formal methods. However, this approach does not indicate how raw data can be collected and transmitted to the top of the PAS hierarchy.

To integrate IoT into the manufacturing process, some work (Alexakos & Kalogeras, 2017; Alexakos, Anagnostopoulos, Fournaris, Koulamas, & Kalogeras, 2018; Shirazi, 2019) presents approaches that combine field device networking and high-level multi-agent systems that contribute to vertical integration. However, the evaluation of such proposals was by simulation only, and it is not considered the impact of IP-based networks that can occur on real-time system deadlines. Other works (Garcia, Irisarri, Perez,

Estevez, & Marcos, 2016; Calderón Godoy & González Pérez, 2018; Llamuca, Garcia, Naranjo, Rosero, Alvarez-M, & Garcia, 2019; Liu, Vengayil, Lu, & Xu, 2019), based on the Open Platform Communications Unified Architecture (OPC-UA) protocol, presents vertical integration architectures whose temporal requirements of real-time systems can be met. However, the need for expensive equipment (unrealistic for small and medium industries) and a server to intermediate communication between the components of these architectures makes such architectures vulnerable in the event of a centralized server failure.

Aiming at making communication and decision making decentralized, a lot of works is applying blockchain technologies in the industry. Blockchain-based smart contracts are being applied across supply chains to improve decision making in control and management processes (Kapitonov, Berman, Lonshakov, & Krupenkin, 2018; Petroni, de Moraes, & Gonçalves, 2018), trusted data generation and privacy (Liang, Shetty, Tosh, Zhao, Li, & Liu, 2018), reliable communication, and between end-user and service provider (Schulz & Freund, 2018; Vatankhah Barenji, Wang, Huang, & Guerra-Zubiaga, 2019). However, such approaches aim at horizontal communication between companies and/or customers. Aiming for vertical integration of the PAS hierarchy, the works (Leang, Kim, & Yoo, 2018; Maw, Adepu, & Mathur, 2019) feature blockchain-based architectures for cyber-physical systems.

The approaches proposed by the works (Leang et al., 2018; Maw et al., 2019) are intended only to monitor data from field devices controlled by the PLC and to record this information on the blockchain to generate an unchanging history. The works (Smirnov & Teslya, 2018; Gallo, Nguyen, Barone, & Van Hien, 2018; Isaja & Soldatos, 2018; Lee, Azamfar, & Singh, 2019; Petroni, Reis, & Gonçalves, 2019) have similar approaches in which the objective is to use blockchain-related technologies to control processes involving devices and businesses. However, the process control of these architectures is implemented through smart contracts, where the execution time is variable (either by network latency or by committing transactions on the blockchain network), making processes unsafe and prone to failures to meet deadlines in real-time systems.

ISSUES AND CHALLENGES IN BLOCKCHAIN-BASED IPAS INTEGRATION

In the previous sections, the authors presented the main aspects of IPAS, blockchain, and smart contracts. The authors presented industrial applications based on the blockchain according to the level of the IPAS hierarchy. Also, the authors introduced the fundamental concepts of blockchain-based smart contracts, conjecturing about their use in replacing a classic approach to the IPAS hierarchy. In this section, the authors discussed the critical issues and challenges in applying and integrating blockchain-based smart contracts platforms in the IPAS hierarchy. Table 1 summary the issues and challenges in blockchain-based IPAS integration.

In the previous section, the authors showed that the integration of IPAS based on blockchain and smart contracts needs investments for a new reality of the hardware and software equipment infrastructure. In this new context, the general agreement in the blockchain-based IIoT ecosystem requires that all stakeholders (both at horizontal and vertical levels) commit to investing and using this new equipment. Therefore, finding low-cost blockchain solutions is a big challenge, as mentioned earlier, small and medium-sized companies/factories are quite resistant to change. In addition, companies should not invest and support these changes because they lack standards for such technologies in the industrial sphere and equipment that demonstrates high durability.

In addition to the problem of investment in infrastructure, there is another problem of investment in staff qualification. Automation engineers and technicians are familiar with the use of ladder logic and do not understand the scripting language, so they feel comfortable working with today's easy-to-use, reliable, proven functional and necessary industrial process control systems. Therefore, while new technologies allow for higher levels of scalability, traceability, integration, manufacturing capacity and autonomous collaboration with other systems, the lack of skills and understanding to explore IIoT and blockchain will bring challenges. In this context, new professions (with skills of industrial process control, blockchain, smart contracts, and contracts and rights) must emerge in order to fill and integrate this gap in the industrial environment.

Although small and medium industries avoid changing their plant of industrial equipment that works perfectly, there will be a natural change in this context soon. This is because IIoT focuses on the development of information throughout the supply chain, optimizing resources and benefiting the productive processes, where equipment, machinery, and suppliers are connected in a network. IIoT allows managers to perceive the loss of productivity and operational processes in advance, making production decisions, contingencies, safety and costs in real time, through an artificial model complemented by IoT, which is why it was introduced in Industry 4.0 (Oztemel & Gursev, 2020).

According to Maqbool Khan et al. (2017), industrial automation is becoming complex gradually, and the data generated in manufacturing alters to big data. Robots, sensors, actuators, switches, industrial devices, and M2M communication are the ore of big data in Industry 4.0. Heavy usage of IIoT brought an immense commute in the era of industries. Industry 4.0 is a blend of modern smart technology and systems which creates a deluge of data, which is quite challenging to handle with classical tools and algorithms. Therefore, in addition to the problems of investment in infrastructure and qualification of the professional team, there is a significant challenge in the transfer and storage of large amounts of IIoT data between the various systems of the IPAS hierarchy.

Recently, big data analysis tools have been proposed for Industry 4.0, which aim to facilitate the cleaning, formatting, and transformation of industrial data generated by systems by different levels of IPAS hierarchy (Rehman, Yaqoob, Salah, Imran, Jayaraman, & Perera, 2019). However, localization and data processing becomes a significant challenge, as the centralized communication architectures used have high network traffic and high latency, due to the large volume of IIoT data. For decentralized communication architectures, the impact on network traffic and latency is greater due to the consensus among nodes of a blockchain network.

Industry 4.0 technologies can benefit from the use of blockchain, but their application also presents challenges in many ways. Deployment a blockchain today can help cloud-based solutions provide redundancy for storage needs, while at the same time this local blockchain deployment is currently challenging to replicate on IIoT nodes due to its memory constraints and computational. In this context, several blockchain approaches to IIoT define the blockchain network above the IIoT device layer (Seok, Park, & Park, 2019; Wan, Li, Imran, & Li, 2019). However, it is essential to assess the impact of this new blockchain layer on the transfer, storage, and control of IIoT data to the other layers above the blockchain network.

In the vast majority of recent approaches to cyber physical systems, the blockchain network is deployed from the level of process control devices in the IPAS hierarchy, allowing integration between synchronous and asynchronous systems. However, in this new context, synchronous IIoT applications acquire new features (data encryption, transaction creation, generation and storage of public and private keys) that can negatively influence the energy consumption of IIoT field devices that are deployed for long periods of time (Barki, Bouabdallah, Gharout, & Traore, 2016). Thus, new encryption schemes and techniques or new lightweight, efficient and robust encryption algorithms must be designed with the aim of reducing energy consumption in IIoT devices.

Another significant challenge in adopting connected IPAS multilayer systems is the integration of asynchronous systems (DER, MER, and SCADA) with process control (PLC and DCS) and real-time oriented synchronous field devices (IIoT devices such as manufacturing machines). In many situations, these IIoT devices have very severe time constraints. For this matter, communication is an essential aspect in which the main challenge is to establish a framework or middleware that allows integration with asynchronous decisions from the top levels of the IPAS hierarchy with synchronous communication on the bottom levels of the IPAS hierarchy. Such blockchain-based solutions that guarantee execution, control, monitoring and decision-making without influencing the real-time systems deadlines, can provide a breakthrough in industry 4.0.

Some recent work, through the results of experimental evaluations, points out that there are problems related to the high and variable blocking time when changing a state in the blockchain network, from the request (made by a requesting client device) to a blockchain node to the commit of the transaction which is the confirmation among all blockchain nodes that the state has been inserted or changed in the ledger (Pongnumkul, Siripanpornchana, & Thajchayapong, 2017; Vatcharatiansakul & Tuwanut, 2019). These results show that the problem is due to the standard operation of the blockchain and its consensus algorithms. Thus, designing fast and reliable consensus algorithms is the key to enabling critical, real-time process controls for IIoT devices. However, seeking the low latency and reliability of a consensus algorithm at the same time is a challenging task. The problem is further compounded by slower and less reliable wireless connectivity compared to wired connections assumed in traditional consensus algorithms (Tramarin, Mok, & Han, 2019).

Communication latency and jitter are very sensitive in the lower layers of the IPAS pyramid. Such delays can mainly influence the monitoring and control of industrial processes. Monitoring, carried out at the supervisory level by shop floor operators, is less sensitive, however, deadlines from data collection to visualization by HMI cannot be changed, with risks of compromising the entire product process. At the process control level, the control performed by PLC is highly sensitive, with low latency and strict deadlines, here a single deadline break can compromise the entire production process chain. Therefore, current blockchain platforms and smart contracts are not suitable for this environment, requiring the design and development of new technologies that do not compromise the strict requirements of the industrial systems of the lower levels of the IPAS pyramid.

In order not to affect the time and strict deadlines of industrial process control systems, some approaches store IIoT data outside the blockchain network and reduce latency with new paradigms. Recent works in the literature apply concepts of fog and edge computing in M2M communication approaches, in which gateways based on the MQTT protocol are used close to field devices as a communication bridge for IIoT data collection and IIoT data hashing only for storage on the blockchain network (Fernández-Caramés & Fraga-Lamas, 2019). However, gateways can increase the delay in delivering sensor and actuator data to higher levels of IPAS, compromising decision making.

In addition to the problems of high and variable block time, other results of experimental evaluations have shown that some blockchain platforms such as Ethereum do not allow parallel operations to be performed (Schäffer, di Angelo, & Salzer, 2019). However, serial execution seems to be necessary: smart contract sharing state and smart contract programming languages have serial semantics in the current operation of the Ethereum system and its four testnets. Although several works in the literature

Table 1. Summary of issues and challenges in blockchain-based IPAS integration

	Issue	Challenge
Ability	Automation technicians and engineers are not professionally qualified or even encouraged to work with blockchain and smart contracts.	Find ways to encourage automation teams to build on the new skills required by blockchain incorporation, or identify new professions based on blockchain, automation and rights.
Investment	The current infrastructure required for the implementation of the blockchain network requires large investments in which not every company or factory is willing to participate and invest.	Find alternatives to reduce investment costs in infrastructure with new platforms and blockchain equipment in a way that guarantees the inclusion of small and medium industries.
Storage	It is necessary to store all IIoT data for application of mining and other techniques, however, storage on the blockchain network can overload the network and devices.	Find IIoT data storage alternatives in a way that does not compromise the blockchain network and guarantees data authenticity and security.
Energy	Encryption algorithms negatively influence the energy consumption of IIoT devices that are deployed for long periods of time.	Find alternatives to encryption schemes or create new lighter, more efficient and more robust encryption algorithms that meet the requirements of IIoT devices.
Time	The time required to complete the insertion of a transaction in the blocks of a blockchain network is high for real-time systems that require 10 to 100 ms times.	Find alternatives to reduce transaction processing time on the blockchain network to incorporate all industrial processes like real-time systems.
Deadline	There is a great jitter in the total time for the transaction process between all nodes of the blockchain network, in which it can compromise the deadlines of the industrial processes.	Find alternatives to reduce the jitter of transaction processing time on the blockchain network to ensure the deadlines of industrial processes.
Scalability	The including transactions in blocks in the blockchain network is serial, not allowing parallel requests by industrial applications.	Find alternatives to increase the number of transaction requests to the blockchain network carried out by the industrial processes.
Mobility	The mobility of IIoT devices reduces opportunities for communication with the blockchain network, negatively influencing synchronous industrial processes.	Find alternatives to ensure the communication of IIoT devices with the blockchain network, even with failures in the communication generated by the mobility of these devices.

present new ways to enable miners and validators to execute smart contracts in parallel, this is still an open problem in this area of research (Saraph & Herlihy, 2019).

Introducing parallelism into blockchain is a challenging task. There is currently an effort in which the classic blockchain architecture is extended to a more sophisticated architecture based on Directed Acyclic Graphs (DAG) (Bai, 2018) and other programming languages used to write smart contracts with mechanisms of concurrency control as presented in modern languages. These approaches lead to parallel transaction validation, which reduces block time by allowing M2M communication closer to real-time requirements. However, DAG increases the complexity of the implementation, and there is no DAG-based solution yet that supports the execution of smart contracts.

Most existing IIoT security systems operate as a set of individual tools and are neither automated nor integrated. Currently, there is a growing consensus about the potential of linking blockchain to IIoT devices (Dai, Zheng, & Zhang, 2019). However, some important questions remain open: Where should blockchain nodes be hosted and located? Hosting blockchain directly on resource-constrained IIoT devices is inadvisable in the literature for the following reasons: lack of computational resources for encryption and basic tasks such as mining; lack of sufficient bandwidth for ledger replication and maintenance; energy saving required.

Another important issue is the mobility of the field devices. With IIoT devices in constant motion, communication with the blockchain network will face high dynamism and, consequently, large amounts of connectivity failures (Lucas-Estañ, Sepulcre, Raptis, Passarella, & Conti, 2018). This scenario will contribute to the reduction of communication opportunities with the blockchain network, increasing the communication delay in the interaction of IIoT devices and blockchain network. Also, if the process control is in the blockchain network layer or higher layers, production may be compromised.

Finally, newer generations of IIoT devices are expected to be equipped with better hardware specifications, which will allow direct communication with smart contracts, reducing communication latency. In this context, the blockchain-based smart contract is expected to operate within an environment in which it must adapt its capabilities to the context of the IIoT devices. This scenario will contribute to the viability of the Pervasive Computing paradigm (Weiser, 1991), where devices run applications and integrate seamlessly with field devices.

CONCLUSION

In a complex industrial ecosystem, several entities are integrated to create, collect, process, transmit and store IIoT data. Industries are resistant to changes in their processes, however, due to rapid advances in technology and innovations in business models, blockchain is expected to be widely applied to the shop floor. In this article, we approach blockchain and IIoT integration from an industrial perspective. A survey of blockchain-based IIoT applications from an industrial process automation and control perspective were presented and discussed. The main applications and challenges are addressed. We also analyzed the research challenges and future trends associated with blockchain-enabled IIoT.

The current use and adoption of blockchain-based smart contracts in Industry 4.0 is in its early stages, as this is an area that has a lot to explore. The cataloged solutions show that most of the related approaches are designed for specific processes designed to automate horizontal IPAS communication. The challenges in horizontal integration are mainly related to the difficulty of changes in processes that work perfectly and a high investment in infrastructure necessary for the new blockchain-based approaches.

On the other hand, vertical blockchain-based integration of IPAS is still in its early stages, in which current approaches do not take advantage of the current manufacturing, supervision and control systems widely used in the industry. Besides, current approaches do not take into account the strict time and deadline requirements related to industrial processes, making the introduction of these approaches on the shop floor unfeasible. In this context, the authors presented several research opportunities and challenges related to blockchain and industrial integration systems.

Finally, it is important to list that there are still many experimental studies to evaluate the behavior of the blockchain network in an industrial environment. Also, such assessments allowed for a deeper analysis of the real application of blockchain in industrial systems, mainly for process control systems that are quite time sensitive. In this context, new consensus algorithms and blockchain platforms are needed to meet the requirements of the industrial environment.

ACKNOWLEDGMENT

We acknowledge the support of the Brazilian research agencies National Council for Scientific and Technological Development (CNPq) and Coordination for the Improvement of Higher Education Personnel (Capes), the Minas Gerais State Research Foundation (FAPEMIG), the Federal Institute of Minas Gerais (IFMG), and the Federal University of Ouro Preto (UFOP).

REFERENCES

Alexakos, C., Anagnostopoulos, C., Fournaris, A., Koulamas, C., & Kalogeras, A. (2018, May). IoT integration for adaptive manufacturing. In *2018 IEEE 21st International Symposium on Real-Time Distributed Computing (ISORC)* (pp. 146-151). IEEE. 10.1109/ISORC.2018.00030

Alexakos, C., & Kalogeras, A. (2017, May). Exposing MES functionalities as enabler for cloud manufacturing. In *2017 IEEE 13th International Workshop on Factory Communication Systems (WFCS)* (pp. 1-4). IEEE. 10.1109/WFCS.2017.7991966

Alladi, T., Chamola, V., Parizi, R. M., & Choo, K. K. R. (2019). Blockchain Applications for Industry 4.0 and Industrial IoT: A Review. *IEEE Access: Practical Innovations, Open Solutions, 7*, 176935–176951. doi:10.1109/ACCESS.2019.2956748

Bagozi, A., Bianchini, D., De Antonellis, V., Garda, M., & Melchiori, M. (2019, July). Services as enterprise smart contracts in the digital factory. In *2019 IEEE International Conference on Web Services (ICWS)* (pp. 224-228). IEEE. 10.1109/ICWS.2019.00046

Bai, C. (2018, November). State-of-the-art and future trends of blockchain based on DAG structure. In *International Workshop on Structured Object-Oriented Formal Language and Method* (pp. 183-196). Springer.

Banerjee, M., Lee, J., & Choo, K. K. R. (2018). A blockchain future for internet of things security: A position paper. *Digital Communications and Networks, 4*(3), 149–160. doi:10.1016/j.dcan.2017.10.006

Barki, A., Bouabdallah, A., Gharout, S., & Traore, J. (2016). M2M security: Challenges and solutions. *IEEE Communications Surveys and Tutorials, 18*(2), 1241–1254. doi:10.1109/COMST.2016.2515516

Bartodziej, C. J. (2017). The concept industry 4.0. In *The concept industry 4.0* (pp. 27–50). Springer Gabler. doi:10.1007/978-3-658-16502-4_3

Calderón Godoy, A. J., & González Pérez, I. (2018). Integration of sensor and actuator networks and the SCADAsystem to promote the migration of the legacy flexible manufacturing system towards the industry 4.0 concept. *Journal of Sensor and Actuator Networks, 7*(2), 23. doi:10.3390/jsan7020023

Candell, R., Kashef, M., Liu, Y., Lee, K. B., & Foufou, S. (2018). Industrial wireless systems guidelines: Practical considerations and deployment life cycle. *IEEE Industrial Electronics Magazine, 12*(4), 6–17. doi:10.1109/MIE.2018.2873820

Cha, S. C., Chen, J. F., Su, C., & Yeh, K. H. (2018). A blockchain connected gateway for BLE-based devices in the internet of things. *IEEE Access: Practical Innovations, Open Solutions*, *6*, 24639–24649. doi:10.1109/ACCESS.2018.2799942

Colombo, A. W., Karnouskos, S., Kaynak, O., Shi, Y., & Yin, S. (2017). Industrial cyberphysical systems: A backbone of the fourth industrial revolution. *IEEE Industrial Electronics Magazine*, *11*(1), 6–16. doi:10.1109/MIE.2017.2648857

Dagher, G. G., Marella, P. B., Milojkovic, M., & Mohler, J. (2018). *BroncoVote: secure voting system using Ethereum's blockchain*. Academic Press.

Dai, H. N., Zheng, Z., & Zhang, Y. (2019). Blockchain for internet of things: A survey. *IEEE Internet of Things Journal*, *6*(5), 8076–8094. doi:10.1109/JIOT.2019.2920987

Di Vaio, A., & Varriale, L. (2020). Blockchain technology in supply chain management for sustainable performance: Evidence from the airport industry. *International Journal of Information Management*, *52*, 102014. doi:10.1016/j.ijinfomgt.2019.09.010

Dinh, T. T. A., Liu, R., Zhang, M., Chen, G., Ooi, B. C., & Wang, J. (2018). Untangling blockchain: A data processing view of blockchain systems. *IEEE Transactions on Knowledge and Data Engineering*, *30*(7), 1366–1385. doi:10.1109/TKDE.2017.2781227

Felser, M. (2005). Real-time ethernet-industry prospective. *Proceedings of the IEEE*, *93*(6), 1118–1129. doi:10.1109/JPROC.2005.849720

Fernández-Caramés, T. M., & Fraga-Lamas, P. (2019). A review on the application of blockchain to the next generation of cybersecure industry 4.0 smart factories. *IEEE Access: Practical Innovations, Open Solutions*, *7*, 45201–45218. doi:10.1109/ACCESS.2019.2908780

Ferreira, C. M. S., Oliveira, R. A. R., Silva, J. S., & da Cunha Cavalcanti, C. F. M. (2020). Blockchain for Machine to Machine Interaction in Industry 4.0. In *Blockchain Technology for Industry 4.0* (pp. 99–116). Springer. doi:10.1007/978-981-15-1137-0_5

Frank, A. G., Dalenogare, L. S., & Ayala, N. F. (2019). Industry 4.0 technologies: Implementation patterns in manufacturing companies. *International Journal of Production Economics*, *210*, 15–26. doi:10.1016/j.ijpe.2019.01.004

Gallo, P., Nguyen, U. Q., Barone, G., & Van Hien, P. (2018, September). DeCyMo: Decentralized Cyber-Physical System for Monitoring and Controlling Industries and Homes. In *2018 IEEE 4th International Forum on Research and Technology for Society and Industry (RTSI)* (pp. 1-4). IEEE.

Garcia, M. V., Irisarri, E., Perez, F., Estevez, E., & Marcos, M. (2016). OPC-UA communications integration using a CPPS architecture. In IEEE Ecuador technical chapters meeting (pp. 1-6). doi:10.1109/ETCM.2016.7750838

Garrocho, C., Ferreira, C. M. S., Junior, A., Cavalcanti, C. F., & Oliveira, R. R. (2019, November). Industry 4.0: Smart Contract-based Industrial Internet of Things Process Management. In Anais do IX Simpósio Brasileiro de Engenharia de Sistemas Computacionais (pp. 137-142). SBC.

Grand View Research. (2019, June). *Industrial internet of things (iiot) market size, share trends analysis report by component, by end use (manufacturing, energy power, oil gas, healthcare, logistics transport, agriculture), and segment forecasts, 2019 - 2025.* Retrieved from https://www.grandviewresearch.com/industry-analysis/industrial-internet-of-things-iiot-market

Hang, L., & Kim, D. H. (2019). Design and implementation of an integrated IoT blockchain platform for sensing data integrity. *Sensors (Basel), 19*(10), 2228. doi:10.339019102228 PMID:31091799

Hasan, H., AlHadhrami, E., AlDhaheri, A., Salah, K., & Jayaraman, R. (2019). Smart contract-based approach for efficient shipment management. *Computers & Industrial Engineering, 136*, 149–159. doi:10.1016/j.cie.2019.07.022

Hill, G., Al-Aqrabi, H., Lane, P., & Aagela, H. (2019, January). Securing Manufacturing Business Intelligence for the Industrial Internet of Things. In *Fourth International Congress on Information and Communication Technology* (p. 174). Springer Singapore.

Isaja, M., & Soldatos, J. (2018, May). Distributed ledger technology for decentralization of manufacturing processes. In *2018 IEEE Industrial Cyber-Physical Systems (ICPS)* (pp. 696-701). IEEE.

Jeschke, S., Brecher, C., Meisen, T., Özdemir, D., & Eschert, T. (2017). Industrial internet of things and cyber manufacturing systems. In *Industrial internet of things* (pp. 3–19). Springer. doi:10.1007/978-3-319-42559-7_1

Kapitonov, A., Berman, I., Lonshakov, S., & Krupenkin, A. (2018, June). Blockchain based protocol for economical communication in industry 4.0. In *2018 Crypto valley conference on blockchain technology (CVCBT)* (pp. 41-44). IEEE.

Kapitonov, A., Lonshakov, S., Krupenkin, A., & Berman, I. (2017, October). Blockchain-based protocol of autonomous business activity for multi-agent systems consisting of UAVs. In *2017 Workshop on Research, Education and Development of Unmanned Aerial Systems (RED-UAS)* (pp. 84-89). IEEE. 10.1109/RED-UAS.2017.8101648

Khan, M., Wu, X., Xu, X., & Dou, W. (2017, May). Big data challenges and opportunities in the hype of Industry 4.0. In *2017 IEEE International Conference on Communications (ICC)* (pp. 1-6). IEEE. 10.1109/ICC.2017.7996801

Kitchenham, B. (2004). Procedures for performing systematic reviews. Keele University.

Ko, T., Lee, J., & Ryu, D. (2018). Blockchain technology and manufacturing industry: Real-time transparency and cost savings. *Sustainability, 10*(11), 4274. doi:10.3390u10114274

Kshetri, N. (2017). Can blockchain strengthen the internet of things? *IT Professional, 19*(4), 68–72. doi:10.1109/MITP.2017.3051335

Leang, B., Kim, R. W., & Yoo, K. H. (2018, July). Real-Time Transmission of Secured PLCs Sensing Data. In *IEEE International Conference on Internet of Things and IEEE Green Computing and Communications and IEEE Cyber, Physical and Social Computing and IEEE Smart Data* (pp. 931-932). 10.1109/Cybermatics_2018.2018.00177

Lee, E. A. (2005). Absolutely positively on time: What would it take? *Computer, 38*(7), 85–87. doi:10.1109/MC.2005.211

Lee, J., Azamfar, M., & Singh, J. (2019). A blockchain enabled Cyber-Physical System architecture for Industry 4.0 manufacturing systems. *Manufacturing Letters, 20*, 34–39. doi:10.1016/j.mfglet.2019.05.003

Liang, X., Shetty, S., Tosh, D. K., Zhao, J., Li, D., & Liu, J. (2018). A Reliable Data Provenance and Privacy Preservation Architecture for Business-Driven Cyber-Physical Systems Using Blockchain. *International Journal of Information Security and Privacy, 12*(4), 68–81. doi:10.4018/IJISP.2018100105

Lin, I. C., & Liao, T. C. (2017). A survey of blockchain security issues and challenges. *International Journal of Network Security, 19*(5), 653–659.

Liu, C., Vengayil, H., Lu, Y., & Xu, X. (2019). A cyber-physical machine tools platform using OPC UA and MTConnect. *Journal of Manufacturing Systems, 51*, 61–74. doi:10.1016/j.jmsy.2019.04.006

Llamuca, J. D., Garcia, C. A., Naranjo, J. E., Rosero, C., Alvarez-M, E., & Garcia, M. V. (2019, November). Integrating ISA-95 and IEC-61499 for Distributed Control System Monitoring. In *Conference on Information Technologies and Communication of Ecuador* (pp. 66-80). Springer.

Lucas-Estañ, M. C., Sepulcre, M., Raptis, T. P., Passarella, A., & Conti, M. (2018). Emerging trends in hybrid wireless communication and data management for the industry 4.0. *Electronics (Basel), 7*(12), 400. doi:10.3390/electronics7120400

Maw, A., Adepu, S., & Mathur, A. (2019). ICS-BlockOpS: Blockchain for operational data security in industrial control system. *Pervasive and Mobile Computing, 59*, 101048. doi:10.1016/j.pmcj.2019.101048

Mehta, B. R., & Reddy, Y. J. (2014). *Industrial process automation systems: design and implementation.* Butterworth-Heinemann.

Mondragon, A. E. C., Mondragon, C. E. C., & Coronado, E. S. (2018, April). Exploring the applicability of blockchain technology to enhance manufacturing supply chains in the composite materials industry. In *2018 IEEE International conference on applied system invention (ICASI)* (pp. 1300-1303). IEEE. 10.1109/ICASI.2018.8394531

Nawari, N. O., & Ravindran, S. (2019). Blockchain and the built environment: Potentials and limitations. *Journal of Building Engineering, 25*, 100832. doi:10.1016/j.jobe.2019.100832

Nguyen, D. D., & Ali, M. I. (2019, June). Enabling On-Demand Decentralized IoT Collectability Marketplace using Blockchain and Crowdsensing. In *2019 Global IoT Summit (GIoTS)* (pp. 1-6). IEEE.

Nilsson, J., Bernhardsson, B., & Wittenmark, B. (1998). Stochastic analysis and control of real-time systems with random time delays. *Automatica, 34*(1), 57–64. doi:10.1016/S0005-1098(97)00170-2

O'donovan, P., Gallagher, C., Bruton, K., & O'Sullivan, D. T. (2018). A fog computing industrial cyber-physical system for embedded low-latency machine learning Industry 4.0 applications. *Manufacturing Letters, 15*, 139–142. doi:10.1016/j.mfglet.2018.01.005

Oktian, Y. E., Witanto, E. N., Kumi, S., & Lee, S. G. (2019, February). BlockSubPay-A Blockchain Framework for Subscription-Based Payment in Cloud Service. In *2019 21st International Conference on Advanced Communication Technology (ICACT)* (pp. 153-158). IEEE. 10.23919/ICACT.2019.8702008

Oztemel, E., & Gursev, S. (2020). Literature review of Industry 4.0 and related technologies. *Journal of Intelligent Manufacturing*, *31*(1), 127–182. doi:10.100710845-018-1433-8

Pal, D., Vain, J., Srinivasan, S., & Ramaswamy, S. (2017, September). Model-based maintenance scheduling in flexible modular automation systems. In *2017 22nd IEEE International Conference on Emerging Technologies and Factory Automation (ETFA)* (pp. 1-6). IEEE. 10.1109/ETFA.2017.8247738

Pedro, A. S., Levi, D., & Cuende, L. I. (2017). *Witnet: A decentralized oracle network protocol.* arXiv preprint arXiv:1711.09756.

Pérez-Lara, M., Saucedo-Martínez, J. A., Marmolejo-Saucedo, J. A., Salais-Fierro, T. E., & Vasant, P. (2018). Vertical and horizontal integration systems in Industry 4.0. *Wireless Networks*, 1–9.

Petroni, B. C. A., de Moraes, E. M., & Gonçalves, R. F. (2018, August). Big Data Analytics for Logistics and Distributions Using Blockchain. In *IFIP International Conference on Advances in Production Management Systems* (pp. 363-369). Springer. 10.1007/978-3-319-99707-0_45

Petroni, B. C. A., Reis, J. Z., & Gonçalves, R. F. (2019, September). Blockchain as an Internet of Services Application for an Advanced Manufacturing Environment. In *IFIP International Conference on Advances in Production Management Systems* (pp. 389-396). Springer. 10.1007/978-3-030-29996-5_45

Pinna, A., & Ibba, S. (2018, July). A blockchain-based Decentralized System for proper handling of temporary Employment contracts. In *Science and information conference* (pp. 1231–1243). Springer.

Pinto, S., Gomes, T., Pereira, J., Cabral, J., & Tavares, A. (2017). IIoTEED: An enhanced, trusted execution environment for industrial IoT edge devices. *IEEE Internet Computing*, *21*(1), 40–47. doi:10.1109/MIC.2017.17

Pongnumkul, S., Siripanpornchana, C., & Thajchayapong, S. (2017, July). Performance analysis of private blockchain platforms in varying workloads. In *2017 26th International Conference on Computer Communication and Networks (ICCCN)* (pp. 1-6). IEEE. 10.1109/ICCCN.2017.8038517

Raikwar, M., Mazumdar, S., Ruj, S., Gupta, S. S., Chattopadhyay, A., & Lam, K. Y. (2018, February). A blockchain framework for insurance processes. In *2018 9th IFIP International Conference on New Technologies, Mobility and Security (NTMS)* (pp. 1-4). IEEE. 10.1109/NTMS.2018.8328731

Rehman, M., Javaid, N., Awais, M., Imran, M., & Naseer, N. (2019, December). Cloud based secure service providing for IoTs using blockchain. *IEEE Global Communications Conference (GLOBCOM)*. 10.1109/GLOBECOM38437.2019.9013413

Rehman, M. H. U., Yaqoob, I., Salah, K., Imran, M., Jayaraman, P. P., & Perera, C. (2019). The role of big data analytics in industrial Internet of Things. *Future Generation Computer Systems*, *99*, 247–259. doi:10.1016/j.future.2019.04.020

Reyna, A., Martín, C., Chen, J., Soler, E., & Díaz, M. (2018). On blockchain and its integration with IoT. Challenges and opportunities. *Future Generation Computer Systems*, *88*, 173–190. doi:10.1016/j.future.2018.05.046

Saraph, V., & Herlihy, M. (2019). *An Empirical Study of Speculative Concurrency in Ethereum Smart Contracts*. arXiv preprint arXiv:1901.01376.

Schäffer, M., di Angelo, M., & Salzer, G. (2019, September). Performance and scalability of private Ethereum blockchains. In *International Conference on Business Process Management* (pp. 103-118). Springer. 10.1007/978-3-030-30429-4_8

Schulz, K. F., & Freund, D. (2018, July). A multichain architecture for distributed supply chain design in industry 4.0. In *International Conference on Business Information Systems* (pp. 277-288). Springer.

Seok, B., Park, J., & Park, J. H. (2019). A Lightweight Hash-Based Blockchain Architecture for Industrial IoT. *Applied Sciences (Basel, Switzerland)*, *9*(18), 3740. doi:10.3390/app9183740

Serpanos, D., & Wolf, M. (2018). Industrial internet of things. In *Internet-of-Things (IoT) Systems* (pp. 37–54). Springer. doi:10.1007/978-3-319-69715-4_5

Sharma, K. L. S. (2016). *Overview of industrial process automation*. Elsevier.

Shih, C. S., & Yang, K. W. (2019, September). Design and implementation of distributed traceability system for smart factories based on blockchain technology. In *Proceedings of the Conference on Research in Adaptive and Convergent Systems* (pp. 181-188). 10.1145/3338840.3355646

Shirazi, B. (2019). Cloud-based architecture of service-oriented MES for subcontracting and partnership exchanges integration: A game theory approach. *Robotics and Computer-integrated Manufacturing*, *59*, 56–68. doi:10.1016/j.rcim.2019.03.006

Sisinni, E., Saifullah, A., Han, S., Jennehag, U., & Gidlund, M. (2018). Industrial internet of things: Challenges, opportunities, and directions. *IEEE Transactions on Industrial Informatics*, *14*(11), 4724–4734. doi:10.1109/TII.2018.2852491

Smirnov, A., & Teslya, N. (2018, July). Robot Interaction Through Smart Contract for Blockchain-Based Coalition Formation. In *IFIP International Conference on Product Lifecycle Management* (pp. 611-620). Springer. 10.1007/978-3-030-01614-2_56

Stodt, J., Jastremskoj, E., Reich, C., Welte, D., & Sikora, A. (2019, September). Formal Description of Use Cases for Industry 4.0 Maintenance Processes Using Blockchain Technology. In *10th IEEE International Conference on Intelligent Data Acquisition and Advanced Computing Systems: Technology and Applications (IDAACS)* (Vol. 2, pp. 1136-1141). IEEE. 10.1109/IDAACS.2019.8924382

Tao, F., Cheng, J., & Qi, Q. (2017). IIHub: An industrial Internet-of-Things hub toward smart manufacturing based on cyber-physical system. *IEEE Transactions on Industrial Informatics*, *14*(5), 2271–2280. doi:10.1109/TII.2017.2759178

Tramarin, F., Mok, A. K., & Han, S. (2019). Real-time and reliable industrial control over wireless LANs: Algorithms, protocols, and future directions. *Proceedings of the IEEE*, *107*(6), 1027–1052. doi:10.1109/JPROC.2019.2913450

Vatankhah Barenji, A., Li, Z., Wang, W. M., Huang, G. Q., & Guerra-Zubiaga, D. A. (2019). Blockchain-based ubiquitous manufacturing: A secure and reliable cyber-physical system. *International Journal of Production Research*, 1–22.

Vatcharatiansakul, N., & Tuwanut, P. (2019, July). A performance evaluation for Internet of Things based on Blockchain technology. In *2019 5th International Conference on Engineering, Applied Sciences and Technology (ICEAST)* (pp. 1-4). IEEE. 10.1109/ICEAST.2019.8802524

Vitturi, S., Zunino, C., & Sauter, T. (2019). Industrial communication systems and their future challenges: Next-generation Ethernet, IIoT, and 5G. *Proceedings of the IEEE, 107*(6), 944–961. doi:10.1109/JPROC.2019.2913443

Voulgaris, S., Fotiou, N., Siris, V. A., Polyzos, G. C., Jaatinen, M., & Oikonomidis, Y. (2019). Blockchain Technology for Intelligent Environments. *Future Internet, 11*(10), 213. doi:10.3390/fi11100213

Wan, J., Li, J., Imran, M., Li, D., & Fazal-e-Amin. (2019). A blockchain-based solution for enhancing security and privacy in smart factory. *IEEE Transactions on Industrial Informatics, 15*(6), 3652–3660. doi:10.1109/TII.2019.2894573

Weiser, M. (1991). The Computer for the 21st Century. *Scientific American, 265*(3), 94–105. doi:10.1038cientificamerican0991-94 PMID:1675486

Wollschlaeger, M., Sauter, T., & Jasperneite, J. (2017). The future of industrial communication: Automation networks in the era of the internet of things and industry 4.0. *IEEE Industrial Electronics Magazine, 11*(1), 17–27. doi:10.1109/MIE.2017.2649104

Xu, L. D., Xu, E. L., & Li, L. (2018). Industry 4.0: State of the art and future trends. *International Journal of Production Research, 56*(8), 2941–2962. doi:10.1080/00207543.2018.1444806

Yan, Y., Duan, B., Zhong, Y., & Qu, X. (2017, October). Blockchain technology in the internet plus: The collaborative development of power electronic devices. In *IECON 2017-43rd Annual Conference of the IEEE Industrial Electronics Society* (pp. 922-927). IEEE.

Yu, Z., Yan, Y., Yang, C., & Dong, A. (2019, March). Design of online audit mode based on blockchain technology. *Journal of Physics: Conference Series, 1176*(4), 042072. doi:10.1088/1742-6596/1176/4/042072

Zhao, Q. (2020). Presents the Technology, Protocols, and New Innovations in Industrial Internet of Things (IIoT). In *Internet of Things for Industry 4.0* (pp. 39–56). Springer. doi:10.1007/978-3-030-32530-5_3

Zheng, Z., Xie, S., Dai, H. N., Chen, X., & Wang, H. (2018). Blockchain challenges and opportunities: A survey. *International Journal of Web and Grid Services, 14*(4), 352–375. doi:10.1504/IJWGS.2018.095647

Zhong, S., Zhong, H., Huang, X., Yang, P., Shi, J., Xie, L., & Wang, K. (2019). *Security and Privacy for Next-Generation Wireless Networks*. Springer International Publishing. doi:10.1007/978-3-030-01150-5

Zhu, Q., & Kouhizadeh, M. (2019). Blockchain technology, supply chain information, and strategic product deletion management. *IEEE Engineering Management Review, 47*(1), 36–44. doi:10.1109/EMR.2019.2898178

Chapter 12
Blockchain in Philanthropic Management:
Trusted Philanthropy With End–to–End Transparency

Sini Anna Alex
Ramaiah Institute of Technology, India

Anita Kanavalli
Ramaiah Institute of Technology, India

Drishya Ramdas
Ramaiah Institute of Technology, India

ABSTRACT

In the world of cutting-edge technology, a buzzword that has been thrown around quite often is blockchain. It has gained prominence in a wide array of fields ranging from the money transfer industry to that of the healthcare sector. The primordial reason for this varied use is the concept of smart contract that makes it intangible and less susceptible to errors. Using this platform of blockchain, the authors propose an avant-garde method of contributing donations to charities through a pivotal body, namely the trust. This application is paramount in the sense that it binds the advancements made on the technological frontier with the social aspect of life, that is, charities in the form of NGO's or other such beneficiaries. This enforces the scrupulous way of donating, ensuring that the money does not get consumed by outsiders or any third-party bodies because ultimately, safeguarding the needs and necessities of the lesser privileged folks is the primary goal, which should be addressed with immediate effect.

DOI: 10.4018/978-1-7998-6694-7.ch012

I. INTRODUCTION

The blockchain wave is one that has consumed the minds of many and is a platform that has piqued the interests of all. A formidable introduction to blockchain will be that it is an incorruptible digital ledger of economic transactions that can be programmed to record not just financial transactions but virtually everything of value. Transactions are congregated into "blocks," and the chain of these is what gives the technology its unique name. Above anything else, the most crucial and substantial area where Blockchain has a major role to play is to develop assurance of validity of a transaction. This is done by recording it not only on a main register but on a connected distributed system of registers, all of which are affixed through a dependable validation technique. The blockchain is a distributed database of records of all transactions or digital events that have taken place and apportioned among participating parties. Each transaction is authenticated by the greater number of partakers of the system. It contains every single record of each settlement.

The blockchain technology promotes the concept of 'trust' in the following manner:

1. Distributed: The distributed ledger is portioned out and is re-equipped with every incoming transaction among the nodes associated to the Blockchain network. All this is done in real-time as there is no eminent server supervising the vital information;
2. Secure: There is no unaccredited ingress to Blockchain made possible through Permissions and Cryptography;
3. Transparent: Since every node or participant in Blockchain has a facsimile of the Blockchain data, they can retrieve all the transaction data. They themselves can validate the identities without the need or necessities for third party entries;
4. Consensus-based: All pertinent network participants must come to the same terms that a transaction is valid. This is materializable through the use of consensus algorithms;
5. Flexible: Smart Contracts which are engineered based on indubitable circumstances can be penned into the platform. Blockchain Network can make headway by pacing exponentially with business operations and undertakings.

With the help of this unique and indispensable way of transacting resulting in a systematic approach of deducting and reimbursing money to the necessary partakers of the consensual network, we levy this as the fundamental platform to go about establishing our proposed methodology.

II. LITERATURE SURVEY

The paper Blockchain for Social Impact-Moving Beyond the hype briefly touches upon the promise and potential of the very famous Blockchain related technology. It goes on to talk about the impact that would be bestowed upon the sectors, primarily the social and humanitarian related ones. It then goes on to deliberate if the technology is promising or just a mere hype. Based on the reports and surveys conducted, the inference that could be drawn is that the various aspects of Blockchain will touch and leave a long-lasting impression on the way people and societies interact which is the fundamental premise of automating the way donations are being made. It comments on the prospective to transform the way these sectors are perceiving technology and how leapfrog infrastructure can be attained through the same. (Galen et al., 2018)

Vishrambh: Trusted Philanthropy with end-to-end Transparency elucidates on how Philanthropy is a massive sector throughout the world and how it is rapidly growing in India. This seems to be critical as it requires a significant amount of attention and care. They have collected data to show the dire condition of these sectors and how the use of Blockchain can be developed to merge the technical, social aspects to resolve and address the challenges currently existing in this domain. They have worked with several payment options to provide an effortless and seamless experience to the donors. (Mehra, 2018)

A Brief Introduction to the Science of Fundraising talks about how the field of philanthropy is an emerging platform and presents few critical insights of the same. The empirical study demonstrated the fact that crafting charitable appeals, contacting donors and promoting annual campaigns produces the best return on investments. It highlights the hope on encouraging collaboration between practitioners and researchers, thereby providing several valuable observations. The donors would like to know if their donation has made an impact and that should be taken care of with utmost importance. Overall, the perceived impact conditions should be addressed and developed sustainably to ensure optimal growth of the economy. (Whillans, 2016)

This paper elaborates on the significance of Social business as a prototype that deals with speculation in order to revolutionize the lives of the lower strata of the society. This can be done for good conviction such as removing penury, enforcing the well-being and not for better profit. The referred paper focuses on the collaborative and compassionate objectives of the varied aspects of fundraising and not on the enterprising domain. Task of Social business is to safeguard invested funds in such a way that spent amount should be proportional to the planned budget. Unfortunately, social business does not have any expedients to obtain funds because of wrong-doing, poor-management and misuse of funds. One of the discussed use cases deals with process of investing funds for nourishment of poor people and growth of society through micro-finances. Conventionally, Social Business acts as a middle man in this process, whose task is collecting funds from the donors and giving it to the much-needed supplicant who is eligible for borrowing. This phenomenon entails some of the problems such as enforcement of trust between the organization and donor, securing private details of donor, donor's visibility to transaction which is carried out by the social business to supplicant and unavailability of funds to fulfil the planned activities. In order to surpass these notable problems, Blockchain technology can be applied as solution through which straightforward and explicit observations can be identified in the transactions. By doing so the trust factor will be taken care of, thereby providing a remarkable rise in the donation amount received. Also, participants involved in business network will be distinguished either through their private or public key so that their personal information is protected and secured. Few of the limitations of Blockchain implementations of social business is being discussed here as well. Firstly, Cryptocurrencies cannot be used for transactions as they have an obvious exchanging problem with normal currencies. Secondly, the users involved in business network have to be trained. Although block chain has few limitations, its implementation is vital in every sphere of life as it leads to an exemplary standard of living among all sections of the society. (Github,)

In previous work, 'radical transparency' proposed by Blockchain technology that overdoes public credulity and mistrust is discussed. The idea of 'smart contracts' is put forward to convey the possibilities of the new business circumstances to fix philanthropy at its fundamental root. It looks at the present state of philanthropy and identifies the dire need of donation to improve the daily lifestyle. An aggregation of the opportunities and ultimatums faced by philanthropic organizations is presented. The problems faced by society and an innovative manner in which charities can raise funds are also proposed. The donation of assets which are intangible in nature, with the help of new models of colored coins that represent such assets is also put forward. This is inculcated, considering the effect Blockchain will have upon the creation and regulation of charities. It builds upon the idea that costs reduce, regulation can be significantly more effective without the need for independent regulatory organizations. We also contemplate that it can be the end of conventional charity regulation in due course of time. (IBM Hyperledger, n.d.)

III. Existing Methodology

The existing system is non-technical and is just a mere prototype of concepts. It is a combination of thoughts and ideas with no practical implementation globally. It is a theory that is implemented well in 'just a handful of countries. Technology for social good is just a concept and not a phenomenon that we see in today's world. There are certain organizations like BitGive that leverage Bitcoin and Blockchain technology to provide greater transparency to donors by sharing the project information only. The drawback is that they do not give the real time statistical information. Since research shows 43% of people don't trust charities, people hope to improve that trust with distributed ledgers, smart contracts, cryptocurrencies and make the nonprofit sector more transparent. Alice, a London based startup has shared the impact data reducing due diligence and reporting costs, thereby helping social organizations collaborate more effectively. The existing methodology fails in the sense that donor does not know whether their money was put to good use and even if it was, where did it exactly go. It is this uncertainty that makes this process impractical and difficult to use. The lack of knowledge and satisfaction brings about an air of curiosity in the heart of the donor which automatically, prevents he/she from donating again the next time. This is how the exponential downgrowth of this sector can be visualized and understood (Medium, n.d.). The rapid decline in this sector has a direct significance in the real world. It can be perceived as a wholesome problem that touches not only the lives of many but enforces a negative impact on their lifestyle and day-to-day activities (Weking & Mandalenakis, 2020). This causes a downfall in the country's economy and most significantly, badly influencing the lives of the larger portion of the society who are economically on the further end of the spectrum.

IV. PROPOSED METHODOLOGY

The problem definition that we are tackling at hand right now is based on the fact that there are several NGO's present in our society and the major problem that they face is; whatever funding they receive, only a tiny amount of it goes directly to the grassroots of the NGO's. This is unacceptable as the money donated for a charitable cause gets misused and does not reach the deserving, the needy and those who are in dire need of it. So, we are developing a system using blockchain to bring about a change in the way donations are made to the organizations who promote social concern and public welfare. Therefore, end result of this project is to generate a platform which will ensure full transparency and accountability in the donations made. Another feature of donating funds to the NGO's whose situation is critical is also taken care of in our project. The implementation is achieved using Hyperledger Fabric (IBM, n.d.). Hyperledger Fabric has become the de-facto standard for enterprise blockchain platforms. It offers a unique approach to consensus that enables performance at scale while preserving privacy to deliver an interoperable network-of-networks. Through open source and open governance, it features innovative new capabilities hardened for use by businesses, ushering in a new era of trust, transparency, and accountability. It also provides a unique platform which has a multitude of features that makes it flexible, attractive, and easy to use in comparison to the existing method. They can be seen as follows:

1. Permissioned network: Establish decentralized trust in a network of known participants rather than a public network with no identity;
2. Confidential transactions: Expose only the data you want to share to the parties you want to share it with;
3. Pluggable architecture: Tailor the blockchain to industry needs with a pluggable architecture rather than a one size fits all approach;
4. Easy to Get Started: Program smart contracts in the languages your team works in today instead of learning custom languages and architectures.

Hyperledger Fabric v1.4 LTS is adding powerful production-focused features to the enterprise-grade, permissioned and distributed ledger framework for developing solutions. Hyperledger Fabric allows components, such as consensus and membership services, to be plug-and-play. Hyperledger Fabric leverages container technology to host smart contracts called "chain code" that comprise the application logic of the system.(Blockchain, n.d.)[8]

The complete problem definition, from the creation of business network to the transfer of funds to the respective NGO's in need, can be scaled down to sequence of steps as follows. Initially, the algorithm depicts the formation of the business network along with the participants. The scenario of block generation once the donation is made by the donor to the trust is proposed by the DBLOCKGENERATION algorithm. In order to distribute the funds to the NGOs who are in a dire need, the scheduling algorithm is invoked by the trust to ensure that the NGOs where an actually necessity is present, receives the funds and it is distributed equally among them. Finally, the funds get transferred to the NGO's and the block is generated, just like the manner it is proposed in the TBLOCKGENERATION algorithm.

The algorithms for the same can be seen as follows:

STEP 1: Start
STEP 2: Create an empty business network
STEP 3: Add participants to the network
STEP 4: Assign access permissions to the participants based on their role in the network.
STEP 5: Initialization of the list COUNT which holds the counters (for each NGO) that records the number of donations made to the respective NGO by the trust.
STEP 6: IF (Donor donates)
Invoke DBLOCKGENERATION()
Invoke SCHEDULING()
STEP 7: ELSE
STEP 7(i): Invoke SCHEDULING()
STEP 7(i.a): Initialize an empty list FINAL to store the selected NGO's that has to be donated to.

STEP 7(i.b): Compares the recent inventory entry of each NGO to decide which has to be donated to, based on the needs.

STEP 7(i.c): IF (Multiple NGO's have the same need)

STEP 7(i.d): IF (NGO's have the same value of the counter)

Add the selected NGOs to the FINAL.

STEP 7(i.e): ELSE

Select the NGO with the lower count.

Add the selected NGO to the FINAL

End IF-ELSE

STEP 7(i.f): ELSE

Add the selected NGO to the FINAL.

End IF-ELSE

END IF-ELSE

STEP 8: Transfer of funds by the trust to the NGO.

STEP 8(i): IF (FINAL is not empty)

STEP 8(i.a): IF (FINAL has only one selected NGO)

Invoke TBLOCKGENERATION()

Increment the counter of the NGO that has been donated.

STEP 8(i.b): ELSE

Divide the funds in an equal manner among the NGOs in FINAL.

WHILE (FINAL is not empty)

Invoke TBLOCKGENERATION()

Increment the counter of the NGOs that have been donated.

END WHILE

END IF-ELSE

STEP 8(ii): ELSE

Save the funds for future needs.

END IF-ELSE

STEP 9: GOTO STEP 6

DBLOCKGENERATION algorithm

STEP 1: IF (Transaction details are valid)

Creation of block with the fields index, timestamp, hash, previous hash, data and nonce.

Block hash generation

Include the participants to the block wherein the sender is the donor and the receiver is the trust.

The block is added to the blockchain network.

STEP 2: ELSE

The transaction gets declined

```
END IF-ELSE.
TBLOCKGENERATION algorithm
STEP 1: IF (Transaction details are valid)
Creation of block with the fields index, timestamp, hash, previous hash, data
and nonce.
Block hash generation
Include the participants to the block wherein the
sender is the trust and the receiver are the NGO's.
The block is added to the blockchain network.
STEP 2: ELSE
The transaction gets declined
END IF-ELSE
```

The algorithm has briefly covered the working of the model in the most basic and brief manner. It is crucial in the sense that, it touches upon all the procedural elements and how each module is connected to the other. It is also highly helpful to understand and analyze the conceptual methodology that is being proposed here. The intricate details of each and every step of the algorithm and how it works in cohesion are explained in detail, diagrammatically below. This can be visualized using the activity diagrams given below depicting different scenarios:

SCENARIO 1

An empty business network is created. In order to be a part of the network, the participant is authenticated and verified. On successful verification, the participant is a part of the network. The access control rules are assigned to each participant who is a part of the network. If the participant is an NGO, then a COUNT is assigned to each NGO to keep track of the number of times the NGO has been donated to by the trust. Overall, a business network with the participants as the donor(s), trust and NGO(s) is formed and a list COUNT is initialised.

SCENARIO 2

This scenario deals with the transfer of funds by the donor to the trust. The donor enters the details of the transaction, upon successful verification of the transaction, a block is generated with a unique transaction id and timestamp. The transaction gets stored in the ledger which can be viewed and verified by all the participants of the network. Overall, it's the functionality of the DBLOCKGENERATION() that is described.

SCENARIO 3

In this scenario, the SCHEDULING() functionality is described. The donated fund is received by the trust. The list FINAL stores the NGO(s) that has to be donated to by the trust. Each NGO maintains an

Figure 1.

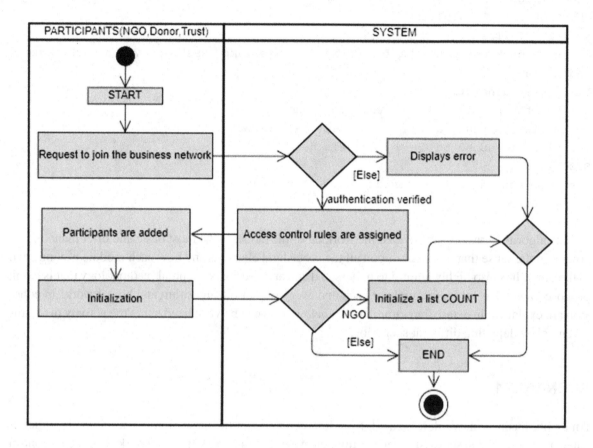

Figure 2.

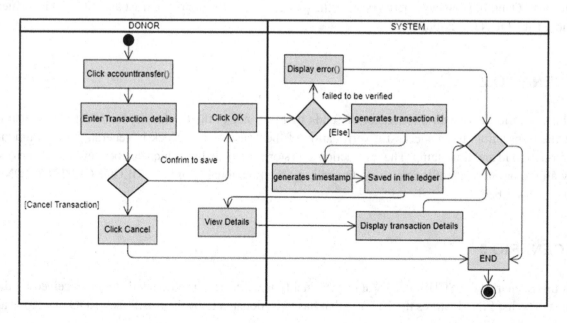

Figure 3.

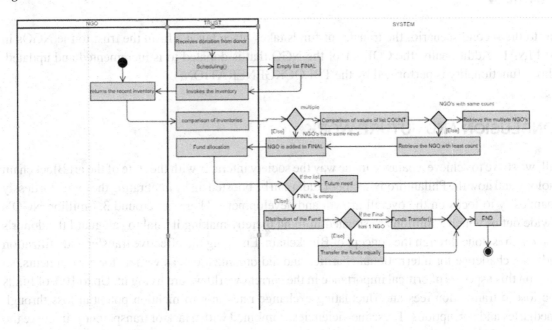

inventory that records the recent needs of the NGO. The trust invokes the recent inventory entry of each NGO and is compared to know the actual needs of the NGO. The NGO in need of the basic necessities is added to the list FINAL. If multiple NGO are in need of the basic necessities, then the COUNT values of respective NGOs is compared. The NGO with the least count is added to list FINAL. If there exists multiple NGOs with the same count, then multiple NGOs gets added to the list FINAL and the funds get distributed equally among them. If at all none of the NGOs are in need and the list FINAL is empty, then the funds are saved for future need.

Figure 4.

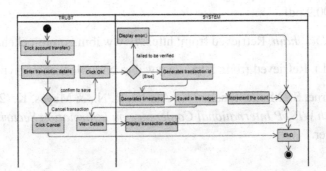

SCENARIO 4

Similar to the second scenario, the transfer of funds takes place but it's from the trust to the NGOs in the list FINAL. Additionally, the COUNT of the NGO that is donated to is incremented and updated. The above functionality is performed by the TBLOCKGENERATION().

V. CONCLUSION AND FUTURE WORK

Overall, we strive to achieve a balance in the way the society interacts with the state of the art Blockchain Technology and how the Philanthropy sector of India can be boosted up by integrating the two effortlessly and seamlessly to focus on the overall growth and development. There are around 3.7 million NGO's worldwide out of which 2 million are situated in India thereby making it vital to safeguard the donor's interest which is done through the concept of Blockchain. Ensuring the effective transfer and utilization of funds is a challenge for international charities and aid organizations as well as for governments, so focusing on this aspect is of critical importance in the current world we are living in. Up to 10% of funds may be lost in transaction fees and fluctuating exchange rates, not to mention potential loss through intermediaries and corruptions. These inefficiencies, combined with a lack of transparency, increase the risk of misuse of funds and perpetuate a lack of trust in the organizations responsible. Moreover, there is always a thought in people as to where their donation went and whether it was put to use effectively or not. Having a novel methodology which ensures transparency and safeguards the interest of the donors as he/she is sure of its proper utilization is indispensable and essential in a variety of ways. The misuse of the donations made will never take place and supposing if it does happen, the required actions can always be taken care of. Retrospectively, this paper can also be used for future implementations using the Hyperledger Fabric to understand what has happened and how it can be put to use for substantial applications and uses.

REFERENCES

Blockchain. (n.d.). Retrieved from: https://blockchaindemo.io/

Galen, Brand, Boucherle, Davis, Do, El-Baz, Kimura, Wharton, & Lee. (2018). Center for Social Innovation. *RippleWorks*.

Github. (n.d.). Retrieved from: https://github.com/alicesi/whitepaper/blob/master/Alice%20white%20paper%20-%20FV%200.9.pdf

IBM. (n.d.). *What is Blockchain*. Retrieved from: https://www.ibm.com/blockchain/what-is-blockchain

IBM Hyperledger. (n.d.). Retrieved from: https://www.ibm.com/blockchain/hyperledger

Jayasinghe, D., Cobourne, S., Markantonakis, K., Akram, R. N., & Mayes, K. (2016). Philanthropy On The Blockchain. In *11th WISTP International Conference on Information Security Theory and Practice (WISTP'2017)*. Springer.

Medium. (n.d.). https://medium.com/bpfoundation/https-medium-com-bpfoundation-charitable-giving-blockchain-case-studies-14f0c9f9d13f

Mehra, A. (2018). Vishrambh: Trusted philanthropy with end-to-end transparency. In HCI for Blockchain: A CHI 2018 workshop on Studying, Critiquing, Designing and Envisioning Distributed Ledger Technologies. Academic Press.

Weking, J., & Mandalenakis, M. (2020). *The impact of blockchain technology on business models – a taxonomy and archetypal patterns. In Electron Markets*. Springer.

Whillans, A. V. (2016). *A Brief Introduction to the Science of Fundraising*. Council for Advancement and Support of Education.

Chapter 13

Blockchain and IoT Integration in Dairy Production to Survive the COVID–19 Situation in Sri Lanka

ruwandi Madhunamali
Sabaragamuwa University of Sri Lanka, Sri Lanka

K. P. N. Jayasena
Sbaragamuwa University of Sri Lanka, Sri Lanka

ABSTRACT

The epidemic crises place massive burdens on our economies. The risk of food supplies is also pushing massive stress on food vendors around the world. There are big problems associated with supply chains framework. Farmers do not receive payment upon delivery of their supplies. The buyers do not have access to finance that will enable them to pay farmers on time. To solve this problem, the authors proposed a dairy production system integration with blockchain and IoT. Blockchain is a decentralized digital ledger technology that allows network participants to trust each other and interact. The dairy product system can check the temperature of the product in real-time by using the website application. Moreover, customers can get notifications when the policy found problems related to temperature values. The blockchain database confirms the information security of the system by using the proof of work algorithm to create the transactions and the blocks. Therefore, the proposed methods can use sensitive data with reasonable time consumption, and no block creation fees are needed.

INTRODUCTION

Every day we consume food products on the basis of the confidence because that providers are produced, warehouse and transported in agreement with the internal and government regulations on food safety. Before reaching the end consumer, food product moving through different phases of supply chain from

DOI: 10.4018/978-1-7998-6694-7.ch013

suppliers to retailers. These intermittent stages contribute to product design, manufacture, delivery, and sales. Although food safety measurements do periodic and provide certifications of the quality, it is often difficult to trust when searching a supply chain scaling across countries with the distribution of technology. For example, The United States stopped imports of meat from Brazil due to the acceptance of bribes by food examiners in Brazil, the horsemeat scandal in Europe, the milk powder of babies' scandal in China and the growing problem of food pollution in India. Over the past decade, these incidents have occurred periodically, pushing consumers and governments to request greater transparency throughout the food supply chain(Bosona & Gebresenbet, 2013)(Aung & Chang, 2014).

Based on Food and Drink research, organizations decide, increasing consideration of the food provenance as a business challenge. They are finding business opportunities through increasing health awareness. Nowadays consumers highly consider the quality of food product so they hesitate to purchase. It is because there is no way to ensure the quality of the food product and less transparency through the supply chain process of the product. So the organizations are identified that customers are always looking for trusted products with verified sources. For that, they are plan to get a competitive advantage by providing service with transparent food supply chain and sustainable manufacturing. For example, Walmart has joined with IBM to study. They were together from February 2018 to test whether the organization can guarantee the Health of food products that they sell in their retail stores. Nevertheless, contemporary repositories for each silo stage of the logistic transportation are ineffective in giving unparalleled trust to the client, because they are not dishonest. A lot of food supply chains today only check their product end of the logistic transportation processes and still there is no way to map their product in source and stages between customers.

Although the different phases of the food supply chain contain many possible adverse results such as Irreversible disruption to the environment, abuse of working conditions, unethical manufacturing practices, counterfeiting and large quantities of agricultural waste attributable to imbalanced sourcing and storage strategies. End users tend to use these programs without realizing the repercussions that they create by their footprint and food supply chains are easily kept hidden with little effort to provide end-to-end access to their stakeholders. Although these challenges, the idea of requiring a single agency to provide data and transaction control in food supply chain was the only realistic solution until recently when a modern system called blockchain provided a whole modern way of addressing food provenance.

BACKGROUND

Supply Chain

Throughout the years, global supply chains are getting increasingly complicated. Therefore, it is very difficult to manage continuously within the industry as sustainable, because the problems many foreign buyers (including large retailers and brand owners) and consumers are concerned about, where monitoring and analysis of their transportation supply networks relies on many suppliers, distributors and delivery centers, some of them uncommon or even one-time. (Venkatesh, Kang, Wang, Zhong, & Zhang, 2020a)(Petri Helo & Shamsuzzoha, 2020). Supply chains are not fixed. It develops and changes in size, shape, and configuration, and in how they are coordinated, controlled and managed. Not only the economic drivers but also the technological drivers affect the changes in the supply chain. As a result of that, digital technology integrates with supply chain management. The new step introduces as "Supply

Chain Digitization". Digitization may play a leverage role in aligning current sourcing strategies as well as developing new sourcing strategies to enhance long-term efficiency, productivity, and competitive advantage overall organizational objectives.

In a dairy supply chain, a network of stakeholders transacts to the end consumer in the form of rising, storing or selling foods. Transport companies act as links which connect these stages and ensure that the right quantity and quality product reaches the right destination at the right time

The stakeholders include:

1. Milk suppliers.
2. The milk processors engaged in the manufacture and sometimes distribution of the milk commodity
3. The distributer active in the sale to end consumers and dealers of the finished product.
4. The end customers engaged in shopping the items, which consists of individuals and markets.

Blockchain

Considered one of the most innovative innovations available, the blockchain first showed up in 2008 when published "Bitcoin: A Peer-to-Peer Electronic Cash System". The scheme suggested was based on cryptographic proof rather than dependency, allowing any two parties to perform transactions without the need of a trustworthy third party. The plan solved the issue of double spending(Kosba, Miller, Shi, Wen, & Papamanthou, 2016)(Wright & De Filippi, 2015). This is the first application of blockchain, Created by Satoshi Nakamoto (Nakamoto, 2008). There are many critical features, that blockchain provides. Such as Decentralized, Traceability, Consensus mechanism, Immutability, Smart contract(Yumna, Murad, Ikram, & Noreen, n.d.)(Madumidha, Ranjani, Varsinee, & Sundari, 2019). Blockchain application contain distributed architecture. That mean of distributed architecture is the program does not rely on any centralized authority but uses a peer-to - peer application server network operated by the owners of decentralized interests (P. Helo & Hao, 2019)(Tezel, Papadonikolaki, Yitmen, & Hilletofth, 2019). Today blockchain is applications further than finance, as in government, health, science, arts and culture(Frizzo-barker et al., 2019)(Pilkington, 2016). A number of applications are already being discussed in the energy market, such as a blockchain based smart grid (Scully & Hobig, 2019). Within that network, Blockchain technology enforces transparency and ensures ultimate, system-wide agreement on the validity of a full transaction history. No major group controls the data in the Blockchain. Any party can see the entire data infrastructure. So that it helps to minimize the bias errors.(Treiblmaier, 2018) Every atutharized person in blockchain can confirm the detail of its transaction followers directly, without a Mediator or ledger unauthorized access or manipulation. Though many are speculating about the effect of blockchain technology on supply chains, the present accepting of its potential remains limited. As this technology is still in its infancy, developing and diffusing (Wang et al., 2018).

Every node inside a blockchain have encrypted keys named public and private key, and each transaction within two nodes contains some important facts about the sender and the receiver, asset information, date, and identifier for the sender 's previous transaction. An asset may be any commodity within a supply chain, or a buyer-seller exchange. A cryptographic hash function named SHA 256 (Secure Hash Algorithm 256) uses the sender's public key and transactional information to produce a 16-digit hexadecimal string called the "tag". The hash done is special to a combination of a public key and transaction information. A group of randomly clustered transactions is one block. This authenticated transaction details is decoded to verify the validity of the transactions and their origin, which can be deciphered only by brute force.

The cycle of hash resolution is called mining, and miners are called nodes that validate certain transactions. When the network generates a block from the pool of unchecked transactions, available miners will be competing to validate the transactions by resolving the cryptographic hash

A consensus algorithm maintain the method of choosing a miner at a blockchain. Some network systems such as the Ethereum and Hyperledger projects are special. Every block within a blockchain contain of 3 important components - a hash (a unique digital identifier), a timestamp, and the hash of the previous block (to compute the account balance). The previous block hash ties the whole block chain together and thus stops any block being changed or added between two authenticated chains. When a transaction is checked, the blockchain records it. Changing a reported transaction value in a decentralized blockchain network such as Bitcoin is quite difficult because an intruder must obtain nearly 51 percent of the entire computing power existing in the framework. Therefore, each subsequent block enhances the verification of the preceding block and ultimately blockchain as a whole. This mechanism holds the blockchain resistant to malicious activities, contributing to the essential immutability attribute. Figure 1 shows blockchain structure.

In Ethereum, the blockchain system is controlled by rules decided upon by the participants in the network in the method of smart contracts and was firstly implemented in Bitcoin for running the mutual accounting ledger. It is commonly used after this initial financial use, when many players with little to no confidence are part of a transaction; for example, fragmented supply chains. Blockchain's three basic features make it an attractive choice for tracking supply chain assets

Figure 1. Blockchain structure

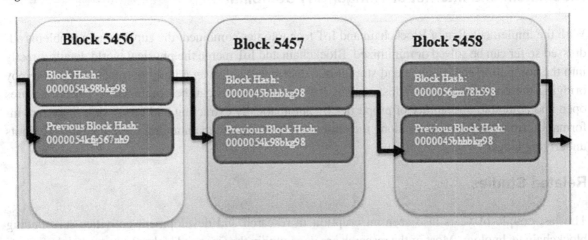

- **Distributed processing:** Does not require a central control system. The process is distributed to all processors or network members inserted in the process.
- **Synchronized records:** The ledger is circulated to all players and so it is fraud-proof.
- **Smart information:** We can build cloud applications that run within the blockchain architecture, allowing us to customize the data format that is available in the supply chain at every point.

Smart contracts

A smart contract is a program that is developed by programmer. Smart contract can activate certain functions robotically if anything predetermined happens. Intelligent contract contacts with the blockchain, the criteria are stored in "contracts" and must be met by the users in order to build a new block. The smart contract is not an integral part of the blockchain protocol itself, but a function on the network that is stored on a database within blockchain in a completely distributed way (Mattila, Seppälä, & Holmström, 2016).

Blockchain Technology in Supply Chain

Blockchains are already generating advantages on supply chains around the world. Real-time visibility can be considered an important benefit to supply chain management (Sheel & Nath, 2019). Furthermore, all transactions can be observable, and consequently. The data is organized into blocks which form a chain. All the transaction of a blockchain operate in a peer-to-peer network, in a decentralized way. Smart contracts inside distributed ledger are responsible for the validate and store transaction data, and it is not needed to have a central person that validates the transactions(Petri Helo & Shamsuzzoha, 2020). Almost all organizations need to take profit of several improvements carried about by blockchain, which spans improved process and operations over the whole supply chain, safer, efficient transactions with transparent and (Kshetri, 2018) and trust and reliability through the network, all processes and captured details being shared by all network members.

Blockchain and Internet of Things(IOT) Combination

With the implementation of Blockchain and IoT technologies combined, the supply chain problems addressed so far can be solved or minimized. Blockchain and IoT merge the physical world details directly into the computing environment and store it in a distributed ledger in a multi partner situation thereby bridging the confidence gap. Whilst various IoT sensor systems can be combined. It system ensures open and auditable traceability of properties by automatically extracting and processing important information from the IoT systems along the entire supply chain and maintaining these data directly in its underlying ledger.

Related Studies

The last couple of years also seen an eruption in research and development activities surrounding blockchain technology. Most of the research are done within the financial technology market. In fact, its intrinsic capacity to deliver immutable and manipulative records, together with its potential of enabling trust and reliability among untrusted peers represents too attractive features, preventing this technology to stay relegated into a single vertical sector. With the population of blockchain characteristics, several industries start researching this. Blockchain technology has already been identified as a driver for a paradigm shift in the financial sector.

Figure 2 Noteworthy, after the year 2015 all selected papers were published. It indicates that selected area to do the research is both new and original. Through all the papers selected, 1 paper (1.61%) has been published in 2016, 2 papers (3.22%) in 2017, 13 papers (20.96%) in 2018 and 46 papers (74.19%) in 2019 when zooming into the distribution year. Which represents increase in blockchain interest.

Figure 2. Publication year of the selected primary papers

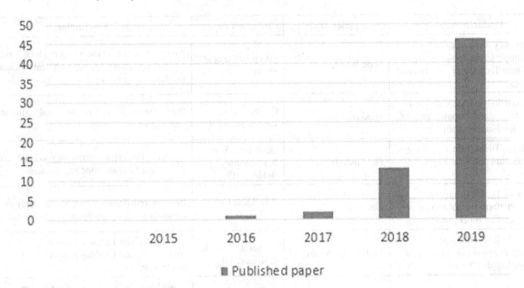

Blockchain technology is still in its infancy of marketing and while there are many industry experts who agree that there is a promising future for the deployment of this technology through industry, many others claim that there is an unrealistic assumption of blockchains that could, in turn, intensify the impact of the inability to implement blockchains in industry. However, while many unsuccessful attempts have been made to use blockchain technology, several successful business cases, such as those listed in this article, have also occurred. The latter provides a rather optimistic view that as more progress is made in overcoming the limits of blockchains, like many other emerging technologies, blockchains can find a position in operation and become popular.

Papers on blockchain, supply chain and blockchain integrated with supply chain management were read and the following results were obtained including the gaps in current studies, requirements in blockchain technology within supply chain management.

Table 1 represent what are the existing research topic and application area of them on supply chain on blockchain

For several specific supply chain scenarios, there are various deployed and conceptual systems, among them the food supply chain has become the hottest topic. The issues relating to food origin and safety are important problems that need to be addressed. There are some ongoing food supply chain projects or food traceability projects. More challenging applications are involving wine and agricultural foods. Pharma and drug industry, Blockchain also helps the electronics industry, since healthcare is also a major social problem.

The Importance of Blockchain Within any Supply Chain Industry

Supply chain management is a term that interaction together for controlling a distribution channel 's total process (Petri Helo & Szekely, 2005). Manage the supply chain is difficult as it involves dispersed practices from upstream, interacting with individuals, physical resources and manufacturing processes to downstream, covering the entire process of marketing; i.e. contracts, sales to customers, distribution and

Table 1. Existing research topics on Blockchain technology with supply chain

Research topic	Applied areas	Research Paper	Key finding
Transparency and Traceability: In Food Supply Chain System using Blockchain Technology with Internet of Things	Food industry	(Madumidha et al., 2019)	An effective system incorporating RFID and Blockchain technology is a technical mechanism for monitoring and locating products
A Blockchain-based decentralized system to ensure the transparency of organic food supply chain	Food industry	(Basnayake & Rajapakse, 2019)	Preparing an efficient and fair food certification architecture
The Rise of Blockchain Technology in Agriculture and Food Supply Chains	Food industry	(Kamilaris, Fonts, & Prenafeta-Boldó, 2019)	Applying blockchain technology to build reliable and secure farm and food supply chains
Framework Design of Financial Service Platform for Tobacco Supply Chain Based on Blockchain	Financial	(Liu, Li, & Cao, 2018)	Build system design for a tobacco supply chain financial service platform based on blockchain
Blockchain-Based Secured Traceability System for Textile and Clothing Supply Chain	Textile and clothing	(Agrawal, Sharma, & Kumar, n.d.)	Blockchain based Secure Traceability System with Textile and Clothing Supply Chain Implementation
Blockchain Framework for Textile Supply Chain Management	Textile	(Elmessiry & Elmessiry, 2018)	A full blockchain-based clothing quality assurance platform that allows cross-chain facts sharing with assured validity and precision in almost real time, allowing for the detection of product faulty lots in all networks as soon as they are identified in a few.
A Blockchain-Based Supply Chain Quality Management Framework	Global supply chains	(Chen et al., 2017)	Using blockchain technology to solve problems caused by lack of trust in the quality management of the supply chain and to achieve sophisticated product quality management
Blockchain in Supply Chain Trading	Global supply chains	(Al Barghuthi, Mohamed, & Said, 2019)	A well-functioning system of supply using a blockchain
Blockchain-based Soybean Traceability in Agricultural Supply Chain	Agriculture	(Salah, Nizamuddin, Jayaraman, & Omar, 2019)	Blockchain and Ethereum smart contracts will map and monitor effectively and make it possible to incorporate busy transactions and workflows in the agricultural supply chain without presence
Blockchains everywhere - a use-case of blockchains in the pharma supply-chain	Pharmaceutical industry	(Bocek, Rodrigues, Strasser, & Stiller, 2017)	Blockchain lets pharmaceutical supply chain to observer temperature and humanity over the distribution of medical products
How the Blockchain Revolution Will Reshape the Consumer Electronics Industry	Electronics industry	(Madhunamali, 2017)	Blockchain can improve efficiency and alignment of processes in consumer electronics supply chain management. Areas in which block chains can impact supply chains include a temper-proof history of product manufacture, handling and maintenance, digital ownership and packaging identification, smart contract sand interaction with customers in the supply chain
Can Blockchain Strengthen the Internet of Things?	Manufacturing/ physical distribution	(It, 2017)	Blockchain can play an important role in tracking sources of insecurity in supply chains and in managing crisis situations such as product recalls that arise after vulnerabilities in safety and security are identified

disposal (Tian, 2016). Aim of the supply chain is to create a multi stakeholder collaborative background through mutual trust, for eliminate communication problems, and ensure that the various companies are connected to pursue routinely the integration of the whole supply network. In the end, linked supply chain stakeholders will increase overall performance and add larger value and benefits to their business (Azzi, Chamoun, & Sokhn, 2019).

Blockchain can solve supply chain problems and even lead to numerous critical objectives of the supply chain management, such as cost, quality, speed, dependability, risk reduction, sustainability and flexibility (Kshetri, 2018)(Basnayake & Rajapakse, 2019)(Al Barghuthi et al., 2019)(Tönnissen & Teuteberg, 2019). Therefore, among the many other operations that are likely to be changed by blockchain the supply chain needs special consideration. Identified profits of applying blockchain in supply chain management are: Improve overall quality, Reduce cost, Shorten delivery time, Reduce risk, and Increase trust. In the following describe problems that address by blockchain in the supply chain.

1. **Differential Pricing:** Companies prefer keeping their pricings a secret, since this allows them to pay lower prices when outsourcing to developing countries.
2. **Numerous Parties Involved:** Mediating between so many parties can be a big problem for logistics-providers, slowing down the delivery of services and creating a large overhead for logistics. Furthermore, a centralized mediator of these parties can misuse power to prefer some parties over others.
3. **Quality & Compliance issues:** Procuring a replacement for defective parts is a long drawn and uncomfortable process.
4. **Inevitable Disruptions:** LEAN "on-demand" manufacturing falls flat in a situation where natural disasters and socio-economic problems are common. For example, Japan (frequently affected by earthquakes) has outsourced most of it's supply chain logistics to other countries.
5. **Centralization:** A central mediator for parties is required, which centralizes power in the hands of a few and is a gateway to misuse of resources.
6. **Fraud by Middlemen:** As number of interacting parties increase, there is a proportional increase in middlemen. They lead to fraud and slow down the supply without adding anything to the network.
7. **Tracking history of any product:** Validating identity vendor and checking for tampering by middlemen is not possible.

Blockchain characteristic for Supply Chain

1. **Quality assurance:** In the perspective of investigation & guidance to adopt required steps for the flawless high-quality production of goods & services, quality assurance makes a remarkable impact to make the business processes easier. (Yadav & Singh, 2019).
2. **Scalability in Supply chain management:** When facts noted in a block of the block chain, this characteristic ensures that it is non-variable & non-volatile. This leads to integrate blockchain without a risk of losing the data consistency.(Tönnissen & Teuteberg, 2019)(Madavi, 2008).
3. **Transparency:** Ensure peer to peer transactions are certified by minor at the end and make sure that the modified data not allow to changed or hacked. Also the assets of changing anything in the ledger stays on it makes the blockchain a transparent system. (Yumna et al., n.d.)(Pe & Llivisaca, n.d.)(Wu et al., 2019)(Casino, Dasaklis, & Patsakis, 2019)

Table 2. How to resolve them by applying blockchain

Problems	Solution
Differential Pricing	Permissioned ledger for confidential transactions between parties
Numerous Parties Involved	Consensus between multiple parties is maintained through Smart contracts
Quality & Compliance issues	Smart contract stores money while all solutions are checked and tested
Inevitable disruptions	Digital ledger is free of geographical constraints like natural disasters, socio-economic issues
Procuring replacements for defective pieces	Smart contract only lets out payments once both parties satisfied
Centralization	Risk of fraud is mitigated by using decentralized nodes for checking delivery status
Fraud by Middlemen	Because of using doubly-signed smart contracts, no financial fraud by middlemen can occur in the system
Tracking history of any product	Using network anyone can verify vendor identity and validity of product

4. **Integrity:** Provides management for the flow of physical goods in supply chain using integration of serial numbers, bar codes, sensors, digital tags like RFID, etc. Following this the flow of blockchain became smoother from manufacturer to end-user.(Yadav & Singh, 2019)(Litke, Anagnostopoulos, & Varvarigou, 2019)

5. **Solving the double spend problem:** Solves the issue of data transaction which cannot be sent to two or more people at the same time. With the help of authenticated peer to peer transaction after the verification by a minor. (Yadav & Singh, 2019)(Bartling & Fecher, 2016)

6. **Immutability and encryption**: After confirming the transaction or data flow from one center to another, changes are not allowed since any change on the block chain cannot be stored without the solidarity of the network (Yumna et al., n.d.)(Schmidt & Wagner, 2019)(Wu et al., 2019).

7. **Efficiency:** The high rate of data flow speed without an intermediator, smart contracts easily traceable and further, it streamlines the process considerably saving time and money. (Pe & Llivisaca, n.d.)(Ahram, Sargolzaei, Sargolzaei, Daniels, & Amaba, 2017).

8. **Security:** Once the creation of block is completed changes or deletion is not applicable. This feature makes the safety of Supply Chain more refine after the adoption of blockchain in the existing traditional methods. (Pe & Llivisaca, n.d.)(Tönnissen & Teuteberg, 2019)(Casino et al., 2019)

9. **Removal of intermediaries:** Blockchain create the platform for a straight business deal eliminating the involvement of intermediaries or a third party(Yadav & Singh, 2019)(Weber et al., 2016)

10. **Reduction in administrative cost:** Reduction in cost of the paper and other consumable items, time-saving, quick discussion, better management, administration & shared databases ease administrative work. (Tönnissen & Teuteberg, 2019)(Osei, Canavari, & Hingley, 2018)

11. **Decentralization:** Blockchain is a system of teaming up gatherings with a database that is decentralized. This implies that most of the gatherings team up on a blockchain have their own duplicate of the considerable number of exchanges that put away on the blockchain.(Yumna et al., n.d.)(Schmidt & Wagner, 2019)(Wu et al., 2019)(Kharlamov, Parry, & Clarke, n.d.)(Lai, 2019)

12. **Traceability and visibility:** Trust-worthy system is imparted by blockchain technology by knowing the origin of a product by offering real-time, live and consistently connected updates(Yumna et al., n.d.)(Kharlamov et al., n.d.)(Venkatesh, Kang, Wang, Zhong, & Zhang, 2020b)(Kamilaris, Fonts, Prenafeta-Boldú, et al., 2019)

The Blockchain based supply chain network focused in reference implementation. This research methodology was chosen in this research because blockchain is still in its infancy. Our goal is to create a model to satisfy the demand for supply chain related operations, while at the same time ensuring that records are safe and transparent across all activities. Nonetheless, it is difficult to transit from modern supply chain to the Blockchain based supply chain as it is not smooth.

Companies must pose the knowledge and capability in blockchain to adopt it. Furthermore, blockchain technology is still in its early stage in terms of industrial application development. It is full of uncertainties such as whether the blockchain is suitable for the required process, whether the practitioners have the working out and required technical development. Moreover, It is important to realize that industrial solutions based on blockchain should start with the willingness of the stakeholders to cooperate and to be involved. They need to reach consensus on building knowledge and capabilities in blockchain with a focus on providing value for all stakeholders. So, creating a culture of collaboration is critical. Scalability is holding back early adoptions of blockchain in supply chains or in other similar areas. By definition, each computer that is connected to the same network will process the transactions. Organizations must compromise productivity to achieve protection. Therefore, in terms of technical infrastructure there is a high demand which will be more expensive than traditional approach.

According to the characteristics of blockchain, stakeholders who use this blockchain based supply chain system will advantage more when the number of joining users grows in this community. When more and more players in the supply chain participate, blockchain becomes more relevant and credible, and develops into market practice. This can be especially difficult as there are legacy processes, regulations and laws that regulate different facets of the company as stakeholders can incur costs as transitioning from legacy systems and combining with new systems and practices. In the future, due to the competitive nature of industry, many companies will be putting effort into the blockchain based logistics network, not just in the private sector but also in public agencies. To ensure interoperability between different blockchain based platforms, it is therefore necessary to establish standards and agreements.

Gaps in Existing Research

If considering the all researches of the study, Most of the identified gaps had to do with outside reasons such as administrative and technical sides.

- The first obstacle is conformity with the laws and the legal barriers restricting Blockchain technology implementation. Common standards for completing transactions are missing (Tribis, El Bouchti, & Bouayad, 2018).
- The second difference is the failure to adapt and acceptance. Mostly society are unaware about how to operates and produce the great difficulty of getting together all parties concerned and convincing supply chain players to change their traditional supply chain to the current blockchain based system(Tribis et al., 2018)(P. Helo & Hao, 2019).

- The third difference relates to scalability and scale. Most of the proposed blockchain-based architectures have been evaluated in a laboratory environment only on a limited scale; including a number of nodes, certain difficulties that occur in scaling blockchains network.
- The latest blockchain implementations are basically small in size. Next gap that identified is Strong computerization demand. Nevertheless, many supply chain participants are not able to adopt blockchain in the developing countries.
- Complexity and uncertainty of the development is the next gap. The delay of transactions that last for several hours until all parties upgrade their ledgers and a smart contract can be access to the public, but the details needed for authentication may or may not be available to everyone.
- Implementation cost of the adaptation is high. For blockchain process, it requires a virtual network and it depends on the electricity, infrastructure and hardware computing systems. These gaps are that most of the frameworks proposed systems were not tested for real world design applications, Researchers should therefore find the viability of blockchain based solutions and test their applicability to industry (Salah et al., 2019).

However, work on t blockchain supply chain management is only in its early stages and should find future applications (Longo, Nicoletti, Padovano, d'Atri, & Forte, 2019)(Yadav & Singh, 2019). Most of the supply chain operations, especially small and medium-sized companies, state they know nothing about blockchain technology, and that they find the influence of blockchain as a menace. To increase understanding of blockchain, a prototype of a blockchain-based logistics monitoring system, frameworks based solution have real performance evaluation in the industrial context(Tribis et al., 2018)(Wamba, 2019).

In Sri Lanka, there is no measurement to measure the readiness to accept blockchain in supply chain management. And also there is less researches have done in this area. This research aims to solve supply chain management challenges with blockchain implementation in the Sri Lankan food supply chain industry. Therefore, for filling some gaps in the literature, this research will be a great support.

MAIN FOCUS OF THE CHAPTER

While the challenges involved in implementing a transparent supply chain are huge, the benefits of applying blockchain to the dairy supply chain far outweigh the disadvantages (initial capital investment cost and maintenance). The advantages of an active blockchain can be narrowly defined as a financial advantage, the benefits of the authorities and the benefits of the food companies. For simplicity's sake, however, the benefits can be classified as enhancing consumer loyalty, improving food crisis management, improving dairy supply chain management, expertise and technical innovation, and contributing to sustainable agriculture. There is an emerging rich network of devices and sensors that build an ecosystem rich in data for efficient monitoring and analysis of properties, which was unlikely in supply chains several years ago. This evolution has now allowed us to use this technology to create a blockchain network that provides as mentioned in this research a lot of possible benefits.

Many of the potential risks and the lack of demonstrable evidence the implementation of blockchain in the supply chain is currently sluggish. Nonetheless, businesses are trying to consider the positives or drawbacks of blockchains in supply chains.

Problem Definition

The emergence of digital businesses transforms conventional market models and, mainly, how we do it. The flow of industry has intensified in a environment today running 24 hours. This has changed the way businesses collaborate, trade and connect with customers, vendors and partners. Suppliers and the supply chain have an effect on everything: from efficiency, distribution and expense, to customer support, loyalty and benefit. Enterprise globalization expanded the difficulty of the supply chain processors. Now it is a main component to improve and integrate the information system. The difficulty of taking decisions needs real-time data sharing (Yu, Wang, Zhong, & Huang, 2016). When information moved in a linear form in conventional supply chains and inefficiencies in one stage influenced the following cascade stages, Digital supply networks are now capable of building interconnected networks capable of overcoming the action-reaction cycle with real-time data and facilitating cooperation. The figure 3 shows the move from the traditional supply chain to the digital supply network (Mussomeli, Gish, & Laaper, 2015).

Figure 3. The evolution of Supply chain

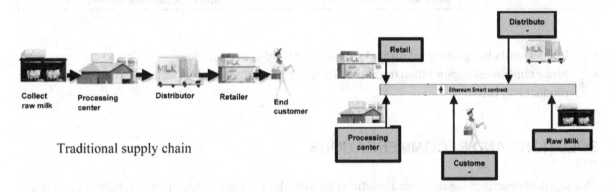

Traditional supply chain

Digital supply chain network

According to this, emphasis on how blockchain affects the supply chain. To have this done, Possible applications and implementation of blockchain are discussed in the supply chain to help businesses understand how to achieve their business goals. Furthermore, A logistics management program based on blockchain is applied to evaluate the viability of applying blockchain in the food supply chain. Accordingly, the major objective of this research is to fill current research gaps, new approaches to integrate blockchain and IoT technology within food supply chain, and food quality management in the Sri Lankan food supply chain system. This study has following objectives also.

- Improve the scalability of any business by increasing customers' experience and more awareness about blockchain.
- Provide Trust for the entire supply chain network through blockchain agreement(consensus)
- Improve the privacy of the supply chain system by facilitating access control over who will have access to the information in the block.

Table 3. Current problems and blockchain impact in supply chain system

Supply chain actor	Current Problems	Blockchain impact
Famer/Supplier	Capability to prove the origin and quality metrics of goods using a global and clear process.	Benefits from the improved trust by maintaining track by raw material production and supply chain from the raw material to the end customer.
Processor	Poor ability to track the goods produced to the final destination. Small ability to analyze measured content from raw material.	Value added from shared facts system with suppliers of raw materials and distribution networks.
Distributor	Customized monitoring devices with limited ability to work together. Limited certification skills and confidence issues.	Ability to have proof of position recorded in the database, and conditions certifications.
Wholesaler	Lack of confidence, and certification of the product path.	Capacity to test the origin of the products and the conditions for transformation or transportation.
Retailer	Lack of confidence, and certification of the product path.	Tracking any single commodity between the wholesaler and the final customer. Capacity to manage the returns of malfunctioning goods efficiently.
Consumer	Lack of trust about the product's compliance with the requirements and origin defined for the origin, quality and enforcement of the product.	Complete and clear view of the sources of the product and its entire journey from the raw material to the purchased finished product.

- Reduce costs by ignoring additional payment for third-party persons.
- Make consumers happier than traditional food supply chain system in terms of transparency of the product and price.

SOLUTIONS AND RECOMMENDATIONS

This segment describes the suggested solution that using blockchain within ethereum network and smart contracts to trace, track, and perform transactions in dairy supply chains. This approach eliminates the need for a trustworthy centralized authority and allows transactions and store the transaction information for food supply chain management. Table 4 describe how blockchain based model address the issues in current dairy supply chain.

The suggested approach would concentrate on the use of autonomously implemented smart contracts on the decentralized blockchain Ethereum network. Functions of the smart contract execution and conduct by thousands of mining nodes. The mining nods are globally distributed, and the execution outcome is agreed by all of the mining nodes.

Additionally, any actor or participant must have an Ethereum account in blockchain and they have to have a unique Ethereum address. This helps to identify the actor in a unique way. The Ethereum account basically consists of the Ethereum address with public and private keys that are used to sign and verify the data integrity within each transaction cryptographically and digitally, and associate each transaction with a specific Ethereum address or account.

Figure 4 shows how combination of IoT blockchains within the food supply chain. This chart describes the process of tracking information from raw milk, processing details, transport information, quality of manufactured product, etc. That will finally bring value in the customer's hands to the finished product.

Table 4. Problems that address by blockchain in the dairy supply chain

Issues in the existing Supply chain system	The solution is given by proposed mechanism
Lack of trust about the product's compliance with the requirements and origin defined for the origin, quality and enforcement of the product.	Complete and clear view of the sources of the product and its entire journey from the raw material to the purchased finished product.
Require a central party to maintain the dairy supply chain transactions.	facilitate the platform for do the transaction directly without the interference of intermediaries or a third party IoT sensors track the data and smart contract validate them and added to the blockchain.
Have to manually enter the data about dairy transaction.	Reduction in paper and another consumable item, time saving. automatically detect and store the data in to blockchain
In traditional dairy supply chain, manually check temperature, volume and quality of milk. It is time consuming.	Information flow speed, no intermediary, smart contracts, simple traceability and ultimately streamlining the processes considerably

This architecture captures information regarding traceability using a range of IoT devices based on the type of event to be recorded. A transaction could be a movement of milk product, processing or store of milk, Distribute. Multiple data recorded from an IoT checkpoint is converted into a transaction and pushed to the Ethereum network. All the transaction data check and validate within the smart contract and then publish to the public ledger. The contract layer monitors every transaction data, to execute the smart contracts when an initial event takes place and it ensures expected data about the raw milk or milk product from the supplier, manufacture and distributor in the supply chain according to terms of trade agreed upon connecting to the blockchain network.

Each entity involved plays a role, relationship, and interactions with the smart contract. Propose model contain only five participating entities. Here describe their role:

Milk Supplier: As per the depiction milk suppliers have access to web applications. Through that application they can view information that they using IoT sensor. IoT will play a key role in the capture and transmission of this information from raw milk to the Blockchain.

Milk Processor: In these premises and storage locations, IoT sensors can significantly improve traceability and support end consumers with information of product storage requirements such as physical density, temperature, volume, etc. The status of several environmental or physical and product related characteristics can help to assess the quality of the finished product before and after manufacture, its freshness and other consuming characteristics. Aberrations can be very dangerous during production and this information isn't available today. This can be made available and evaluated with the IoT network system, which help to determine the root cause causes if anything goes wrong or any complications found through random sample checks.

Distributer: Nowadays consumer can get only few information about transporting these products. Capturing IoT data at the time of travel or factory exit analysis will greatly help close this significant gap. The sensors will capture the physical storage conditions in the trucks / ocean freight warehouse and make it accessible in the blockchain network. Diverse partners can access this information and produce informed product decisions based on smart contracts. Where authenticity and transparency are required, and also this information can be rendered to end customers.

Retailer: The emphasis on product safety and freshness is of vital importance for a retailer. Data are available in blockchain that can be traced and analyzed right from farm to fork. In addition to that, the IoT Blockchain architecture can help to obtain the information from source / origin until final consumption.

Customer: The customer is the end user who buys and uses the retailer's product.

Figure 4. Supply chain solution with IoT Blockchain model architecture

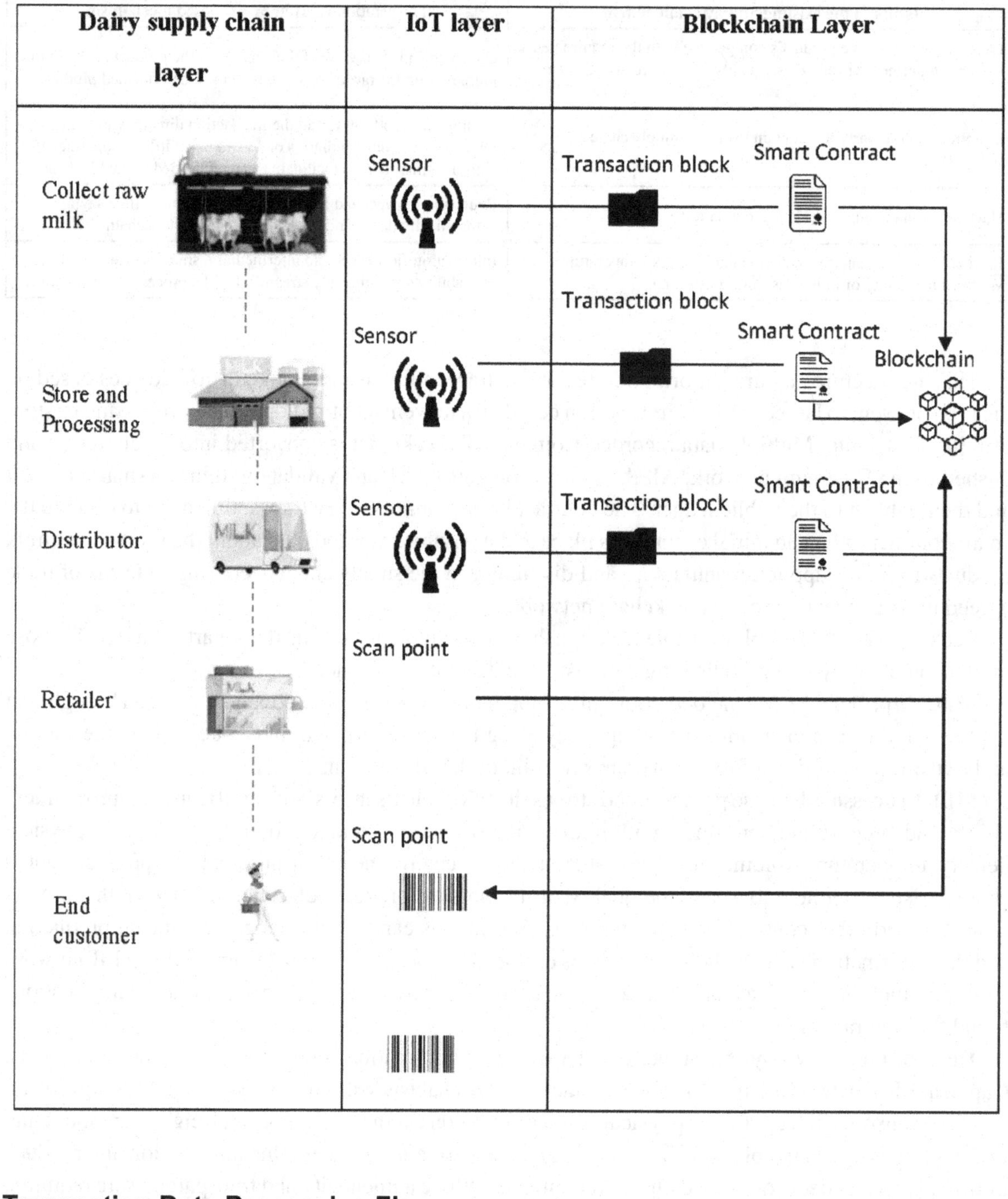

Transaction Data Processing Flow

Figure 5 describe the transaction data processing flow of storing data in the blockchain. IoT devices generate data such as density, temperature, volume, etc. After digital signing and the hashing, such data

Figure 5. Transaction Data Processing Flow

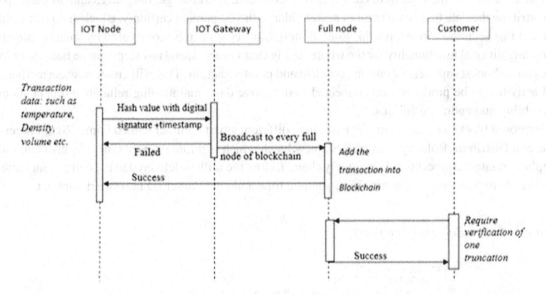

will be sent directly or through the IoT gateways to the entire blockchain network nodes, where they are verified, connected to the Transaction Pool and stored in blockchain.

Customers can access and validate all transaction data via their laptops or mobile phones. For example, one buys a package of milk from a supermarket and then he or she can use a mobile to check the 2-D barcode to gather all the transaction data relevant to it, including the farm from which the milk was made, the day and time it was delivered, the cow ID on the farm, the workers ID processing the milk, the collection of computer information, the packaging information, all the temperature. All of that information can be verified without human intervention by the blockchain system.

Traceable Functionality

Using our suggested blockchain based approach utilizing smart contracts, the benefit of using traceable technology in the dairy supply chain is that all actors without a core authority within the supply chain have verifiable and non-modifiable details accessible. The whole volume of milk products sold between subsequent entities is logged to the next echelon starting with supplier and manufacturing transactions, and all transactions can be verified. For example, with the agreed terms, it is impossible to alter or change the volume of milk sold between entities. In addition, milk with various quality standards cannot be combined together for sale, because all stakeholders are aware with total quantity.

The use of traceable identifiers per lot and the ability to trace all relevant transactions between stakeholders further ensure continuous quality enforcement monitoring. It is also possible to monitor the quality of the milk and conditions using IoT enabled containers and packages equipped with sensors, cameras, GPS locator, and 4G communication with blockchain, such knowledge and verification cannot be changed or tampered with, and usable automatically and open to all stakeholders in a transparent and decentralized way, without intermediaries.

It should be remembered that a stakeholder can steal or may transact and record fraudulent data. The blockchain, in this situation, marks the data as such with a validated reference to the source data (i.e. the real stakeholder). If the data were caught to be incorrect at a later stage, the judges and all participants can attribute the data to a given actor or stakeholder with 100 percent certainty. Blockchain can identify fraud in that scenario. To resolve this kind of theft, blockchain can be configured by smart contracts to provide additional functionality for the whole supply chain process, and any steps can be taken to enforce fines on dishonest suppliers or take appropriate and punitive action. This will create new corrective data and activities to be produced and connected to deceptive data, maintaining reliable and unchallenged traceability and audit capabilities.

Proposed blockchain based model have three different smart contract named FamerRoal, Processor-Role and DistributerRole. System creates a new batch which is initial stage of dairy supply chain. Milk supplier initiate the process of dairy supply chain. Before the milk is delivered to the dairy manufacturer, capture the temperature of the raw milk, volume, time and date, famer ID into smart contract.

Figure 6. FarmerRole smart contract

```
uint256 public temp;
using Roles for Roles.Role;
event FarmerAdded(address indexed account);
event FarmerRemoved(address indexed account);
Roles.Role private farmers;

constructor() public {
  _addFarmer(msg.sender);
}
modifier onlyFarmer() {
  require(isFarmer(msg.sender), "Caller is not a farmer.");
  _;
}
function isFarmer(address account) public view returns (bool) {
  return farmers.has(account);
}
function addFarmer(address account) public onlyOwner {
  _addFarmer(account);
}
function renounceFarmer() public onlyOwner {
  _removeFarmer(msg.sender);
}
function _addFarmer(address account) internal {
  farmers.add(account);
  emit FarmerAdded(account);
}
function _removeFarmer(address account) internal {
  farmers.remove(account);
  emit FarmerRemoved(account);
}
function setTemperature(uint256 temp) public {
    temp = temp;
  }
function getTemperature() external view returns (uint256) {
    return temp;
  }
function checkTemp() external view returns (string){
    if(temp<=5 ){
        return "Correct temperature";
    }else{
        return "Incorrect temperature";
```

Figure 6 shows FarmerRole smart contract. The initial contractual state is determined, the smart contract checks to confirm that the applicant farmer is already registered, the temperature of the raw milk and volume. If the scenario is successful, then the contractual state will change to ProcessorRole. Famer state changes to manufacture and first block added to the blockchain. ProcessorRole smart contract same as the farmer role contract in this stage describes the process of milk product. Most important criteria to consider in this stage are packaging date time, processor name, unique Id of the milk product and check the temperature of raw milk for the product. At this stage, the contract has to check two condition. First one is the requesting milk processor is a registered entity and second one is the quality of the milk is agreed (temperature, volume). If these two requirements are valid or met, the contract state will be changed to DistributorRole. Manufacture state change to distributer. In the other case, if the above two conditions are not fulfilled, change the contract state to ProcessorRoleFail, processor state changes to RequestFailure, the cancel the process.

At the distributor stage retailer buy the product from distributer. The date of manufacture of the product and the amount sold are some important parameters to keep a check. The distributor and retailers will have their Ethereum addresses identified. For execute the DistributerRole smart contract, authorized distributer have to input date about transport information and warehouse information of the milk product. Then smart contract check and validate distributor role. Above each and every success transaction add a new block to the blockchain. This is how the dairy supply chain complete for one batch. In this way store all the batch information into blockchin database. Using smart tag with barcode reader batch information can show for the outside user. Retailer and customer are final role of the system. They can verify the entire history of a product before buying it in a transparent manner. Each package may be associated with smart tags, so retailers and consumers can easily retrieve the entire product history.

FUTURE RESEARCH DIRECTIONS

Future research efforts can concentrate on defining the different compensation mechanisms to be used within the blockchain network to promote a consistent transfer of power as to how the transactional data can be used within the food supply chain. A major technological transition such as the introduction of blockchains is only possible if it is driven by the company in certain stages of the value chain with a larger impact on the sector. Therefore it would be interesting to find out how the power balance between retailers and food processors would change the blockchain model proposed. Another possible research problem to answer is blockchain scalability.

CONCLUSION

Food provenance is one of the most challenging questions that companies in the food supply chain are trying to solve today and this research is a small contribution to answering that question. The primary aim of this research is to establish a blockchain platform that can be applied within a food supply chain and include its advantages and disadvantages in terms of food provenance and product traceability over conventional tracking systems It is clear from this research initiative that blockchains can be more effective in monitoring food provenance, avoiding significant degradation of food items, detecting and eliminating the source of foodborne disease in seconds, whereas contemporary systems may take as many weeks. It would also provide greater customer confidence that reflects the satisfaction of sales and customers.

REFERENCES

Agrawal, T. K., Sharma, A., & Kumar, V. (n.d.). *Blockchain-Based Secured Traceability Chain*. Academic Press.

Ahram, T., Sargolzaei, A., Sargolzaei, S., Daniels, J., & Amaba, B. (2017). Blockchain technology innovations. *2017 IEEE Technology and Engineering Management Society Conference. TEMSCON, 2017*, 137–141. Advance online publication. doi:10.1109/TEMSCON.2017.7998367

Al Barghuthi, N. B., Mohamed, H. J., & Said, H. E. (2019). Blockchain in Supply Chain Trading. *ITT 2018 - Information Technology Trends: Emerging Technologies for Artificial Intelligence*, 336–341. doi:10.1109/CTIT.2018.8649523

Aung, M. M., & Chang, Y. S. (2014). Traceability in a food supply chain: Safety and quality perspectives. *Food Control*, *39*(1), 172–184. doi:10.1016/j.foodcont.2013.11.007

Madhunamali, A. T. H. E. (2017). *How the Blockchain Revolution Will Reshape the Consumer Electronics Industry*. Academic Press.

Azzi, R., Chamoun, R. K., & Sokhn, M. (2019). Computers & Industrial Engineering The power of a blockchain-based supply chain. *Computers & Industrial Engineering, 135*(August), 582–592. doi:10.1016/j.cie.2019.06.042

Bartling, S., & Fecher, B. (2016). Could Blockchain provide the technical fix to solve science's reproducibility crisis? *Impact of Social Sciences Blog*.

Basnayake, B. M. A. L., & Rajapakse, C. (2019). A Blockchain-based decentralized system to ensure the transparency of organic food supply chain. *Proceedings - IEEE International Research Conference on Smart Computing and Systems Engineering, SCSE 2019*, 103–107. 10.23919/SCSE.2019.8842690

Bocek, T., Rodrigues, B. B., Strasser, T., & Stiller, B. (2017). *Blockchains Everywhere - A Use-case of Blockchains in the Pharma Supply-Chain*. Academic Press.

Bosona, T., & Gebresenbet, G. (2013). Food traceability as an integral part of logistics management in food and agricultural supply chain. *Food Control*, *33*(1), 32–48. Advance online publication. doi:10.1016/j.foodcont.2013.02.004

Casino, F., Dasaklis, T. K., & Patsakis, C. (2019). A systematic literature review of blockchain-based applications: Current status, classification and open issues. *Telematics and Informatics*, *36*, 55–81. doi:10.1016/j.tele.2018.11.006

Chen, S., Shi, R., Ren, Z., Yan, J., Shi, Y., & Zhang, J. (2017). A Blockchain-Based Supply Chain Quality Management Framework. *Proceedings - 14th IEEE International Conference on E-Business Engineering, ICEBE 2017 - Including 13th Workshop on Service-Oriented Applications, Integration and Collaboration, SOAIC 207*, 172–176. 10.1109/ICEBE.2017.34

Elmessiry, M., & Elmessiry, A. (2018). *Blockchain Framework for Textile Supply Chain Management*. doi:10.1007/978-3-319-94478-4

Frizzo-barker, J., Chow-white, P. A., Adams, P. R., Mentanko, J., Ha, D., & Green, S. (2019). International Journal of Information Management Blockchain as a disruptive technology for business : A systematic review. *International Journal of Information Management, 0–1*(April). Advance online publication. doi:10.1016/j.ijinfomgt.2019.10.014

Helo, P., & Hao, Y. (2019). Blockchains in operations and supply chains: A model and reference implementation. *Computers & Industrial Engineering, 136*(July), 242–251. doi:10.1016/j.cie.2019.07.023

Helo, P., & Shamsuzzoha, A. H. M. (2018, December). Real-time supply chain—A blockchain architecture for project deliveries. *Robotics and Computer-integrated Manufacturing, 63*, 101909. doi:10.1016/j.rcim.2019.101909

Helo, P., & Szekely, B. (2005, January). Logistics information systems: An analysis of software solutions for supply chain co-ordination. *Industrial Management & Data Systems, 105*(1), 5–18. Advance online publication. doi:10.1108/02635570510575153

It, S. (2017). *Can Blockchain Strengthen the Internet of Things?* Academic Press.

Kamilaris, A., Fonts, A., & Prenafeta-Boldú, F. X. (2019). The rise of blockchain technology in agriculture and food supply chains. *Trends in Food Science & Technology, 91*, 640–652. doi:10.1016/j.tifs.2019.07.034

Kamilaris, A., Fonts, A., Prenafeta-Boldú, F. X., Kamble, S. S., Gunasekaran, A., Sharma, R., ... Beynon-Davies, P. (2019). How the blockchain enables and constrains supply chain performance. *Supply Chain Management, 24*(4), 376–397. doi:10.1108/IJPDLM-02-2019-0063

Kharlamov, A., Parry, G., & Clarke, A. C. (n.d.). *Advanced Supply Chains : Visibility, Blockchain and Human Behaviour*. Academic Press.

Kosba, A., Miller, A., Shi, E., Wen, Z., & Papamanthou, C. (2016). Hawk: The Blockchain Model of Cryptography and Privacy-Preserving Smart Contracts. *Proceedings - 2016 IEEE Symposium on Security and Privacy, SP 2016*. 10.1109/SP.2016.55

Kshetri, N. (2018). Blockchain's roles in meeting key supply chain management objectives. *International Journal of Information Management, 39*(June), 80–89. doi:10.1016/j.ijinfomgt.2017.12.005

Lai, J. (2019). Research on Cross-Border E-Commerce Logistics Supply under Block Chain. *Proceedings - 2nd International Conference on Computer Network, Electronic and Automation, ICCNEA 2019*, 214–218. 10.1109/ICCNEA.2019.00049

Litke, A., Anagnostopoulos, D., & Varvarigou, T. (2019). Blockchains for Supply Chain Management: Architectural Elements and Challenges Towards a Global Scale Deployment. *Logistics, 3*(1), 5. doi:10.3390/logistics3010005

Liu, H., Li, Z., & Cao, N. (2018). *Framework Design of Financial Service Platform for Tobacco Supply Chain Based on Blockchain* (Vol. 2). doi:10.1007/978-3-030-05234-8

Longo, F., Nicoletti, L., Padovano, A., d'Atri, G., & Forte, M. (2019). Blockchain-enabled supply chain: An experimental study. *Computers & Industrial Engineering, 136*(July), 57–69. doi:10.1016/j.cie.2019.07.026

Madavi, D. (2008). *A Comprehensive Study on Blockchain Technology.* International Research Journal of Engineering and Technology.

Madumidha, S., Ranjani, P. S., Varsinee, S. S., & Sundari, P. S. (2019). Transparency and traceability: In food supply chain system using blockchain technology with internet of things. *Proceedings of the International Conference on Trends in Electronics and Informatics, ICOEI 2019*, 983–987. 10.1109/ICOEI.2019.8862726

Mattila, J., Seppälä, T., & Holmström, J. (2016). Product-centric Information Management. *A Case Study of a Shared Platform with Blockchain Technology.*

Mussomeli, A., Gish, D., & Laaper, S. (2015). The Rise of the Digital Supply network. *Deloitte.*

Nakamoto, S. (2008). *Bitcoin: A Peer-to-Peer Electronic Cash SyNakamoto, S. (2008). Bitcoin: A Peer-to-Peer Electronic Cash System. Consulted.* Consulted. doi:10.100710838-008-9062-0stem

Osei, R. K., Canavari, M., & Hingley, M. (2018). An Exploration into the Opportunities for Blockchain in the Fresh Produce Supply Chain. doi:10.20944/preprints201811.0537.v1

Pe, M., & Llivisaca, J. (n.d.). Advances in Emerging Trends and Technologies. *Blockchain and Its Potential Applications in Food Supply Chain Management in Ecuador., 3*, 101–112. doi:10.1007/978-3-030-32022-5

Pilkington, M. (2016). Blockchain technology: Principles and applications. Research Handbooks on Digital Transformations. doi:10.4337/9781784717766.00019

Salah, K., Nizamuddin, N., Jayaraman, R., & Omar, M. A. (2019). Blockchain-Based Soybean Traceability in Agricultural Supply Chain. *Blockchain-based Soybean Traceability in Agricultural Supply Chain, 7*(May), 73295–73305. Advance online publication. doi:10.1109/ACCESS.2019.2918000

Schmidt, C. G., & Wagner, S. M. (2019). Journal of Purchasing and Supply Management Blockchain and supply chain relations : A transaction cost theory perspective. *Journal of Purchasing and Supply Management, 25*(4), 100552. doi:10.1016/j.pursup.2019.100552

Scully, P., & Hobig, M. (2019). Exploring the impact of blockchain on digitized Supply Chain flows: A literature review. *2019 6th International Conference on Software Defined Systems, SDS 2019*, 278–283. 10.1109/SDS.2019.8768573

Sheel, A., & Nath, V. (2019). Effect of blockchain technology adoption on supply chain adaptability, agility, alignment and performance. *Management Research Review, 42*(12), 1353–1374. Advance online publication. doi:10.1108/MRR-12-2018-0490

Tezel, A., Papadonikolaki, E., Yitmen, I., & Hilletofth, P. (2019). *Preparing Construction Supply Chains for Blockchain : An Exploratory Preparing Construction Supply Chains for Blockchain : An Exploratory.* Academic Press.

Tian, F. (2016). An agri-food supply chain traceability system for China based on RFID & blockchain technology. *2016 13th International Conference on Service Systems and Service Management, ICSSSM 2016*. 10.1109/ICSSSM.2016.7538424

Tönnissen, S., & Teuteberg, F. (2019). Analysing the impact of blockchain-technology for operations and supply chain management: An explanatory model drawn from multiple case studies. *International Journal of Information Management, 0–1*(January). Advance online publication. doi:10.1016/j.ijin-fomgt.2019.05.009

Treiblmaier, H. (2018). The impact of the blockchain on the supply chain: A theory-based research framework and a call for action. *Supply Chain Management, 23*(6), 545–559. doi:10.1108/SCM-01-2018-0029

Tribis, Y., El Bouchti, A., & Bouayad, H. (2018). Supply chain management based on blockchain: A systematic mapping study. *MATEC Web of Conferences, 200*. 10.1051/matecconf/201820000020

Venkatesh, V. G., Kang, K., Wang, B., Zhong, R. Y., & Zhang, A. (2020). System architecture for blockchain based transparency of supply chain social sustainability. *Robotics and Computer-Integrated Manufacturing, 63*(November), 101896. doi:10.1016/j.rcim.2019.101896

Wamba, S. F. (2019). *Continuance Intention in Blockchain-Enabled Supply Chain Applications : Modelling the Moderating Effect of Supply Chain Stakeholders Trust*. doi:10.1007/978-3-030-11395-7

Wang, Y., Han, J. H., Beynon-davies, P., Wang, Y., Han, J. H., & Beynon-davies, P. (2018). *Understanding blockchain technology for future supply chains : a systematic literature review and research agenda*. doi:10.1108/SCM-03-2018-0148

Weber, I., Xu, X., Riveret, R., Governatori, G., Ponomarev, A., & Mendling, J. (2016). *Untrusted business process monitoring and execution using blockchain*. Lecture Notes in Computer Science. Including Subseries Lecture Notes in Artificial Intelligence and Lecture Notes in Bioinformatics. doi:10.1007/978-3-319-45348-4_19

Wright, A., & De Filippi, P. (2015). Decentralized Blockchain Technology and the Rise of Lex Cryptographia. SSRN *Electronic Journal*. doi:10.2139srn.2580664

Wu, H., Cao, J., Yang, Y., Tung, C. L., Jiang, S., Tang, B., . . . Deng, Y. (2019). Data management in supply chain using blockchain: challenges and a case study. *Proceedings - International Conference on Computer Communications and Networks, ICCCN*, 1–8. 10.1109/ICCCN.2019.8846964

Yadav, S., & Singh, S. P. (2019). *Blockchain critical success factors for sustainable supply chain Resources, Conservation & Recycling*. doi:10.1016/j.resconrec.2019.104505

Yu, Y., Wang, X., Zhong, R. Y., & Huang, G. Q. (2016). E-commerce Logistics in Supply Chain Management: Practice Perspective. *Procedia CIRP, 52*, 179–185. Advance online publication. doi:10.1016/j.procir.2016.08.002

Yumna, H., Murad, M., Ikram, M., & Noreen, S. (n.d.). *Use of blockchain in Education: A systematic Literature Review*. Academic Press.

KEY TERMS AND DEFINITIONS

Cryptography: The practice and study of secure communication techniques in the presence of third parties known as adversaries.

Decentralization: Process by which an organization's activities, in particular those relating to planning and decision-making, are distributed or delegated from a central, authoritative place or group.

Distributed Ledger: A consensus of geographically spread replicated, shared, and synchronized digital data across multiple sites, countries, or institutions.

Double Spend: Potential flaw in a digital cash scheme where the same digital token can be spent more than once.

Ethereum: Decentralized open source blockchain featuring smart contract functionality.

Immutability: Design pattern where something can't be modified after being instantiated.

Smart Contract: Computer program or transaction protocol that is intended to automatically execute, control, or document events and actions legally relevant under the terms of a contract or agreement.

Chapter 14
The Role of Blockchain Technology and Its Usage in Various Sectors in the Modern Age:
Various Roles of Blockchain and Use Cases in Different Sectors

Amrit Sahani
Siksha O Anusandhan (Deemed), India

Sushree BibhuPrada B. Priyadarshini
Siksha O Anusandhan (Deemed), India

Suchismita Chinara
National Institute of Technology, Rourkela, India

ABSTRACT

A decade earlier, the basic guiding theory of the blockchain was implemented. It took a few years for the technology to be widely recognized outside the computer science sector in industry and academic communities. Since then, several scientific institutions have taken up the topic. Through this chapter, the authors focus not only on the working mechanism of the technology but also towards the use cases in varied industries. Blockchain implementations are an effective way to actively move business expertise to study goals that support both technical growth and testing through analysis, design, and research approach.

DOI: 10.4018/978-1-7998-6694-7.ch014

1. INTRODUCTION

Blockchains have risen as a platform to allow money exchanging facilities removing the cause for a trustworthy mediator for notarization, also validating these exchange transactions or facilities, while safeguarding the privacy and the protection of data. There are many new systems of blockchains that have been developed for the fulfilment in varied fields such as safety, tourism, retail, health care and many other industries using supply chain management. The emphasis of this paper is the Blockchains usage in online health and health records management and sharing to permit patients, hospitals, clinics and other health actors to connect and enhance interoperability of knowledge among themselves (Nakamoto, 2008).

The essence of the unified structure used depends on the individuals participating in the network. There are also issues that, through the use of blockchains, would alleviate confusion and provide doctors a solution, given specific clinical data that could breach the privacy of patients and ultimately weaken the entire of the stakeholder network. In this chapter, we discuss the different features of blockchains, evaluate current problems and suggest alternative solutions. They focus on issues that can expose patients' wellbeing and safety in future attacks by Blockchains.

The framework of blockchain gained popularity, beginning the journey from a distributed ledger framework based on the "Bitcoin white paper published in October 2008(Nakamoto, 2008)." Blockchain's main technology as a "Cryptocurrency" allows consumers, without the need for a single, trustworthy third party, to quickly swap electronic coins on a regional Network. In typical situations, transactions between individuals or companies involving the exchanging of electronic money have relied, as mediators, on trustworthy third parties like a bank. For a number of reasons, confidence in the TTP is not sufficient. The TTP, thus, undermines the network, as a point of failure. Any third party trustee can malfunction or make the finance system inaccessible or vulnerable. A TTP also pays prices for production and sets external operating constraints. Therefore, the driving force behind Bitcoins is to resolve the shortcomings of TTP dependency on online transactions.

Bitcoin development has been released years since the publication from the renowned research project " Bitcoin White Paper ", with the Application published as an open-source, which allows other users to alter and improve the Application and create new generation innovations carried out in the context of BlockChain. The wave which instinctively started from the tokens carried out on the part of the blockchain, for example, for bitcoin is the initial step in the application of creation of decentralised medium known as blockchain 1.0 (Hauxe, 2006). Several 1.0 technologies like "Monero (Monero Project, n.d.), Dash (Dash Official Website, n.d.) and Litecoin (Litecoin—Open Source P2P Digital Currency, n.d.)", to name a handful used the conceptualisation of Blockchain.

The subsequent phase of blockchain creation followed by the first one (blockchain 2.0) applies to the establishment of intellectual possessions and contracts based on distribution (Forrest, 2016). Smart property is the immaterial properties or assets to be run through a blockchain network, and the software programs based on smart contracts which code how smart property is governed and handled. " Ethereum (Forrest, 2016), "Ethereum, Ethereum Classic, (Ethereum Classic, 2018) NEO (NEO Smart Economy, 2018) and QTUM (Qtum, 2018) are representations of blockchain 2,0 cryptocurrencies " ".

On the basis of the above, version 3.0 of blockchain now gets concerned in the purpose of non-financial blockchain applications (Monero Project, n.d.). Throughout this purpose, attempts were conducted to expand the network to other sectors, including banking, so that the revolutionary features of blockchain would be exploited for other businesses and use scenarios. As a result, blockchain is known as the general-purpose technology(Burniske et al., 2016; Jovanovic & Rousseau, 2005), which has evolved

Figure 1. Usage of Blockchain in various Sectors

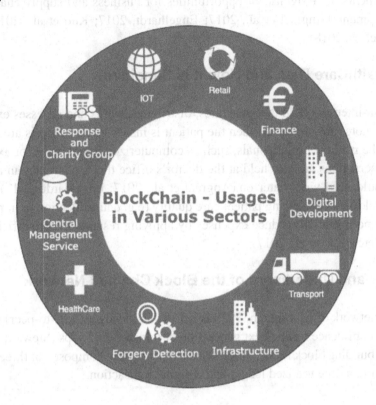

and used different fields, for example, identity management, dispute resolution, contract management, supply chains, insurance and healthcare(Androulaki et al., 2018; Burniske et al., 2016).

Growing demand for and deployment in different companies in the blockchain and in healthcare is a significant area in which a variety of uses of blockchain technologies have been found. Since blockchain is very young technology, but, with much excitement in the mainstream and in the grey mainstream as opinion pieces, commentaries, blog posts, interviews, etc., the potential usage of blockchain in the health sector is highly misleading. Members and professional study organizations would like to know the particular fields of blockchain adoption or application in the healthcare industry, and what blockchain-based healthcare applications have been built for such specified use cases? What are the challenges and drawbacks of blockchain healthcare networks and how are they currently addressed and improved?

1.1 Different Sectors and Divisions Which Uses Blockchain

Blockchain's appeal stems from its potential to promote open data exchange, optimize business operations, reducing operational costs, enhancing collective productivity and creating a network which, for example in the cases of supply chains, does not involve directly incorporation of confidence into its controls. Fig. 1 shows the usage of blockchain in different sectors. It also offers different ways of renewable development, as well as tracking and processing data-related emissions and environmental destruction practices, and for prompt decision-making in real-time, the gathering and review of renewable and low carbon data.

These advancements offer significant opportunities for business and supply chain innovation and sustainable development. (Angraal et al., 2017; Engelhardt, 2017; Kuo et al., 2017; Mettler, 2016; Roman-Belmonte et al., 2018)

1.2 What is HealthCare Data and How it is Sensitive?

Healthcare is a data-intensive field that generates, distributes, stores and accesses extensive data on a daily basis. Firstly, notes are produced when the patient is inspected and reports are transmitted to the x-ray and then to the medical professionals, such as computerized tomography, or axial scans.(Hauxe, 2006). Visiting observations are also held at the doctor's office that a pharmacy in another pharmacy in the network would need views later on.(Angraal et al., 2017; Engelhardt, 2017). Technology can certainly play a vital role in enhancing patient care quality (e.g. data collection to improve professional decision-making) and potentially reduce expenses by applying resources more efficiently to supplies, supplies, services, etc. (Kuo et al., 2017).

1.3 Technology and Underliners of the Block Chained Network

The decentralised network of Blockchain (P2P) is a distributed ledger (peer-to-peer) platform to create accountability and confidence for the next generation of transactional apps (Steward, 2005).

Blockchain is a building block for Bitcoin and a design structure composed of three key components: a centralized network, a decentralized ledger and a digital transaction.

2. FRAMEWORK OF DISTRIBUTED NETWORKS

The Framework of distributed network for BlockChain is a decentralized P2P network user node system. -- network member holds the same copy of blockchain and helps to validate digital transactions on a mutual basis for network validation and certification (Bit Fury Group, 2016).

2.1 Ledger

Shared Ledger members record digital transactions in a distributed network in a shared directory. The representatives of the network operate algorithms to test and validate a suggested transaction in order to add transactions. If any participants of the network believe that the transaction is legitimate, a mutual directory will be attached to the new transaction. Improvements to the public ledger are seen in all versions of the blockchain in minutes or even seconds. It can not be changed or removed once the transaction has been added after a transaction. No one has the capacity to alter or modify records, as the blockchain network is completely shared across all network participants (Bit Fury Group, 2016; Blockchain,).

2.2 Digital Transactions

Digital transactions Both quantity of knowledge and physical artefacts in a blockchain may be stored, and the network that implements a blockchain determines the identification of the transaction data. To ensure authenticity and precision, information shall be authenticated and digitally registered. Transactions are organized into blocks, and each block offers the previous block an authenticated hash. The numerical, series of the lines is added.(Blockchain, ; Rodriguez, 2015)

3. APPLICATIONS

Blockchain for open data storage has the ability for non-financial technology applications. A report written in the Harvard Business Review refers to numerous possible uses for blockchain, extending from the validation of the artwork to the checking of the voting documents, electronic records for patients. (Roman-Belmonte et al., 2018; Steward, 2005). This broad interest has given birth to a broad interest that has given rise to a range of firms, including the firms IBM, Microsoft, Accenture and other businesses. This passion is largely inspired by the belief that blockchain-enabled digital innovation could save the financial services industry $15 to $20 billion annually over the next five years.

4. DIFFERENT CATEGORIES OF BLOCKCHAIN AND BACKGROUND DETAILS

The first creator for the cryptocurrency coin named the common name 'Bitcoin' is known to be the "Satoshi Nakamoto", the first Blockchains application(Nakamoto, 2008). The Bitcoin concept was launched for the first time in 2008 to allow two individuals to execute transactions without a trustworthy third party. Instead of confidence or fear (Hauxe, 2006; Monero Project, n.d.; Nakamoto, 2008), the scheme is based on cryptographic evidence. Although the first Blockchains models have been accessibly accessible without special permits to Web users, since then businesses have effectively introduced additional instances in the permitted ecosystem restricting the role of assessing blocks with sufficient permits to select carefully identified individuals((Leader/Randomization/Signature)-free Byzantine Consensus for Consortium Blockchains, n.d.).

4.1. Blockchains Which do not Need Authorisation

Open blockchains are a kind of decentralized mechanism that enables a number of nodes to access the network and carry out transactions with no trustworthy third parties. Public blockchains are deemed illegal because not all nodes are excluded. To check, store and preserve the background of the transaction network, blockchains are used. Such transactions are processed in a single database in cubes. Each interaction between different nodes is checked and forwarded by a number of nodes to the blockchain. "Ether (Ethereum currency)" is used to reward the node which is used as the starting node which effectively mines the block ((Leader/Randomization/Signature)-free Byzantine Consensus for Consortium Blockchains, n.d.). If a block is authenticated and attached to the chain, it is difficult to delete the block. Adjust or alter a block involves a re-calculation of the intended block's hash value and all of the blocks that result in an intruder finding it incredibly difficult to forge (Hauxe, 2006; Nakamoto, 2008). In fact, the attackers can not alter a blockchain since the database is spread in many nodes. The introduction of a new component to a ledger can be seen in Fig 2.

Adjusting or altering a block involves a re-calculation of the intended block's hash value and all of the blocks that result in an intruder finding it incredibly difficult to forge (Roman-Belmonte et al., 2018; Steward, 2005). In fact, the attackers can not alter a blockchain since the database is spread in many nodes.

Figure 2. Introduction of a New Component to a Ledger

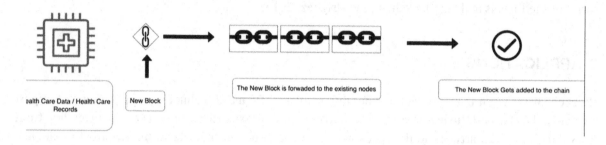

The introduction of a new component to a ledger can be seen ((Leader/Randomization/Signature)-free Byzantine Consensus for Consortium Blockchains, n.d.; Block Chain Technology Beyond Bitcoin, n.d.). The Fig. 3 represents the forwarding of new block to existing node.

Figure 3. Forwarding to new block to Existing node

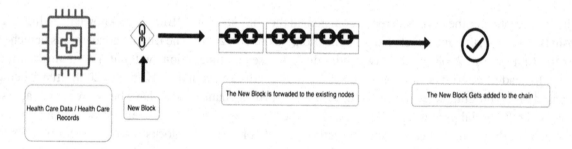

Recently several public healthcare research projects have been carried out by Blockchains. One of the new model was coined as MedRec as mentioned in the research project quoted in (Azaria et al., 2016). A shared network of medical information sharing focused on intelligent contracts is developed in accordance with the MedRec model. It facilitates the exchange of medical data between different clients, doctors and other people who process medical and safety data. Health care professionals may include information for patients at any given time, but patients will determine what MedRec recommends with two separate types of mining(Azaria et al., 2016). Firstly, the usage of Ether for researchers; secondly, the use of aggregated and anonymised data to enable the researchers to use and firstly, the connection to a block to the required data is given by the first node.

4.2. Blockchains Which Need Authorisation

Although some of Blockchains' features are appropriate for distributed applications like smart healthcare, Blockchains can not be used without sufficient protection to store and exchange private data such as health records. Public blockchains have as their primary objective little protection; they are built to render the data open to view, validate and forgive(Kadena: Confidentiality in Private Blockchain, n.d.). Furthermore, large-scale and widely-used Blockchain applications such as healthcare are concerned with scalability via the decentralised medium in transmission and data storage for BlockChain Applications(Blockchain For Health Data and Its Potential Use in Health IT and Health Care Related Research, n.d.). In addition to the basic functionalities offered on the initial Blockchain network the approved blockchains will be enhanced to defend, protect privacy and be more scalable(Consensus-as-a-Service: A Brief Report on the Emergence of Permissioned, Distributed Ledger Systems, n.d.; Kadena: The First Scalable, High Performance Private Blockchain, n.d.; On Public and Private Blockchains, n.d.). This means the industry is implementing a revamped version of an earlier framework named approved Blockchains or blockchains which need authorisation.

Two kinds of approved Blockchains are available: private Blockchains and consortium Blockchains. The difference between proprietary (private) and Blockchains has been marginally stressed as they all run on a proprietary network(Bit Fury Group, 2016; Blockchain, ; Rodriguez, 2015). Both are blockchains enabled for direct disclosure and transaction submission of Blockchains results, both are restricted to predefined individuals((Leader/Randomization/Signature)-free Byzantine Consensus for Consortium Blockchains, n.d.) where blockchains are approved. There are two groups of permitted Blockchains: the "Private Blockchains Community" and the "Consortium Blockchains community." ((Leader/Randomization/Signature)-free Byzantine Consensus for Consortium Blockchains, n.d.).

4.3 Private BlockChain

Private blockchains are blockchains, in which written rights are essential for one organization / entity, whereas reading allowances can be arbitrarily restricted or accessible. Private(Exklusive) Blockchains are built with the intention of ensuring the transparency and compliance of rules on the transactions of specified parties to Blockchains service and allowing safe mining without proof of work(Gideon Greenspan, 2015). Thanks to published and understood limits on permissions in private blockchains, strong confidentiality is feasible. The downside of private Blockchains in a distinction to public Blockchains(On Public and Private Blockchains, n.d.) is that a business-owned Blockchains firms will easily alter and restore laws and transactions. Furthermore, manual interference in tightly linked nodes can solve errors, and chain members can control block-size limitations that solve problems of scalability.

The summarisation suggests, a private blockchain is nothing but a defined distributed network that records an agreement between approved parties on transactions in blocks. A transaction or block will be generated by an accepted Node. In need of cryptographic hatching, the contract is checked and transmitted by the arbiter. Fig 4 illustrates how private Blockchains can operate in a medical environment (On Public and Private Blockchains, n.d.).

The arbiter is liable for the introduction of new documents and the preservation of central, public ledger of private blockchains. Interest is focused on one arbiter. However, reading permissions to other nodes that to some degree be restricted or constrained. In every contract, the nodes concerned remind the arbiter of the contract and update the server. The trust exists all nodes in private Blockchains. Personal Blockchains are also somewhat close to the public standard blockchain.

4.4 Consortium Blockchains

Consortium Blockchains are blockchains that have a pre-select group of secret nodes in the consensus process (What Is Ether, n.d.). When a party from a pre-selected node-set has reached an agreement, a block shall be added to the chain. For example, when five known / trustful connections are on the chain,

Figure 4. Private Blockchain in Medical Environment

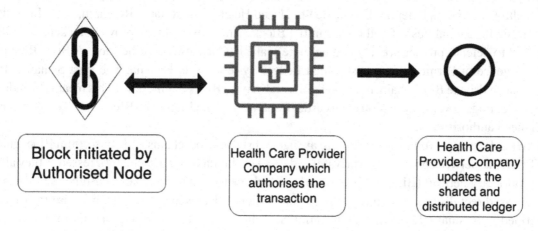

at least three individuals sign a contract for allowing the block to be appended to the chain to attach or move to each block. Fig.5 previews an overview of how a three-step aspect is implemented in the healthcare system to the chain.

Figure 5. Implementation of three-step aspect in Health care system

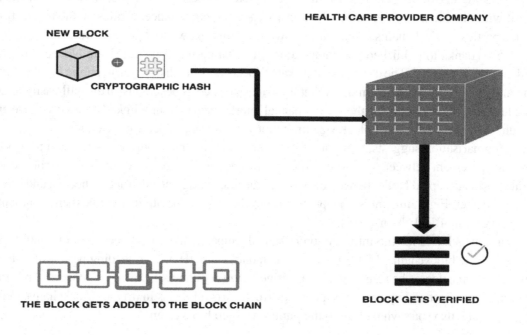

In the Blockchain Community, members are only allowed to have a privilege to interpret the ledger. Furthermore, unlike proprietary Blockchains the consortium Blockchains are partly decentralized. A network architecture in a group appears to draw businesses because, as opposed to proprietary block-chains, it is shared (MedChain, n.d.). For the healthcare industry, a blockchain network will be set up by introducing a blockchain that will enable health institutions to exchange EMR patients via a centralized ledger through a centralized database (MedChain, n.d.; ModelChain, n.d.). On a blockchain network, 'there is no chance of breaches in the confidentiality of confidential health records because the details can only be obtained by people who have historically been provided with this knowledge' (BlockIsure, n.d.). For example, only identity records of all patients are accessible for the receptionist, whilst the caregiver may only access his patients' medical documentation. Any of the previous construction projects of the Blockchains community for healthcare have been built such as MedChain (MedChain, n.d.), ModelChain (ModelChain, n.d.) and BlockInsure (BlockIsure, n.d.).

5. TECHNICAL BACKGROUND

Bitcoin is one of the more common blockchain implementations. Digital asset transfers (e.g. bitcoin) within the blockchain was done as a transaction between a seller / paid person (Figure ()). Such transactions are distributed to all pees linked to the blockchain network where users, named miners, are utilizing cryptocurrencies. (figure ()). This confirmation addresses two key issues with digital currency trading before: guarantee the survival of the digital commodity and it's not spent. A contract is assumed to be successful when a miner assumes it is well constructed (only the fields specified in the protocol include the input and outputs), and the outputs he tries to pass remain. Miners are not licensed so everyone who spends their money is free to do so. The incentive for mine owners is in the form of a block of approved transactions created which rewards the mine owners. The appropriate software required for running of the framework or the systems of Blockchain is available for free download and simple to use. When a transaction is authenticated by a configurable number of customers, it is stored in a block containing details of the authenticated transactions along with the time stamp and the encrypted hash (mathematically generated alphanumeric string).

Fig. 6 depicts a process of the mechanism of blockchain.

The block with transaction details followed by the transfer of the assets to the receiving party is added to the end of the blockchain. The single-way hash is an vital element of the blockchain, since it reflects a cryptographic digital signature that is unique to the current data block and generated using the previous block hash (Figure [B]). It is an integral element of the blockchain. Since all blocks are closely linked with the hash in the previous block, illegal modifications in the blockchain have been avoided. Immutability of Blockchain is an integral feature (Casino et al., 2019). Fig. 7 represents transaction in case of blockchains.

This methodology varies from conventional money management in many functional terms. For example, after a transaction of a credit card is made, the retailer's payment processor will check the available funds and accept the money and pass it on to the retailer for several days. The goal of blockchain is to remove such intermediaries by building up a digital trust to render transaction management more effective. The network itself validates the transaction in a blockchain system, secures the background of the transaction and enables the exchange of properties to be exchanged automatically directly between parties (Casino et al., 2019).

Compared to conventional distributed repositories for applications of bio-medical and safety technologies, the common benefits of BlockChain are -

Figure 6. Whole Mechanism of Blockchain

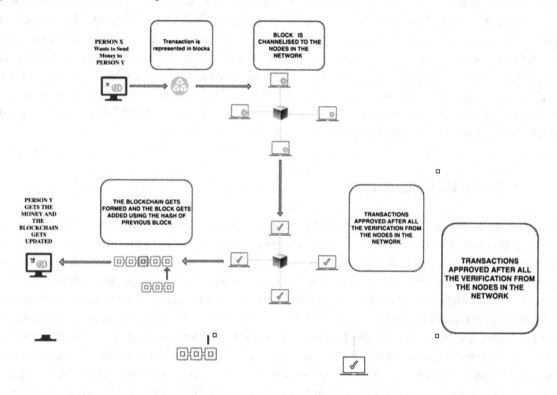

1.   Through contrasting this with the traditional centralized database management framework, we identify the main benefits or comparable gain of blockchain, to help explain how biomedical and

Figure 7. Transactions in Blockchain

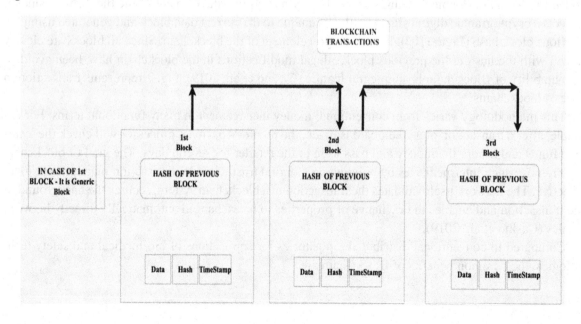

medical technologies will embrace the distributed ledger network.

2. The traditional database framework includes the frameworks which use structured query language, Apache frameworks and the most popular database Oracle systems.

3. Transparency regulation is the first key benefit of blockchain. DBMSs are centrally controlled (i.e. consumers logically assume that they have a central database, but the actual machines will be distributable physically), while blockchain is an inter-peer, shared database management network (Kuo et al., 2016; McConaghy et al., n.d.).

4. Blockchain thus is suitable for implementations where healthcare and wellness actors separately controlled (e.g. clinics, suppliers, patients and payers) choose to operate together without handing access to a central management intermediary (Kuo et al., 2016; McConaghy et al., n.d.; ONC/NIST Use of Blockchain in Healthcare and Research Workshop, 2016).

5. The source of results. Digital asset ownership can be altered by the device administrator in DDBMS, although ownership can only be altered in blockchain by the user adopting cryptographic protocols(Kuo et al., 2016). In addition, it is possible to trace assets origins (e.g. sources or the data and data can be confirmed).(ONC/NIST Use of Blockchain in Healthcare and Research Workshop, 2016) Blockchain is, therefore, suitable for use in the management of critical digital assets (eg patient consent records)(Martin, n.d.), increasing the reusability of verified data(Martin, n.d.).

6. The last point focuses not on the root of the results. Digital object ownership may be modified by the network admin on DDBMS, whereas ownership on blockchain may be adjusted by the owner only, following the cryptographing protocols,45 the root of properties (e.g. source data or information can be confirmed) may even be traced,(ONC/NIST Use of Blockchain in Healthcare and Research Workshop, 2016) raising the reusability of the validated data (e.g., for insurance transactions)(Lorenz et al., n.d.).

Robustness and flexibility are the fourth advantages. While DDBMS and blockchain are focused on distributor technologies and therefore have no single point limitation, it would be expensive for DDBMS to achieve a high standard of blockchain replication (i.e. every node includes copies of all background of information data) (Martin, n.d.; McConaghy et al., n.d.).

In addition, Bitcoin blockchain uses the 256-bit Elliptic Curve Digital Signature Algorithm, an asymmetric cryptography algorithm described in US Federal Information Processing Standards 180-4.73, to produce and validate high-security public and private keys as digital signatures, maintaining control of digital properties as with patient records (FIPS PUB 180-4 Secure Hash Standard (SHS), n.d.). The hash algorithm plays a vital role in the dominance of blockchain. In addition, Bitcoin blockchain uses a "256-bit "Elliptic Curve Digital Signature" Algorithm to produce and validate public, and private, high-security keys as digital signatures, maintaining digital property controls as well as patient records (FIPS PUB 180-4 Secure Hash Standard (SHS), n.d.). The Curve Bitcoin blockchain also uses the 256-bit Elliptic Curve Digital Signature Algorithm. Fig. 8 describes a scenario of patient data and digitization.

Every blockchain of healthcare has to be transparent, with technological alternatives to three main elements: scalable, controlled connection and data protection. The above three features form important terminology in the aspect of the blockchain model.

Figure 8. Patient data and digitisation

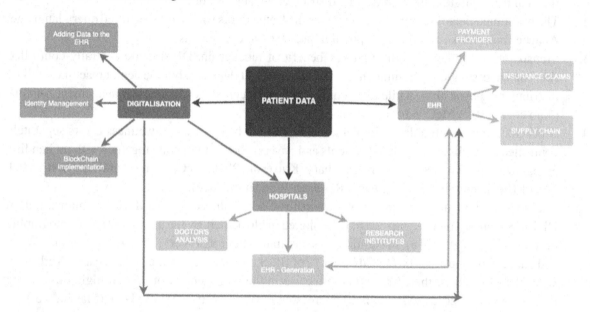

5.1 Adaptivity and Scalability

A centralized database including medical history, documentation, photographs will have consequences for data access and application output limitations. Each user of the global blockchain health care network will be presented with a replica of each patient register for every person residing, if based on the Bitcoin blockchain. Since health documents are complex and vast, it will require bandwidth-intensive replicating of all the health information for specific users of the network. Blockchain has to serve as a network to view patient data and knowledge and consider the implications of Blockchain in the health sector.

5.2 Privacy in Data and Secured Access to Users

The consumer will have direct access to his details and power over the distribution of his knowledge. The consumer will grant access rights to his blockchain and indicate who may scan and sort the data. A smartphone portal system will allow users to see who can access their blockchain. The customer may even display an audit file, showing when and what information was accessed, by whom his database was accessed. It will also allow the consumer to provide, cancel access to any individual with a specific identity.

6. VARIOUS CHALLENGING TASKS TAKEN UP BY THE USE OF BLOCKCHAIN

6.1 Validation Process

Validation process of the Blockchain Proof of Research (Nakamoto, 2008) is also recognized as the mining step of blockchain. This process normally requires a consensus algorithm that also specifies the rules to be followed by the nodes for validation of such chains. The Consensus Protocol will insure that all nodes involved in validation provide a appropriate solution by following the order in which the transactions are to be processed. In other terms, the block is to be inserted into the chain (Pîrlea & Sergey, 2018; Sankar et al., 2017). Consensus protocols that offer a more robust network are built for block validation in the blockchain. We outline the following key protocols contained in healthcare literature for blockchain:

6.2 Analysis Proof (PoW)

The nodes (meaning miners) engaged in the study strip each other to overcome a cryptographic mystery. The node to find a solution first has the privilege to verify the block and create a new block for transactions. It should also be borne in mind that other PoW algorithm implementations like Bitcoin will compensate for the winner (Nakamoto, 2008).

6.3 Proof of Stake

Validation of the number of network members is chosen. Evidence of Stake (POS) The more coins they have, the more blocks will be verified, and thus the legitimacy of the block is assessed by this node (King & Nadal, 2012; Mingxiao et al., 2017).

6.4 PBFT

The server and client are made up of two nodes, the functional Byzantine fault tolerance (PBFT). A server node moves the application to another server node, who decides whether or not it is valid; (iii) the node forwards a preparation response to other nodes if the server node approves the application; (iii) the server node transmits a preparation clarification to other nodes. The PBFT approach follows many stages of validity.

While the transaction is validated by an adequate number of nodes, it is alerted to "validity," (iv) each node that has been validated sends a communication message to the network confirming its action and (v) a message to the node transmitter has been recognized that the transaction has been or is not valid (Blockchain For Health Data and Its Potential Use in Health IT and Health Care Related Research, n.d.; Miller & Sim, 2004).

6.5 Smart Contracts

With the launch of the Ethereum network, smart contracts on Blockchain 2.0 have been developed (Buterin, 2014). Today it is popular for smart contracts, thanks to the tools available to build a Blockchain app in solidity language. An intelligent arrangement is a provision that provides standards for automated, electronic enforcement (Chatterjee et al., 2018; Szabo, 1997) during the contract phase. Implementing intelligent trading contracts will render the transactions more safe, efficient and easier. If they trade other properties for cryptocurrencies. Once a settlement interest is balanced by a provision that is specified therein, contracts are performed automatically. This knowledge can help to automatically recognise incoherences (e.g. infringements). Intelligent contracts can allow online purchases more versatile as they can play a role in the judicial environment (Lorenz et al., n.d.; Nakamoto, 2008).

7. CHALLENGES

Challenges in using Blockchain in health care may be implemented in growing ways, but it is multidisciplinary and challenging (Swan, 2015). The impact of these adverse factors is attempted by researchers in this field. In the field of healthcare (ONC/NIST Use of Blockchain in Healthcare and Research Workshop, 2016; Swan, 2015; Szabo, 1997; Yli-Huumo et al., 2016) we mention several problems (i.e., technological challenge) of blockchain technology: Performance Throughput: As the amount of transactions and network nodes grows, more restrictions would be needed to create a networking bottleneck. Fast production is a concern in dealing with healthcare services. This may have a detrimental effect on a treatment that will improve someone's lives if there is no easy access. (ONC/NIST Use of Blockchain in Healthcare and Research Workshop, 2016; Swan, 2015; Szabo, 1997; Yli-Huumo et al., 2016)

1. **Latency:** The block validation process takes around 10 minutes, weakening the protection capabilities of your network as successful attacks will occur during this cycle. Health networks are dynamic and can be tracked constantly because a break is harmful to research results.
2. **Security:** It may be exploited if an person may access 51 per cent of the network computing resources. This requires further focus as a broken health infrastructure can lead to the health organizations' loss of credibility. (ONC/NIST Use of Blockchain in Healthcare and Research Workshop, 2016; Swan, 2015; Szabo, 1997; Yli-Huumo et al., 2016)
3. **Consumption of Resource:** The use of this technique continues to contribute to significant wealth loss, particularly when a large amount of energy is spent on mining. Energy costs in the healthcare sector are very high because various methods for monitoring patients are important but the usage of the blockchain can also require major energy and calculation costs. Organizations have difficulty in managing these prices.
4. **Accessibility:** Accessibility of such systems is also a concern, as they are quite easy to manage. Moreover, it is important to build an API with user-friendly functionality for applications (application programming interfaces). The programs will be clear and understandable because health care practitioners are not as experienced as IT practitioners.
5. **Centralisation:** Although blockchain is a decentralized system, other methods prefer to centralize miners such that networking capacity is that. This centre of knowledge can be obtained by malicious attacks as it is fragile and can be abused (Zheng et al., 2018).
6. **Anonymity:** The software of Bitcoin is generally considered to preserve the anonymity of its nodes. This argument was therefore refuted by the findings of(Zheng et al., 2018). In order to deliver this ability for blockchain-based applications, strategies are often required(Zheng et al., 2018). Thanks to data security regulations and rules, Blockchain-based networks are regulated by the General Data Protection Regulation (GDPR).

8. INFORMATION MANAGEMENT THROUGH HEALTH

After researching basic blockchain technology concepts, this section explores how it can be used in the medical industry — primarily to secure the health data, which provides an immense advantage in the healthcare environment when coping with sensitive patient information. The knowledge of HealthCare Management is of great socio-economic value for education, as its performance would greatly enhance the standard of life. In line with this line of reasoning, the calculation should mitigate the implications of other problems in this field.

For eg, computing helps simplify health records by allowing data exchange, recording and use more efficient in other sectors(Azaria et al., 2016; Wechsler et al., 2003; Xia et al., 2017). The consistency of medical treatment significantly impacts the handling of health knowledge, whether through clinical reports or other methods. The evidence collection will increase the time needed for diagnosis, and help the practitioner focus on the effects of the patient (Miller & Sim, 2004). Each segment is meant to address topics relating to patient knowledge management. It will demonstrate how blockchain technologies will aid in the distribution and management of health records, including exchanging and handling details from IoT apps on patient surveillance.

8.1 Health Care Records Sharing

Health care shared details One of the first and most common healthcare apps in the blockchain is the exchange of health records. Health records are difficult to share since they are classified as sensitive details and deal with patients' medical data. The major publications in literature discussing this usage of blockchain technologies include Dubovitskaya et al. (Dubovitskaya et al., 2017), Azaria et al. (Azaria et al., 2016) and Xia et al. (Xia et al., 2017). Blockchain-based systems may provide differing capabilities for the exchange of electronic health information. Azaria et al. (Azaria et al., 2016) explore one of the most ancient frameworks of literature. Many recent articles in the literature referenced this, utilizing it as a basis for constructing many similar architectures. Any of such systems, cited in (Alwen et al., 2017; Azaria et al., 2016; Xia et al., 2017), was influenced by Azaría et al. (Azaria et al., 2016). MedRec, which uses a Blockchain-based system to store electronic health information, would be the first networking platform to be addressed. The aim of MedRec is to resolve issues such as data access reaction times, interoperability, and enhanced data quality for health research(Angraal et al., 2017).

To learn the techniques used while designing the MedRec architecture, it deployed a private P2P network and used smart contracts using the Ethereum platform to control and monitor the network's state transformations. One feature of the MedRec system is its availability of clinical information enabling patients to be consulted of health choices by a consultative organization. Another distinction is that they require health data to be centralized as they are versatile and provide open data requirements in several various ways. The usage of health data management systems in this form of design is promising as it provides better protection and a shared vocabulary for clinical data sharing (Azaria et al., 2016; Dubovitskaya et al., 2017), while the paper from Azaria et al.(Azaria et al., 2016) still aims to carry out the testing and observational work across a wide variety of users. Briefly, MedRec is a practical approach utilized in the exchange and collaboration of clinical data for doctors, physicians and professional professionals. The recorded data could thus reduce incoherence in various hospital systems. As stated by Dubovitskaya et al (Dubovitskaya et al., 2017), the solution includes cloud storage, and can also help to create new technologies to exchange health information through blockchain through designing secure and more efficient clinical healthcare networks.

The authors propose a blockchain-based cloud-based architecture that connects the communication network to nodes. This study by Dubovitskaya et al.(Dubovitskaya et al., 2017) shows how blockchain software is used to handle the exchange of health records by means of intelligent contract principles and open, immutable bookkeeping.

Dubovitskaya et al. (Dubovitskaya et al., 2017) also pointed out that Cloud Junction and blockchain technologies function together to enhance network access control. For examples, the author used radiation oncology department data for research. It establishes policies of access control with two critical roles (doctor and patient) and smart contracts to describe the nature of transaction. One of the potential priorities for these forms of infrastructure is the exchange of radiological data and the monitoring of actual patients(Dubovitskaya et al., 2017). The research papers in healthcare concerning blockchain introduce a network or device concept and plan to build a working framework for experiments of actual users in future research. In addition to researching concerns pertaining to cloud technology-based health data exchange blockchain systems, it is therefore important for the auditing details () to be addressed. Xia et al. (Xia et al., 2017) (MedShare) is one of the writers who answer this issue as there is a debate on seeking a workaround for record-sharing in cloud providers. This technology allows to enhance environmental surveillance, control access to documentation and even the development of an interview layer to link the blockchain network utilizing authentication triggers to conduct smart contract research (Alwen et al., 2017; Xia et al., 2017). The software even includes an interactive interface for querying databases.

The MedShare-based approach includes a four-layer architecture: I User-layer: a graphical interface to the application; (ii) application database layer: a set of systems that handle and address question requests throughout the network; (iii) an architecture bases infrastructure: a network bases framework through which only a few specialist entities can be accessed; (iv) data structure;

` The key aim of the approach form, such as MedShare, is to make it easier to utilize some aspects in health systems. The characteristics can include data root, auditing and improved device reliability. Therefore, the approach facilitates the monitoring and cancellation of consumer access rights and therefore a patient knowledge archive to be developed that can be used for big data research. Thus, the device may be appropriate to meet high data demand because it uses cloud processing(Xia et al., 2017).

8.2 Sharing Imaging Scans at the HealthCare

All sorts of data and photographs will describe health knowledge. At present, photos can often pose certain issues with exchanging health records(de Oliveira Guedes Bastos, 2011). An architecture of this sort can be identified in (Patel, 2018) with other meanings underlying this concept. They essentially plan to introduce an architecture to exchange pictures from this work. The patient has a secure and managed means of sharing his pictures. This system is focused on a centralized network established but built in a decentralized fashion by the Radiological Society of North America (RSNA). The Image Share Network (ISN) aims to solve the problems in the RSNA networks: to store images in studio repositories for safe viewing. Photos will be used as long as they are viewed by the owner of the registered pictures ().

Exploring the architecture(), it was designed as a collection of nodes creating a chord-type P2P network representing an individual in the healthcare system identified in each node of the network. (ii) the patient who has full access levels under his / her pictures, so that he / she may decide who they share with. (iii) health care: has the level of read-only access to the pictures that a patient specifies; and (iv) personal records for healthcare: it represents the medicinal records and all kinds of recitals.

The principal role of the design for picture sharing focuses on the principles used in the validation process. The method is performed using the agreement proof-of-stake algorithm because it protects the participants from the low load. And the public and private cryptographic key principles are used for safe transition. Overall, the proposed design will support health networks, which allow blockchain technology to provide more protection and reliability. But, since they are personal details, they primarily have drawbacks linked to the protection of photos. The writers hope for guidance in this respect from prospective researchers (Patel, 2018). In short, (Patel, 2018) can be a beneficial approach since an agent is not necessary and patients themselves may administer their data and keys. The (Patel, 2018) model can be similar to that of (Ge et al., 2013), which offers a structure for patient-oriented picture sharing (i.e. own patients are liable for sharing their images). It relies, however, on the central unit transmitting the data to other network nodes. The central server may be targeted or disabled, hindering the network's successful efficiency. (Ge et al., 2013)

8.3 Management of Logs/Records in Healthcare Systems

For computational systems, log management is an important concept as logs allow the generation of historical data which can help in an error analysis, intrusion detection and other services(Gupta, 2015). Healthcare systems also need such management to provide users with more control over access to patient information (Wechsler et al., 2003). This management is necessary. However, as the logs generated by conventional systems we currently use run the risk of being manipulated, a technological system has to be introduced that can resolve this issue and blockchain can do this. For saved data (like the logs themselves), blockchain immutability characteristics can ensure that they are not manipulated in the ledger. Such principles have been discussed in Anderson's research in the healthcare environment(Anderson, 2018).

It adopts an approach focused on blockchain to verify the logs generated by entry. The plan also aims to perform audits, standardize data and promote collaboration through an authorized blockchain system. The protection audit reporting is quite difficult, as it may often not be helpful or miss critical details (Anderson, 2018; Wechsler et al., 2003). In the Anderson(Anderson, 2018) report, they explored a log control method known as "AuditChain," which effectively solves interoperability concerns and offers electronic record storage facilities. The IBM platform and Hyperledger Fabric3 promote the blockchain-based building development method were used as the components for this approach.

In the Anderson report (Anderson, 2018), they examined the so-called "AuditChain" method for log control which resolves interoperability issues and offers electronic record storage facilities. As components of this solution, the IBM framework and Hyperledger Fabric3 support the construction process focused on blockchain. The audit chain utilizes asymmetrically cryptography using a set of keys to protect the details involved in the process when operating in a blockchain-based system. And where a data-related security issue occurs in the blockchain network, the JavaScript Entity Notation (JSON) format of the users that may access this program is simulated. This would be included by the user's account as a digital signature. Nonetheless, the usage of AuditChain is restricted, as is the complexity of locating logs for a single person. It is also necessary to create a query script when performing the procedure, meaning the process is not very intuitive. Another critical aspect was the inability to execute the experiments carried out for applications in the actual world, so the indicators used not be most optimal for real-life operation (Anderson, 2018).

8.4 Management of Supply Chain

One of the management mechanisms for the organization's growth is the Supply Chain Managence (SCM), insofar as a network of collaborators links from the raw material supplier to the delivery business. SCM networks include growing sectors, such as emergency facilities, as well as other interconnected devices, including blockchain technologies, as a consequence of technological advances (Lambert et al., 1998).

It will also help to monitor and record properties in the supply chain. The segment is also intended to address several important aspects in which blockchain will help supply chain management in the health field. Supervision of the supply chain specializes of managing products of a decent condition and on schedule from the manufacturing line to its sale to the final customer (Lambert et al., 1998). For certain industries such as hospitals and the pharmaceutical sector, the market plan is a vital aspect. Provided that the standard of medicines in this sort of company must be enhanced because the lack of assets that conflict with the social climate, it is important to investigate those medicines for the quality of life of certain citizens. They may not conduct their usual business without them (Sousa et al., 2011). This review would concentrate on two points: I blockchain and IoT for the medication control supply chain and (ii) blockchain-based safety asset management in the supply chain.

8.5 Monitoring of Patients

Because of the need to ensure the protection of such sensors, as IoT and sensors work in a specific setting and even in laboratories, hospitals and other medical centres, (Cha et al., 2018). The sensors may be inserted in patients with intelligent bracelets or any other equipment in the hospital. Blockchain is a technology to enhance the safety of these devices, as sensitive personal information is generated through the sensors when monitoring patients. There are rules for securing personal details that need to be complied with, such as the Lei Geral de Proteção a Dados(LGPD) in Brazil (Cha et al., 2018; Mulholland, 2018), the GDPR in Europe(Forrest, 2016), and HIPAA in the U.S.(U.S. Department of Health & Human Services (HHS), 2013). These guidelines say that the applications will maintain the data security of patients and the blockchain will, therefore, help to safeguard their privacy.

Many innovations have been developed to upgrade and improve existing programs. Any of these innovations like IoT, sensor networks and connected apps. Those developments are also feasible for medicine, for example, utilizing the concept of the Wireless Body Region Networks (WBANs). This principle applies to a personal network consisting of several implanted and wearable sensors and the central data transmission system(NEO Smart Economy, 2018). This principle applies. A streamlined WBAN network for blockchain patient surveillance() is shown in Fig. 9.

The professional community's patient monitoring is a critical procedure as it allows the specialist to track the health of the individual. This means the compatibility of WBANS and its requirements with the core features such as smart devices and gateways is improved. However, security, efficiency and accuracy remain limited in terms of the capacity to share patient details on a safe medium (Ren et al., 2010), and many emerging innovations such as blockchain will add to these challenges. Such a system will thereby improve the degree of protection in the transmission of information as it provides the secure sharing of information among the nodes of the network and employs principles like immutability and data privacy. On the basis of the above factors, blockchain can help to track patients through the creation of frameworks that can boost the efficiency of the operation. In their paper, Linn and Koo (Linn & Koo, 2016) propose a blockchain-based system built to exchange sensors' safety details that has all the advantages of blockchain. The framework thereby improves the degree of confidentiality as knowledge is passed on as it guarantees safe information exchange between the network nodes and utilizes concepts such as immutability and data privacy.

Based on the reasons listed above, blockchain will help monitor patients by creating systems that will increase the operations' performance. Linn and Koo (Ashraf Uddin, 2018) are introducing a blockchain-based network intended to share the protection information of sensors with all the advantages of

Figure 9. A streamlined WBAN network for blockchain patient surveillance

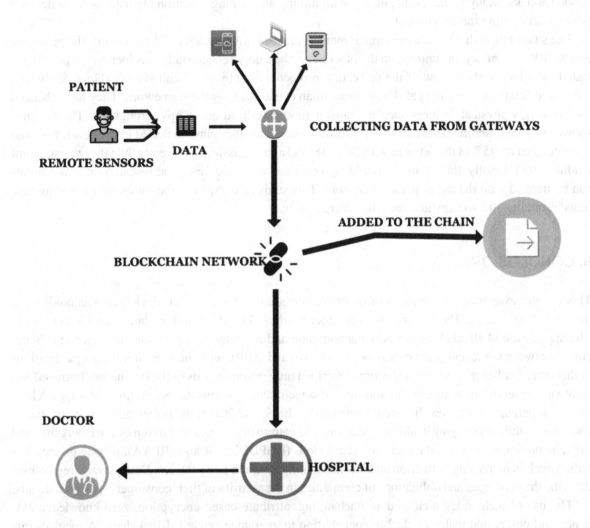

blockchain. There was another case of blockchain patient surveillance by (Ashraf Uddin, 2018). They analyze patients' remote surveillance via personal sensor networks. In fact, this device utilizes blockchain technologies to pass sensor data to the different layers of the proposed architecture. This reduces information complexity and requires documents to be transmitted without the need for a trustworthy third party, and provides consistency and immutability (Halamka et al., 2017; Stagnaro, 2017). There are two types of architecture built by Uddin et al.(Ashraf Uddin, 2018): I the first is the flow regulation, and the second the central health data unit is managed. The system is designed through a specific patient sensor network through which data produced was transmitted to a medical data provider (e.g. smartphone). The generated data is sent to a server that works as a patient data agent and manages the data framework, the data mining framework and data protection. It should also be noted that, when exchanging data, it is important to move through the blockchain network system before entering the end-users in order to ensure better protection and reliability(Ashraf Uddin, 2018). Uddin et al. (Ashraf Uddin, 2018)'s software conducts experiments to assess their output in many circumstances. Some of the research was performed on other forms of threats, such as individual assaults in the middle and denial of service attacks. Many variables, beginning with mining and mining selection algorithms, were decided prior to performing the experiments.

The study found that there were three miners in the grid utilizing about 25 per cent of the processor and 98 MB of memory. In contrast, on the other hand, the safety-related study was focused on previously stated assaults and the review of the protection protocols used by Gope and Hwang (Gope & Hwang, 2016) and Balasubramanian et al.(Balasubramanian et al., 2011) as the framework. They have checked the network's physical features such as transfer time, overhead and Kbps throughput. The findings showed reduced running costs and lower turnover relative to other plays included in the benchmark and compensated for 45% of the network with 26 nodes and a transmission rate greater than the others(Ashraf Uddin, 2018). Finally, this segment should lay out a range of guidelines and research on how patients can be tracked with the aid of personal sensors. This study also explores measures for improving data transfer quality and security and reducing energy costs.

9. CONCLUSION

This chapter examined several areas of literature surrounding the usage of blockchain technologies in the area of healthcare. The inquiry involved other co-related fields including data security and health. The application of Blockchain is a new phenomenon and its usage in the healthcare sector mostly occurred between the recent years mostly between(2016 and 2019), with the most significant publications in this area. Studies in this field, therefore, described only general words in the beginning. Initial efforts were subsequently made to use this tool to exchange diagnostic knowledge, control the supply chain and track patients' processes. In recent years (2017, 2018, and 2019), the policy addressed guarantees anonymity while exchanging health information. The pattern has increased. Driven by the emergence and implementation of personal data security regulations (LGPD, GDPR and HIPAA), private privacy is a topic which is increasing in traction and has fascinating research perspectives. Data privacy regulations describe the privileges and obligations of companies in the security of their consumers' personal details.

The use of techniques such as data unchanging, attribute-based encryption, zero-knowledge evidence and others that make a valuable contribution to guarantee privacy. Blockchain. A focus of this analysis is the scope of trust protocols for blockchain-based medical applications. Most widely used are the PBFT (PoW) and Proof of Operation, as they can be found in systems such as Etherum and Hyper-Guide Manufacturing. A study of these procedures (begun in the PoW) found that the cost to the health care system is huge and unworkable. In order to retain this provision in a network, hospitals will need to expend a lot of money on equipment and, since it is a legal system, user protection may be violated. Even as a matter of caution for material, it should be noted that most papers covered in this technique are theoretical and application is still a theory. The protocol that would be appropriate for use in healthcare applications will then become PBFT, as its protocol is approved and has another justification for support, low computing costs and mineralization.

Summarized, this analysis attempted to include a collection of studies on the introduction of blockchain-based healthcare networks by scholars. We have addressed several technologies that provide drawbacks and advantages for developing blockchain-based healthcare applications.

We conclude that the exchange of healthcare knowledge, the use of the PBFT consensus algorithm and the usage of this Hyperledger Fabric network form part of our work. However, if the researcher is concerned about the outcome in the future, the medication supply chain and the patient management network where blockchain and IoT may be merged should be taken into consideration. Through the research, we will see the blockchain can be extended to various areas of healthcare. The healthcare facilities tracking combined with IoT is one of them worth investigating further. With these technologies, it is interesting that the full spectrum of smart health devices currently emerging allows for greater safety for the fitness and mental health control environments. Any issues relating to the confidentiality and protection of medical data may be mitigated with the help of blockchain technologies. Finally, we have outlined a few health strategies and solutions that cover each of the fields of expertise described in this analysis via blockchain.

REFERENCES

Alwen, Blocki, & Harsha. (2017). *Practical Graphs for Optimal Side-Channel Resistant Memory- Hard Functions*. Cryptology ePrint Archive, Report 2017/443. Retrieved September 20, 2018 from https:// eprint.iacr. org/2017/443

Anderson, J. (2018). *Securing, Standardizing, and Simplifying Electronic Health Record Audit Logs through Per- missioned Blockchain Technology* (Ph.D. Dissertation). Dartmouth College. https://www. cs.dartmouth.edu/~trdata/ reports/abstracts/TR2018- 854/

Androulaki, E., Barger, A., Bortnikov, V., Cachin, C., Christidis, K., De Caro, A., Enyeart, D., Ferris, C., Laventman, G., & Manevich, Y. (2018). Hyperledger Fabric: A Distributed Operating System for Permissioned Blockchains. In *Proceedings of the Thirteenth EuroSys Conference; EuroSys '18*. Association for Computing Machinery. https://dl.acm.org/doi/10.1145/3190508.3190538

Angraal, S., Krumholz, H. M., & Schulz, W. L. (2017). Blockchain Technology Applications in Health Care. *Circulation: Cardiovascular Quality and Outcomes*, *10*(9), e003800. doi:10.1161/CIRCOUT-COMES.117.003800 PMID:28912202

Ashraf Uddin, M. (2018). Continuous patient monitoring with a patient centric agent: A block architecture. *IEEE Access: Practical Innovations, Open Solutions*, *6*, 32700–32726. doi:10.1109/AC-CESS.2018.2846779

Azaria, A., Ekblaw, A., Vieira, T., & Lippman, A. (2016). MedRec: Using Blockchain for Medical Data Access and Permission Management. *2016 2nd International Conference on Open and Big Data (OBD)*, 25-30. 10.1109/OBD.2016.11

Balasubramanian, V., Hoang, D. B., & Zia, T. A. (2011). Addressing the confidentiality and integrity of assistive care loop framework using wireless sensor networks. In *2011 21st International Conference on Systems Engineering*. IEEE. 10.1109/ICSEng.2011.82

Bit Fury Group. (2016). *Digital Assets on Public Blockchains*. Bit Fury Group Limited.

Block Chain Technology Beyond Bitcoin. (n.d.). Available at http://scet.berkeley.edu/wp-content/uploads/ AIR-2016- Blockchain.pdf

Blockchain. (n.d.). Retrieved 7 2016, from Wikipedia: https://en.wikipedia.org/wiki/Blockchain

Blockchain For Health Data and Its Potential Use in Health IT and Health Care Related Research. (n.d.). Available at https://www.healthit.gov/sites/default/files/11-74- ablockchainforhealthcare.pdf

BlockIsure. (n.d.). Available at https://oncprojectracking.healthit.gov/wiki/download/attachments/14582699/70-BlockInsure_Pieces_Tech%20%282%29.pdf

Burniske, C., Vaughn, E., Cahana, A., & Shelton, J. (2016). *How Blockchain Technology Can Enhance Electronic Health Record Operability*. Ark Invest.

Buterin, V. (2014). *A Next-Generation Smart Contract and Decentralized Application Platform*. Retrieved August 20, 2018 from https://github.com/ethereum/wiki/wiki/White-Paper

Casino, F., Dasaklis, T. K., & Patsakis, C. (2019). A systematic literature review of blockchain-based applications: Current status, classification and open issues. *Telematics and Informatics*, *36*, 55–81. doi:10.1016/j.tele.2018.11.006

Cha, S., Chen, J., Su, C., & Yeh, K. (2018). A blockchain connected gateway for BLE-based devices in the Internet of Things. *IEEE Access: Practical Innovations, Open Solutions*, *6*, 24639–24649. doi:10.1109/ACCESS.2018.2799942

Chatterjee, K., Goharshady, A. K., & Velner, Y. (2018). Quantitative analysis of smart contracts. *Springer International Publishing*.

Consensus-as-a-Service: A Brief Report on the Emergence of Permissioned, Distributed Ledger Systems. (n.d.). Available at http://www.ofnumbers.com/2015/04/06/consensus-as-a-service- a-brief-report-on-the-emergence-of-permissioned-distributed- ledger-systems/

Dash Official Website. (n.d.). *Dash Crypto Currency—Dash*. Available online: https://www.dash.org/

de Oliveira Guedes Bastos. (2011). *Quality of Health Information on Acute Myocardial Infarction and Stroke in the World Wide Web* (Master's Thesis). Universidade do Porto.

Dubovitskaya, A., Xu, Z., Ryu, S., Schumacher, M., & Wang, F. (2017). *Secure and trustable electronic medical records sharing using blockchain*. https://arxiv.org/abs/1709.06528

Engelhardt, M. A. (2017). Hitching Healthcare to the Chain: An Introduction to Blockchain Technology in the Healthcare Sector. *Technology Innovation Management Review*, *7*(10), 22–34. doi:10.22215/timreview/1111

Ethereum Classic. (2018). *A Smarter Blockchain that Takes Digital Assets Further*. Available online: https: //ethereumclassic.org/

FIPS PUB 180-4 Secure Hash Standard (SHS). (n.d.). https://nvlpubs.nist.gov/nistpubs/FIPS/NIST.FIPS.180-4.pdf

Forrest, P. (2016). Blockchain and non financial services use cases. *Linkedin*. https://www.linkedin.com/pulse/blockchain-non-financial-services-use-cases-paul-forrest

Ge, Y., Ahn, D. K., Unde, B., Gage, H. D., & Carr, J. J. (2013, January). Patient-controlled sharing of medical imaging data across unaffiliated healthcare organizations. *Journal of the American Medical Informatics Association*, *20*(1), 157–163. doi:10.1136/amiajnl-2012-001146 PMID:22886546

Gideon Greenspan. (2015). *Multi Chain Private Blockchain—White Paper*. Available: http://www.multichain.com/download/MultiChain-White- Paper.pdf

Gope, P., & Hwang, T. (2016, March). BSN-Care: A secure IoT-based modern healthcare system using body sensor network. *IEEE Sensors Journal*, *16*(5), 1368–1376. doi:10.1109/JSEN.2015.2502401

Gupta, U. (2015). *Secure management of logs in internet of things*. https://arxiv.org/abs/1507.05085

Halamka, J. D., Lippman, A., & Ekblaw, A. (2017). *The Potential for Blockchain to Transform Electronic Health Records*. Retrieved September 30, 2018 from https://hbr.org/2017/03/the-potential-for-blockchain-to-transform-electronic-health- records

Hauxe, R. (2006). Health Information Systems—Past, Present, Future. *International Journal of Medical Informatics*, *75*(3–4), 268–281. doi:10.1016/j.ijmedinf.2005.08.002 PMID:16169771

Häyrinena, K. (2008). Definition, Structure, Content, Use and Impacts of Electronic Health Records: A Review of the Research Literature. *International Journal of Medical Informatics*, *77*(5), 291–304. doi:10.1016/j.ijmedinf.2007.09.001 PMID:17951106

Jovanovic, B., & Rousseau, P. L. (2005). General Purpose Technologies. In *Handbook of Economic Growth*. Elsevier. doi:10.1016/S1574-0684(05)01018-X

Kadena: Confidentiality in Private Blockchain. (n.d.). Available at http://kadena.io/docs/Kadena-ConfidentialityWhitepaper- Aug2016.pdf

Kadena: The First Scalable, High Performance Private Blockchain. (n.d.). Available at http://kadena.io/docs/Kadena- ConsensusWhitePaper-Aug2016.pdf

King & Nadal. (2012). *Ppcoin: Peer-to-peer Crypto-Currency with Proof-of-Stake*. Retrieved October 31, 2018 from https://peercoin.net/960assets/paper/peercoin-paper.pdf

Kuo, T.-T., Hsu, C.-N., & Ohno-Machado, L. (2016). *ModelChain: Decentralized Privacy-Preserving Healthcare Predictive Modeling Framework on Private Blockchain Networks*. In ONC/NIST Use of Blockchain for Healthcare and Research Workshop, Gaithersburg, MD.

Kuo, T. T., Kim, H. E., & Ohno-Machado, L. (2017). Blockchain Distributed Ledger Technologies for Biomedical and Health Care Applications. *Journal of the American Medical Informatics Association: JAMIA*, *24*(6), 1211–1220. doi:10.1093/jamia/ocx068 PMID:29016974

Lambert, Cooper, & Pagh. (1998). Supply chain management: Implementation issues and research opportunities. *International Journal of Logistics Management*, *9*(2), 1–20. doi:10.1108/09574099810805807

(Leader/Randomization/Signature)-free Byzantine Consensus for Consortium Blockchains. (n.d.). Available at http://poseidon.it.usyd.edu.au/~concurrentsystems/doc/Consensu sRedBellyBlockchain.pdf

Linn & Koo. (2016). *Blockchain for Health Data and Its Potential Use in Health IT and Health Care Related Research*. Academic Press.

Litecoin—Open Source P2P Digital Currency. (n.d.). Available online: https://litecoin.org/

Lorenz, J.-T., Münstermann, B., Higginson, M., Olesen, P. B., Bohlken, N., & Ricciardi, V. (n.d.). *Blockchain in Insurance – Opportunity or Threat?* McKinsey & Company. http://www.mckinsey.com/~/media/McKinsey/Industries/Financial Services/Our Insights/Blockchain in insurance opportunity or threat/Blockchain-in-insurance-opportunity-or-threat.ashx

Martin, L. (n.d.). *Blockchain vs. Relational Database: Which is right for your Application?* TechBeacon. https://techbeacon.com/Blockchain-relational-database-which-right-for-your-application

McConaghy, T., Marques, R., & Müller, A. (n.d.). *BigchainDB: A Scalable Blockchain Database.* https://www.bigchaindb.com/whitepaper/

MedChain. (n.d.). *Secure, Decentralized, Interoperable Medication Reconciliation Using the Blockchain.* Available at https://oncprojectracking.healthit.gov/wiki/download/attachment s/14582699/36-20160808-blockchain-medrec-whitepaper- final.pdf

Mettler, M. (2016). Blockchain Technology in Healthcare the Revolution Starts Here. *Proceedings of the 2016 IEEE 18th International Conference on E-Health Networking, Applications and Services (Healthcom),* 520–522. 10.1109/HealthCom.2016.7749510

Miller. & Sim. (2004). Physicians' use of electronic medical records: Barriers and solutions. *Health Affairs, 23*(2), 116–126. Doi:10.1377/hlthaff.23.2.116

Mingxiao, D., Xiaofeng, M., Zhe, Z., Xiangwei, W., & Qijun, C. (2017). A review on consensus algorithm of blockchain. In *2017 IEEE International Conference on Systems, Man, and Cybernetics (SMC'17).* IEEE. 10.1109/SMC.2017.8123011

ModelChain. (n.d.). *Decentralized Privacy-Preserving Healthcare Predictive Modeling Framework on Private Blockchain Networks.* Available at https://www.healthit.gov/sites/default/files/10-30-ucsd-dbmi-onc-blockchain-challenge.pdf

Monero Project. (n.d.). Available online: https://getmonero.org/the-monero-project/

Mulholland, C. S. (2018). Dados pessoais sensíveis e a tutela de direitos fundamentais: Uma análise à luz da lei geral de proteção de dados (Lei 13.709/18). *Revista de Direitos e Garantias Fundamentais, 19*(3), 159–180. doi:10.18759/rdgf.v19i3.1603

Nakamoto, S. (2008). *Bitcoin: A Peer-to-Peer Electronic Cash System.* Available online: www.bitcoin.org

NEO Smart Economy. (2018). Available online: https://neo.org/

On Public and Private Blockchains. (n.d.). Available at https://blog.ethereum.org/2015/08/07/on-public-and-private- blockchains/

ONC/NIST Use of Blockchain in Healthcare and Research Workshop. (2016). https://oncprojectracking.healthit.gov/wiki/display/TechLabI/Use+of+Blockchain+in+Healthcare+and+Research+Workshop

Patel, V. (2018). A framework for secure and decentralized sharing of medical imaging data via blockchain consensus. *Health Informatics Journal, 25*(4), 1398–1411. doi:10.1177/1460458218769699

Pîrlea, & Sergey. (2018). Mechanising blockchain consensus. In *Proceedings of the 7th ACM SIGPLAN International Conference on Certified Programs and Proofs.* ACM. 10.1145/3167086

Qtum. (2018). Available online: https://qtum.org/en

Ren, Y., Werner, R., Pazzi, N., & Boukerche, A. (2010). Monitoring patients via a secure and mobile healthcare system. *IEEE Wireless Communications, 17*(1), 59–65. doi:10.1109/MWC.2010.5416351

Rodriguez, J. (2015). *Building an IOT Platform: Centralized vs. Decentralized Models.* Retrieved from https://jrodthoughts.com/tag/enterprisesoftware/page/2/

Roman-Belmonte, J. M., De la Corte-Rodriguez, H., Rodriguez-Merchan, E. C. C., la Corte-Rodriguez, H., & Carlos Rodriguez-Merchan, E. (2018). How Blockchain Technology Can Change Medicine. *Postgraduate Medicine, 130*(4), 420–427. doi:10.1080/00325481.2018.1472996 PMID:29727247

Sankar, L. S., Sindhu, M., & Sethumadhavan, M. (2017). Survey of consensus protocols on blockchain applications. In *2017 4th International Conference on Advanced Computing and Communication Systems (ICACCS'17).* IEEE. 10.1109/ICACCS.2017.8014672

Sousa, Liu, Papageorgiou, & Shah. (2011). Global supply chain planning for pharmaceuticals. *Chemical Engineering Research and Design, 89*(11), 2396–2409. DOI:.2011.04.005 doi:10.1016/j.cherd

Stagnaro, C. (2017). *White Paper: Innovative Blockchain Uses in Health Care.* Retrieved September 28, 2018 from https://www.freedassociates.com/wp-content/uploads/2017/08/Blockchain_White_Paper.pdf

Steward, M. (2005). Electronic Medical Records. *Journal of Legal Medicine, 26*(4), 491–506. doi:10.1080/01947640500364762 PMID:16303736

Swan, M. (2015). *Blockchain: Blueprint for a New Economy* (1st ed.). O'Reilly Media, Inc.

Szabo. (1997). Formalizing and securing relationships on public networks. *First Monday, 2*(9), 22. doi:10.5210/fm.v2i9.548

U.S. Department of Health & Human Services (HHS). (2013). *Summary of the HIPAA Privacy Rule.* Retrieved February 4, 2019 from https://www.hhs.gov/hipaa/for-professionals/privacy/laws-regulations/index.html

Wechsler, R., Anção, M. S., de Campos, C. J. R., & Sigulem, D. (2003). A Informática no consultório Médico. *Jornal de Pediatria, 79*, 1–10. doi:10.1590/S0021-75572003000700002

What Is Ether. (n.d.). Available: https://ethereum.org/ether

Xia, Q., Sifah, E. B., Asamoah, K. O., Gao, J., Du, X., & Guizani, M. (2017). MeDShare: Trust-less medical data sharing among cloud service providers via blockchain. *IEEE Access: Practical Innovations, Open Solutions, 5*, 14757–14767. doi:10.1109/ACCESS.2017.2730843

Yli-Huumo, Ko, Choi, Park, & Smolander. (2016). Where is current research on blockchain technology? A systematic review. *PLoS One, 11*, 1–27. DOI:.0163477 doi:10.1371/journal.pone

Zheng, Z., Xie, S., Dai, H.-N., Chen, X., & Wang, H. (2018). Blockchain challenges and opportunities: A survey. *International Journal of Web and Grid Services, 14*(4), 352–375. doi:10.1504/IJWGS.2018.095647

Chapter 15
Blockchain and IoT–Based Diary Supply Chain Management System for Sri Lanka

K. Pubudu Nuwnthika Jayasena
Sbaragamuwa University of Sri Lanka, Sri Lanka

Poddivila Marage Nimasha Ruwandi Madhunamali
Sabaragamuwa University of Sri Lanka, Sri Lanka

ABSTRACT

The central problem to be addressed in this research is to investigate how blockchain technology can be used in today's food supply chains to deliver greater traceability of assets. The aim is to create a blockchain model in the dairy supply chain that can be implemented across any food supply chains and present the advantages and limitations in its implementation. Blockchain allows monitoring all types of transactions in a supply chain more safely and transparently. Acceptance of blockchain in the supply chain and logistics is slow right now because of related risks and the lack of demonstrable models. The proposed solution removes the need for a trusted centralized authority, intermediaries and provides records of transactions, improving high integrity, reliability, and security efficiency and protection. All transactions are registered and maintained in the unchangeable database of the blockchain with access to a shared file network.

INTRODUCTION

Every day we consume food products on the basis of the confidence because that providers are produced, transported and warehouse in accordance with the internal and government regulations on food safety. Before reaching the end consumer, food product moving through different phases of supply chain from suppliers to retailers. These intermittent stages contribute to product design, manufacture, delivery, and sales. Although food safety measurements do periodic measure of food safety and provide certifications of the quality, it is often difficult to trust when searching a supply chain scaling across countries with

DOI: 10.4018/978-1-7998-6694-7.ch015

the distribution of technology. For example, The United States stopped imports of meat from Brazil due to the acceptance of bribes by food examiners in Brazil, the horsemeat scandal in Europe, the milk powder of babies scandal in China and the growing problem of food pollution in India. Over the past decade, these incidents have occurred periodically, pushing consumers and governments to request greater transparency throughout the food supply chain(Aung & Chang, 2014)(Bosona & Gebresenbet, 2013).

Based on Food and Drink research, organizations decide, increasing consideration of the food provenance as a business challenge. They are finding business opportunities through increasing health awareness. Nowadays consumers highly consider the quality of food product so they hesitate to purchase. It is because there is no way to ensure the quality of the food product and less transparency through the supply chain process of the product. Nowadays organizations are identified that customers are always looking for trusted products with verified sources. For that, they are plan to get a competitive advantage by providing a transparent supply chain and sustainable manufacturing. For example, Walmart has joined with IBM to study as of February 2018 to test whether the organization can guarantee the Health of food products that they sell in their retail stores. Nevertheless, contemporary repositories for each silo stage of the logistic transportation are ineffective in giving unparalleled trust to the client, because they are not dishonest. A lot of food supply chains today only check their product end of the logistic transportation processes and still there is no way to map their product in source and stages between customers.

Although the different phases of the food supply chain has many possible adverse results such as Irreversible disruption to the environment, abuse of working conditions, unethical manufacturing practices, counterfeiting and large quantities of agricultural waste attributable to imbalanced sourcing and storage strategies. End users tend to use these programs without realizing the repercussions that they create by their footprint and food supply chains are easily kept hidden with little effort to provide end-to-end access to their stakeholders. Although these challenges, the idea of requiring a single agency to provide data and transaction control in food supply chain was the only realistic solution until recently when a modern system called blockchain provided a whole modern way of addressing food provenance

BACKGROUND

Supply Chain

Global Supply Chains are becoming progressively difficult over the years. Therefore, it has become more challenging to manage social sustainability problems which are concerned by many foreign buyers (including large retailers and brand owners) and consumers, where monitoring and analysis of their transportation supply networks relies on many suppliers, distributors and delivery centers, some of them uncommon or even one-time. (Venkatesh, Kang, Wang, Zhong, & Zhang, 2020a)(Petri Helo & Shamsuzzoha, 2020). Supply chains are not fixed. It develops and changes in size, shape, and configuration, and in how they are coordinated, controlled and managed. Not only the economic drivers but also the technological drivers affect the changes in the supply chain. As a result of that, digital technology integrates with supply chain management. The new step introduces as "Supply Chain Digitization". Digitization may play a leverage role in aligning current sourcing strategies as well as developing new sourcing strategies to enhance long-term efficiency, productivity, and competitive advantage overall organizational objectives.

In a dairy supply chain, a network of stakeholders transacts to the end consumer in the form of rising, storing or selling foods. Transport companies act as links which connect these stages and ensure that the right quantity and quality product reaches the right destination at the right time

The stakeholders include:

1. Milk suppliers.
2. The milk processors engaged in the manufacture and sometimes distribution of the milk commodity
3. The distributer active in the sale to end consumers and dealers of the finished product.
4. The end customers engaged in shopping the items, which consists of individuals and markets.

Blockchain

Considered one of the most innovative innovations available, the blockchain first showed up in 2008 when published "Bitcoin: A Peer-to-Peer Electronic Cash System". The scheme suggested was based on cryptographic proof rather than dependency, allowing any two parties to perform transactions without the need of a trustworthy third party. The plan solved the issue of double spending(Kosba, Miller, Shi, Wen, & Papamanthou, 2016)(Wright & De Filippi, 2015). This is the first application of blockchain, Created by Satoshi Nakamoto (Nakamoto, 2008). There are many critical features, that blockchain provides. Such as Decentralized, Traceability, Consensus mechanism, Immutability, Smart contract(Yumna, Murad, Ikram, & Noreen, n.d.)(Madumidha, Ranjani, Varsinee, & Sundari, 2019). Blockchain application contain distributed architecture. That mean of distributed architecture is the system does not depend on any centralized authority but uses a peer-to-peer network of computer servers maintained by decentralized interest owners(P. Helo & Hao, 2019)(Tezel, Papadonikolaki, Yitmen, & Hilletofth, 2019). Today blockchain is applications further than finance, as in government, health, science, arts and culture(Frizzo-barker et al., 2019)(Pilkington, 2016).A range of implementations is already being explored such as a blockchain based smart grid in the energy sector(Scully & Hobig, 2019).In such a network, blockchain technology enforces transparency and guarantees ultimate, system-wide accord on the validity of a complete history of transactions. In the blockchain, no single party controls the data. The whole data infrastructure is visible to all parties. So that it helps to minimize the bias errors. (Treiblmaier, 2018) Every party can confirm the records of its transaction followers directly, without an intermediary or ledger unauthorized access or manipulation. Although many speculate about the impact of blockchain technology upon supply chains, the current understanding of its potential remains limited. As the development and diffusion of this technology is still in its infancy (Wang et al., 2018).

Every node inside a blockchain have encrypted keys named public and private key, and each transaction within two nodes contains some important information about the sender and the receiver, asset information, date, and identifier for the sender 's previous transaction. An asset may be any commodity within a supply chain, or a buyer-seller exchange. A cryptographic hash function named SHA 256 (Secure Hash Algorithm 256) uses the sender's public key and transactional information to produce a 16-digit hexadecimal string called the "tag". The hash done is special to a combination of a public key and transaction information. A group of randomly clustered transactions is one block. This authenticated transaction information is decoded to verify the validity of the transactions and their origin, which can only be decrypted by brute force. The cycle of hash resolution is called mining, and miners are called nodes that validate certain transactions. When the network generates a block from the pool of unchecked transactions, available miners will be competing to validate the transactions by resolving the cryptographic hash

A consensus algorithm controls the method of choosing a miner at a blockchain. Some network systems such as the Ethereum and Hyperledger projects are special. Every block within a blockchain contain of 3 important components - a hash (a unique digital identifier), a timestamp, and the hash of the previous block (to compute the account balance). The previous block hash ties the whole block chain together and thus stops any block being changed or added between two authenticated chains. When a transaction is checked, the blockchain records it. Changing a reported transaction value in a decentralized blockchain network such as Bitcoin is quite difficult because an intruder must obtain nearly 51 percent of the entire computing power existing in the framework. Therefore each subsequent block enhances the verification of the preceding block and ultimately blockchain as a whole. This mechanism holds the blockchain resistant to malicious activities, contributing to the essential immutability attribute.

In Ethereum, the blockchain system is controlled by rules decided upon by the participants in the network in the method of smart contracts and was firstly implemented in Bitcoin for running the mutual accounting ledger. It is commonly used after this initial financial use, when many players with little to no confidence are part of a transaction; for example, fragmented supply chains. Blockchain's three basic features make it an attractive choice for tracking supply chain assets

Figure 1.

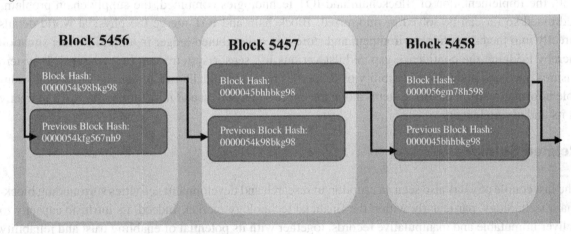

- **Distributed processing:** Does not require a central control system. The process is distributed to all processors or network participants embedded in the process.
- **Synchronized records:** The ledger is circulated to all players and so it is fraud-proof.
- **Smart information:** We can build cloud applications that run on top of the blockchain architecture, allowing us to customize the data format that is available in the supply chain at every point.

Smart contracts

A smart contract can be defined as a program which can activate certain functions automatically if anything predetermined happens. Intelligent contract contact with the blockchain, the criteria are stored in "contracts" and must be met by the users in order to build a new block. A smart contract is not an intrinsic part of the blockchain protocol itself, but a function on the network that is stored on a blockchain database in a completely distributed manner (Mattila, Seppälä, & Holmström, 2016).

Blockchain Technology in Supply Chain

Blockchains are already generating advantages on supply chains around the world. Real-time visibility can be considered an important benefit to supply chain management (Sheel & Nath, 2019). Moreover, all transactions can be traceable, and consequently. The data are organized into blocks that shape a chain. Blockchain transactions operate in a peer-to-peer network, in a decentralized way. In other words, the transactions are validated and stored by a distributed ledger, and it is not necessary to have a central entity that validates the transactions(Petri Helo & Shamsuzzoha, 2020). Almost all organizations need to take profit of several improvements brought about by blockchain, which spans improved process and operations over the whole supply chain, safer, transparent and efficient transactions(Kshetri, 2018) and trust and reliability through the network, all processes and related information being shared by all network participants.

Blockchain and Internet of Things(IOT) Combination

With the implementation of Blockchain and IOT technologies combined, the supply chain problems addressed so far can be solved or minimized. Blockchain and IOT merge the physical world details directly into the computing environment and store it in a distributed ledger in a multi partner situation thereby bridging the confidence gap. Whilst various IoT sensor systems can be combined. It system ensures open and auditable traceability of properties by automatically extracting and processing valuable information from the IoT systems along the entire supply chain and maintaining these data directly in its underlying ledger.

Related Studies

The last couple of years also seen an eruption in research and development activities surrounding blockchain technology, particularly within the financial technology market. Indeed, its intrinsic capacity to deliver immutable and manipulative records, together with its potential of enabling trust and reliability among untrusted peers represents too attractive features, preventing this technology to stay relegated into a single vertical sector. For this reason, several industries beyond the financial technology sector have already identified Blockchain technology as a driver for a paradigm shift.

Figure 3 remarkably, all the selected papers were published after the year 2015. It indicates that this area of research is both new and original. Through all the papers selected, 1 papers (1.61%) were published in 2016, 2 papers (3.22%) in 2017, 13 papers (20.96%)in 2018 and 46 papers (74.19%) in 2019 when zooming into the distribution year. Which represents increase in blockchain interest.

Blockchain technology is still in the early stages of marketing and while there are many industry experts who agree that there is a promising future for the deployment of this technology through industry, many others claim that there is an unrealistic assumption of blockchains that could, in turn, intensify the impact of the inability to implement blockchains in industry. However, while many unsuccessful attempts have been made to use blockchain technology, several successful business cases, such as those listed

Figure 2. Publication year of the selected primary papers

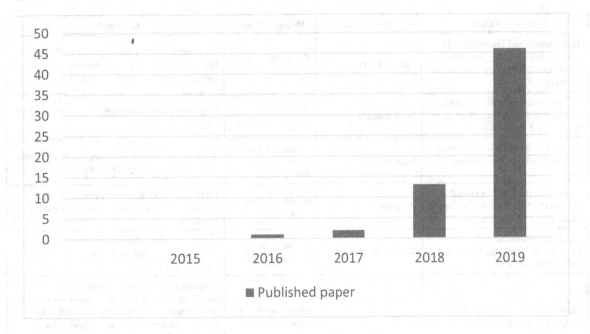

in this article, have also occurred. The latter provides a rather optimistic view that as more progress is made in overcoming the limits of blockchains, like many other emerging technologies, blockchains can find a position in operation and become popular.

Papers on blockchain, supply chain and blockchain with supply chain management were read and the following results were obtained including the gaps in current studies, requirements in blockchain technology within supply chain management.

Table 1 represent what are the existing research topic and application area of them on supply chain on blockchain

For several specific supply chain scenarios, there are many deployed and conceptual systems, among them the food supply chain is the hottest topic. The issues of food provenance and safety are important issues that need to be addressed. There are some ongoing food supply chain projects or food traceability projects. More challenging applications are involving wine and agricultural foods. Pharma and drug industry, Blockchain also helps the electronics industry, since healthcare is also a major social problem

The significance of blockchain for the supply chain

Supply chain management is an integrative term for controlling a distribution channel 's total process (Petri Helo & Szekely, 2005). The supply chain is complex as it involves dispersed practices from upstream, interacting with individuals, physical resources and manufacturing processes to downstream, covering the entire process of selling; i.e. contracts, sales to customers, distribution and disposal(Tian, 2016). The supply chain aims to create a multi-stakeholder collaborative environment through mutual trust, to eliminate communication problems, and ensure that the various companies are connected to pursue routinely the integration of the whole supply network. In the end, linked supply chain stakeholders

Table 1. Existing research topics on supply chain based on blockchain

Research topic	Applied areas	Research Paper	Key finding
Transparency and Traceability: In Food Supply Chain System using Blockchain Technology with Internet of Things	Food industry	(Madumidha et al., 2019)	An effective system incorporating RFID and Blockchain technology is a technical mechanism for monitoring and locating products
A Blockchain-based decentralized system to ensure the transparency of organic food supply chain	Food industry	(Basnayake & Rajapakse, 2019)	Preparing a transparent and efficient architecture for food certification
The Rise of Blockchain Technology in Agriculture and Food Supply Chains	Food industry	(Kamilaris, Fonts, & Prenafeta-Boldú, 2019)	Applying blockchain technology to build reliable and secure farm and food supply chains
Framework Design of Financial Service Platform for Tobacco Supply Chain Based on Blockchain	Financial	(Liu, Li, & Cao, 2018)	Build framework design of financial service platform for tobacco supply chain based on blockchain
Blockchain-Based Secured Traceability System for Textile and Clothing Supply Chain	Textile and clothing	(Agrawal, Sharma, & Kumar, n.d.)	Blockchain-Based Secured Traceability System with implementation for textile and clothing supply chain
Blockchain Framework for Textile Supply Chain Management	Textile	(Elmessiry & Elmessiry, 2018)	A full blockchain-based clothing quality assurance platform that allows cross-chain information sharing with assured validity and precision in almost real time, allowing for the detection of product faulty lots in all networks as soon as they are identified in a few.
A Blockchain-Based Supply Chain Quality Management Framework	Global supply chains	(Chen et al., 2017)	Using blockchain technology to solve problems caused by lack of trust in the quality management of the supply chain and to achieve sophisticated product quality management
Blockchain in Supply Chain Trading	Global supply chains	(Al Barghuthi, Mohamed, & Said, 2019)	A well-function supply system using a blockchain technology
Blockchain-based Soybean Traceability in Agricultural Supply Chain	Agriculture	(Salah, Nizamuddin, Jayaraman, & Omar, 2019)	Blockchain and Ethereum smart contracts will map and monitor effectively and make it possible to incorporate busy transactions and workflows in the agricultural supply chain without presence
Blockchains everywhere - a use-case of blockchains in the pharma supply-chain	Pharmaceutical industry	(Bocek, Rodrigues, Strasser, & Stiller, 2017)	Blockchain allows pharmaceutical supply chain to monitor temperature and humanity over the transport of medical products
How the Blockchain Revolution Will Reshape the Consumer Electronics Industry	Electronics industry	(Jayasena, 2017)	Transparency and process integration in consumer electronics supply chain management will be enhanced by blockchain. Areas where blockchains can affect supply chains include a tamper-proof history of product manufacturing, handling and maintenance, digital identity for ownership and packaging, tendering across the supply chain through smart contract sand engagement with consumers
Can Blockchain Strengthen the Internet of Things?	Manufacturing/ physical distribution	(It, 2017)	Blockchain can play a key role in tracking the sources of insecurity in supply chains and in handling crisis situations like product recalls that occur after safety and security vulnerabilities are found

will increase overall performance and add greater value and benefits to their business (Azzi, Chamoun, & Sokhn, 2019).

Blockchain can solve supply chain problems and even lead to numerous critical supply chain management objectives, such as cost, quality, speed, dependability, risk reduction, sustainability and flexibility(Kshetri, 2018)(Basnayake & Rajapakse, 2019)(Al Barghuthi et al., 2019)(Tönnissen & Teuteberg, 2019). Therefore, among the many other operations that are likely to be changed by blockchain the supply chain needs special consideration. Identified profits of applying blockchain in supply chain management are Improve overall quality, Reduce cost, Shorten delivery time, Reduce risk, Increase trust. In the following describe problems that address by blockchain in the supply chain.

1. **Differential Pricing:** Companies prefer keeping their pricings a secret, since this allows them to pay lower prices when outsourcing to developing countries.
2. **Numerous Parties Involved:** Mediating between so many parties can be a big problem for logistics-providers, slowing down the delivery of services and creating a large overhead for logistics. Furthermore, a centralized mediator of these parties can misuse power to prefer some parties over others.
3. **Quality & Compliance issues:** Procuring a replacement for defective parts is a long drawn and uncomfortable process.
4. **Inevitable Disruptions:** LEAN "on-demand" manufacturing falls flat in a situations where natural disasters and socio-economic problems are common. For example, Japan (frequently affected by earthquakes) has outsourced most of it's supply chain logistics to other countries.
5. **Centralization:** A central mediator for parties is required, which centralizes power in the hands of a few and is a gateway to misuse of resources.
6. **Fraud by Middlemen:** As number of interacting parties increase, there is a proportional increase in middlemen. They lead to fraud and slow down the supply without adding anything to the network.
7. **Tracking history of any product:** Validating identity vendor and checking for tampering by middlemen is not possible.

Blockchain characteristic for Supply Chain

1. **Quality assurance:** In the perspective of investigation & guidance to adopt required steps for the flawless high-quality production of goods & services, quality assurance makes a remarkable impact to make the business processes easier. (Yadav & Singh, 2019).
2. **Scalability in Supply chain management:** When an information recorded in a block of the block chain, this characteristic ensures that it is non-variable & non-volatile. This leads to integrate blockchain without a risk of losing the data consistency.(Tönnissen & Teuteberg, 2019)(Madavi, 2008).
3. **Transparency:** Ensure peer to peer transactions are verified at the minor end & make sure that the updated data cannot be changed/hacked. Also the property of *changing anything in the ledger stays on it* makes the blockchain a transparent system. (Yumna et al., n.d.)(Pe & Llivisaca, n.d.) (Wu et al., 2019)(Casino, Dasaklis, & Patsakis, 2019)
4. **Integrity:** Provides management for the flow of physical goods in supply chain using integration of serial numbers, bar codes, sensors, digital tags like RFID, etc. Following this the flow of blockchain

Table 2. How to resolve them by applying blockchain

Problems	Solution
Differential Pricing	Permissioned ledger for confidential transactions between parties
Numerous Parties Involved	Consensus between multiple parties is maintained through Smart contracts
Quality & Compliance issues	Smart contract stores money while all solutions are checked and tested
Inevitable disruptions	Digital ledger is free of geographical constraints like natural disasters, socio-economic issues
Procuring replacements for defective pieces	Smart contract only lets out payments once both parties satisfied
Centralization	Risk of fraud is mitigated by using decentralized nodes for checking delivery status
Fraud by Middlemen	Because of using doubly-signed smart contracts, no financial fraud by middlemen can occur in the system
Tracking history of any product	Using network anyone can verify vendor identity and validity of product

became smoother from manufacturer to end-user.(Yadav & Singh, 2019)(Litke, Anagnostopoulos, & Varvarigou, 2019)

5.   **Solving the double spend problem:** Solves the issue of data transaction which cannot be sent to two or more people at the same time. With the help of authenticated peer to peer transaction after the verification by a minor. (Yadav & Singh, 2019)(Bartling & Fecher, 2016)

6.   **Immutability and encryption**: After confirming the transaction or data flow from one center to another, changes are not allowed since any change on the block chain cannot be stored without the solidarity of the network (Yumna et al., n.d.)(Schmidt & Wagner, 2019)(Wu et al., 2019).

7.   **Efficiency:** The high rate of information flow speed without an intermediary, smart contracts easily traceable & further, it streamlines the process considerably saving time & money. (Pe & Llivisaca, n.d.)(Ahram, Sargolzaei, Sargolzaei, Daniels, & Amaba, 2017).

8.   **Security:** Once the creation of block is completed changes or deletion is not applicable. This feature makes the security of Supply Chain more refine after the adoption of blockchain in the existing traditional methods. (Pe & Llivisaca, n.d.)(Tönnissen & Teuteberg, 2019)(Casino et al., 2019)

9.   **Removal of intermediaries:** Blockchain create the platform for a direct transaction eliminating the interference of intermediaries or a third party(Yadav & Singh, 2019)(Weber et al., 2016)

10.   **Reduction in administrative cost:** Reduction in cost of the paper and other consumable items, time-saving, quick discussion, better management, administration & shared databases ease administrative work. (Tönnissen & Teuteberg, 2019)(Osei, Canavari, & Hingley, 2018)

11.   **Decentralization:** Blockchain is a system of teaming up gatherings with a database that is decentralized. This implies that most of the gatherings team up on a blockchain have their own duplicate of the considerable number of exchanges that put away on the blockchain.(Yumna et al., n.d.)(Schmidt & Wagner, 2019)(Wu et al., 2019)(Kharlamov, Parry, & Clarke, n.d.)(Lai, 2019)

12.   **Traceability and visibility:** Trust-worthy system is imparted by blockchain technology by knowing the origin of a product by offering real-time, live and consistently connected updates(Yumna

et al., n.d.)(Kharlamov et al., n.d.)(Venkatesh, Kang, Wang, Zhong, & Zhang, 2020b)(Kamilaris, Fonts, Prenafeta-Boldú, et al., 2019)

The blockchain-based supply chain system focused in this research is a very explorative in reference implementation. This research approach was chosen because blockchain is still in its nascent stage. Our purpose is to set up a platform to meet the demand of supply chain related operations, and at the same time to guarantee the security and transparency of the records in all activities. However, it is difficult to transit from traditional supply chain to the blockchain-based supply chain as it is not smooth.

Companies must poses the knowledge and capability in blockchain to adopt it. Moreover, blockchain technology is still in its early stage in terms of industrial application development. It is full of uncertainties such as whether the blockchain is suitable for the required process, whether the practitioners have the training and required technical development. Furthermore, it is important to realize that blockchain-based industrial solutions should start from the stakeholders' willingness to collaborate and be involved. They must reach a consensus on building blockchain knowledge and capabilities with a focus on driving value for all stakeholders. So that it is critical to create a culture of collaboration. Scalability is holding back early adoptions of blockchain in supply chains or in other similar areas. By definition, every computer connected to the network needs to process the transactions. Organizations have to sacrifice efficiency to obtain security. Therefore, there is a high demand in terms of the technical infrastructure which will be more expensive than the traditional approach.

According to the characteristics of blockchain, stakeholders who use this blockchain based supply chain system will benefit more when the number of participating users grows in this community. As more and more supply chain stakeholders participate, blockchain becomes more valuable and more authentic, evolving into industry practice. This will be particularly tricky when there are legacy processes, regulations and laws governing various aspects of the business, as stakeholders will incur costs when migrating from legacy systems and integrating with new systems and practices. In the future, many organizations, not only in the private sector but also in public departments, will put effort into the blockchain-based logistics system, due to the competitive nature of business. Therefore, itis important to determine standards and agreements to ensure the interoperability between different blockchain-based platforms.

Gaps in Existing Research

If considering the all researches of the study, Most of the identified gaps had to do with outside reasons such as administrative and technical aspects.

- The first obstacle is conformity with the laws and the legal barriers restricting Blockchain technology implementation. Common standards for completing transactions are missing (Tribis, El Bouchti, & Bouayad, 2018).
- The second difference is the failure to adapt and acceptance. Mostly society are unaware about how to operates and produce the great difficulty of getting together all parties concerned and convincing supply chain players to change their traditional supply chain to the current blockchain based system(Tribis et al., 2018)(P. Helo & Hao, 2019).
- The third difference relates to scalability and scale. Most of the proposed blockchain-based architectures have been evaluated in a laboratory environment only on a limited scale; including a number of nodes, certain difficulties that occur in scaling blockchains network.

- The latest blockchain implementations are basically small in size. Next gap that identified is Strong computerization demand. Nevertheless, many supply chain participants are not able to adopt blockchain in the developing countries.
- Complexity and uncertainty of the development is the next gap. The delay of transactions that last for several hours until all parties upgrade their ledgers and the smart contract can be accessible to the public, but the details needed for authentication may or may not be available to everyone.
- Implementation cost of the adaptation is high. For blockchain process, it requires a virtual network and it depends on the electricity, infrastructure and hardware computing systems. These gaps are that most of the frameworks proposed were not evaluated to design systems for real-world applications, Researchers should therefore find the viability of blockchain based solutions and test their applicability to industry (Salah et al., 2019).

However, work on blockchain supply chain management is still in its early stage and should find future applications (Longo, Nicoletti, Padovano, d'Atri, & Forte, 2019)(Yadav & Singh, 2019). Most of the supply chain oparations, especially small and medium-sized companies, state they know nothing about blockchain, and that they find the impact of blockchain as a menace. To increase understanding of blockchain, a prototype of a blockchain-based logistics monitoring system, Frameworks-based solution have real performance evaluation in the industrial context(Tribis et al., 2018)(Wamba, 2019).

In Sri Lanka, there is no measurement to measure the readiness to accept blockchain in supply chain management. And also there is less researches have done in this area. This research aims to solve supply chain management challenges with blockchain implementation in the Sri Lankan food supply chain industry. Therefore for filling some gaps in the literature, this research will be a great support.

MAIN FOCUS OF THE CHAPTER

While the challenges involved in implementing a transparent supply chain are huge, The benefits of applying blockchain to the dairy supply chain far outweigh the disadvantages (initial capital investment cost and maintenance). The advantages of an active blockchain can be narrowly defined as a financial advantage, the benefits of the authorities and the benefits of the food companies. For simplicity's sake, however, the benefits can be classified as enhancing consumer loyalty, improving food crisis management, improving dairy supply chain management, expertise and technical innovation, and contributing to sustainable agriculture. There is an emerging rich network of devices and sensors that build an ecosystem rich in data for efficient monitoring and analysis of properties, which was unlikely in supply chains several years ago. This evolution has now allowed us to use this technology to create a blockchain network that provides as mentioned in this research a lot of possible benefits.

Many of the potential risks and the lack of demonstrable evidence the implementation of blockchain in the supply chain is currently sluggish. Nonetheless, businesses are trying to consider the positives or drawbacks of blockchains in supply chains.

Problem Definition

The emergence of digital businesses transforms conventional market models and, mainly, how we do it. The flow of industry has intensified in a environment today running 24 hours. This has changed the way businesses collaborate, trade and connect with customers, vendors and partners. Suppliers and the supply chain have an effect on everything: from efficiency, distribution and expense, to customer support, loyalty and benefit. Enterprise globalization expanded the difficulty of the supply chain processors. Now it is a main component to improve and integrate the information system. The difficulty of taking decisions needs real-time data sharing (Yu, Wang, Zhong, & Huang, 2016). When information moved in a linear form in conventional supply chains and inefficiencies in one stage influenced the following cascade stages, Digital supply networks are now capable of building interconnected networks capable of overcoming the action-reaction cycle with real-time data and facilitating cooperation. The figure 3 shows the shift from the traditional supply chain to the digital supply network(Mussomeli, Gish, &

Figure 3. The evolution of Supply chain

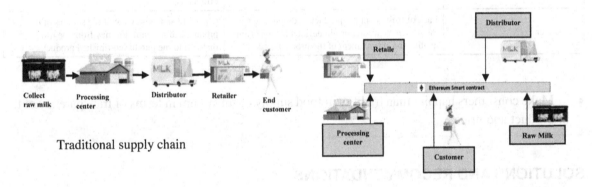

Traditional supply chain

Digital supply chain network

Laaper, 2015).

According to this, emphasis on how blockchain affects the supply chain. To have this done, Possible applications and implementation of blockchain are discussed in the supply chain to help businesses understand how to achieve their business goals. Furthermore, A logistics management program based on blockchain is applied to evaluate the viability of applying blockchain in the food supply chain. Accordingly, The major objective of this research is to fill current research gaps, new approaches to integrate blockchain and IoT technology within food supply chain, and food quality management in the Sri Lankan food supply chain system. This study has following objectives also.

- Improve the scalability of any business by increasing customers' experience and more awareness about blockchain.
- Provide Trust for the entire supply chain network through blockchain agreement(consensus)
- Improve the privacy of the supply chain system by facilitating access control over who will have access to the information in the block.
- Reduce costs by ignoring additional payment for third-party persons.

Table 3. Current problems and blockchain impact in supply chain system

Supply chain actor	Current Problems	Blockchain impact
Famer/Supplier	Capability to prove the origin and quality metrics of goods using a global and clear process.	Benefits from the improved trust by maintaining track by raw material production and supply chain from the raw material to the end customer.
Processor	Poor ability to track the goods produced to the final destination. Small ability to analyze measured content from raw material.	Value added from shared facts system with suppliers of raw materials and distribution networks.
Distributor	Customized monitoring devices with limited ability to work together. Limited certification skills and confidence issues.	Ability to have proof of position recorded in the database, and conditions certifications.
Wholesaler	Lack of confidence, and certification of the product path.	Capacity to test the origin of the products and the conditions for transformation or transportation.
Retailer	Lack of confidence, and certification of the product path.	Tracking any single commodity between the wholesaler and the final customer. Capacity to manage the returns of malfunctioning goods efficiently.
Consumer	Lack of trust about the product's compliance with the requirements and origin defined for the origin, quality and enforcement of the product.	Complete and clear view of the sources of the product and its entire journey from the raw material to the purchased finished product.

• Make consumers happier than traditional food supply chain system in terms of transparency of the product and price.

SOLUTIONS AND RECOMMENDATIONS

This segment describes the suggested solution that using blockchain within ethereum network and smart contracts to trace, track, and perform transactions in dairy supply chains. This approach eliminates the need for a trustworthy centralized authority and allows transactions and store the transaction information for food supply chain management.. Table 4 describe how blockchain based model address the issues in current dairy supply chain.

Table 4. Problems that address by blockchain in the dairy supply chain

Issues in the existing Supply chain system	The solution is given by proposed mechanism
Lack of trust about the product's compliance with the requirements and origin defined for the origin, quality and enforcement of the product.	Complete and clear view of the sources of the product and its entire journey from the raw material to the purchased finished product.
Require a central party to maintain the dairy supply chain transactions.	provides the platform for a direct transaction without the interference of intermediaries or a third party IoT sensors track the data and smart contract validate them and added to the blockchain.
Have to manually enter the data about dairy transaction.	Reduction in paper and another consumable item, time-saving. automatically detect and store the data in to blockchain
In traditional dairy supply chain, manually check temperature, volume and quality of milk. It is time consuming.	Information flow speed, no intermediary is required, smart contracts, easily traceable and finally it streamlines the processes considerably

The suggested approach would concentrate on the use of autonomously implemented smart contracts on the decentralized blockchain Ethereum network. Functions of the smart contract execution and conductby thousands of mining nodes. Mining nods are globally distributed, and the execution outcome is agreed by all of the mining nodes.

Additionally, any actor or participant must have an Ethereum account in blockchain and they have to have a unique Ethereum address. This helps to identify the actor in a unique way. The Ethereum account basically consists of the Ethereum address with public and private keys that are used to sign and verify the data integrity within each transaction cryptographically and digitally, and associate each transaction with a specific Ethereum address or account.

Table 5 shows how combination of IOT blockchains within the food supply chain. This chart describe the process of tracking information from raw milk, processing details, transport information, quality of manufactured product, etc. That will finally bring value in the customer's hands to the finished product.

This architecture captures information regarding traceability using a range of IoT devices based on the type of event to be recorded. A transaction could be a movement of milk product, processing or store of milk, Distribute. Multiple data recorded from an IoT checkpoint is converted into a transaction and pushed to the etheteum network. All the transaction data check and validate within the smart contract and then publish to the public ledger. The contract layer monitors every transaction data, to execute the smart contracts when an initial event takes place and it ensures expected data about the raw milk or milk product from the supplier, manufacture and distributor in the supply chain according to terms of trade agreed upon connecting to the blockchain network.

Each entity involved plays a role, relationship, and interactions with the smart contract. Propose model contain only five participating entities. Here describe their role:

Milk Supplier: As per the depiction milk suppliers have access to web applications. Through that application they can view information that they using IOT sensor. IOT will play a key role in capturing this information from the raw milk and transmitting it to the Blockchain.

Milk Processor: IOT sensors in those premises and storage locations can greatly enhance the traceability and help end customers with information of products storage criteria like the physical conditions of density, temperature, volume, etc. The status of various environmental / physical and product-related characteristics can help to assess the quality of the finished product before and after manufacture, its freshness and other consuming characteristics. Aberrations can be very dangerous during production and this information isn't available today. This can be made available and evaluated with the IOT network system, which help to determine the root cause causes if anything goes wrong or any complications found through random sample checks.

Distributer: Nowadays consumer can get only few information about transporting these products. Capturing IOT data at the time of travel or factory exit analysis will greatly help close this significant gap. The sensors will capture the physical storage conditions in the trucks / ocean freight warehouse and make it accessible in the blockchain network. Various partners can access this information and make informed product decisions based on smart contracts. Where authenticity and transparency are required, even this information can be rendered to end customers.

Retailer: The emphasis on product safety and freshness is of vital importance for a retailer. Data are available in blockchain that can be traced and analyzed right from farm to fork. In addition to that, the IOT Blockchain architecture can help to obtain the information from source / origin until final consumption.

Customer: The customer is the end-user who buys and uses the retailer's product.

Table 5. Supply chain solution with IOT Blockchain model architecture

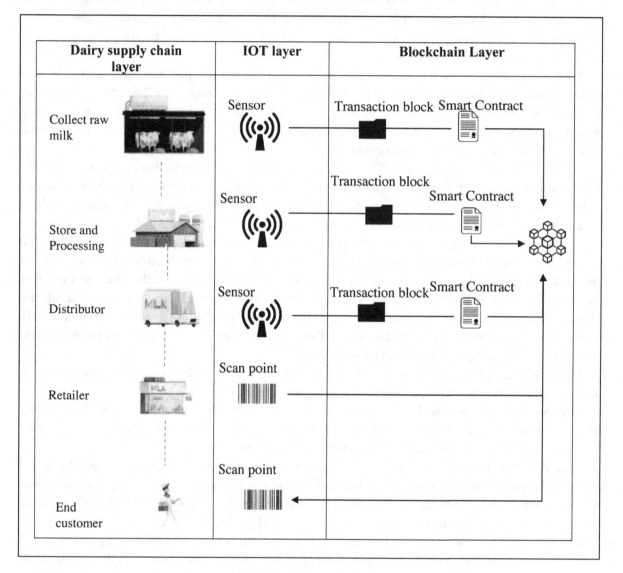

Transaction Data Processing Flow

Figure 4 describe the transaction data processing flow of storing data in the blockchain. IoT devices generate data such as density, temperature, volume, etc. After digital signing and the hashing,

Such data will be sent directly or through the IoT gateways to the entire blockchain network nodes, Where they are verified, connected to the Transaction Pool and stored in blockchain.

Customers can access and validate all transaction data via their laptops or mobile phones. For example, one buys a package of milk from a supermarket and then he / she can use a mobile to check the 2-D barcode to gather all the transaction data relevant to it, including the farm from which the milk was made, the day and time it was delivered, the cow ID on the farm, the workers ID processing the milk,

Figure 4. Transaction Data Processing Flow

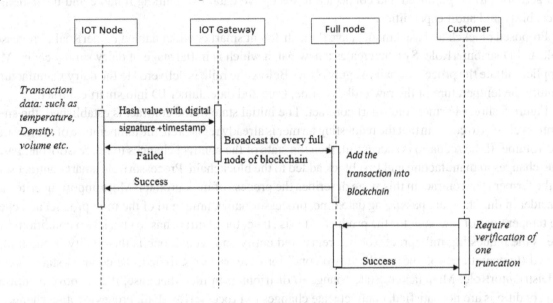

the collection of computer information, the packaging information, all the temperature. All of those information can be verified without human intervention by the blockchain system.

Traceable Functionality

Using our suggested blockchain-based approach utilizing smart contracts, the benefit of using traceable technology in the dairy supply chain is that all actors without a central authority within the supply chain have verifiable and non-modifiable details accessible. The total volume of milk products sold between subsequent entities is logged to the next echelon starting with supplier and manufacturing transactions, and all transactions can be verified. For example, with the agreed terms, it is impossible to alter or change the volume of milk sold between entities. In addition, milk with various quality standards cannot be combined together for sale, because all stakeholders are aware with total quantity.

The use of traceable identifiers per lot and the ability to trace all corresponding transactions between stakeholders further ensure continuous monitoring for quality compliance. It is also possible to monitor the quality of the milk and conditions using IoT-enabled containers and packages equipped with sensors, cameras, GPS locator, and 4G communication With blockchain, such knowledge and verification cannot be changed or tampered with, and usable automatically and open to all stakeholders in a transparent and decentralized way, without intermediaries.

It should be remembered that a stakeholder can steal or may transact and record fraudulent data. The blockchain, in this situation, marks the data as such with a validated reference to the source data (i.e. the real stakeholder). If the data were caught to be incorrect at a later stage, the judges and all participants can attribute the data to a given actor or stakeholder with 100 percent certainty. Blockchain can identify fraud in that scenario. To resolve this kind of theft, blockchain can be configured by smart contracts to provide additional functionality for the whole supply chain process, and any steps can be taken to enforce fines on dishonest suppliers or take appropriate and punitive action. This will create new corrective data and activities to be produced and connected to deceptive data, maintaining reliable and unchallenged traceability and audit capabilities.

Proposed blockchain based model have three different smart contract named FamerRoal,, Processor-Role and DistributerRole. System creates a new batch which is initial stage of dairy supply chain. Milk supplier initiate the process of dairy supply chain. Before the milk is delivered to the dairy manufacturer, capture the temperature of the raw milk, volume, time and date, famer ID into smart contract.

Figure 5 shows FarmerRole smart contract. The initial state of the contract is established, the smart contract checks to confirm that the requesting farmer is already registered, the temperature of the raw milk and volume. If the scenario is successful, then the state of the contract changes to ProcessorRole. Famer state changes to manufacture and first block added to the blockchain. ProcessorRole smart contract same as the farmer role contract in this stage describes the process of milk product. Most important criteria to consider in this stage are packaging date time, processor name, unique Id of the milk product and check the temperature of raw milk for the product. At this stage, the contract has to check two condition. First one is the requesting milk processor is a registered entity and second one is the quality of the milk is agreed (temperature, volume). If these two conditions are true or satisfied, the contract state changes to DistributorRole. Manufacture state change to distributer. In the other case, if the above mentioned two conditions are not satisfied, contract state changes to ProcessorRoleFail, processor state chenges to RequestFailure, the cancel the process.

At the distributor stage retailer buy the product from distributer. Date of product manufacture and quantity sold are some important parameters to keep a check. The distributer and retailers will be identified with their Ethereum addresses. For execute the DistributerRole smart contract, authorized distributer have to input date about transport information and warehouse information of the milk product. Then smart contract check and validate distributor role. Above each and every success transaction add a new block to the blockchain. This is how the dairy supply chain complete for one batch. In this way store all the batch information into blockchin database. Using smart tag with barcode reader batch information can show for the outside user. Retailer and customer are final role of the system. They are able to transparently verify the whole history of a product before buying it. Smart-tags can be associated to each package, so that retailers and consumers can easily retrieve the whole history of the product.

IoT Implementation

The proposed system contain two type of IoT devices to integrate. One of them is sensors that used to collect data like temperature, volume, density. Although preparations were being made for integrating actuators into the system, the work performed here ended up only covering sensor usage for readings. Nevertheless, theoretically, the same kind of platform used for sensor-Blockchain connectivity may also be used for actuators.

For the purpose of integrating IoT devices into proposed model, first need to resolve the question about where our Blockchain client should be operating. Most IoT sensors are intended to have low processing capacity due to energy usage and cost constraints. Clients of Blockchain, moreover, are heavy programs that need massive quantities of data and computing capacity to run. As a result, the simplest way to integrate an IoT device to a Blockchain at the moment is by a gateway machine running the Blockchain client and connecting only with IoT device through another protocol.

Second one is to connect with the Blockchain, each system contain user account or a private and public key combination. Then system have to decide where it keep the secret keys that is used to sign

Figure 5. FarmerRole smart contract

```
contract FarmerRole is Ownable {

    uint256 public temp;
    using Roles for Roles.Role;
    event FarmerAdded(address indexed account);
    event FarmerRemoved(address indexed account);
    Roles.Role private farmers;

    constructor() public {
        _addFarmer(msg.sender);
    }
    modifier onlyFarmer() {
        require(isFarmer(msg.sender), "Caller is not a farmer.");
        _;
    }
    function isFarmer(address account) public view returns (bool) {
        return farmers.has(account);
    }
    function addFarmer(address account) public onlyOwner {
        _addFarmer(account);
    }
    function renounceFarmer() public onlyOwner {
        _removeFarmer(msg.sender);
    }
    function _addFarmer(address account) internal {
        farmers.add(account);
        emit FarmerAdded(account);
    }
    function _removeFarmer(address account) internal {
        farmers.remove(account);
        emit FarmerRemoved(account);
    }
    function setTemperature(uint256 temp) public {
        temp = temp;
    }
    function getTemperature() external view returns (uint256) {
        return temp;
    }
function checkTemp() external view returns (string){
    if(temp<=5 ){
        return "Correct temperature";
    }else{
        return "Incorrect temperature";
    }
```

transfers and invest the currency of the account. Realizing that executing transactions are challenging in terms of computing capacity, and that keeping a private key in the system itself can prove dangerous because there is no access control over its memory storage, system have opted to use a Blockchain wallet program in the gateway module of its own to improve the protection of that key.

When create a new batch, when parsing each and every process, it access a method in the smart contract, next fire event to start reading input data. Then gateway unit is listening to the Blockchain network. Store the data received into the system when reserved it. Finally before moving to the next phase. Consider the tracked data and it validate automatically by smart contract according to the requested quality of food.

The proposed system architecture integrate with NodeMCU for IoT implementation. It has ability receive real time data from different censers at the different level, store that data and process them into actionable insights. Using nodeMCU can store data in a place where it can be readily accessed for further analysis. It is open source, interactive, programmable, low cost, simple to complement, smart and Wi-Fi enabled device. Not only has that it also taken advantage with the building-in API to data transmit.

Here use only Waterproof a LM35 temperature sensor. That have selected in proposed model to track the temperature of raw milk and milk product in different stage of the dairy supply chain. Temperature sensor module LM35 has been selected because it needs no calibration and is compatible with NodeMCU, waterproof and even low power consumption. Other important factors of dairy supply chain can track using different sensors as the measure temperature.

Figure 6. Algorithm 1

Algorithm 1 FarmerRole

1: **INPUT:**
2:       F is the list of registered farmers
3:       EthereumAddress(EA) of Farmer
4:       t is the TemperatureOfRawMilk
5: Contractsate is **FarmerRole**
6: Restrict access to only

$$farmer \in F$$

   i.e., registered Farmer
7: **if** farmer = registered **then**
8:      Change State of farmer to WaitForMilk
9:      **if** $t \geq 5C^{r0}$ **then**
10:         Create a notification message stating the success of process
11:      **end if**
12: **end if**

Figure 7. Algorithm 2

Algorithm 2 ProcessorRole

1: **INPUT:**
2:        P is the list of registered Processors
3:        EthereumAddress(EA) of Milk Processors
4:        t TemperatureOfRawMilk
5:        DatePurchesed , Quality
6: Contractsate is **ProcessorRole**
7: Restrict access to only

$$Processor \in P$$

8: **if** Processor = registered **then**
9:     Change State of processer to WaitForMilkProduct
10:     **if** $t \geq 5C^{\circ0}$ AND Quality **then**
11:         Create a notification message stating the success
12:            of process
13:     **end if**
14: **end if**

3.7. Implementation Process

The proposed Blockchain-based model has three different smart contracts named FamerRoal,, ProcessorRole and DistributerRole. The system creates a new batch which is the initial stage of the dairy supply chain. Milk supplier initiates the process of the dairy supply chain. Before the milk is delivered to the dairy manufacturer, capture the temperature of the raw milk, volume, time and date, famer ID into a smart contract.

Figure 6 Algorithm 1 shows FarmerRole smart contract. The initial contractual state is determined, the smart contract checks to confirm that the applicant farmer is already registered, the temperature of the raw milk and volume. If the scenario is successful, then the contractual state will change to ProcessorRole. Famer state changes to manufacture and first block added to the Blockchain. Figure 7, Algorithm 2 describes ProcessorRole smart contract. It the same as the farmer role contract in this stage describes the process of milk production. The most important criteria to consider in this stage are packaging date-time, processor name, unique Id of the milk product and check the temperature of raw milk for the product. At this stage, the contract has to check two conditions. The first one is the requesting milk processor is a registered entity and the second one is the quality of the milk is agreed (temperature, volume). If these two requirements are valid or met, the contract state will be changed to DistributorRole. Figure 7, Algorithm 3 describes DistributorRole. In the other case, if the above two conditions are not fulfilled, change the contract state to ProcessorRoleFail, processor state changes to RequestFailure, the cancel the process.

At the distributor, stage the retailer buys the product from the distributor. The date of manufacture of the product and the amount sold are some important parameters to keep a check. The distributor and retailers will have their Ethereum addresses identified. To execute the DistributerRole smart contract,

Figure 8. Algorithm 3

Algorithm 3 DistributorRole

1: **INPUT:**
2:       D is the list of registered Distributors
3:       EthereumAddress(EA) of Distributors
4:       TransportCondition, WarehouseCondition,
5:       DateManufactured
6: Contractsate is **DistributorRole**
7: Restrict access to only

$$Distributor \in D$$

8: **if** Distributor = registered **then**
9:     Change State of distributor to WaitForDistribute
10:     Create a notification message stating the success of process
11: **end if**

---

authorized distributors have to input date about transport information and warehouse information of the milk product. Then smart contract checks and validates the distributor role. Above each and every success transaction add a new block to the Blockchain. This is how the dairy supply chain complete for one batch. In this way store all the batch information into the Blockchain database. Using a smart tag with barcode reader batch information can show for the outside user. Retailers and customers are final

Figure 9. Admin Dashboard

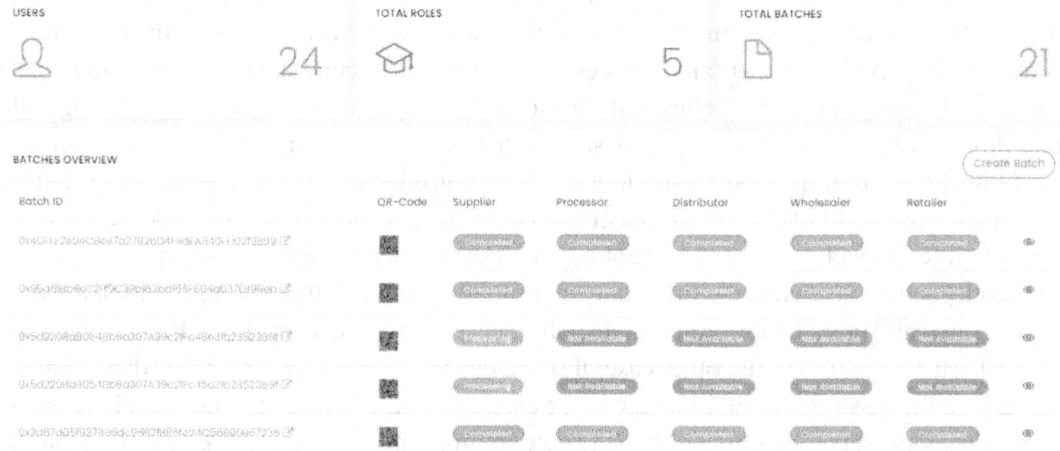

Figure 10. Create New Batch

roles of the system. They can verify the entire history of a product before buying it in a transparent manner. Each package may be associated with smart tags, so retailers and consumers can easily retrieve the entire product history.

RESULT AND FINDING

An overview of the framework built and applied will be made in this portion. First, the experiments presented here will establish whether the reference implemented system performs as it should when users communicate with its processes. An overview of the built web applications is given here. That provides ability to track the origin of the milk product.

For validate the proposed model, create simple web application. If permissioned user want to gain information form Blockchain network. It provide admin dashboard and it display Total Number of User, Total Roles, Total Batch, and Batch Overview. Figure 9 shows admin dashboard.

In batches overview section provide information about the progress of each batch. By clicking on button Create Batch, system can create new batch for dairy supply chain. Complete that process user have to provide basic information of batch like Supplier Registration Number, Supplier's Name, and Supplier's Address.

Each and every process detail of the particular batch in the supply chain, user can find by pressing on eye icon. It shows as figure below. Here user can read complete details of each transaction.

With the complete details of each transaction, create RFID tag for each and product. Customers can access and validate all transaction data using that RFID tag.

Figure 11. Batch Details

FUTURE RESEARCH DIRECTIONS

Future research efforts can concentrate on defining the different compensation mechanisms to be used within the blockchain network to promote a consistent transfer of power as to how the transactional data can be used within the food supply chain. A major technological transition such as the introduction of blockchains is only possible if it is driven by the company in certain stages of the value chain with a larger impact on the sector. Therefore it would be interesting to find out how the power balance between retailers and food processors would change the blockchain model proposed. Another possible research problem to answer is blockchain scalability.

CONCLUSION

Food provenance is one of the most challenging questions that companies in the food supply chain are trying to solve today and this research is a small contribution to answering that question. The primary aim of this research is to establish a blockchain platform that can be applied within a food supply chain and include its advantages and disadvantages in terms of food provenance and product traceability over conventional tracking systems It is clear from this research initiative that blockchains can be more effective in monitoring food provenance, avoiding significant degradation of food items, detecting and eliminating the source of foodborne disease in seconds, whereas contemporary systems may take as many weeks. It would also provide greater customer confidence that reflects the satisfaction of sales and customers.

REFERENCES

Agrawal, T. K., Sharma, A., & Kumar, V. (n.d.). *Blockchain-Based Secured Traceability Chain*. Academic Press.

Ahram, T., Sargolzaei, A., Sargolzaei, S., Daniels, J., & Amaba, B. (2017). Blockchain technology innovations. *2017 IEEE Technology and Engineering Management Society Conference. TEMSCON, 2017*, 137–141. Advance online publication. doi:10.1109/TEMSCON.2017.7998367

Al Barghuthi, N. B., Mohamed, H. J., & Said, H. E. (2019). Blockchain in Supply Chain Trading. *ITT 2018 - Information Technology Trends: Emerging Technologies for Artificial Intelligence*, 336–341. doi:10.1109/CTIT.2018.8649523

Aung, M. M., & Chang, Y. S. (2014). Traceability in a food supply chain: Safety and quality perspectives. *Food Control*, *39*(1), 172–184. doi:10.1016/j.foodcont.2013.11.007

Jayasena. (2017). *How the Blockchain Revolution Will Reshape the Consumer Electronics Industry*. Academic Press.

Azzi, R., Chamoun, R. K., & Sokhn, M. (2019). Computers & Industrial Engineering The power of a blockchain-based supply chain. *Computers & Industrial Engineering, 135*(August), 582–592. doi:10.1016/j.cie.2019.06.042

Bartling, S., & Fecher, B. (2016). Could Blockchain provide the technical fix to solve science's reproducibility crisis? *Impact of Social Sciences Blog.*

Basnayake, B. M. A. L., & Rajapakse, C. (2019). A Blockchain-based decentralized system to ensure the transparency of organic food supply chain. *Proceedings - IEEE International Research Conference on Smart Computing and Systems Engineering, SCSE 2019*, 103–107. 10.23919/SCSE.2019.8842690

Bocek, T., Rodrigues, B. B., Strasser, T., & Stiller, B. (2017). *Blockchains Everywhere - A Use-case of Blockchains in the Pharma Supply-Chain.* Academic Press.

Bosona, T., & Gebresenbet, G. (2013). Food traceability as an integral part of logistics management in food and agricultural supply chain. *Food Control, 33*(1), 32–48. Advance online publication. doi:10.1016/j.foodcont.2013.02.004

Casino, F., Dasaklis, T. K., & Patsakis, C. (2019). A systematic literature review of blockchain-based applications: Current status, classification and open issues. *Telematics and Informatics, 36*, 55–81. doi:10.1016/j.tele.2018.11.006

Chen, S., Shi, R., Ren, Z., Yan, J., Shi, Y., & Zhang, J. (2017). A Blockchain-Based Supply Chain Quality Management Framework. *Proceedings - 14th IEEE International Conference on E-Business Engineering, ICEBE 2017 - Including 13th Workshop on Service-Oriented Applications, Integration and Collaboration, SOAIC 207*, 172–176. 10.1109/ICEBE.2017.34

Elmessiry, M., & Elmessiry, A. (2018). *Blockchain Framework for Textile Supply Chain Management.* doi:10.1007/978-3-319-94478-4

Frizzo-barker, J., Chow-white, P. A., Adams, P. R., Mentanko, J., Ha, D., & Green, S. (2019). A systematic review. *International Journal of Information Management, 0–1*(April). Advance online publication. doi:10.1016/j.ijinfomgt.2019.10.014

Helo, P., & Hao, Y. (2019). Blockchains in operations and supply chains: A model and reference implementation. *Computers & Industrial Engineering, 136*(July), 242–251. doi:10.1016/j.cie.2019.07.023

Helo, P., & Shamsuzzoha, A. H. M. (2018, December). Real-time supply chain—A blockchain architecture for project deliveries. *Robotics and Computer-integrated Manufacturing, 63*, 101909. doi:10.1016/j.rcim.2019.101909

Helo, P., & Szekely, B. (2005, January). Logistics information systems: An analysis of software solutions for supply chain co-ordination. *Industrial Management & Data Systems, 105*(1), 5–18. Advance online publication. doi:10.1108/02635570510575153

It, S. (2017). *Can Blockchain Strengthen the Internet of Things?* Academic Press.

Kamilaris, A., Fonts, A., & Prenafeta-Boldó, F. X. (2019). The rise of blockchain technology in agriculture and food supply chains. *Trends in Food Science & Technology, 91*, 640–652. doi:10.1016/j.tifs.2019.07.034

Kamilaris, A., Fonts, A., Prenafeta-Boldó, F. X., Kamble, S. S., Gunasekaran, A., Sharma, R., ... Beynon-Davies, P. (2019). How the blockchain enables and constrains supply chain performance. *Supply Chain Management, 24*(4), 376–397. doi:10.1108/IJPDLM-02-2019-0063

Kharlamov, A., Parry, G., & Clarke, A. C. (n.d.). *Advanced Supply Chains : Visibility, Blockchain and Human Behaviour*. Academic Press.

Kosba, A., Miller, A., Shi, E., Wen, Z., & Papamanthou, C. (2016). Hawk: The Blockchain Model of Cryptography and Privacy-Preserving Smart Contracts. *Proceedings - 2016 IEEE Symposium on Security and Privacy, SP 2016*. 10.1109/SP.2016.55

Kshetri, N. (2018). Blockchain's roles in meeting key supply chain management objectives. *International Journal of Information Management, 39*(June), 80–89. doi:10.1016/j.ijinfomgt.2017.12.005

Lai, J. (2019). Research on Cross-Border E-Commerce Logistics Supply under Block Chain. *Proceedings - 2nd International Conference on Computer Network, Electronic and Automation, ICCNEA 2019*, 214–218. 10.1109/ICCNEA.2019.00049

Litke, A., Anagnostopoulos, D., & Varvarigou, T. (2019). Blockchains for Supply Chain Management: Architectural Elements and Challenges Towards a Global Scale Deployment. *Logistics, 3*(1), 5. doi:10.3390/logistics3010005

Liu, H., Li, Z., & Cao, N. (2018). *Framework Design of Financial Service Platform for Tobacco Supply Chain Based on Blockchain* (Vol. 2). doi:10.1007/978-3-030-05234-8

Longo, F., Nicoletti, L., Padovano, A., d'Atri, G., & Forte, M. (2019). Blockchain-enabled supply chain: An experimental study. *Computers & Industrial Engineering, 136*(July), 57–69. doi:10.1016/j.cie.2019.07.026

Madavi, D. (2008). *A Comprehensive Study on Blockchain Technology. International Research Journal of Engineering and Technology*.

Madumidha, S., Ranjani, P. S., Varsinee, S. S., & Sundari, P. S. (2019). Transparency and traceability: In food supply chain system using blockchain technology with internet of things. *Proceedings of the International Conference on Trends in Electronics and Informatics, ICOEI 2019*, 983–987. 10.1109/ICOEI.2019.8862726

Mattila, J., Seppälä, T., & Holmström, J. (2016). Product-centric Information Management. *A Case Study of a Shared Platform with Blockchain Technology*.

Mussomeli, A., Gish, D., & Laaper, S. (2015). The Rise of the Digital Supply network. *Deloitte*.

Nakamoto, S. (2008). *Bitcoin: A Peer-to-Peer Electronic Cash System. Consulted*. Consulted. doi:10.100710838-008-9062-0stem

Osei, R. K., Canavari, M., & Hingley, M. (2018). An Exploration into the Opportunities for Blockchain in the Fresh Produce Supply Chain. doi:10.20944/preprints201811.0537.v1

Pe, M., & Llivisaca, J. (n.d.). Advances in Emerging Trends and Technologies. *Blockchain and Its Potential Applications in Food Supply Chain Management in Ecuador., 3*, 101–112. doi:10.1007/978-3-030-32022-5

Pilkington, M. (2016). Blockchain technology: Principles and applications. Research Handbooks on Digital Transformations. doi:10.4337/9781784717766.00019

Salah, K., Nizamuddin, N., Jayaraman, R., & Omar, M. A. (2019). Blockchain-Based Soybean Traceability in Agricultural Supply Chain. *Blockchain-based Soybean Traceability in Agricultural Supply Chain*, *7*(May), 73295–73305. Advance online publication. doi:10.1109/ACCESS.2019.2918000

Schmidt, C. G., & Wagner, S. M. (2019). A transaction cost theory perspective. *Journal of Purchasing and Supply Management*, *25*(4), 100552. doi:10.1016/j.pursup.2019.100552

Scully, P., & Hobig, M. (2019). Exploring the impact of blockchain on digitized Supply Chain flows: A literature review. *2019 6th International Conference on Software Defined Systems, SDS 2019*, 278–283. 10.1109/SDS.2019.8768573

Sheel, A., & Nath, V. (2019). Effect of blockchain technology adoption on supply chain adaptability, agility, alignment and performance. *Management Research Review*, *42*(12), 1353–1374. Advance online publication. doi:10.1108/MRR-12-2018-0490

Tezel, A., Papadonikolaki, E., Yitmen, I., & Hilletofth, P. (2019). *Preparing Construction Supply Chains for Blockchain : An Exploratory*. Academic Press.

Tian, F. (2016). An agri-food supply chain traceability system for China based on RFID & blockchain technology. *2016 13th International Conference on Service Systems and Service Management, ICSSSM 2016*. 10.1109/ICSSSM.2016.7538424

Tönnissen, S., & Teuteberg, F. (2019). Analysing the impact of blockchain-technology for operations and supply chain management: An explanatory model drawn from multiple case studies. *International Journal of Information Management*, *0–1*(January). Advance online publication. doi:10.1016/j.ijinfomgt.2019.05.009

Treiblmaier, H. (2018). The impact of the blockchain on the supply chain: A theory-based research framework and a call for action. *Supply Chain Management*, *23*(6), 545–559. doi:10.1108/SCM-01-2018-0029

Tribis, Y., El Bouchti, A., & Bouayad, H. (2018). Supply chain management based on blockchain: A systematic mapping study. *MATEC Web of Conferences, 200*. 10.1051/matecconf/201820000020

Venkatesh, V. G., Kang, K., Wang, B., Zhong, R. Y., & Zhang, A. (2020). System architecture for blockchain based transparency of supply chain social sustainability. *Robotics and Computer-Integrated Manufacturing, 63*(November), 101896. doi:10.1016/j.rcim.2019.101896

Wamba, S. F. (2019). *Continuance Intention in Blockchain-Enabled Supply Chain Applications : Modelling the Moderating Effect of Supply Chain Stakeholders Trust*. doi:10.1007/978-3-030-11395-7

Wang, Y., Han, J. H., Beynon-davies, P., Wang, Y., Han, J. H., & Beynon-davies, P. (2018). *Understanding blockchain technology for future supply chains : a systematic literature review and research agenda*. doi:10.1108/SCM-03-2018-0148

Weber, I., Xu, X., Riveret, R., Governatori, G., Ponomarev, A., & Mendling, J. (2016). *Untrusted business process monitoring and execution using blockchain*. Lecture Notes in Computer Science. Including Subseries Lecture Notes in Artificial Intelligence and Lecture Notes in Bioinformatics. doi:10.1007/978-3-319-45348-4_19

Wright, A., & De Filippi, P. (2015). Decentralized Blockchain Technology and the Rise of Lex Cryptographia. SSRN *Electronic Journal*. doi:10.2139srn.2580664

Wu, H., Cao, J., Yang, Y., Tung, C. L., Jiang, S., Tang, B., . . . Deng, Y. (2019). Data management in supply chain using blockchain: challenges and a case study. *Proceedings - International Conference on Computer Communications and Networks, ICCCN,* 1–8. 10.1109/ICCCN.2019.8846964

Yadav, S., & Singh, S. P. (2019). *Blockchain critical success factors for sustainable supply chain Resources, Conservation & Recycling.* doi:10.1016/j.resconrec.2019.104505

Yu, Y., Wang, X., Zhong, R. Y., & Huang, G. Q. (2016). E-commerce Logistics in Supply Chain Management: Practice Perspective. *Procedia CIRP, 52,* 179–185. Advance online publication. doi:10.1016/j.procir.2016.08.002

Yumna, H., Murad, M., Ikram, M., & Noreen, S. (n.d.). *Use of blockchain in Education : A systematic Literature Review*. Academic Press.

KEY TERMS AND DEFINITIONS

Cryptography: The practice and study of secure communication techniques in the presence of third parties known as adversaries.

Decentralization: Process by which an organization's activities, in particular those relating to planning and decision-making, are distributed or delegated from a central, authoritative place or group.

Distributed Ledger: A consensus of geographically spread replicated, shared, and synchronized digital data across multiple sites, countries, or institutions.

Double Spend: Potential flaw in a digital cash scheme where the same digital token can be spent more than once.

Ethereum: Decentralized open source blockchain featuring smart contract functionality.

Immutability: Design pattern where something can't be modified after being instantiated.

Smart Contract: Computer program or transaction protocol that is intended to automatically execute, control, or document events and actions legally relevant under the terms of a contract or agreement.

Compilation of References

Bodkhe, U., Bhattacharya, P., Tanwar, S., Tyagi, S., Kumar, N., & Obaidat, M. S. (2019, August). Blohost: Blockchain enabled smart tourism and hospitality management. In *2019 International Conference on Computer, Information and Telecommunication Systems (CITS)* (pp. 1-5). IEEE. 10.1109/CITS.2019.8862001

Burniske, C., Vaughn, E., Cahana, A., & Shelton, J. (2016). *How Blockchain Technology Can Enhance Electronic Health Record Operability*. Ark Invest.

Dannen, C. (2017). *Introducing Ethereum and Solidity: Foundations of Cryptocurrency and Blockchain Programming for Beginners* (1st ed.). Apress., doi:10.1007/978-1-4842-2535-6

Lu, Q., & Xu, X. (2017, November/December). Adaptable blockchain-based systems: A case study for product traceability. *IEEE Software*, *34*(6), 21–27. doi:10.1109/MS.2017.4121227

Weking, J., & Mandalenakis, M. (2020). *The impact of blockchain technology on business models – a taxonomy and archetypal patterns. In Electron Markets*. Springer.

Blockchain: The India Strategy. (n.d.). https://niti.gov.in/sites/default/files/2020-01/Blockchain_The_India_Strategy_Part_I.pdf

Dorri, A., Steger, M., Kanhere, S. S., & Jurdak, R. (2017, December). BlockChain: A distributed solution to automotive security and privacy. *IEEE Communications Magazine*, *55*(12), 119–125. doi:10.1109/MCOM.2017.1700879

Hardwick, F. S., Gioulis, A., Akram, R. N., & Markantonakis, K. (2018, July). E-voting with blockchain: An e-voting protocol with decentralisation and voter privacy. In *2018 IEEE International Conference on Internet of Things (iThings) and IEEE Green Computing and Communications (GreenCom) and IEEE Cyber, Physical and Social Computing (CPSCom) and IEEE Smart Data (SmartData)* (pp. 1561-1567). IEEE.

Jovanovic, B., & Rousseau, P. L. (2005). General Purpose Technologies. In *Handbook of Economic Growth*. Elsevier. doi:10.1016/S1574-0684(05)01018-X

Androulaki, E., Barger, A., Bortnikov, V., Cachin, C., Christidis, K., De Caro, A., Enyeart, D., Ferris, C., Laventman, G., & Manevich, Y. (2018). Hyperledger Fabric: A Distributed Operating System for Permissioned Blockchains. In *Proceedings of the Thirteenth EuroSys Conference; EuroSys '18*. Association for Computing Machinery. https://dl.acm.org/doi/10.1145/3190508.3190538

Dinh & Thai. (2018). AI and Blockchain: A Disruptive Integration. *Computer, 51*(9), 48-53.

Khandelwal, A. (2019, February). Blockchain implimentation on E-voting System. In *2019 International Conference on Intelligent Sustainable Systems (ICISS)* (pp. 385-388). IEEE. 10.1109/ISS1.2019.8907951

Swan, M. (2014). Blockchain-Enforced Friendly AI. In *Crypto Money Expo*. http://cryptomoneyexpo.com/expos/inv2/#schedule

Angraal, S., Krumholz, H. M., & Schulz, W. L. (2017). Blockchain Technology Applications in Health Care. *Circulation: Cardiovascular Quality and Outcomes, 10*(9), e003800. doi:10.1161/CIRCOUTCOMES.117.003800 PMID:28912202

Nakamoto. (2008). *Bitcoin: A peer-to-peer electronic cash system*. Academic Press.

Salah, K., Habib ur Rehman, M., Nizamuddin, N., & Al-Fuqaha, A. (2018). Blockchain for AI: Review and Open Research Challenges. *IEEE Access*. doi:10.1109/ACCESS.2018.2890507

Zhang, A., & Lin, X. (2018). Towards secure and privacy-preserving data sharing in e-health systems via consortium blockchain. *Journal of Medical Systems, 42*(8), 140. doi:10.100710916-018-0995-5 PMID:29956061

Engelhardt, M. A. (2017). Hitching Healthcare to the Chain: An Introduction to Blockchain Technology in the Healthcare Sector. *Technology Innovation Management Review, 7*(10), 22–34. doi:10.22215/timreview/1111

Panarello, A., Tapas, N., Merlino, G., Longo, F., & Puliafito, A. (2018). Blockchain and IoT Integration: A Systematic Survey. *Sensors (Basel), 18*(8), 2575. doi:10.339018082575 PMID:30082633

Sabah, S., Mahdi, N., & Majeed, I. (2019). *The road to the blockchain technology: Concept and types*. Academic Press.

Yuan, Y., & Wang, F. Y. (2018). Blockchain and cryptocurrencies: Model, techniques, and applications. *IEEE Transactions on Systems, Man, and Cybernetics. Systems, 48*(9), 1421–1428. doi:10.1109/TSMC.2018.2854904

McKendrick, J. (2017). *Blockchain as Blockbuster: Still Too Soon to Tell*. But Get Ready, Forbes.

Mettler, M. (2016). Blockchain Technology in Healthcare the Revolution Starts Here. *Proceedings of the 2016 IEEE 18th International Conference on E-Health Networking, Applications and Services (Healthcom)*, 520–522. 10.1109/HealthCom.2016.7749510

Notheisen, B., Hawlitschek, F., & Weinhardt, C. (2017). Breaking down the blockchain hype – Towards a blockchain market engineering approach. In *Proceedings of the 25th European Conference on Information Systems (ECIS)* (pp. 1062-1080). https://aisel.aisnet.org/ecis2017_rp/69

Tasatanattakool, P., & Techapanupreeda, C. (2018, January). Blockchain: Challenges and applications. In *2018 International Conference on Information Networking (ICOIN)* (pp. 473-475). IEEE. 10.1109/ICOIN.2018.8343163

Alketbi, A., Nasir, Q., & Talib, M. A. (2018, February). Blockchain for government services—Use cases, security benefits and challenges. In *2018 15th Learning and Technology Conference (L&T)* (pp. 112-119). IEEE.

Blockchain and Emerging Digital Technologies for Enhancing Post-2020 Climate Markets. (n.d.). *World Bank*. http://documents1.worldbank.org/curated/en/942981521464296927/pdf/124402-WP-Blockchainandemergingdigitaltechnologiesforenhancingpostclimatemarkets-PUBLIC.pdf

Kuo, T. T., Kim, H. E., & Ohno-Machado, L. (2017). Blockchain Distributed Ledger Technologies for Biomedical and Health Care Applications. *Journal of the American Medical Informatics Association: JAMIA, 24*(6), 1211–1220. doi:10.1093/jamia/ocx068 PMID:29016974

Wood, G. (2014). Ethereum: A secure decentralised generalised transaction ledger. Ethereum Project Yellow Paper, 151, 1–32.

Birch, D. (2020). *The Digital Currency Revolution*. https://responsiblefinanceforum.org/wp-content/uploads/2020/04/Birch_02-20_v81-April2020.pdf

Hassan, F., Ali, A., Latif, S., Qadir, J., Kanhere, S., Singh, J., & Crowcroft, J. (2019). *Blockchain And The Future of the Internet: A Comprehensive Review.* Available online: https://www.researchgate.net/publication/331730251_Blockchain_And_The_Future_of_the_Internet_A_Comprehensive_Review

Hughes, L., Dwivedi, Y. K., Misra, S. K., Rana, N. P., Raghavan, V., & Akella, V. (2019). Blockchain research, practice and policy: Applications, benefits, limitations, emerging research themes and research agenda. *International Journal of Information Management, 49*, 114–129. doi:10.1016/j.ijinfomgt.2019.02.005

Roman-Belmonte, J. M., De la Corte-Rodriguez, H., Rodriguez-Merchan, E. C. C., la Corte-Rodriguez, H., & Carlos Rodriguez-Merchan, E. (2018). How Blockchain Technology Can Change Medicine. *Postgraduate Medicine, 130*(4), 420–427. doi:10.1080/00325481.2018.1472996 PMID:29727247

Blockchain: Powering the Value of Internet. (2020). https://blockchainlab.com/pdf/bank-2020---blockchain-powering-the-internet-of-value---whitepaper.pdf

Kshetri, N., & Voas, J. (2018). Blockchain-enabled e-voting. *IEEE Software, 35*(4), 95–99. doi:10.1109/MS.2018.2801546

Li, Z., Kang, J., Yu, R., Ye, D., Deng, Q., & Zhang, Y. (2018). Consortium blockchain for secure energy trading in industrial internet of things. *IEEE Transactions on Industrial Informatics, 14*(8), 3690–3700.

Steward, M. (2005). Electronic Medical Records. *Journal of Legal Medicine, 26*(4), 491–506. doi:10.1080/01947640500364762 PMID:16303736

Burchardi, K., Mikhalev, I., Song, B., & Alexander Kok, S. (2020). Get ready for the future of money. *BCG.* https://www.bcg.com/publications/2020/get-ready-for-the-future-of-money.aspx

Häyrinena, K. (2008). Definition, Structure, Content, Use and Impacts of Electronic Health Records: A Review of the Research Literature. *International Journal of Medical Informatics, 77*(5), 291–304. doi:10.1016/j.ijmedinf.2007.09.001 PMID:17951106

Savelyev, A. (2018). Copyright in the blockchain era: Promises and challenges. *Computer Law & Security Review, 34*(3), 550–561. doi:10.1016/j.clsr.2017.11.008

Szabo, N. (n.d.). *Formalizing and Securing Relationships on Public Networks.* Available online: http://ojphi. org/ojs/index.php/fm/article/view/548/469

Choudhury, T., Gupta, A., Pradhan, S., Kumar, P., & Rathore, Y. S. (2017). Privacy and Security of Cloud-Based Internet of Things (IoT). *International Conference on Computational Intelligence and Networks*, 41-45. 10.1109/CINE.2017.28

Dinh, T. T. A., Liu, R., Zhang, M., Chen, G., Ooi, B. C., & Wang, J. (2018, July 1). Untangling Blockchain: A Data Processing View of Blockchain Systems. *IEEE Transactions on Knowledge and Data Engineering, 30*(7), 1366–1385. doi:10.1109/TKDE.2017.2781227

Dunphy, P., & Petitcolas, F. A. (2018). A first look at identity management schemes on the blockchain. *IEEE Security and Privacy, 16*(4), 20–29. doi:10.1109/MSP.2018.3111247

Galen, Brand, Boucherle, Davis, Do, El-Baz, Kimura, Wharton, & Lee. (2018). Center for Social Innovation. *RippleWorks.*

Nakamoto, S. (2008). *Bitcoin: A Peer-to-Peer Electronic Cash System.* Available online: www.bitcoin.org

Stephan, L., Steffen, S., Moritz, S., & Bela, G. (2019). A Review on Blockchain Technology and Blockchain Projects Fostering Open Science. *Frontiers in Blockchain, 2*, 16. doi:10.3389/fbloc.2019.00016

Barrutia Barreto, I., Urquizo Maggia, J. A., & Acevedo, S. I. (2019). Cryptocurrencies and blockchain in tourism as a strategy to reduce poverty. RETOS. *Revista de Ciencias de la Administración y Economía, 9*(18), 287–302.

Bit Fury Group. (2016). *Digital Assets on Public Blockchains*. Bit Fury Group Limited.

Deloitte. (2020). *5 Blockchain Trends for 2020*. CS suits briefing. https://www2.deloitte.com/content/dam/Deloitte/ie/Documents/Consulting/Blockchain-Trends-2020-report.pdf

Wolfson, R. (2018, November). Diversifying Data With Artificial Intelligence And Blockchain Technology. *Forbes*. Retrieved from: https://www.forbes.com/sites/rachelwolfson/2018/11/20/diversifying-data-with-artificial-intelligence-and-blockchain-technology/#338157b74dad

Blockchain. (n.d.). Retrieved 7 2016, from Wikipedia: https://en.wikipedia.org/wiki/Blockchain

CIO's Guide to Blockchain. (2020). https://www.gartner.com/smarterwithgartner/the-cios-guide-to-blockchain/#:~:text=Gartner%20estimates%20blockchain%20will%20generate,be%20exploring%20the%20technology%20now

Fusco, F., Lunesu, M. I., Pani, F. E., & Pinna, A. (2018). Crypto-voting, a Blockchain based e-Voting System. In KMIS (pp. 221-225). doi:10.5220/0006962102230227

Restuccia, F., d'Oro, S., Kanhere, S., Melodia, T., & Das, S. (2018). *Blockchain for the Internet of Things: Present and Future*. Available online: https://www.researchgate.net/publication/329044700_Blockchain_for_the_Internet_of_Things_Present_and_Future

Blockchain-Based Applications in Education: A Systematic Review. (n.d.). College of Computing and Informatics, Saudi Electronic University.

Konstantinidis, I., Siaminos, G., Timplalexis, C., Zervas, P., Peristeras, V., & Decker, S. (2018). *Blockchain for Business Applications: A Systematic Literature Review*. . doi:10.1007/978-3-319-93931-5_28

Mehta, R., Kapoor, N., Sourav, S., & Shorey, R. (2019, January). Decentralised Image Sharing and Copyright Protection using Blockchain and Perceptual Hashes. In *2019 11th International Conference on Communication Systems & Networks (COMSNETS)* (pp. 1-6). IEEE. 10.1109/COMSNETS.2019.8711440

Rodriguez, J. (2015). *Building an IOT Platform: Centralized vs. Decentralized Models*. Retrieved from https://jrod-thoughts.com/tag/enterprisesoftware/page/2/

(Leader/Randomization/Signature)-free Byzantine Consensus for Consortium Blockchains. (n.d.). Available at http://poseidon.it.usyd.edu.au/~concurrentsystems/doc/Consensu sRedBellyBlockchain.pdf

Arenas, R., & Fernandez, P. (2018). CredenceLedger: A Permissioned Blockchain for Verifiable Academic Credentials. *Proceedings of the 2018 IEEE International Conference on Engineering, Technology and Innovation (ICE/ITMC)*, 1–6. 10.1109/ICE.2018.8436324

Avital, M. (2018). Peer review: Toward a blockchain-enabled market-based ecosystem. *Communications of the Association for Information Systems*, 42(1), 646–653. doi:10.17705/1CAIS.04228

Xu, J., Xue, K., Li, S., Tian, H., Hong, J., Hong, P., & Yu, N. (2019). Healthchain: A blockchain-based privacy preserving scheme for large-scale health data. *IEEE Internet of Things Journal*, 6(5), 8770–8781. doi:10.1109/JIOT.2019.2923525

Beck, R., Avital, M., Rossi, M., & Thatcher, J. B. (2017). Blockchain technology in business and information systems research. *Business & Information Systems Engineering*, 59(6), 381–384. doi:10.100712599-017-0505-1

Block Chain Technology Beyond Bitcoin. (n.d.). Available at http://scet.berkeley.edu/wp-content/uploads/AIR-2016-Blockchain.pdf

Fan, K., Wang, S., Ren, Y., Li, H., & Yang, Y. (2018). Medblock: Efficient and secure medical data sharing via block-chain. *Journal of Medical Systems, 42*(8), 136. doi:10.100710916-018-0993-7 PMID:29931655

Han, M., Li, Z., He, J. S., Wu, D., Xie, Y., & Baba, A. (2018). A Novel Blockchain-based Education Records Verification Solution. *Proceedings of the 19th Annual SIG Conference on Information Technology Education*, 178–183. 10.1145/3241815.3241870

Hjálmarsson, F. Þ., Hreiðarsson, G. K., Hamdaqa, M., & Hjálmtýsson, G. (2018). Blockchain-Based E-Voting System. *2018 IEEE 11th International Conference on Cloud Computing (CLOUD)*, 983-986. 10.1109/CLOUD.2018.00151

Pawar, D., Sarode, P., Santpure, S., Thore, P., & Nimbalkar, P. (n.d.). *Secure Voting System using Blockchain*. Academic Press.

Artificial Intelligence and Privacy. (2018). *Datatilsynet (Norwegian Data Protection Authority)*. Available at: https://www.datatilsynet.no/globalassets/global/english/ai-and-privacy.pdf

Deshpande, A., Stewart, K., Lepetit, L., & Gunashekar, S. (2017). *Distributed Ledger Technologies/Blockchain: Challenges, Opportunities and the Prospects for Standards*. Technical report, The British Standards Institution (BSI). Available online at: https://bit.ly/32QxvKp

Kadena: Confidentiality in Private Blockchain. (n.d.). Available at http://kadena.io/docs/Kadena-ConfidentialityWhitepaper- Aug2016.pdf

Wohrer, M., & Zdun, U. (2018, March). Smart contracts: security patterns in the ethereum ecosystem and solidity. In *2018 International Workshop on Blockchain Oriented Software Engineering (IWBOSE)* (pp. 2-8). IEEE. 10.1109/IWBOSE.2018.8327565

Blockchain For Health Data and Its Potential Use in Health IT and Health Care Related Research. (n.d.). Available at https://www.healthit.gov/sites/default/files/11-74- ablockchainforhealthcare.pdf

Filimonau, V., & Naumova, E. (2020). The blockchain technology and the scope of its application in hospitality operations. *International Journal of Hospitality Management, 87*, 102383. doi:10.1016/j.ijhm.2019.102383

Internet Security & the Trust Working Group. (2018). Big data, machine learning, consumer protection and privacy. ITU. Available at: https://www.itu.int/en/ITU- T/extcoop/figisymposium/2019/ Documents/Presentations/Big %20data,%20 Machine%20learning,%20Consumer%20protection%20and%20Privacy.pdf

Tama, B. A., Kweka, B. J., Park, Y., & Rhee, K. H. (2017). A Critical Review of Blockchain and Its Current Applications. *International Conference on Electrical Engineering and Computer Science*, 109–113. 10.1109/ICECOS.2017.8167115

Alienor, L. (2018). *What is Data Silo and Why it is Bad for Your Organisation*. Retrieved from https://www.plixer.com/blog/data-silo-what-is-it-why-is-it-bad/

Crosby, M., Nachiappan, P., Verma, S., & Kalyanaraman, V. (2016). Blockchain beyond bitcoin. Applied Innovation Review, (2).

Kadena: The First Scalable, High Performance Private Blockchain. (n.d.). Available at http://kadena.io/docs/Kadena-ConsensusWhitePaper-Aug2016.pdf

Zhao, Y., & Duncan, B. (2018, July). The Impact of Crypto-Currency Risks on the Use of Blockchain for Cloud Security and Privacy. In *2018 International Conference on High Performance Computing & Simulation (HPCS)* (pp. 677-684). IEEE. 10.1109/HPCS.2018.00111

Consensus-as-a-Service: A Brief Report on the Emergence of Permissioned, Distributed Ledger Systems. (n.d.). Available at http://www.ofnumbers.com/2015/04/06/consensus-as-a-service- a-brief-report-on-the-emergence-of-permissioned-distributed- ledger-systems/

Hawlitschek, F., Notheisen, B., & Teubner, T. (2018). The limits of trust-free systems: A literature review on blockchain technology and trust in the sharing economy. *Electronic Commerce Research and Applications*, *29*, 50–63. doi:10.1016/j.elerap.2018.03.005

How to Breakdown Data Silos. (n.d.). *Problems and Solutions*. Retrieved from https://status.net/articles/data-silos-information-silos/

The Future of Blockchain. (2020). https://www.finextra.com/researcharticle/136/the-future-of-blockchain-2020

Hauxe, R. (2006). Health Information Systems—Past, Present, Future. *International Journal of Medical Informatics*, *75*(3–4), 268–281. doi:10.1016/j.ijmedinf.2005.08.002 PMID:16169771

Hussain, F., Hussain, R., Hassan, S. A., & Hossain, E. (2018). Machine Learning in IoT Security: Current Solutions and Future Challenges. Academic Press.

Lin, I.-C., & Liao, T.-C. (2017). A survey of blockchain security issues and challenges. *International Journal of Network Security*, *19*, 653–659. doi:10.6633/IJNS.201709.19(5).01

Makridakis, S., Polemitis, A., & Giaglis, G. (2018). *Blockchain: The Next Breakthrough in the Rapid Progress of AI*. *Robot Autom Eng J*.

Mehra, A. (2018). Vishrambh: Trusted philanthropy with end-to-end transparency. In HCI for Blockchain: A CHI 2018 workshop on Studying, Critiquing, Designing and Envisioning Distributed Ledger Technologies. Academic Press.

Xie, J., Tang, H., Huang, T., Yu, F. R., Xie, R., Liu, J., & Liu, Y. (2019). A survey of blockchain technology applied to smart cities: Research issues and challenges. *IEEE Communications Surveys and Tutorials*, *21*(3), 2794–2830. doi:10.1109/COMST.2019.2899617

Choudhary, D. (2019). *Human Bias in AI*. Retrieved from https://www.infosys.com/services/incubating-emerging-technologies/offerings/Documents/human-bias.pdf

Gatteschi, V., Lamberti, F., Demartini, C., Pranteda, C., & Santamaria, V. (2018). To blockchain or not to blockchain: That is the question. *IT Professional*, *20*(2), 62–74. doi:10.1109/MITP.2018.021921652

On Public and Private Blockchains. (n.d.). Available at https://blog.ethereum.org/2015/08/07/on-public-and-private-blockchains/

Calvaresi, D., Leis, M., Dubovitskaya, A., Schegg, R., & Schumacher, M. (2019). Trust in tourism via blockchain technology: results from a systematic review. In *Information and communication technologies in tourism 2019* (pp. 304–317). Springer. doi:10.1007/978-3-030-05940-8_24

Gideon Greenspan. (2015). *Multi Chain Private Blockchain—White Paper*. Available: http://www.multichain.com/download/MultiChain-White- Paper.pdf

Srivastava, A., Bhattacharya, P., Singh, A., & Mathur, A. (2018). *A Systematic Review on Evolution of Blockchain Generations*. Academic Press.

Deshpande, A. (2017). *Distributed ledger technologies/blockchain: Challenges, opportunities and the prospects for standards*. British Standards Inst. Available: https://www.bsigroup.com/LocalFiles/zh-tw/InfoSec-newsletter/No201706/download/BSI_Blockchain_D LT_Web.pdf

What Is Ether. (n.d.). Available: https://ethereum.org/ether

Dinh, T. T., Wang, J., Chen, G., Liu, R., Ooi, B. C., & Tan, K.-L. (2017). Blockbench: A framework for analyzing private blockchains. *Proceedings of the 2017 ACM International Conference on Management of Data*, 1085-1100. 10.1145/3035918.3064033

MedChain. (n.d.). *Secure, Decentralized, Interoperable Medication Reconciliation Using the Blockchain.* Available at https://oncprojectracking.healthit.gov/wiki/download/attachment s/14582699/36-20160808-blockchain-medrec-whitepaper- final.pdf

ModelChain. (n.d.). *Decentralized Privacy-Preserving Healthcare Predictive Modeling Framework on Private Block-chain Networks.* Available at https://www.healthit.gov/sites/default/files/10-30-ucsd-dbmi- onc-blockchain-challenge.pdf

Zheng, Z., Xie, S., Dai, H.-N., Chen, X., & Wang, H. (2017). *An Overview of Blockchain Technology: Architecture.* Consensus, and Future Trends. doi:10.1109/BigDataCongress.2017.85

BlockIsure. (n.d.). Available at https://oncprojectracking.healthit.gov/wiki/download/attachments/14582699/70-Block-Insure_Pieces_Tech%20%282%29.pdf

Dib, O., Brousmiche, K.-L., Durand, A., Thea, E., & Hamida, E. (2018). Consortium Blockchains: Overview, Applications and Challenges. *International Journal On Advances in Telecommunications, IARIA, 2018*, 51–64.

Alharby, M., Aldweesh, A., & Moorsel, A. v. (2018). Blockchain-based Smart Contracts: A Systematic Mapping Study of Academic Research. *International Conference on Cloud Computing, Big Data and Blockchain (ICCBB)*, 1-6. 10.1109/ICCBB.2018.8756390

Hu, Y., Liyanage, M., Manzoor, A., Thilakarathna, K., Jourjon, G., & Seneviratne, A. (2019). *Blockchain-based Smart Contracts - Applications and Challenges.* Retrieved from: https://arxiv.org/abs/1810.04699

Meinert, E., Alturkistani, A., Foley, K., Osama, T., Car, J., Majeed, A., Van Velthoven, M., Wells, G., & Brindley, D. (2018). *Blockchain Implementation in Health Care: Protocol for a Systematic Review.* . doi:10.2196/10994

Cognizant. (2017). *Retail: Opening the Doors to Blockchain.* Available at: https://www.cognizant.com/whitepapers/retail-opening-the-doors-to-blockchain-codex2879.pdf

McConaghy, T., Marques, R., & Müller, A. (n.d.). *BigchainDB: A Scalable Blockchain Database.* https://www.big-chaindb.com/whitepaper/

Feng, Q., He, D., Zeadally, S., Khan, M. K., & Kumar, N. (2019). A survey on privacy protection in blockchain system. *Journal of Network and Computer Applications*, *126*, 45–58. doi:10.1016/j.jnca.2018.10.020

Holotescu, C. (2018). Understanding blockchain technology and how to get involved. The 14th International Scientific Conference eLearning and Software for Education, 19-20.

Li, X., Jiang, P., Chen, T., Luo, X., & Wen, Q. (2017). A survey on the security of blockchain systems. *Future Generation Computer Systems.*

Monero Project. (n.d.). Available online: https://getmonero.org/the-monero-project/

Nakamoto. (2009). *Bitcoin: A peer-to-peer electronic cash system.* url:http://www.bitcoin.org/bitcoin.pdf

Whillans, A. V. (2016). *A Brief Introduction to the Science of Fundraising.* Council for Advancement and Support of Education.

Kuo, T.-T., Hsu, C.-N., & Ohno-Machado, L. (2016). *ModelChain: Decentralized Privacy-Preserving Healthcare Predictive Modeling Framework on Private Blockchain Networks*. In ONC/NIST Use of Blockchain for Healthcare and Research Workshop, Gaithersburg, MD.

USDofE. (2017). *Reimagining the Role of Technology in Education: 2017 National Education Technology Plan Update*. U.S. Department of Education. Retrieved From: https://tech.ed.gov/files/2017/01/NETP17.pdf

Hardwick, F. S., Akram, R. N., & Markantonakis, K. (2018). *E-voting with blockchain: An e-voting protocol with decentralisation and voter privacy*. Available: https://arxiv.org/abs/1805.10258

ONC/NIST Use of Blockchain in Healthcare and Research Workshop. (2016). https://oncprojecttracking.healthit.gov/wiki/display/TechLabI/Use+of+Blockchain+in+Healthcare+and+Research+Workshop

Andoni, M., Robu, V., Flynn, D., Abram, S., Geach, D., Jenkins, D., McCallum, P., & Peacock, A. (2019, February). Blockchain technology in the energy sector: A systematic review of challenges and opportunities. *Renewable & Sustainable Energy Reviews*, *100*, 143–174. doi:10.1016/j.rser.2018.10.014

Lorenz, J.-T., Münstermann, B., Higginson, M., Olesen, P. B., Bohlken, N., & Ricciardi, V. (n.d.). *Blockchain in Insurance – Opportunity or Threat?* McKinsey & Company. http://www.mckinsey.com/~/media/McKinsey/Industries/Financial Services/Our Insights/Blockchain in insurance opportunity or threat/Blockchain-in-insurance-opportunity-or-threat.ashx

Martin, L. (n.d.). *Blockchain vs. Relational Database: Which is right for your Application?* TechBeacon. https://techbeacon.com/Blockchain-relational-database-which-right-for-your-application

Zhou, Q., Huang, H., & Zheng, Z. (2020). *Solutions to Scalability of Blockchain: A Survey*. IEEE Access. doi:10.1109/ACCESS.2020.2967218

FIPS PUB 180-4 Secure Hash Standard (SHS). (n.d.). https://nvlpubs.nist.gov/nistpubs/FIPS/NIST.FIPS.180-4.pdf

Habib ur Rehman, M., Salah, K., Damiani, E., & Svetinovic, D. (2020). *Towards Blockchain-Based Reputation-Aware Federated Learning*. Academic Press.

Zhang, R., Xue, R., & Liu, L. (2019). Security and privacy on blockchain. ACM Computing Survey. doi:10.1145/3316481

Monrat, A. A., Schelén, O., & Andersson, K. (2019). Survey of Blockchain from the Perspectives of Applications, Challenges and Opportunities. *IEEE Access*. . doi:10.1109/ACCESS.2019.2936094

Pîrlea, & Sergey. (2018). Mechanising blockchain consensus. In *Proceedings of the 7th ACM SIGPLAN International Conference on Certified Programs and Proofs*. ACM. 10.1145/3167086

Sankar, L. S., Sindhu, M., & Sethumadhavan, M. (2017). Survey of consensus protocols on blockchain applications. In *2017 4th International Conference on Advanced Computing and Communication Systems (ICACCS'17)*. IEEE. 10.1109/ICACCS.2017.8014672

Shi, P., Wang, H., Yang, S., Chen, C., & Yang, W. (2019). Blockchain-based trusted data sharing among trusted stakeholders in IoT. *Software, Practice & Experience*, spe.2739. Advance online publication. doi:10.1002pe.2739

Jimi, S. (2018). Blockchain: What are nodes and masternodes? *Medium*. https://medium.com/coinmonks/blockchain-what-is-a-node-or-masternode-and-what-does-it-do-4d9a4200938f

King & Nadal. (2012). *Ppcoin: Peer-to-peer Crypto-Currency with Proof-of-Stake*. Retrieved October 31, 2018 from https://peercoin.net/960assets/paper/peercoin-paper.pdf

Chen, G., Xu, B., Lu, M., & Chen, N.-S. (2018). Exploring blockchain technology and its potential applications for education. *Smart Learning Environments.*, *5*(1), 1. Advance online publication. doi:10.118640561-017-0050-x

Mingxiao, D., Xiaofeng, M., Zhe, Z., Xiangwei, W., & Qijun, C. (2017). A review on consensus algorithm of blockchain. In *2017 IEEE International Conference on Systems, Man, and Cybernetics (SMC'17)*. IEEE. 10.1109/SMC.2017.8123011

Dash Official Website. (n.d.). *Dash Crypto Currency—Dash*. Available online: https://www.dash.org/

Github. (n.d.). Retrieved from: https://github.com/alicesi/whitepaper/blob/master/Alice%20white%20paper%20-%20 FV%200.9.pdf

Niranjanamurthy, M., Nithya, B. N., & Jagannatha, S. (2019). Analysis of Blockchain technology: Pros, cons and SWOT. *Cluster Computing*, 22(6), 14743–14757. doi:10.100710586-018-2387-5

Swan. (2015). *Blockchain: Blueprint for a New Economy* (1st ed.). O'Reilly Media, Inc.

Swan, M. (2015). *Blockchain: Blueprint for a new economy*. O'Reilly Media, Inc.

Waseem, A. (2017, September 30). Blockchain Technology: Challenges and Future Prospects. *International Journal of Advanced Research in Computer Science*, 08(9), 642–644. doi:10.26483/ijarcs.v8i9.4950

Finck, M. (2019, May). Smart contracts as a form of solely automated processing under the GDPR. *International Data Privacy Law*, 9(2), 78–94. doi:10.1093/idpl/ipz004

Miller. & Sim. (2004). Physicians' use of electronic medical records: Barriers and solutions. *Health Affairs*, 23(2), 116–126. Doi:10.1377/hlthaff.23.2.116

Buterin, V. (2014). *A Next-Generation Smart Contract and Decentralized Application Platform*. Retrieved August 20, 2018 from https://github.com/ethereum/wiki/wiki/White-Paper

Pandl, K. D., Tiebes, S., Schmidt-Kraepelin, M., & Sunyaev, A. (2020). *On the convergence of artifcial intelligence and distributed ledger technology: A scoping review and future research agenda*. arXiv preprint arXiv:2001.11017.

Chatterjee, K., Goharshady, A. K., & Velner, Y. (2018). Quantitative analysis of smart contracts. *Springer International Publishing*.

Hileman, G., & Rauchs, M. (2017) Global Blockchain Benchmarking Study. SSRN *Electron. J.* doi:10.2139srn.3040224

Szabo. (1997). Formalizing and securing relationships on public networks. *First Monday*, 2(9), 22. doi:10.5210/fm.v2i9.548

Yli-Huumo, Ko, Choi, Park, & Smolander. (2016). Where is current research on blockchain technology? A systematic review. *PLoS One, 11*, 1–27. DOI:.0163477 doi:10.1371/journal.pone

Dubovitskaya, A., Xu, Z., Ryu, S., Schumacher, M., & Wang, F. (2017). *Secure and trustable electronic medical records sharing using blockchain*. https://arxiv.org/abs/1709.06528

IBM Hyperledger. (n.d.). Retrieved from: https://www.ibm.com/blockchain/hyperledger

Litecoin—Open Source P2P Digital Currency. (n.d.). Available online: https://litecoin.org/

Miraz, M. H., & Donald, D. C. (2018, August). Application of blockchain in booking and registration systems of securities exchanges. In *2018 International Conference on Computing, Electronics & Communications Engineering (iCCECE)* (pp. 35-40). IEEE. 10.1109/iCCECOME.2018.8658726

Nakamoto, S. (2009). *Bitcoin: A Peer-to-Peer Electronic Cash System*. https://metzdowd.com

Nian, L. P., & Chuen, D. (2015). *Introduction to bitcoin, Handbook of Digital Currency: Bitcoin*. Innovation, Financial Instruments, and Big Data.

Xu, M., Chen, X., & Kou, G. (2019). A systematic review of blockchain. Financ Innov, 5, 27. doi:10.118640854-019-0147-z

Wechsler, R., Anção, M. S., de Campos, C. J. R., & Sigulem, D. (2003). A Informática no consultório Médico. *Jornal de Pediatria, 79*, 1–10. doi:10.1590/S0021-75572003000700002

Xia, Q., Sifah, E. B., Asamoah, K. O., Gao, J., Du, X., & Guizani, M. (2017). MeDShare: Trust-less medical data sharing among cloud service providers via blockchain. *IEEE Access: Practical Innovations, Open Solutions, 5*, 14757–14767. doi:10.1109/ACCESS.2017.2730843

Alwen, Blocki, & Harsha. (2017). *Practical Graphs for Optimal Side-Channel Resistant Memory- Hard Functions.* Cryptology ePrint Archive, Report 2017/443. Retrieved September 20, 2018 from https://eprint.iacr. org/2017/443

de Oliveira Guedes Bastos. (2011). *Quality of Health Information on Acute Myocardial Infarction and Stroke in the World Wide Web* (Master's Thesis). Universidade do Porto.

Patel, V. (2018). A framework for secure and decentralized sharing of medical imaging data via blockchain consensus. *Health Informatics Journal, 25*(4), 1398–1411. doi:10.1177/1460458218769699

Ge, Y., Ahn, D. K., Unde, B., Gage, H. D., & Carr, J. J. (2013, January). Patient-controlled sharing of medical imaging data across unaffiliated healthcare organizations. *Journal of the American Medical Informatics Association, 20*(1), 157–163. doi:10.1136/amiajnl-2012-001146 PMID:22886546

Gupta, U. (2015). *Secure management of logs in internet of things.* https://arxiv.org/abs/1507.05085

Anderson, J. (2018). *Securing, Standardizing, and Simplifying Electronic Health Record Audit Logs through Per- missioned Blockchain Technology* (Ph.D. Dissertation). Dartmouth College. https://www.cs.dartmouth.edu/~trdata/ reports/ abstracts/TR2018- 854/

Lambert, Cooper, & Pagh. (1998). Supply chain management: Implementation issues and research opportunities. *International Journal of Logistics Management, 9*(2), 1–20. doi:10.1108/09574099810805807

Sousa, Liu, Papageorgiou, & Shah. (2011). Global supply chain planning for pharmaceuticals. *Chemical Engineering Research and Design, 89*(11), 2396–2409. DOI:.2011.04.005 doi:10.1016/j.cherd

Blockchain Terminology. (n.d.). A glossary for beginners. In *CompTIA.* Blockchain Advisory Council. https:// comptiacdn.azureedge.net/webcontent/docs/default-source/research-reports/07576-blockchain-glossary-of-terms-r3. pdf?sfvrsn=7df7462a_0

Forrest, P. (2016). Blockchain and non financial services use cases. *Linkedin.* https://www.linkedin.com/pulse/blockchain-non-financial-services-use-cases-paul-forrest

IBM. (n.d.). *What is Blockchain.* Retrieved from: https://www.ibm.com/blockchain/what-is-blockchain

Lamport, L., Shostak, R., & Pease, M. (1982, July). The Byzantine Generals problem. *ACM Transactions on Programming Languages and Systems, 4*(3), 382–401. doi:10.1145/357172.357176

Marwala, T., & Xing, B. (2018). *Blockchain and Artificial Intelligence.* ArXiv, volume=abs/1802.04451.

Swati, V., & Prasad, A. S. (2018, December). Application of Blockchain Technology in Travel Industry. In *2018 International Conference on Circuits and Systems in Digital Enterprise Technology (ICCSDET)* (pp. 1-5). IEEE.

Mulholland, C. S. (2018). Dados pessoais sensíveis e a tutela de direitos fundamentais: Uma análise à luz da lei geral de proteção de dados (Lei 13.709/18). *Revista de Direitos e Garantias Fundamentais, 19*(3), 159–180. doi:10.18759/ rdgf.v19i3.1603

U.S. Department of Health & Human Services (HHS). (2013). *Summary of the HIPAA Privacy Rule*. Retrieved February 4, 2019 from https://www.hhs.gov/hipaa/for-professionals/privacy/laws-regulations/index.html

Ren, Y., Werner, R., Pazzi, N., & Boukerche, A. (2010). Monitoring patients via a secure and mobile healthcare system. *IEEE Wireless Communications*, *17*(1), 59–65. doi:10.1109/MWC.2010.5416351

Linn & Koo. (2016). *Blockchain for Health Data and Its Potential Use in Health IT and Health Care Related Research*. Academic Press.

Ashraf Uddin, M. (2018). Continuous patient monitoring with a patient centric agent: A block architecture. *IEEE Access: Practical Innovations, Open Solutions*, *6*, 32700–32726. doi:10.1109/ACCESS.2018.2846779

Halamka, J. D., Lippman, A., & Ekblaw, A. (2017). *The Potential for Blockchain to Transform Electronic Health Records*. Retrieved September 30, 2018 from https://hbr.org/2017/03/the-potential-for-blockchain-to-transform-electronic-health-records

Stagnaro, C. (2017). *White Paper: Innovative Blockchain Uses in Health Care*. Retrieved September 28, 2018 from https://www.freedassociates.com/wp-content/uploads/2017/08/Blockchain_White_Paper.pdf

Gope, P., & Hwang, T. (2016, March). BSN-Care: A secure IoT-based modern healthcare system using body sensor network. *IEEE Sensors Journal*, *16*(5), 1368–1376. doi:10.1109/JSEN.2015.2502401

Balasubramanian, V., Hoang, D. B., & Zia, T. A. (2011). Addressing the confidentiality and integrity of assistive care loop framework using wireless sensor networks. In *2011 21st International Conference on Systems Engineering*. IEEE. 10.1109/ICSEng.2011.82

Blockchain. (n.d.). Retrieved from: https://blockchaindemo.io/

Castro, M., & Liskov, B. (2002, November). Practical Byzantine fault tolerance and proactive recovery. *ACM Transactions on Computer Systems*, *20*(4), 398–461. doi:10.1145/571637.571640

Ethereum Classic. (2018). *A Smarter Blockchain that Takes Digital Assets Further*. Available online: https://ethereum-classic.org/

Kang, J., Yu, R., Huang, X., Wu, M., Maharjan, S., Xie, S., & Zhang, Y. (2018). Blockchain for secure and efficient data sharing in vehicular edge computing and networks. *IEEE Internet of Things Journal*, *6*(3), 4660–4670. doi:10.1109/JIOT.2018.2875542

Narayanan, A., Bonneau, J., Felten, E., Miller, A., & Goldfeder, S. (2016). *Bitcoin and Cryptocurrency Technologies*. Princeton University Press.

Wang, K., Dong, J., Wang, Y., & Yin, H. (2019). Securing Data With Blockchain and AI. *IEEE Access: Practical Innovations, Open Solutions*, *7*, 77981–77989. doi:10.1109/ACCESS.2019.2921555

Casino, F., Dasaklis, K. T., & Patsakis, C. (2019). A systematic literature review of blockchain-based applications: Current status, classification and open issues. *Telematics and Informatics, 36*, 55-81. doi:10.1016/j.tele.2018.11.006

Ferrag, M. A., Derdour, M., Mukherjee, M., Derhab, A., Maglaras, L., & Janicke, H. (2018). Blockchain technologies for the internet of things: Research issues and challenges. *IEEE Internet of Things Journal*, *6*(2), 2188–2204. doi:10.1109/JIOT.2018.2882794

Jayasinghe, D., Cobourne, S., Markantonakis, K., Akram, R. N., & Mayes, K. (2016). Philanthropy On The Blockchain. In *11th WISTP International Conference on Information Security Theory and Practice (WISTP'2017)*. Springer.

Nakamoto, S. (2008). *Bitcoin: A peer-to-peer electronic cash system*. https://bitcoin.org/bitcoin.pdf

NEO Smart Economy. (2018). Available online: https://neo.org/

Sgantzos, K., & Grigg, I. (2019). Artificial Intelligence Implementations on the Blockchain. Use Cases and Future Applications. *Future Internet*, *11*(8), 170. doi:10.3390/fi11080170

Dasoriya, R., Rajpopat, J., Jamar, R., & Maurya, M. (2018). The Uncertain Future of Artificial Intelligence. *2018 8th International Conference on Cloud Computing, Data Science & Engineering (Confluence)*, 458-461. 10.1109/CONFLUENCE.2018.8442945

Medium. (n.d.). https://medium.com/bpfoundation/https-medium-com-bpfoundation-charitable-giving-blockchain-case-studies-14f0c9f9d13f

Ostern, N. (2020). Blockchain in the IS research discipline: A discussion of terminology and concepts. *Electronic Markets*, *30*(2), 195–210. doi:10.100712525-019-00387-2

Qtum. (2018). Available online: https://qtum.org/en

Vasin, P. (2014). *Blackcoin's proof-of-stake protocol v2*. https://blackcoin.co/blackcoin-pos-protocol-v2- whitepaper.pdf

A, B., & K, M. V. (2016). Blockchain platform for industrial internet of things. *Journal of software Engineering and Applications*, *9*(10), 533.

Abd El-Latif, A., Abd-El-Atty, B., Venegas-Andraca, S., Elwahsh, H., Piran, M., Bashir, A., ... Mazurczyk, W. (2020). Providing End-to-End Security Using Quantum Walks in IoT Networks. *IEEE Access: Practical Innovations, Open Solutions*, *8*, 92687–92696. doi:10.1109/ACCESS.2020.2992820

Abeyratne, S. A., & Monfared, R. P. (2016). Blockchain ready manufacturing supply chain using distributed ledger. *Int. J. Res. Eng. Technol.*, *5*(9), 1–10.

Abeyratne, S. A., & Monfared, R. P. (2016). Blockchain ready manufacturing supply chain using distributed ledger. *International Journal of Research in Engineering and Technology*, *5*(9), 1–10. doi:10.15623/ijret.2016.0509001

Abou Jaoude, J., & George Saade, R. (2019). Blockchain applications - Usage in different domains. *IEEE Access: Practical Innovations, Open Solutions*, *7*, 45360–45381. https://doi.org/10.1109/ACCESS.2019.2902501

Abramov, R., & Herzberg, A. (2011). TCP ack storm DoS attacks. In *IFIP International Information Security Conference* (pp. 29-40). Springer. 10.1007/978-3-642-21424-0_3

Agrawal, T. K., Sharma, A., & Kumar, V. (n.d.). *Blockchain-Based Secured Traceability Chain*. Academic Press.

Ahmad, J., Larijani, H., Emmanuel, R., & Mannion, M. (2018). *Secure occupancy monitoring system for iot using lightweight intertwining logistic map. In 10th Computer Science and Electronic Engineering (CEEC)*. IEEE.

Ahram, T., Sargolzaei, A., Sargolzaei, S., Daniels, J., & Amaba, B. (2017). Blockchain technology innovations. *2017 IEEE Technology and Engineering Management Society Conference. TEMSCON*, *2017*, 137–141. Advance online publication. doi:10.1109/TEMSCON.2017.7998367

Ahram, T., Sargolzaei, A., Sargolzaei, S., Daniels, J., & Amaba, B. (2017). Blockchain technology innovations. *Proc. IEEE Technol. Eng. Manag. Conf.*, 1-6.

Aitzhan, N. Z., & Svetinovic, D. (2018). Security and Privacy in Decentralized Energy Trading Through Multi-Signatures, Blockchain and Anonymous Messaging Streams. *IEEE Transactions on Dependable and Secure Computing*, *15*(5), 840–852. https://doi.org/10.1109/TDSC.2016.2616861

Ajao, L. A., Agajo, J., Adedokun, E. A., & Karngong, L. (2019). Crypto hash algorithm-based blockchain technology for managing decentralized ledger database in oil and gas industry. *J—Multidisciplinary Scientific Journal, 2*(3), 300-325.

Akyildiz, I. F., & Jornet, J. M. (2010). The internet of nano-things. *IEEE Wireless Communications, 17*(6), 58–63.

Al Barghuthi, N. B., Mohamed, H. J., & Said, H. E. (2019). Blockchain in Supply Chain Trading. *ITT 2018 - Information Technology Trends: Emerging Technologies for Artificial Intelligence*, 336–341. doi:10.1109/CTIT.2018.8649523

Aldaej, A. (2019). Enhancing Cyber Security in Modern Internet of Things (IoT) Using Intrusion Prevention Algorithm for IoT (IPAI). *IEEE Access : Practical Innovations, Open Solutions*. Advance online publication. doi:10.1109/ACCESS.2019.2893445

Alexakos, C., & Kalogeras, A. (2017, May). Exposing MES functionalities as enabler for cloud manufacturing. In *2017 IEEE 13th International Workshop on Factory Communication Systems (WFCS)* (pp. 1-4). IEEE. 10.1109/WFCS.2017.7991966

Alexakos, C., Anagnostopoulos, C., Fournaris, A., Koulamas, C., & Kalogeras, A. (2018, May). IoT integration for adaptive manufacturing. In *2018 IEEE 21st International Symposium on Real-Time Distributed Computing (ISORC)* (pp. 146-151). IEEE. 10.1109/ISORC.2018.00030

Ali, A., & Jan, S. (n.d.). [*A Comparative Analysis of Blockchain Architecture and Its Applications: Problems and Recommendations.* Academic Press.]. *Nadeem, & Alghamdi.*

Al-Jaroodi, J., & Mohamed, N. (2019). Blockchain in Industries: A survey. *IEEE Access: Practical Innovations, Open Solutions, 7*, 36500–36515.

Al-Jaroodi, J., & Mohamed, N. (2019). Blockchain in Industries: A Survey. *IEEE Access: Practical Innovations, Open Solutions, 7*, 36500–36515. https://doi.org/10.1109/ACCESS.2019.2903554

Alladi, T., Chamola, V., Parizi, R. M., & Choo, K. K. R. (2019). Blockchain Applications for Industry 4.0 and Industrial IoT: A Review. *IEEE Access: Practical Innovations, Open Solutions, 7*, 176935–176951. doi:10.1109/ACCESS.2019.2956748

Ambika, N. (2020). Methodical IoT-Based Information System in Healthcare. In C. Chakraborthy (Ed.), Smart Medical Data Sensing and IoT Systems Design in Healthcare (pp. 155-177). Bangalore, India: IGI Global.

Ambika, N. (2020). Encryption of Data in Cloud-Based Industrial IoT Devices. In S. Pal & V. G. Díaz (Eds.), *IoT: Security and Privacy Paradigm* (pp. 111–129). CRC press, Taylor & Francis Group.

Ananth, M. D., & Sharma, R. (2016, December). Cloud management using network function virtualization to reduce capex and opex. In *2016 8th International Conference on Computational Intelligence and Communication Networks (CICN)* (pp. 43-47). IEEE. 10.1109/CICN.2016.17

Ananth, M. D., & Sharma, R. (2017, January). Cost and performance analysis of network function virtualization based cloud systems. In *2017 IEEE 7th International Advance Computing Conference (IACC)* (pp. 70-74). IEEE. 10.1109/IACC.2017.0029

Andrews, C., Broby, D., Paul, G., & Whitfield, I. (2020). *Utilising Financial Blockchain Technologies in Advanced Manufacturing*. Available: https://strathprints.strath.ac.uk/ 61982/

Androulaki, E., Barger, A., Bortnikov, V., Cachin, C., Christidis, K., De Caro, A., Enyeart, D., Ferris, C., Laventman, G., Manevich, Y., Muralidharan, S., Murthy, C., Nyugen, B., Sethi, M., Singh, G., Smith, K., Sorniotti, A., Stathakopoulou, C., Vukolic, M., ... Yellick, J. (2018). Hyperledger Fabric: A Distributed Operating System for Permissioned Blockchains. *Proceedings of the Thirteenth EuroSys Conference*. 10.1145/3190508.3190538

Arcelus, A., Jones, M. H., Goubran, R., & Knoefel, F. (2007). Integration of smart home technologies in a health monitoring system for the elderly. In *21st International Conference on Advanced Information Networking and Applications Workshops (AINAW'07)* (*vol. 2*, pp. 820-825). Niagara Falls, Canada: IEEE. 10.1109/AINAW.2007.209

Atlam, H. F., & Wills, G. B. (2019). Technical aspects of blockchain and IoT. In Role of Blockchain Technology in IoT Applications (Vol. 115). doi:10.1016/bs.adcom.2018.10.006

Aung, M. M., & Chang, Y. S. (2014). Traceability in a food supply chain: Safety and quality perspectives. *Food Control, 39*(1), 172–184. doi:10.1016/j.foodcont.2013.11.007

Azaria, A., Ekblaw, A., Vieira, T., & Lippman, A. (2016). MedRec: Using blockchain for medical data access and permission management. *Proceedings - 2016 2nd International Conference on Open and Big Data, OBD 2016*, 25–30. doi:10.1109/OBD.2016.11

Azzi, R., Chamoun, R. K., & Sokhn, M. (2019). The power of a blockchain-based supply chain. *Computers & Industrial Engineering, 135*, 582–592. doi:10.1016/j.cie.2019.06.042

Bagozi, A., Bianchini, D., De Antonellis, V., Garda, M., & Melchiori, M. (2019, July). Services as enterprise smart contracts in the digital factory. In *2019 IEEE International Conference on Web Services (ICWS)* (pp. 224-228). IEEE. 10.1109/ICWS.2019.00046

Bai, C. (2018, November). State-of-the-art and future trends of blockchain based on DAG structure. In *International Workshop on Structured Object-Oriented Formal Language and Method* (pp. 183-196). Springer.

Bai, L., Hu, M., Liu, M., & Wang, J. (2019). BPIIoT: A light-weighted blockchain-based platform for Industrial IoT. *IEEE Access: Practical Innovations, Open Solutions, 7*, 58381–58393. doi:10.1109/ACCESS.2019.2914223

Balraj. (2018). *Crypto currency: Everything You Need to Know about It*. Retrieved May 13, 2020, from https://pepnewz.com/2018/02/24/cryptocurrency-everything-need-know

Banerjee, M., Lee, J., & Choo, K. K. R. (2018). A blockchain future for internet of things security: A position paper. *Digital Communications and Networks, 4*(3), 149–160. doi:10.1016/j.dcan.2017.10.006

Barki, A., Bouabdallah, A., Gharout, S., & Traore, J. (2016). M2M security: Challenges and solutions. *IEEE Communications Surveys and Tutorials, 18*(2), 1241–1254. doi:10.1109/COMST.2016.2515516

Bartling, S., & Fecher, B. (2016). Could Blockchain provide the technical fix to solve science's reproducibility crisis? *Impact of Social Sciences Blog*.

Bartodziej, C. J. (2017). The concept industry 4.0. In *The concept industry 4.0* (pp. 27–50). Springer Gabler. doi:10.1007/978-3-658-16502-4_3

Basnayake, B. M. A. L., & Rajapakse, C. (2019). A Blockchain-based decentralized system to ensure the transparency of organic food supply chain. *Proceedings - IEEE International Research Conference on Smart Computing and Systems Engineering, SCSE 2019*, 103–107. 10.23919/SCSE.2019.8842690

Benchoufi, M., & Ravaud, P. (2017). Blockchain technology for improving clinical research quality. *Trials, 18*(1), 335.

Berge, J. (2018, April). Digital Transformation and IIoT for Oil and Gas Production. In *Offshore Technology Conference*. Offshore Technology Conference. 10.4043/28643-MS

Bernal Bernabe, J., Canovas, J. L., Hernandez-Ramos, J. L., Torres Moreno, R., & Skarmeta, A. (2019). Privacy-Preserving Solutions for Blockchain: Review and Challenges. *IEEE Access: Practical Innovations, Open Solutions, 7*, 164908–164940.

Bharani . (2019). *What is IoT (Internet of Things)? IoT Architecture*. Retrieved May 13, 2020, from https://www.edureka.co/blog/what-is-iot

Bhushan, B., Khamparia, A., Sagayam, K. M., Sharma, S. K., Ahad, M. A., & Debnath, N. C. (2020). Blockchain for smart cities: A review of architectures, integration trends and future research directions. *Sustainable Cities and Society, 61*. doi:10.1016/j.scs.2020.102360

Blackstock, M., & Lea, R. (2014). Toward a distributed data flow platform for the web of things (distributed node-red). *Proceedings of the 5th International Workshop on Web of Things*. 10.1145/2684432.2684439

Blockchain and the Internet of Things: the IoT blockchain opportunity and challenge. (n.d.). Retrieved May 13, 2020 from https://www.i-scoop.eu/internet-of-things-guide/blockchain-iot

Bocek, T., Rodrigues, B. B., Strasser, T., & Stiller, B. (2017). *Blockchains Everywhere - A Use-case of Blockchains in the Pharma Supply-Chain*. Academic Press.

Bond, F., Amati, F., & Blousson, G. (2015). *Blockchain, academic verification use case*. https://s3.amazonaws.com/signatura-usercontent/blockchain_academic_verification_use_case.pdf

Bosona, T., & Gebresenbet, G. (2013). Food traceability as an integral part of logistics management in food and agricultural supply chain. *Food Control, 33*(1), 32–48. Advance online publication. doi:10.1016/j.foodcont.2013.02.004

Boutros, A., Hesham, S., Georgey, B., & Abd El Ghany, M. A. (2017). Hardware acceleration of novel chaos-based image encryption for IoT applications. In *29th International Conference on Microelectronics (ICM)* (pp. 1-4). Beirut, Lebanon: IEEE. 10.1109/ICM.2017.8268833

Brewster, C., Roussaki, I., Kalatzis, N., Doolin, K., & Ellis, K. (2017). IoT in agriculture: Designing a Europe-wide large-scale pilot. *IEEE Communications Magazine, 55*(9), 26–33. doi:10.1109/MCOM.2017.1600528

Cachin, C. (2016). Architecture of the hyperledger blockchain fabric. In *Workshop on distributed cryptocurrencies and consensus ledgers* (*Vol. 310*, p. 4). Academic Press.

Calderón Godoy, A. J., & González Pérez, I. (2018). Integration of sensor and actuator networks and the SCADA system to promote the migration of the legacy flexible manufacturing system towards the industry 4.0 concept. *Journal of Sensor and Actuator Networks, 7*(2), 23. doi:10.3390/jsan7020023

Candell, R., Kashef, M., Liu, Y., Lee, K. B., & Foufou, S. (2018). Industrial wireless systems guidelines: Practical considerations and deployment life cycle. *IEEE Industrial Electronics Magazine, 12*(4), 6–17. doi:10.1109/MIE.2018.2873820

Caro, M. P., Ali, M. S., Vecchio, M., & Giaffreda, R. (2018, May). Blockchain-based traceability in Agri-Food supply chain management: A practical implementation. In *2018 IoT Vertical and Topical Summit on Agriculture-Tuscany (IOT Tuscany)* (pp. 1-4). IEEE. doi:10.1109/IOT-TUSCANY.2018.8373021

Casino, F., Dasaklis, T. K., & Patsakis, C. (2019). A systematic literature review of blockchain-based applications: Current status, classification and open issues. *Telematics and Informatics, 36*, 55–81.

Chain.co. (2014). https://chain.com/docs/1.2/protocol/papers/whitepaper

Chandel, V., Sinharay, A., Ahmed, N., & Ghose, A. (2016). Exploiting IMU Sensors for IOT Enabled Health Monitoring. In *First Workshop on IoT-enabled Healthcare and Wellness Technologies and Systems* (pp. 21-22). Singapore: ACM. 10.1145/2933566.2933569

Cha, S. C., Chen, J. F., Su, C., & Yeh, K. H. (2018). A blockchain connected gateway for BLE-based devices in the internet of things. *IEEE Access: Practical Innovations, Open Solutions, 6*, 24639–24649. doi:10.1109/ACCESS.2018.2799942

Chen, L., Xu, L., Shah, N., Gao, Z., Lu, Y., & Shi, W. (2017). On security analysis of proof-of-elapsed-time (PoET). *Lecture Notes in Computer Science (Including Subseries Lecture Notes in Artificial Intelligence and Lecture Notes in Bioinformatics), 10616 LNCS*, 282–297. doi:10.1007/978-3-319-69084-1_19

Chen, S., Shi, R., Ren, Z., Yan, J., Shi, Y., & Zhang, J. (2017). A Blockchain-Based Supply Chain Quality Management Framework. *Proceedings - 14th IEEE International Conference on E-Business Engineering, ICEBE 2017 - Including 13th Workshop on Service-Oriented Applications, Integration and Collaboration, SOAIC 207*, 172–176. 10.1109/ICEBE.2017.34

Chen, B., Wu, L., Kumar, N., Choo, K. K., & He, D. (2019). Lightweight searchable public-key encryption with forward privacy over IIoT outsourced data. *IEEE Transactions on Emerging Topics in Computing*, 1–1. doi:10.1109/TETC.2019.2921113

Chen, W., Zhang, Z., Hong, Z., Chen, C., Wu, J., Maharjan, S., Zheng, Z., & Zhang, Y. (2019). Cooperative and distributed computation offloading for blockchain-empowered industrial Internet of Things. *Internet of Things Journal, 6*(5), 8433–8446. doi:10.1109/JIOT.2019.2918296

Christopher, M., & Ryals, L. (1999). Supply Chain Strategy: Its Impact on Shareholder Value. *International Journal of Logistics Management, 10*(1), 1–10. https://doi.org/10.1108/09574099910805897

Clauson, K. A., Breeden, E. A., Davidson, C., & Mackey, T. K. (2018). Leveraging blockchain technology to enhance supply chain management in healthcare: an exploration of challenges and opportunities in the health supply chain. *Blockchain in Healthcare Today, 1*(3), 1-12.

Colombo, A. W., Karnouskos, S., Kaynak, O., Shi, Y., & Yin, S. (2017). Industrial cyberphysical systems: A backbone of the fourth industrial revolution. *IEEE Industrial Electronics Magazine, 11*(1), 6–16. doi:10.1109/MIE.2017.2648857

Cooper, M. C., Lambert, D. M., & Pagh, J. D. (1997). Supply Chain Management: More Than a New Name for Logistics. *International Journal of Logistics Management, 8*(1), 1–14. https://doi.org/10.1108/09574099710805556

Dagher, G. G., Marella, P. B., Milojkovic, M., & Mohler, J. (2018). *BroncoVote: secure voting system using Ethereum's blockchain.* Academic Press.

Dai, F., Shi, Y., Meng, N., Wei, L., & Ye, Z. (2017, November). From Bitcoin to cybersecurity: A comparative study of blockchain application and security issues. In *2017 4th International Conference on Systems and Informatics (ICSAI)* (pp. 975-979). IEEE. 10.1109/ICSAI.2017.8248427

Dai, H. N., Zheng, Z., & Zhang, Y. (2019). Blockchain for Internet of Things: A Survey. *IEEE Internet of Things Journal, 6*(5), 8076–8094. doi:10.1109/JIOT.2019.2920987

Dai, Zheng, & Zhang. (2019). Blockchain for Internet of Things: A Survey. *IEEE Internet of Things Journal.*

Daley. (2019). *Blockchain and IoT: 8 examples making our future smarter.* Retrieved May 13, 2020 from https://builtin.com/blockchain/blockchain-iot-examples

Das, Zeadally, & He. (n.d.). Taxonomy and analysis of security protocols for Internet of Things. *Future Generation Computer Systems.*

Dasgupta, D., Shrein, J. M., & Gupta, K. D. (2019). A survey of blockchain from security perspective. *Journal of Banking and Financial Technology, 3*(1), 1–17. https://doi.org/10.1007/s42786-018-00002-6

De Angelis, S., Aniello, L., Baldoni, R., Lombardi, F., Margheri, A., & Sassone, V. (2018). PBFT vs proof-of-authority: Applying the CAP theorem to permissioned blockchain. *CEUR Workshop Proceedings, 2058.*

Dedeoglu, V., Jurdak, R., Dorri, A., Lunardi, R. C., Michelin, R. A., Zorzo, A. F., & Kanhere, S. S. (2020). Blockchain technologies for iot. In *Advanced Applications of Blockchain Technology* (pp. 55–89). Springer.

Dennis, R., & Owen, G. (2016). Rep on the block: A next generation reputation system based on the blockchain. *2015 10th International Conference for Internet Technology and Secured Transactions, ICITST 2015*, 131–138. doi:10.1109/ICITST.2015.7412073

Di Vaio, A., & Varriale, L. (2020). Blockchain technology in supply chain management for sustainable performance: Evidence from the airport industry. *International Journal of Information Management, 52*, 102014. doi:10.1016/j.ijinfomgt.2019.09.010

Dinh, T. N., & Thai, M. T. (2018). Ai and blockchain: A disruptive integration. *Computer, 51*(9), 48–53. doi:10.1109/MC.2018.3620971

Dorri, A., Kanhere, S. S., & Jurdak, R. (2017, April). Towards an optimized blockchain for IoT. In *2017 IEEE/ACM Second International Conference on Internet-of-Things Design and Implementation (IoTDI)* (pp. 173-178). IEEE.

Ekblaw, A., Azaria, A., Halamka, J. D., & Lippman, A. (2016, August). A Case Study for Blockchain in Healthcare:"MedRec" prototype for electronic health records and medical research data. In *Proceedings of IEEE open & big data conference* (*Vol. 13*, p. 13). Academic Press.

Elhoseny, M., Ramírez-González, G., Abu-Elnasr, O. M., Shawkat, S. A., Arunkumar, N., & Farouk, A. (2018). Secure medical data transmission model for IoT-based healthcare systems. *IEEE Access: Practical Innovations, Open Solutions, 6*, 20596–20608. doi:10.1109/ACCESS.2018.2817615

Elmessiry, M., & Elmessiry, A. (2018). *Blockchain Framework for Textile Supply Chain Management*. doi:10.1007/978-3-319-94478-4

Esposito, C., De Santis, A., Tortora, G., Chang, H., & Choo, K. K. R. (2018). Blockchain: A panacea for healthcare cloud-based data security and privacy? *IEEE Cloud Computing, 5*(1), 31–37. doi:10.1109/MCC.2018.011791712

Ethereum. (2016). *White Paper - Ethereum/WiKi*. Available: https:github.com/Ethereum/wiki/wiki/White-Paper

Felser, M. (2005). Real-time ethernet-industry prospective. *Proceedings of the IEEE, 93*(6), 1118–1129. doi:10.1109/JPROC.2005.849720

Ferdous, M. S., Chowdhury, M. J. M., Hoque, M. A., & Colman, A. (2020). *Blockchain consensus algorithms: a survey*. ArXiv.

Fernández-Caramés, T. M., & Fraga-Lamas, P. (2018). A Review on the Use of Blockchain for the Internet of Things. *IEEE Access : Practical Innovations, Open Solutions, 6*, 32979–33001.

Fernández-Caramés, T. M., & Fraga-Lamas, P. (2018). A Review on the Use of Blockchain for the Internet of Things. *IEEE Access: Practical Innovations, Open Solutions, 6*, 32979–33001.

Fernández-Caramés, T. M., & Fraga-Lamas, P. (2019). A review on the application of blockchain to the next generation of cybersecure industry 4.0 smart factories. *IEEE Access: Practical Innovations, Open Solutions, 7*, 45201–45218. doi:10.1109/ACCESS.2019.2908780

Fernandez-Carames, T. M., & Fraga-Lamas, P. (2019). A Review on the Application of Blockchain to the Next Generation of Cybersecure Industry 4.0 Smart Factories. *IEEE Access: Practical Innovations, Open Solutions, 7*, 45201–45218. https://doi.org/10.1109/ACCESS.2019.2908780

Ferreira, C. M. S., Oliveira, R. A. R., Silva, J. S., & da Cunha Cavalcanti, C. F. M. (2020). Blockchain for Machine to Machine Interaction in Industry 4.0. In *Blockchain Technology for Industry 4.0* (pp. 99–116). Springer. doi:10.1007/978-981-15-1137-0_5

Fraga-Lamas, P., & Fernández-Caramés, T. M. (2019). A review on blockchain technologies for an advanced and cyber-resilient automotive industry. *IEEE Access: Practical Innovations, Open Solutions*, 7, 17578–17598.

Francisco, K. & Swanson, D. (2018). The Supply Chain Has No Clothes: Technology Adoption of Blockchain for Supply Chain Transparency. *Digital Logistics*, 1-13.

Frank, A. G., Dalenogare, L. S., & Ayala, N. F. (2019). Industry 4.0 technologies: Implementation patterns in manufacturing companies. *International Journal of Production Economics*, 210, 15–26. doi:10.1016/j.ijpe.2019.01.004

Frizzo-barker, J., Chow-white, P. A., Adams, P. R., Mentanko, J., Ha, D., & Green, S. (2019). International Journal of Information Management Blockchain as a disruptive technology for business : A systematic review. *International Journal of Information Management*, 0–1(April). Advance online publication. doi:10.1016/j.ijinfomgt.2019.10.014

Fuller, J. R. (2016). *The 4 stages of an IoT architecture*. Retrieved May 13, 2020, from https://techbeacon.com/enterprise-it/4-stages-iot-architecture

Gallo, P., Nguyen, U. Q., Barone, G., & Van Hien, P. (2018, September). DeCyMo: Decentralized Cyber-Physical System for Monitoring and Controlling Industries and Homes. In *2018 IEEE 4th International Forum on Research and Technology for Society and Industry (RTSI)* (pp. 1-4). IEEE.

Garcia, M. V., Irisarri, E., Perez, F., Estevez, E., & Marcos, M. (2016). OPC-UA communications integration using a CPPS architecture. In IEEE Ecuador technical chapters meeting (pp. 1-6). doi:10.1109/ETCM.2016.7750838

Garderen, P. V. (2016). *Introduction to Blockchain and Recordkeeping, Recordkeeping Roundtable*. http://www.interpares.org/display_file.cfm?doc=ip1_dissemination_ss_van-garderen_rr_2016.pdf

Garrocho, C., Ferreira, C. M. S., Junior, A., Cavalcanti, C. F., & Oliveira, R. R. (2019, November). Industry 4.0: Smart Contract-based Industrial Internet of Things Process Management. In Anais do IX Simpósio Brasileiro de Engenharia de Sistemas Computacionais (pp. 137-142). SBC.

Gebrekiros, Y., & Doorman, G. (2014, February 10). Optimal transmission capacity allocation for cross-border exchange of Frequency Restoration Reserves (FRR). *Proceedings - 2014 Power Systems Computation Conference, PSCC 2014*. doi:10.1109/PSCC.2014.7038426

Ghosh, D., & Tan, A. (2020). *A Framework for Implementing Blockchain Technologies to Improve Supply Chain Performance*. Available: https://dspace.mit.edu/handle/1721.1/113244

Giang, N. K., Blackstock, M., Lea, R., & Leung, V. C. (2015). Developing iot applications in the fog: A distributed dataflow approach. In *2015 5th International Conference on the Internet of Things (IOT)* (pp. 155-162). IEEE. 10.1109/IOT.2015.7356560

Gill, S. S., Chana, I., & Buyya, R. (2017). IoT based agriculture as a cloud and big data service: The beginning of digital India. *Journal of Organizational and End User Computing*, 29(4), 1–23. doi:10.4018/JOEUC.2017100101

Gobel, J., & Krzesinski, A. E. (2017). Increased block size and Bitcoin blockchain dynamics. *2017 27th International Telecommunication Networks and Applications Conference, ITNAC 2017*, 1–6. doi:10.1109/ATNAC.2017.8215367

Golatowski, F., Butzin, B., Brockmann, T., Schulz, T., Kasparick, M., Li, Y., ... Aydemir, Ö. (2019, May). Challenges and research directions for blockchains in the internet of things. In *2019 IEEE International Conference on Industrial Cyber Physical Systems (ICPS)* (pp. 712-717). IEEE. 10.1109/ICPHYS.2019.8780270

Gopinath, T., Kumar, A. R., & Sharma, R. (2013, April). Performance evaluation of TCP and UDP over wireless ad-hoc networks with varying traffic loads. In *2013 International Conference on Communication Systems and Network Technologies* (pp. 281-285). IEEE. 10.1109/CSNT.2013.66

Grand View Research. (2019, June). *Industrial internet of things (iiot) market size, share trends analysis report by component, by end use (manufacturing, energy power, oil gas, healthcare, logistics transport, agriculture), and segment forecasts, 2019 - 2025.* Retrieved from https://www.grandviewresearch.com/industry-analysis/industrial-internet-of-things-iiot-market

Grieves, M. (2020). *Digital Twin: Manufacturing Excellence Through Virtual Factory Replication.* Available: http://www.apriso.com

Gupta, S., Sinha, S., & Bhushan, B. (2020). Emergence of Blockchain Technology: Fundamentals, Working and its Various Implementations. *SSRN Electronic Journal.* doi:10.2139srn.3569577

Gura, N., Patel, A., Wander, A., Eberle, H., & Shantz, S. C. (2004). Comparing Elliptic Curve Cryptography and RSA on 8-bit CPUs. *Proceedings of the International Workshop on Cryptographic Hardware and Embedded Systems.*

Habib, M., Mehmood, T., Ullah, F., & Ibrahim, M. (2009). Performance of WiMAX Security Algorithm (The Comparative Study of RSA Encryption Algorithm with ECC Encryption Algorithm). *Proceedings of the 2009 International Conference on Computer Technology and Development, 2,* 108-112.

Hafid, A., Hafid, A. S., & Samih, M. (2020). Scaling Blockchains: A Comprehensive Survey. *IEEE Access: Practical Innovations, Open Solutions, 8,* 125244–125262. https://doi.org/10.1109/ACCESS.2020.3007251

Hang, L., & Kim, D. H. (2019). Design and implementation of an integrated IoT blockchain platform for sensing data integrity. *Sensors (Basel), 19*(10), 2228. doi:10.339019102228 PMID:31091799

Hao, Y., Li, Y., Dong, X., Fang, L., & Chen, P. (2018). Performance Analysis of Consensus Algorithm in Private Blockchain. *IEEE Intelligent Vehicles Symposium, Proceedings,* 280–285. doi:10.1109/IVS.2018.8500557

Haque, A. B., Najmul Islam, A. K. M., Hyrynsalmi, S., Naqvi, B., & Smolander, K. (2021). GDPR Compliant Blockchains – A Systematic Literature Review. *IEEE Access,* 1–1. doi:10.1109/ACCESS.2021.3069877

Haque, A. K. M. B., & Rahman, M. (2020). Blockchain Technology : Methodology, Application and Security Issues. *International Journal of Computer Science and Network Security, 20*(2), 21–30. https://www.researchgate.net/publication/339973150_Blockchain_Technology_Methodology_Application_and_Security_Issues/citations

Hasan, H., AlHadhrami, E., AlDhaheri, A., Salah, K., & Jayaraman, R. (2019). Smart contract-based approach for efficient shipment management. *Computers & Industrial Engineering, 136,* 149–159. doi:10.1016/j.cie.2019.07.022

Helo, P., & Hao, Y. (2019). Blockchains in operations and supply chains: A model and reference implementation. *Computers & Industrial Engineering, 136*(July), 242–251. doi:10.1016/j.cie.2019.07.023

Helo, P., & Shamsuzzoha, A. H. M. (2018, December). Real-time supply chain—A blockchain architecture for project deliveries. *Robotics and Computer-integrated Manufacturing, 63,* 101909. doi:10.1016/j.rcim.2019.101909

Helo, P., & Szekely, B. (2005, January). Logistics information systems: An analysis of software solutions for supply chain co-ordination. *Industrial Management & Data Systems, 105*(1), 5–18. Advance online publication. doi:10.1108/02635570510575153

Hijro. (n.d.). Retrieved April 1, 2021, from https://hijro.com/

Hill, G., Al-Aqrabi, H., Lane, P., & Aagela, H. (2019, January). Securing Manufacturing Business Intelligence for the Industrial Internet of Things. In *Fourth International Congress on Information and Communication Technology* (p. 174). Springer Singapore.

Hossain, M., & Muhammad, G. (2016). Cloud-assisted industrial internet of things (iiot)–enabled framework for health monitoring. *Computer Networks*, *101*, 192–202. doi:10.1016/j.comnet.2016.01.009

Hou, H. (2017, September 14). The application of blockchain technology in E-government in China. *2017 26th International Conference on Computer Communications and Networks, ICCCN 2017*. doi:10.1109/ICCCN.2017.8038519

Huang, J., Kong, L., Chen, G., Wu, M. Y., Liu, X., & Zeng, P. (2019). Towards secure industrial IoT: Blockchain system with credit-based consensus mechanism. *IEEE Transactions on Industrial Informatics*, *15*(6), 3680–3689. doi:10.1109/TII.2019.2903342

Hyperledger. (2019). *Hyperledger – Open Source Blockchain Technologies*. Hyperledger. https://www.hyperledger.org/

Isaja, M., & Soldatos, J. (2018, May). Distributed ledger technology for decentralization of manufacturing processes. In *2018 IEEE Industrial Cyber-Physical Systems (ICPS)* (pp. 696-701). IEEE.

Islam, I., Munim, K. M., Oishwee, S. J., Islam, A. K. M. N., & Islam, M. N. (2020). A Critical Review of Concepts, Benefits, and Pitfalls of Blockchain Technology Using Concept Map. *IEEE Access: Practical Innovations, Open Solutions*, *8*, 68333–68341. https://doi.org/10.1109/ACCESS.2020.2985647

Ismail, A., & Shehab, A. (2019). Security in Smart Cities: Models, Applications, and Challenges.). *Future Generation Computer Systems*, *9*(November).

It, S. (2017). *Can Blockchain Strengthen the Internet of Things?* Academic Press.

Ivanov, D., Dolgui, A., & Sokolov, B. (2019). The impact of digital technology and industry 4.0 on the ripple effect and supply chain risk analytics. *International Journal of Production Research*, *57*(3), 829–846.

Jain, M., Kaushik, N., & Jayavel, K. (2017, February). Building automation and energy control using IoT-Smart campus. In *2017 2nd International Conference on Computing and Communications Technologies (ICCCT)* (pp. 353-359). IEEE. 10.1109/ICCCT2.2017.7972303

Jamil, F., Hang, L., Kim, K., & Kim, D. (2019). A novel medical blockchain model for drug supply chain integrity management in a smart hospital. *Electronics (Basel)*, *8*(5), 505. doi:10.3390/electronics8050505

Jayaram, A. (2016, December). Lean six sigma approach for global supply chain management using industry 4.0 and IIoT. In *2016 2nd international conference on contemporary computing and informatics (IC3I)* (pp. 89-94). IEEE.

Jayasena. (2017). *How the Blockchain Revolution Will Reshape the Consumer Electronics Industry*. Academic Press.

Jeschke, S., Brecher, C., Meisen, T., Özdemir, D., & Eschert, T. (2017). Industrial internet of things and cyber manufacturing systems. In *Industrial internet of things* (pp. 3–19). Springer. doi:10.1007/978-3-319-42559-7_1

Johnston, W. M., Hanna, J. P., & Millar, R. J. (2004). Advances in dataflow programming languages. *ACM Computing Surveys*, *36*(1), 1–34. doi:10.1145/1013208.1013209

Judmayer, A., Stifter, N., Krombholz, K., & Weippl, E. (2017). Blocks and Chains: Introduction to Bitcoin, Cryptocurrencies, and Their Consensus Mechanisms. *Synthesis Lectures on Information Security, Privacy, and Trust*, *9*(1), 1–123. doi:10.220000773ed1v01y201704spt020

Kamilaris, A., Fonts, A., & Prenafeta-Boldú, F. X. (2019). The rise of blockchain technology in agriculture and food supply chains. *Trends in Food Science & Technology*, *91*, 640–652. doi:10.1016/j.tifs.2019.07.034

Kamilaris, A., Fonts, A., Prenafeta-Boldú, F. X., Kamble, S. S., Gunasekaran, A., Sharma, R., ... Beynon-Davies, P. (2019). How the blockchain enables and constrains supply chain performance. *Supply Chain Management, 24*(4), 376–397. doi:10.1108/IJPDLM-02-2019-0063

Kapitonov, A., Berman, I., Lonshakov, S., & Krupenkin, A. (2018, June). Blockchain based protocol for economical communication in industry 4.0. In *2018 Crypto valley conference on blockchain technology (CVCBT)* (pp. 41-44). IEEE.

Kapitonov, A., Lonshakov, S., Krupenkin, A., & Berman, I. (2017, October). Blockchain-based protocol of autonomous business activity for multi-agent systems consisting of UAVs. In *2017 Workshop on Research, Education and Development of Unmanned Aerial Systems (RED-UAS)* (pp. 84-89). IEEE. 10.1109/RED-UAS.2017.8101648

Kastner, W., Kofler, M., Jung, M., Gridling, G., & Weidinger, J. (2014, September). Building Automation Systems Integration into the Internet of Things The IoT6 approach, its realization and validation. In *Proceedings of the 2014 IEEE Emerging Technology and Factory Automation (ETFA)* (pp. 1-9). IEEE. 10.1109/ETFA.2014.7005197

Khan, J., Li, J. P., Ahamad, B., Parveen, S., Haq, A. U., Khan, G. A., & Sangaiah, A. K. (2020). SMSH: Secure Surveillance Mechanism on Smart Healthcare IoT System With Probabilistic Image Encryption. *IEEE Access: Practical Innovations, Open Solutions, 8*, 15747–15767. doi:10.1109/ACCESS.2020.2966656

Khan, M. A., & Salah, K. (2018). IoT security: Review, blockchain solutions, and open challenges. *Future Generation Computer Systems, 82*, 395–411. doi:10.1016/j.future.2017.11.022

Khan, M., Wu, X., Xu, X., & Dou, W. (2017, May). Big data challenges and opportunities in the hype of Industry 4.0. In *2017 IEEE International Conference on Communications (ICC)* (pp. 1-6). IEEE. 10.1109/ICC.2017.7996801

Khan, P. W., & Byun, Y. (2020). A Blockchain-Based Secure Image Encryption Scheme for the Industrial Internet of Things. *Entropy (Basel, Switzerland), 22*(175), 1–26. doi:10.3390/e22020175 PMID:33285950

Kharlamov, A., Parry, G., & Clarke, A. C. (n.d.). *Advanced Supply Chains : Visibility, Blockchain and Human Behaviour*. Academic Press.

Khorov, E., Lyakhov, A., Ivanov, A., & Akyildiz, I. F. (2020). Modeling of real-time multimedia streaming in Wi-Fi networks with periodic reservations. *IEEE Access : Practical Innovations, Open Solutions, 8*, 55633–55653.

Kiel, D., Arnold, C., & Voigt, K. I. (2017). The influence of the Industrial Internet of Things on business models of established manufacturing companies–A business level perspective. *Technovation, 68*, 4–19. doi:10.1016/j.technovation.2017.09.003

Kim, H. M., & Laskowski, M. (2018). Agriculture on the blockchain: Sustainable solutions for food, farmers, and financing. In *Supply Chain Revolution*. Barrow Books.

King, S., & Nadal, S. (2012). *PPCoin: Peer-to-Peer Crypto-Currency with Proof-of-Stake*. Academic Press.

Kitchenham, B. (2004). Procedures for performing systematic reviews. Keele University.

Knirsch, F., Unterweger, A., & Engel, D. (2018). Privacy-preserving blockchain-based electric vehicle charging with dynamic tariff decisions. *Computer Science -. Research for Development, 33*(1–2), 71–79. https://doi.org/10.1007/s00450-017-0348-5

Kobzan, T., Biendarra, A., Schriegel, S., Herbst, T., Müeller, T., & Jasperneite, J. (2018). Utilising blockchain technology in industrial manufacturing with the help of network simulation. *Proc. 16th Int. Conf. Ind. Informat.*, 152-159.

Koç, A. K., Yavuz, E., Çabuk, U. C., & Dalkiliç, G. (2018). Towards secure e-voting using ethereum blockchain. *6th International Symposium on Digital Forensic and Security, ISDFS 2018 - Proceeding*, 1–6. doi:10.1109/ISDFS.2018.8355340

Kohad, H. (2020). Scalability Issues of Blockchain Technology. *International Journal of Engineering and Advanced Technology*.

Kosba, A., Miller, A., Shi, E., Wen, Z., & Papamanthou, C. (2016). Hawk: The Blockchain Model of Cryptography and Privacy-Preserving Smart Contracts. *Proceedings - 2016 IEEE Symposium on Security and Privacy, SP 2016*. 10.1109/SP.2016.55

Ko, T., Lee, J., & Ryu, D. (2018). Blockchain technology and manufacturing industry: Real-time transparency and cost savings. *Sustainability*, *10*(11), 4274. doi:10.3390u10114274

Kounelis, I., Steri, G., Giuliani, R., Geneiatakis, D., Neisse, R., & Nai-Fovino, I. (2017, August 23). Fostering consumers' energy market through smart contracts. *Energy and Sustainability in Small Developing Economies, ES2DE 2017 - Proceedings*. doi:10.1109/ES2DE.2017.8015343

Krishnan, P., Najeem, J. S., & Achuthan, K. (2017, August). SDN framework for securing IoT networks. In *International Conference on Ubiquitous Communications and Network Computing* (pp. 116-129). Springer.

Kshetri, N. (2018). Blockchain's roles in meeting key supply chain management objectives. *International Journal of Information Management*, *39*(June), 80–89. doi:10.1016/j.ijinfomgt.2017.12.005

Kshetri, N. (2017). Can blockchain strengthen the internet of things? *IT Professional*, *19*(4), 68–72.

Ku, I., Lu, Y., Gerla, M., Gomes, R. L., Ongaro, F., & Cerqueira, E. (2014, June). Towards software-defined VANET: Architecture and services. In *2014 13th annual Mediterranean ad hoc networking workshop (MED-HOC-NET)* (pp. 103-110). IEEE.

Kumar, E. S., Kusuma, S. M., & Kumar, B. V. (2014, April). An intelligent defense mechanism for security in wireless sensor networks. In *2014 International Conference on Communication and Signal Processing* (pp. 275-279). IEEE

Kumar, N. M., & Mallick, P. K. (2018, January). Blockchain technology for security issues and challenges in IoT. *Procedia Computer Science*, *132*, 1815–1823.

Kwon, J. (2014). TenderMint : Consensus without Mining. In *The-Blockchain.Com* (Vol. 6). tendermint.com/docs/tendermint.pdf

La Londe, B. J., & Masters, J. M. (1994). Emerging Logistics Strategies: Blueprints for the Next Century. *International Journal of Physical Distribution & Logistics Management*, *24*(7), 35–47. https://doi.org/10.1108/09600039410070975

Laabs, M., & Dukanovic, S. (2018). "Blockchain in industrie 4.0: Beyond' cryptocurrency. *IT-Inf. Technol.*, *60*(3), 143–153.

Labazova, O., Dehling, T., & Sunyaev, A. (2019). From Hype to Reality: A Taxonomy of Blockchain Applications. *Proceedings of the 52nd Hawaii International Conference on System Sciences*. doi:10.24251/hicss.2019.552

Lai, J. (2019). Research on Cross-Border E-Commerce Logistics Supply under Block Chain. *Proceedings - 2nd International Conference on Computer Network, Electronic and Automation, ICCNEA 2019*, 214–218. 10.1109/ICCNEA.2019.00049

Lambrechts & Sinha. (2016). *Micro sensing Networks for Sustainable Cities: Pollution as a Key Driving Factor*. https://link.springer.com/chapter/10.1007/978-3-319-28358-6_1

Lamport, L. (1998). The Part-Time Parliament. *ACM Transactions on Computer Systems*, *16*(2), 133–169.

Lamport, L., Shostak, R., & Pease, M. (2008). The byzantine generals problem. *Dr. Dobb's Journal*, *33*(4), 30–36. https://doi.org/10.1145/3335772.3335936

Laszka, A., Dubey, A., Walker, M., & Schmidt, D. (2017). Providing privacy, safety, and security in IoT-based transactive energy systems using distributed ledgers. *ACM International Conference Proceeding Series*, 1–8. doi:10.1145/3131542.3131562

Leang, B., Kim, R. W., & Yoo, K. H. (2018, July). Real-Time Transmission of Secured PLCs Sensing Data. In *IEEE International Conference on Internet of Things and IEEE Green Computing and Communications and IEEE Cyber, Physical and Social Computing and IEEE Smart Data* (pp. 931-932). 10.1109/Cybermatics_2018.2018.00177

Lee, J., Azamfar, M. & Singh, J. (2019). A blockchain-enabled cyber-physical system architecture for industry 4.0 manufacturing systems. *Manuf. Lett., 20*, 34-39.

Lee, E. A. (2005). Absolutely positively on time: What would it take? *Computer, 38*(7), 85–87. doi:10.1109/MC.2005.211

Lee, J., Azamfar, M., & Singh, J. (2019). A blockchain enabled Cyber-Physical System architecture for Industry 4.0 manufacturing systems. *Manufacturing Letters, 20*, 34–39. doi:10.1016/j.mfglet.2019.05.003

Lee, J., & Pilkington, M. (2017, July). How the blockchain revolution will reshape the consumer electronics industry. *IEEE Consum. Electron. Mag., 6*(3), 19–23.

Leiding, B., Memarmoshrefi, P., & Hogrefe, D. (2016). Self-managed and blockchain-based vehicular ad-hoc networks. *UbiComp 2016 Adjunct - Proceedings of the 2016 ACM International Joint Conference on Pervasive and Ubiquitous Computing*, 137–140. doi:10.1145/2968219.2971409

Lemieux, V. L., Hofman, D., Batista, D., & Joo, A. (2019). Blockchain technology & recordkeeping. *ARMA International Educational Foundation, May, 30*.

Leng, J, Zhang, H., Yan, D., Liu, Q., Chen, X. & Zhang, D. (2019). Digital twin-driven manufacturing cyber-physical system for parallel controlling of smart workshop. *J. Ambient Intell. Hum. Computer., 10*, 1155-1166.

Leng, J. (2020, January). ManuChain: Combining permissioned blockchain with a holistic optimisation model as bi-level intelligence for smart manufacturing. *IEEE Transactions on Systems, Man, and Cybernetics. Systems, 50*(1), 182–192.

Liang, X., Shetty, S., Tosh, D. K., Zhao, J., Li, D., & Liu, J. (2018). A Reliable Data Provenance and Privacy Preservation Architecture for Business-Driven Cyber-Physical Systems Using Blockchain. *International Journal of Information Security and Privacy, 12*(4), 68–81. doi:10.4018/IJISP.2018100105

Li, L., Liu, J., Cheng, L., Qiu, S., Wang, W., Zhang, X., & Zhang, Z. (2018). CreditCoin: A Privacy-Preserving Blockchain-Based Incentive Announcement Network for Communications of Smart Vehicles. *IEEE Transactions on Intelligent Transportation Systems, 19*(7), 2204–2220. https://doi.org/10.1109/TITS.2017.2777990

Lin, I. C., & Liao, T. C. (2017). A survey of blockchain security issues and challenges. *International Journal of Network Security, 19*(5), 653–659.

Litke, A., Anagnostopoulos, D., & Varvarigou, T. (2019). Blockchains for Supply Chain Management: Architectural Elements and Challenges Towards a Global Scale Deployment. *Logistics, 3*(1), 5. doi:10.3390/logistics3010005

Liu, H., Li, Z., & Cao, N. (2018). *Framework Design of Financial Service Platform for Tobacco Supply Chain Based on Blockchain* (Vol. 2). doi:10.1007/978-3-030-05234-8

Liu, C., Vengayil, H., Lu, Y., & Xu, X. (2019). A cyber-physical machine tools platform using OPC UA and MTConnect. *Journal of Manufacturing Systems, 51*, 61–74. doi:10.1016/j.jmsy.2019.04.006

Liu, D., Alahmadi, A., Ni, J., Lin, X., & Shen, X. (2019). Anonymous reputation system for IIoT-enabled retail marketing atop PoS blockchain. *IEEE Transactions on Industrial Informatics, 15*(6), 3527–3537. doi:10.1109/TII.2019.2898900

Liu, M., Yu, F. R., Teng, Y., Leung, V. C., & Song, M. (2019). Performance optimization for blockchain-enabled industrial Internet of Things (IIoT) systems: A deep reinforcement learning approach. *IEEE Transactions on Industrial Informatics, 15*(6), 3559–3570. doi:10.1109/TII.2019.2897805

Liu, Y., Wang, K., Lin, Y., & Xu, W. (2019). A Lightweight Blockchain System for Industrial Internet of Things. *IEEE Transactions on Industrial Informatics, 15*(6), 3571–3581. doi:10.1109/TII.2019.2904049

Li, X., Jiang, P., Chen, T., Luo, X., & Wen, Q. (2020). A survey on the security of blockchain systems. *Future Generation Computer Systems, 107*, 841–853. https://doi.org/10.1016/j.future.2017.08.020

Li, Z., Kang, J., Yu, R., Ye, D., Deng, Q., & Zhang, Y. (2017). Consortium blockchain for secure energy trading in industrial internet of things. *IEEE Transactions on Industrial Informatics, 14*(8), 3690–3700. doi:10.1109/TII.2017.2786307

Llamuca, J. D., Garcia, C. A., Naranjo, J. E., Rosero, C., Alvarez-M, E., & Garcia, M. V. (2019, November). Integrating ISA-95 and IEC-61499 for Distributed Control System Monitoring. In *Conference on Information Technologies and Communication of Ecuador* (pp. 66-80). Springer.

Lödding, H., Yu, K. W., & Wiendahl, H. P. (2003). Decentralised WIPoriented manufacturing control (DEWIP). *Production Planning and Control, 14*(1), 42–54.

Longo, F., Nicoletti, L., Padovano, A., d'Atri, G., & Forte, M. (2019). Blockchain-enabled supply chain: An experimental study. *Computers & Industrial Engineering, 136*(July), 57–69. doi:10.1016/j.cie.2019.07.026

Lucas-Estañ, M. C., Sepulcre, M., Raptis, T. P., Passarella, A., & Conti, M. (2018). Emerging trends in hybrid wireless communication and data management for the industry 4.0. *Electronics (Basel), 7*(12), 400. doi:10.3390/electronics7120400

Lu, H., Guo, L., Azimi, M., & Huang, K. (2019). Oil and Gas 4.0 era: A systematic review and outlook. *Computers in Industry, 111*, 68–90. doi:10.1016/j.compind.2019.06.007

Lu, H., Huang, K., Azimi, M., & Guo, L. (2019). Blockchain technology in the oil and gas industry: A review of applications, opportunities, challenges, and risks. *IEEE Access: Practical Innovations, Open Solutions, 7*, 41426–41444. doi:10.1109/ACCESS.2019.2907695

Luo, B., Li, X., Weng, J., Guo, J., & Ma, J. (2020). Blockchain Enabled Trust-Based Location Privacy Protection Scheme in VANET. *IEEE Transactions on Vehicular Technology, 69*(2), 2034–2048. https://doi.org/10.1109/TVT.2019.2957744

Lu, Y. (2018). Blockchain and the related issues: A review of current research topics. *J. Manag. Anal., 5*(4), 231–255.

Lu, Y. (2018). Blockchain: A Survey on Functions, Applications and Open Issues. *Journal of Industrial Integration and Management, 03*(04), 1850015. https://doi.org/10.1142/s242486221850015x

Lu, Y., Li, J., & Zhang, Y. (2019). Privacy-Preserving and Pairing-Free Multirecipient Certificateless Encryption With Keyword Search for Cloud-Assisted IIoT. *IEEE Internet of Things Journal, 7*(4), 2553–2562. doi:10.1109/JIOT.2019.2943379

Lv, S., Liu, Y., & Sun, J. (2019). IMES: An Automatically Scalable Invisible Membrane Image Encryption for Privacy Protection on IoT Sensors. In *International Symposium on Cyberspace Safety and Security* (pp. 265-273). Guangzhou, China: Springer.

Madaan, G., Bhushan, B., & Kumar, R. (2021). Blockchain-Based Cyberthreat Mitigation Systems for Smart Vehicles and Industrial Automation. Springer. https://doi.org/10.1007/978-981-15-7965-3_2.

Madavi, D. (2008). *A Comprehensive Study on Blockchain Technology*. International Research Journal of Engineering and Technology.

Madhunamali, A. T. H. E. (2017). *How the Blockchain Revolution Will Reshape the Consumer Electronics Industry.* Academic Press.

Madumidha, S., Ranjani, P. S., Varsinee, S. S., & Sundari, P. S. (2019). Transparency and traceability: In food supply chain system using blockchain technology with internet of things. *Proceedings of the International Conference on Trends in Electronics and Informatics, ICOEI 2019*, 983–987. 10.1109/ICOEI.2019.8862726

Ma, M., He, D., Kumar, N., Choo, K. K., & Chen, J. (2017). Certificateless searchable public key encryption scheme for industrial internet of things. *IEEE Transactions on Industrial Informatics*, *14*(2), 759–767.

Mattila, J., Seppälä, T., & Holmström, J. (2016). Product-centric Information Management. *A Case Study of a Shared Platform with Blockchain Technology.*

Maw, A., Adepu, S., & Mathur, A. (2019). ICS-BlockOpS: Blockchain for operational data security in industrial control system. *Pervasive and Mobile Computing*, *59*, 101048. doi:10.1016/j.pmcj.2019.101048

Mazlan, A. A., Daud, S. M., Sam, S. M., Abas, H., Rasid, S. Z. A., & Yusof, M. F. (2020). Scalability Challenges in Healthcare Blockchain System-A Systematic Review. *IEEE Access: Practical Innovations, Open Solutions*, *8*, 23663–23673.

Meghdadi, M., Özdemir, S., & Güler, İ. (2008). Kablosuz Algılayıcı Ağlarında Güvenlik: Sorunlar ve Çözümler. *Bilişim Teknolojileri Dergisi*, *1*(1).

Mehta, B. R., & Reddy, Y. J. (2014). *Industrial process automation systems: design and implementation.* Butterworth-Heinemann.

Mendiboure, L., Chalouf, M. A., & Krief, F. (2020). Survey on blockchain-based applications in internet of vehicles. *Computers & Electrical Engineering*, *84*, 106646. doi:10.1016/j.compeleceng.2020.106646

Mengelkamp, E., Gärttner, J., Rock, K., Kessler, S., Orsini, L., & Weinhardt, C. (2018). Designing microgrid energy markets: A case study: The Brooklyn Microgrid. *Applied Energy*, *210*, 870–880. https://doi.org/10.1016/j.apenergy.2017.06.054

Mengelkamp, E., Notheisen, B., Beer, C., Dauer, D., & Weinhardt, C. (2018). A blockchain-based smart grid: Towards sustainable local energy markets. *Computer Science -. Research for Development*, *33*(1–2), 207–214. https://doi.org/10.1007/s00450-017-0360-9

Mentzer, J. T., DeWitt, W., Keebler, J. S., Min, S., Nix, N. W., Smith, C. D., & Zacharia, Z. G. (2001). Defining Supply Chain Management. *Journal of Business Logistics*, *22*(2), 1–25. https://doi.org/10.1002/j.2158-1592.2001.tb00001.x

Miglani, A., Kumar, N., Chamola, V., & Zeadally, S. (2020). Blockchain for Internet of Energy management: Review, solutions, and challenges. *Computer Communications*, *151*, 395–418. doi:10.1016/j.comcom.2020.01.014

Milani, F., García-Bañuelos, L., & Dumas, M. (2016). *Blockchain and Business Process Improvement.* BPTrends. www.bptrends.com

Min, H. (2019). Blockchain technology for enhancing supply chain resilience. *Business Horizons*, *62*(1), 35–45.

Moghaddam, M., Cadavid, M. N., Kenley, C. R., & Deshmukh, A. V. (2018). Reference architectures for smart manufacturing: A critical review. *Journal of Manufacturing Systems*, *49*, 215–225.

Mohamed, N., & Al-Jaroodi, J. (2019). Applying blockchain in industry 4.0 applications. *Proc. IEEE 9th Annu. Comput. Commun. Workshop Conf.*, 852-858.

Mondragon, A. E. C., Mondragon, C. E. C., & Coronado, E. S. (2018, April). Exploring the applicability of blockchain technology to enhance manufacturing supply chains in the composite materials industry. In *2018 IEEE International conference on applied system invention (ICASI)* (pp. 1300-1303). IEEE. 10.1109/ICASI.2018.8394531

Mourtzis, D., & Doukas, M. (2012, September). Decentralised manufacturing systems review: Challenges and outlook. *Logist. Res.*, *5*, 113–121.

Muhammad, K., Hamza, R., Ahmad, J., Lloret, J., Wang, H., & Baik, S. W. (2018). Secure surveillance framework for IoT systems using probabilistic image encryption. *IEEE Transactions on Industrial Informatics*, *14*(8), 3679–3689. doi:10.1109/TII.2018.2791944

Mussomeli, A., Gish, D., & Laaper, S. (2015). The Rise of the Digital Supply network. *Deloitte.*

Nakamoto, S. (2008). *Bitcoin: A peer-to-peer Electronic Cash System.* https://bitcoin.org/bitcoin.pdf

Nakamoto, S. (2008). *Bitcoin: A Peer-to-Peer Electronic Cash System.* https://bitcoin.org/bitcoin.pdf

Nakamoto, S. (2008). *Bitcoin: A Peer-to-Peer Electronic Cash SyNakamoto, S. (2008). Bitcoin: A Peer-to-Peer Electronic Cash System. Consulted.* Consulted. doi:10.100710838-008-9062-0stem

Nakasumi, M. (2017). Information sharing for supply chain management based on block chain technology. *Proceedings - 2017 IEEE 19th Conference on Business Informatics, CBI 2017, 1*, 140–149. doi:10.1109/CBI.2017.56

Nawari, N. O., & Ravindran, S. (2019). Blockchain and the built environment: Potentials and limitations. *Journal of Building Engineering*, *25*, 100832. doi:10.1016/j.jobe.2019.100832

Nejad, H. T. N., Nobuhiro, S., & Iwamura, K. (2011). Agent-based dynamic integrated process planning and scheduling in flexible manufacturing systems. *International Journal of Production Research*, *49*(5), 1373–1389.

Nguyen, D. D., & Ali, M. I. (2019, June). Enabling On-Demand Decentralized IoT Collectability Marketplace using Blockchain and Crowdsensing. In *2019 Global IoT Summit (GIoTS)* (pp. 1-6). IEEE.

Nguyen, G. T., & Kim, K. (2018). A survey about consensus algorithms used in Blockchain. *Journal of Information Processing Systems*, *14*(1), 101–128. https://doi.org/10.3745/JIPS.01.0024

Nilsson, J., Bernhardsson, B., & Wittenmark, B. (1998). Stochastic analysis and control of real-time systems with random time delays. *Automatica*, *34*(1), 57–64. doi:10.1016/S0005-1098(97)00170-2

NIST. (n.d.). https://www.nist.gov

Nitsche, T., Cordeiro, C., Flores, A. B., Knightly, E. W., Perahia, E., & Widmer, J. C. (2014). IEEE 802.11 ad: Directional 60 GHz communication for multi-Gigabit-per-second Wi-Fi. *IEEE Communications Magazine*, *52*(12), 132–141. doi:10.1109/MCOM.2014.6979964

Noura, H., Chehab, A., Sleem, L., Noura, M., Couturier, R., & Mansour, M. M. (2018). One round cipher algorithm for multimedia IoT devices. *Multimedia Tools and Applications*, *77*(14), 18383–18413. doi:10.100711042-018-5660-y

O'donovan, P., Gallagher, C., Bruton, K., & O'Sullivan, D. T. (2018). A fog computing industrial cyber-physical system for embedded low-latency machine learning Industry 4.0 applications. *Manufacturing Letters*, *15*, 139–142. doi:10.1016/j.mfglet.2018.01.005

Oktian, Y. E., Witanto, E. N., Kumi, S., & Lee, S. G. (2019, February). BlockSubPay-A Blockchain Framework for Subscription-Based Payment in Cloud Service. In *2019 21st International Conference on Advanced Communication Technology (ICACT)* (pp. 153-158). IEEE. 10.23919/ICACT.2019.8702008

Ometov, A., Petrov, V., Bezzateev, S., Andreev, S., Koucheryavy, Y., & Gerla, M. (2019). Challenges of multi-factor authentication for securing advanced IoT applications. *IEEE Network*, *33*(2), 82–88. doi:10.1109/MNET.2019.1800240

Ongaro, D., & Ousterhout, J. (2019). In search of an understandable consensus algorithm. *Proceedings of the 2014 USENIX Annual Technical Conference, USENIX ATC 2014*.

Osei, R. K., Canavari, M., & Hingley, M. (2018). An Exploration into the Opportunities for Blockchain in the Fresh Produce Supply Chain. doi:10.20944/preprints201811.0537.v1

Ownest. (n.d.). Retrieved April 1, 2021, from https://ownest.io/

Oztemel, E., & Gursev, S. (2020). Literature review of Industry 4.0 and related technologies. *Journal of Intelligent Manufacturing, 31*(1), 127–182. doi:10.100710845-018-1433-8

Pal, D., Vain, J., Srinivasan, S., & Ramaswamy, S. (2017, September). Model-based maintenance scheduling in flexible modular automation systems. In *2017 22nd IEEE International Conference on Emerging Technologies and Factory Automation (ETFA)* (pp. 1-6). IEEE. 10.1109/ETFA.2017.8247738

Pal, K. (2017). A Semantic Web Service Architecture for Supply Chain Management, In the Proceeding of the 8th International Conference on Ambient Systems, Networks and Technologies (ANT 2017), Portugal, Procedia Computer Science, 999-1004.

Pal, K. (2019). Algorithmic Solutions for RFID Tag Anti-Collision Problem in Supply Cain Management, In the proceeding of 9th International Symposium on Frontier in Ambient and Mobile Systems (FAMS), 29 April – 2 May 2019, Leuven, Belgium, Procedia Computer Science, 929-934.

Pal, K. (2020a). Internet of Things and blockchain technology in apparel manufacturing supply chain data management. *Procedia Computer Science, 170*, 450–457.

Pal, K. (2020b). *Information sharing for manufacturing supply chain management based on blockchain technology*. In I. Williams (Ed.), *Cross-Industry Use of Blockchain Technology and Opportunities for the Future* (pp. 1–17). IGI Global.

Pan, X., Pan, X., Song, M., Ai, B. & Ming, Y. (2020). Blockchain technology and enterprise operational capabilities: An empirical test. *Int. J. Inf. Manag., 52*.

Panetto, H., Iung, B., Ivanov, D., Weichhart, G., & Wang, X. (2019). Challenges for the cyber-physical manufacturing enterprises of the future. *Annual Reviews in Control, 47*, 200–213.

Pauw, C. (2018). *How Significant Is Blockchain in Internet of Things?* https://cointelegraph.com/news/how-significant-is-blockchain-in-internet-of-things

Pavithran, Shaalan, Al-Karaki, & Gawanmeh. (2020). Towards building a blockchain framework for IoT. *Cluster Computing*.

Pedro, A. S., Levi, D., & Cuende, L. I. (2017). *Witnet: A decentralized oracle network protocol.* arXiv preprint arXiv:1711.09756.

Pe, M., & Llivisaca, J. (n.d.). Advances in Emerging Trends and Technologies. *Blockchain and Its Potential Applications in Food Supply Chain Management in Ecuador., 3*, 101–112. doi:10.1007/978-3-030-32022-5

Perahia, E., & Gong, M. X. (2011). Gigabit wireless LANs: An overview of IEEE 802.11 ac and 802.11 ad. *Mobile Computing and Communications Review, 15*(3), 23–33. doi:10.1145/2073290.2073294

Pérez-Lara, M., Saucedo-Martínez, J. A., Marmolejo-Saucedo, J. A., Salais-Fierro, T. E., & Vasant, P. (2018). Vertical and horizontal integration systems in Industry 4.0. *Wireless Networks*, 1–9.

Petroni, B. C. A., de Moraes, E. M., & Gonçalves, R. F. (2018, August). Big Data Analytics for Logistics and Distributions Using Blockchain. In *IFIP International Conference on Advances in Production Management Systems* (pp. 363-369). Springer. 10.1007/978-3-319-99707-0_45

Petroni, B. C. A., Reis, J. Z., & Gonçalves, R. F. (2019, September). Blockchain as an Internet of Services Application for an Advanced Manufacturing Environment. In *IFIP International Conference on Advances in Production Management Systems* (pp. 389-396). Springer. 10.1007/978-3-030-29996-5_45

Pilkington, M. (2016). Blockchain technology: Principles and applications. In Research Handbooks on Digital Transformations (pp. 225–253). Edward Elgar Publishing Ltd. https://doi.org/10.4337/9781784717766.00019.

Pilkington, M. (2016). Blockchain technology: Principles and applications. Research Handbooks on Digital Transformations. doi:10.4337/9781784717766.00019

Pinna, A., & Ibba, S. (2018, July). A blockchain-based Decentralized System for proper handling of temporary Employment contracts. In *Science and information conference* (pp. 1231–1243). Springer.

Pinto, S., Gomes, T., Pereira, J., Cabral, J., & Tavares, A. (2017). IIoTEED: An enhanced, trusted execution environment for industrial IoT edge devices. *IEEE Internet Computing, 21*(1), 40–47. doi:10.1109/MIC.2017.17

Pongnumkul, S., Siripanpornchana, C., & Thajchayapong, S. (2017, July). Performance analysis of private blockchain platforms in varying workloads. In *2017 26th International Conference on Computer Communication and Networks (ICCCN)* (pp. 1-6). IEEE. 10.1109/ICCCN.2017.8038517

Popov, S. (2016). *The tangle*. Academic Press.

Prashanth Joshi, A., Han, M., & Wang, Y. (2018). A survey on security and privacy issues of blockchain technology. *Mathematical Foundations of Computing, 1*(2), 121–147. doi:10.3934/mfc.2018007

Prockl, G., Bhakoo, V., & Wong, C. (2017). Supply chains and electronic markets - impulses for value co-creation across the disciplines. *Electronic Markets, 27*(2), 135–140. https://doi.org/10.1007/s12525-017-0253-6

Quentson, A. (2016). *Bitcoin Magazine*. https://bitcoinmagazine.com/%0Aarticles/how-bitcoin-and-blockchain-can-avert-systemic-bank-collapses-1461170796/

Raikwar, M., Mazumdar, S., Ruj, S., Gupta, S. S., Chattopadhyay, A., & Lam, K. Y. (2018, February). A blockchain framework for insurance processes. In *2018 9th IFIP International Conference on New Technologies, Mobility and Security (NTMS)* (pp. 1-4). IEEE. 10.1109/NTMS.2018.8328731

Rehman, M. H. U., Yaqoob, I., Salah, K., Imran, M., Jayaraman, P. P., & Perera, C. (2019). The role of big data analytics in industrial Internet of Things. *Future Generation Computer Systems, 99*, 247–259. doi:10.1016/j.future.2019.04.020

Rehman, M., Javaid, N., Awais, M., Imran, M., & Naseer, N. (2019, December). Cloud based secure service providing for IoTs using blockchain. *IEEE Global Communications Conference (GLOBCOM)*. 10.1109/GLOBECOM38437.2019.9013413

Ren, L., Zheng, S., & Zhang, L. (2018). A blockchain model for industrial Internet. *Proc. IEEE Int. Conf. Internet Things (iThings) Green Comput. Commun. (GreenCom) Cyber Phys. Soc. Comput. (CPSC) Smart Data (SmartData) iThings/GreenCom/CPSCòm/SmartData*, 791-794.

Reyna, A., Martín, C., Chen, J., Soler, E., & Díaz, M. (2018). On blockchain and its integration with IoT. Challenges and opportunities. *Future Generation Computer Systems, 88*, 173–190. doi:10.1016/j.future.2018.05.046

Rinki, S. (2014). *Simulation studies on effects of dual polarisation and directivity of antennas on the performance of MANETs* (Doctoral dissertation). Coventry University.

Rivest, R. L., Shamir, A., & Adleman, L. (1978). A method for obtaining digital signatures and public-key cryptosystems. *Communications of the ACM, 21*(2), 120–126. doi:10.1145/359340.359342

Rizvi, S., Kurtz, A., Pfeffer, J., & Rizvi, M. (2018, August). Securing the Internet of Things (IoT): A security taxonomy for IoT. In *2018 17th IEEE International Conference On Trust, Security And Privacy In Computing And Communications/12th IEEE International Conference On Big Data Science And Engineering (TrustCom/BigDataSE)* (pp. 163-168). IEEE.

Ross, D. F. (1998). Competing Through Supply Chain Management. In *Competing Through Supply Chain Management.* Springer US. doi:10.1007/978-1-4757-4816-1

S. A. A. (2016). Blockchain Ready Manufacturing Supply Chain Using Distributed Ledger. *International Journal of Research in Engineering and Technology, 05*(09).

Saad, M., Spaulding, J., Njilla, L., Kamhoua, C., Shetty, S., Nyang, D. H., & Mohaisen, D. (2020). Exploring the Attack Surface of Blockchain: A Comprehensive Survey. *IEEE Communications Surveys and Tutorials, 22*(3), 1977–2008. https://doi.org/10.1109/COMST.2020.2975999

Saghiri, A. M. HamlAbadi, K. G., & Vahdati, M. (2020). The internet of things, artificial intelligence, and blockchain: implementation perspectives. In Advanced applications of blockchain technology (pp. 15-54). Springer, Singapore.

Sahraoui, S., & Bilami, A. (2014, May). Compressed and distributed host identity protocol for end-to-end security in the IoT. In *2014 International Conference on Next Generation Networks and Services (NGNS)* (pp. 295-301). IEEE.

Sakız, B., & Gencer, A. H. (2019). Blockchain Technology and its Impact on the Global Economy. *International Conference on Eurasian Economies 2019.* doi:10.36880/c11.02258

Salah, K., Nizamuddin, N., Jayaraman, R., & Omar, M. (2019). Blockchain-based soybean traceability in agricultural supply chain. *IEEE Access: Practical Innovations, Open Solutions, 7,* 73295–73305. doi:10.1109/ACCESS.2019.2918000

Salman, T., Zolanvari, M., Erbad, A., Jain, R., & Samaka, M. (2019). Security services using blockchains: A state of the art survey. *IEEE Communications Surveys and Tutorials, 21*(1), 858–880. https://doi.org/10.1109/COMST.2018.2863956

Sanseverino, E. R., Di Silvestre, M. L., Gallo, P., Zizzo, G., & Ippolito, M. (2018). The blockchain in microgrids for transacting energy and attributing losses. *Proceedings - 2017 IEEE International Conference on Internet of Things, IEEE Green Computing and Communications, IEEE Cyber, Physical and Social Computing, IEEE Smart Data, IThings-GreenCom-CPSCom-SmartData 2017, 925*–930. doi:10.1109/iThings-GreenCom-CPSCom-SmartData.2017.142

Saraph, V., & Herlihy, M. (2019). *An Empirical Study of Speculative Concurrency in Ethereum Smart Contracts.* arXiv preprint arXiv:1901.01376.

Saxena, S., Bhushan, B., & Yadav, D. (2020). Blockchain-powered Social Media Analytics in Supply Chain Management. *SSRN Electronic Journal.* doi:10.2139srn.3598906

Schäffer, M., di Angelo, M., & Salzer, G. (2019, September). Performance and scalability of private Ethereum blockchains. In *International Conference on Business Process Management* (pp. 103-118). Springer. 10.1007/978-3-030-30429-4_8

Schmidt, C. G., & Wagner, S. M. (2019). Journal of Purchasing and Supply Management Blockchain and supply chain relations : A transaction cost theory perspective. *Journal of Purchasing and Supply Management, 25*(4), 100552. doi:10.1016/j.pursup.2019.100552

Schneider, S. (2017). The industrial internet of things (iiot) applications and taxonomy. *Internet of Things and Data Analytics Handbook, 41-81.*

Schulz, K. F., & Freund, D. (2018, July). A multichain architecture for distributed supply chain design in industry 4.0. In *International Conference on Business Information Systems* (pp. 277-288). Springer.

Scully, P., & Hobig, M. (2019). Exploring the impact of blockchain on digitized Supply Chain flows: A literature review. *2019 6th International Conference on Software Defined Systems, SDS 2019*, 278–283. 10.1109/SDS.2019.8768573

Seitz, A., Henze, D., Miehle, D., Bruegge, B., Nickles, J., & Sauer, M. (2018). Fog computing as enabler for blockchain-based IIoT app marketplaces-A case study. In *Fifth international conference on internet of things: systems, management and security* (pp. 182-188). Valencia, Spain: IEEE.

Sengupta, J., Ruj, S., & Bit, S. D. (2020). A Comprehensive survey on attacks, security issues and blockchain solutions for IoT and IIoT. *Journal of Network and Computer Applications*, *149*, 102481. doi:10.1016/j.jnca.2019.102481

Seok, B., Park, J., & Park, J. H. (2019). A lightweight hash-based blockchain architecture for industrial IoT. *Applied Sciences (Basel, Switzerland)*, *9*(18), 1–17. doi:10.3390/app9183740

Serpanos, D., & Wolf, M. (2018). Industrial internet of things. In *Internet-of-Things (IoT) Systems* (pp. 37–54). Springer. doi:10.1007/978-3-319-69715-4_5

Sethi, R., Bhushan, B., Sharma, N., Kumar, R., & Kaushik, I. (2021). Applicability of Industrial IoT in Diversified Sectors: Evolution, Applications and Challenges. Springer. https://doi.org/10.1007/978-981-15-7965-3_4

Shah, A. (2019). *The chain gang. In Mechanical Engineering*. Springer.

Sharama, R., Shankar, J. U., & Rajan, S. T. (2014, April). Effect of Number of Active Nodes and Inter-node Distance on the Performance of Wireless Sensor Networks. In *2014 Fourth International Conference on Communication Systems and Network Technologies* (pp. 69-73). IEEE. 10.1109/CSNT.2014.22

Sharma, R., & Reddy, H. (2019, December). Effect of Load Balancer on Software-Defined Networking (SDN) based Cloud. In *2019 IEEE 16th India Council International Conference (INDICON)* (pp. 1-4). IEEE.

Sharma, R., Kadambi, G. R., Vershinin, Y. A., & Mukundan, K. N. (2015, April). Multipath Routing Protocol to Support Dual Polarised Directional Communication for Performance Enhancement of MANETs. In *2015 Fifth International Conference on Communication Systems and Network Technologies* (pp. 258-262). IEEE. 10.1109/CSNT.2015.105

Sharma, K. L. S. (2016). *Overview of industrial process automation*. Elsevier.

Sharma, P. K., Chen, M. Y., & Park, J. H. (2018). A Software Defined Fog Node Based Distributed Blockchain Cloud Architecture for IoT. *IEEE Access: Practical Innovations, Open Solutions*, *6*, 115–124. https://doi.org/10.1109/AC-CESS.2017.2757955

Sharma, R., Gupta, S. K., Suhas, K. K., & Kashyap, G. S. (2014, April). Performance analysis of Zigbee based wireless sensor network for remote patient monitoring. In *2014 Fourth International Conference on Communication Systems and Network Technologies* (pp. 58-62). IEEE. 10.1109/CSNT.2014.21

Sharma, R., Kadambi, G. R., Vershinin, Y. A., & Mukundan, K. N. (2015, April). Dual Polarised Directional Communication based Medium Access Control Protocol for Performance Enhancement of MANETs. In *2015 Fifth International Conference on Communication Systems and Network Technologies* (pp. 185-189). IEEE. 10.1109/CSNT.2015.104

Sheel, A., & Nath, V. (2019). Effect of blockchain technology adoption on supply chain adaptability, agility, alignment and performance. *Management Research Review*, *42*(12), 1353–1374. Advance online publication. doi:10.1108/MRR-12-2018-0490

Shen, C., & Pena-Mora, F. (2018). Blockchain for Cities - A Systematic Literature Review. *IEEE Access: Practical Innovations, Open Solutions*, *6*, 76787–76819. https://doi.org/10.1109/ACCESS.2018.2880744

Shen, W. (2002, January/February). Distributed manufacturing scheduling using intelligent agents. *IEEE Intelligent Systems, 17*(1), 88–94.

Shih, C. S., & Yang, K. W. (2019, September). Design and implementation of distributed traceability system for smart factories based on blockchain technology. In *Proceedings of the Conference on Research in Adaptive and Convergent Systems* (pp. 181-188). 10.1145/3338840.3355646

Shirazi, B. (2019). Cloud-based architecture of service-oriented MES for subcontracting and partnership exchanges integration: A game theory approach. *Robotics and Computer-integrated Manufacturing, 59*, 56–68. doi:10.1016/j.rcim.2019.03.006

Shrestha, R., Bajracharya, R., Shrestha, A. P., & Nam, S. Y. (2020). A new type of blockchain for secure message exchange in VANET. *Digital Communications and Networks, 6*(2), 177–186. doi:10.1016/j.dcan.2019.04.003

Shrestha, R., & Kim, S. (2019). *Integration of IoT with blockchain and homomorphic encryption: Challenging issues and opportunities.* Elsevier BV.

Singh, S. K., Rathore, S., & Park, J. H. (2020). Blockiotintelligence: A blockchain-enabled intelligent IoT architecture with artificial intelligence. *Future Generation Computer Systems, 110*, 721–743.

Sisinni, E., Saifullah, A., Han, S., Jennehag, U., & Gidlund, M. (2018). Industrial internet of things: Challenges, opportunities, and directions. *IEEE Transactions on Industrial Informatics, 14*(11), 4724–4734. doi:10.1109/TII.2018.2852491

Smirnov, A., & Teslya, N. (2018, July). Robot Interaction Through Smart Contract for Blockchain-Based Coalition Formation. In *IFIP International Conference on Product Lifecycle Management* (pp. 611-620). Springer. 10.1007/978-3-030-01614-2_56

Sousa, J., Bessani, A., & Vukolic, M. (2018). A byzantine fault-tolerant ordering service for the hyperledger fabric blockchain platform. In *2018 48th annual IEEE/IFIP international conference on dependable systems and networks (DSN)* (s. 51-58), IEEE. 10.1109/DSN.2018.00018

Steiner, J., & Baker, J. (2015). *Blockchain: the solution for supply chain transparency.* Provenance. https://www.provenance.org/whitepaper

Stodt, J., Jastremskoj, E., Reich, C., Welte, D., & Sikora, A. (2019, September). Formal Description of Use Cases for Industry 4.0 Maintenance Processes Using Blockchain Technology. In *10th IEEE International Conference on Intelligent Data Acquisition and Advanced Computing Systems: Technology and Applications (IDAACS)* (Vol. 2, pp. 1136-1141). IEEE. 10.1109/IDAACS.2019.8924382

Stouffer, K. A., Zimmerman, T., Tang, C., McCarthy, J., & Cichonski, J. (2020). *Cybersecurity for Smart Manufacturing Systems.* Available: nist.gov/programs-projects/cybersecuritysmart-manufacturing-systems

Sturm, L. D., Williams, C. B., Camelio, J. A., White, J., & Parker, R. (2017, July). Cyber-physical vulnerabilities in additive manufacturing systems: A case study attack on the. STL file with human subjects. *Journal of Manufacturing Systems, 44*, 154–164.

Suter, A. (2019). *How is the Internet Of Things Making Life Safer?* Retrieved May 13, 2020 from https://techstory.in/internet-of-things-making-life-safe

Szilágyi, P. (2017). *Clique PoA protocol & Rinkeby PoA testnet · Issue #225 · ethereum/EIPs.* https://github.com/ethereum/EIPs/issues/225

Tama, B. A. (2015). Learning to Prevent Inactive Student of Indonesia Open University. *Journal of Information Processing Systems, 11*(2), 165–172. https://doi.org/10.3745/JIPS.04.0015

Tama, B. A., & Rhee, K. H. (2019). Tree-based classifier ensembles for early detection method of diabetes: An exploratory study. *Artificial Intelligence Review*, *51*(3), 355–370. https://doi.org/10.1007/s10462-017-9565-3

Tanwar, S., Parekh, K., & Evans, R. (2020). Blockchain-based electronic healthcare record system for healthcare 4.0 applications. *Journal of Information Security and Applications*, *50*, 102407. https://doi.org/10.1016/j.jisa.2019.102407

Tao, F., Cheng, J., & Qi, Q. (2017). IIHub: An industrial Internet-of-Things hub toward smart manufacturing based on cyber-physical system. *IEEE Transactions on Industrial Informatics*, *14*(5), 2271–2280. doi:10.1109/TII.2017.2759178

Tariq, N., Asim, M., Al-Obeidat, F., Zubair Farooqi, M., Baker, T., Hammoudeh, M., & Ghafir, I. (2019). The security of big data in fog-enabled IoT applications including blockchain: A survey. *Sensors (Basel)*, *19*(8), 1788. doi:10.339019081788 PMID:31013993

Tasca, P., & Tessone, C. J. (2017). *Taxonomy of blockchain technologies. Principles of identification and classification.* doi:10.5195/ledger.2019.140

Taş, O., & Kíaní, F. (2018). Blok zinciri teknolojisine yapılan saldırılar üzerine bir inceleme. *Bilişim Teknolojileri Dergisi*, *11*(4), 369–382. doi:10.17671/gazibtd.451695

Teslya, N., & Ryabchikov, I. (2017, November). Blockchain-based platform architecture for industrial IoT. In *2017 21st Conference of Open Innovations Association (FRUCT)* (pp. 321-329). IEEE. 10.23919/FRUCT.2017.8250199

Tezel, A., Papadonikolaki, E., Yitmen, I., & Hilletofth, P. (2019). *Preparing Construction Supply Chains for Blockchain : An Exploratory Preparing Construction Supply Chains for Blockchain : An Exploratory.* Academic Press.

Tezel, A., Papadonikolaki, E., Yitmen, I., & Hilletofth, P. (2019). *Preparing Construction Supply Chains for Blockchain : An Exploratory.* Academic Press.

Thakore, R., Vaghashiya, R., Patel, C., & Doshi, N. (2019). Blockchain - based IoT: A Survey. *Proceedings of the 2nd International Workshop on Recent advances on Internet of Things: Technology and Application Approaches (IoT-T&A 2019) 2019.*

Thriveni, H. B., Kumar, G. M., & Sharma, R. (2013, April). Performance evaluation of routing protocols in mobile ad-hoc networks with varying node density and node mobility. In *2013 International Conference on Communication Systems and Network Technologies* (pp. 252-256). IEEE. 10.1109/CSNT.2013.60

Tian, F. (2016, August 9). An agri-food supply chain traceability system for China based on RFID & blockchain technology. *2016 13th International Conference on Service Systems and Service Management, ICSSSM 2016.* doi:10.1109/ICSSSM.2016.7538424

Tijan, E., Aksentijevic, A., Ivani, K., & Jardas, M. (2019). Blockchain tech-ontology implementation in logistics. *Sustainability (Basel)*, *11*(4), 1185.

Tomov, Y. K. (2019, September 1). Bitcoin: Evolution of blockchain technology. *2019 28th International Scientific Conference Electronics, ET 2019 - Proceedings.* doi:10.1109/ET.2019.8878322

Tönnissen, S., & Frank, T. (2020). Analysing the impact of blockchain technology for operations and supply chain management: An explanatory model drawn from multiple case studies. *International Journal of Information Management*, *52*(June), 2020.

Tönnissen, S., & Teuteberg, F. (2019). Analysing the impact of blockchain-technology for operations and supply chain management: An explanatory model drawn from multiple case studies. *International Journal of Information Management*, *0–1*(January). Advance online publication. doi:10.1016/j.ijinfomgt.2019.05.009

Tramarin, F., Mok, A. K., & Han, S. (2019). Real-time and reliable industrial control over wireless LANs: Algorithms, protocols, and future directions. *Proceedings of the IEEE, 107*(6), 1027–1052. doi:10.1109/JPROC.2019.2913450

Treiblmaier, H. (2018). The impact of the blockchain on the supply chain: A theory-based research framework and a call for action. *Supply Chain Management, 23*(6), 545–559. doi:10.1108/SCM-01-2018-0029

Tribis, Y., El Bouchti, A., & Bouayad, H. (2018). Supply chain management based on blockchain: A systematic mapping study. *MATEC Web of Conferences, 200.* 10.1051/matecconf/201820000020

Tripoli, M., & Schmidhuber, J. (2018). *Emerging Opportunities for the Application of Blockchain in the Agri-food Industry.* FAO and ICTSD: Rome and Geneva. Licence: CC BY-NC-SA, 3.

Turkanović, M., Hölbl, M., Košič, K., Heričko, M., & Kamišalić, A. (2018). EduCTX: A blockchain-based higher education credit platform. *IEEE Access: Practical Innovations, Open Solutions, 6*, 5112–5127. https://doi.org/10.1109/ACCESS.2018.2789929

Tyagi, S., Agarwal, A., & Maheshwari, P. (2016, January). A conceptual framework for IoT-based healthcare system using cloud computing. In 2016 6th International Conference-Cloud System and Big Data Engineering (Confluence) (pp. 503-507). IEEE. doi:10.1109/CONFLUENCE.2016.7508172

Vatankhah Barenji, A., Li, Z., Wang, W. M., Huang, G. Q., & Guerra-Zubiaga, D. A. (2019). Blockchain-based ubiquitous manufacturing: A secure and reliable cyber-physical system. *International Journal of Production Research*, 1–22.

Vatcharatiansakul, N., & Tuwanut, P. (2019, July). A performance evaluation for Internet of Things based on Blockchain technology. In *2019 5th International Conference on Engineering, Applied Sciences and Technology (ICEAST)* (pp. 1-4). IEEE. 10.1109/ICEAST.2019.8802524

Venkatesh, V. G., Kang, K., Wang, B., Zhong, R. Y., & Zhang, A. (2020). System architecture for blockchain based transparency of supply chain social sustainability. *Robotics and Computer-Integrated Manufacturing, 63*(November), 101896. doi:10.1016/j.rcim.2019.101896

Vitturi, S., Zunino, C., & Sauter, T. (2019). Industrial communication systems and their future challenges: Next-generation Ethernet, IIoT, and 5G. *Proceedings of the IEEE, 107*(6), 944–961. doi:10.1109/JPROC.2019.2913443

Voulgaris, S., Fotiou, N., Siris, V. A., Polyzos, G. C., Jaatinen, M., & Oikonomidis, Y. (2019). Blockchain Technology for Intelligent Environments. *Future Internet, 11*(10), 213. doi:10.3390/fi11100213

Vujičić, D., Jagodić, D., & Randić, S. (2018). Blockchain technology, bitcoin, and Ethereum: A brief overview. *2018 17th International Symposium on INFOTEH-JAHORINA, INFOTEH 2018 - Proceedings*, 1–6. doi:10.1109/INFOTEH.2018.8345547

Wamba, S. F. (2019). *Continuance Intention in Blockchain-Enabled Supply Chain Applications : Modelling the Moderating Effect of Supply Chain Stakeholders Trust.* doi:10.1007/978-3-030-11395-7

Wang, X., Weili, J., & Chai, J. (2018). The Research on the Incentive Method of Consortium Blockchain Based on Practical Byzantine Fault Tolerant. *Proceedings - 2018 11th International Symposium on Computational Intelligence and Design, ISCID 2018, 2*, 154–156. doi:10.1109/ISCID.2018.10136

Wang, Y., Han, J. H., Beynon-davies, P., Wang, Y., Han, J. H., & Beynon-davies, P. (2018). *Understanding blockchain technology for future supply chains : a systematic literature review and research agenda.* doi:10.1108/SCM-03-2018-0148

Wang, E. K., Liang, Z., Chen, C. M., Kumari, S., & Khan, M. K. (2020). PoRX: A reputation incentive scheme for blockchain consensus of IIoT. *Future Generation Computer Systems, 102*, 140–151. doi:10.1016/j.future.2019.08.005

Wang, Q., Zhu, X., Ni, Y., Gu, L., & Zhu, H. (2020). Blockchain for the IoT and industrial IoT: A review. *Internet of Things*, *10*, 100081.

Wang, W., Hoang, D. T., Hu, P., Xiong, Z., Niyato, D., Wang, P., Wen, Y., & Kim, D. I. (2019). A Survey on Consensus Mechanisms and Mining Strategy Management in Blockchain Networks. *IEEE Access: Practical Innovations, Open Solutions*, *7*, 22328–22370. https://doi.org/10.1109/ACCESS.2019.2896108

Wan, J., Li, J., Imran, M., Li, D., & Fazal-e-Amin. (2019). A blockchain-based solution for enhancing security and privacy in smart factory. *IEEE Transactions on Industrial Informatics*, *15*(6), 3652–3660. doi:10.1109/TII.2019.2894573

Wazid, M., Das, A. K., Shetty, S., & Jo, M. (2020). A Tutorial and Future Research for Building a Blockchain-Based Secure Communication Scheme for Internet of Intelligent Things. *IEEE Access: Practical Innovations, Open Solutions*.

Weber, I., Xu, X., Riveret, R., Governatori, G., Ponomarev, A., & Mendling, J. (2016). Untrusted business process monitoring and execution using blockchain. *Lecture Notes in Computer Science (Including Subseries Lecture Notes in Artificial Intelligence and Lecture Notes in Bioinformatics)*, *9850 LNCS*, 329–347. doi:10.1007/978-3-319-45348-4_19

Weiser, M. (1991). The Computer for the 21st Century. *Scientific American*, *265*(3), 94–105. doi:10.1038cientificamerican0991-94 PMID:1675486

Weyer, S., Schmitt, M., Ohmer, M., & Gorecky, D. (2015). Towards Industry 4.0-Standardization as the crucial challenge for highly modular, multi-vendor production systems. *IFAC-PapersOnLine*, *48*(3), 579–584. doi:10.1016/j.ifacol.2015.06.143

Wollschlaeger, M., Sauter, T., & Jasperneite, J. (2017). The future of industrial communication: Automation networks in the era of the internet of things and industry 4.0. *IEEE Industrial Electronics Magazine*, *11*(1), 17–27. doi:10.1109/MIE.2017.2649104

Wright, A., & De Filippi, P. (2015). Decentralized Blockchain Technology and the Rise of Lex Cryptographia. SSRN *Electronic Journal*. doi:10.2139srn.2580664

Wright, C. S. (2019). Bitcoin: A Peer-to-Peer Electronic Cash System. *SSRN Electronic Journal*. doi:10.2139srn.3440802

Wu, H., Cao, J., Yang, Y., Tung, C. L., Jiang, S., Tang, B., . . . Deng, Y. (2019). Data management in supply chain using blockchain: challenges and a case study. *Proceedings - International Conference on Computer Communications and Networks, ICCCN*, 1–8. 10.1109/ICCCN.2019.8846964

Wu, M., Wang, K., Cai, X., Guo, S., Guo, M., & Rong, C. (2019). A Comprehensive Survey of Blockchain: From Theory to IoT Applications and beyond. *IEEE Internet of Things Journal*, *6*(5), 8114–8154. doi:10.1109/JIOT.2019.2922538

Wu, T. Y., Fan, X., Wang, K. H., Lai, C. F., Xiong, N., & Wu, J. M. (2019). A DNA Computation-Based Image Encryption Scheme for Cloud CCTV Systems. *IEEE Access: Practical Innovations, Open Solutions*, *7*, 181434–181443. doi:10.1109/ACCESS.2019.2946890

Wu, T.-Y., Chen, C.-M., Wang, K.-H., & Wu, J. M.-T. (2019). Security Analysis and Enhancement of a Certificateless Searchable Public Key Encryption Scheme for IIoT Environments. *IEEE Access: Practical Innovations, Open Solutions*, *7*, 49232–49239. doi:10.1109/ACCESS.2019.2909040

Xie, J., Tang, H., Huang, T., Yu, F. R., Xie, R., Liu, J., & Liu, Y. (2019). A Survey of Blockchain Technology Applied to Smart Cities: Research Issues and Challenges. *IEEE Communications Surveys and Tutorials*, *21*(3), 2794–2830. https://doi.org/10.1109/COMST.2019.2899617

Xu, X., Weber, I., & Staples, M. (2019). Architecture for Blockchain Applications. In *Architecture for Blockchain Applications*. Springer International Publishing. doi:10.1007/978-3-030-03035-3

Xu, L. D., Xu, E. L., & Li, L. (2018). Industry 4.0: State of the art and future trends. *International Journal of Production Research*, *56*(8), 2941–2962. doi:10.1080/00207543.2018.1444806

Xu, Y., Ren, J., Wang, G., Zhang, C., Yang, J., & Zhang, Y. (2019). A blockchain-based nonrepudiation network computing service scheme for industrial IoT. *IEEE Transactions on Industrial Informatics*, *15*(6), 3632–3641. doi:10.1109/TII.2019.2897133

Yadav, S., & Singh, S. P. (2019). *Blockchain critical success factors for sustainable supply chain Resources, Conservation & Recycling*. doi:10.1016/j.resconrec.2019.104505

Yan, Y., Duan, B., Zhong, Y., & Qu, X. (2017, October). Blockchain technology in the internet plus: The collaborative development of power electronic devices. In *IECON 2017-43rd Annual Conference of the IEEE Industrial Electronics Society* (pp. 922-927). IEEE.

Yang, Z., Yang, K., Lei, L., Zheng, K., & Leung, V. C. M. (2019). Blockchain-based decentralized trust management in vehicular networks. *IEEE Internet of Things Journal*, *6*(2), 1495–1505. doi:10.1109/JIOT.2018.2836144

Yan, H., Chen, Z., & Jia, C. (2019). SSIR: Secure similarity image retrieval in IoT. *Information Sciences*, *479*, 153–163. doi:10.1016/j.ins.2018.11.046

Yassein, M. B., Shatnawi, F., Rawashdeh, S., & Mardin, W. (2019). Blockchain technology: Characteristics, security and privacy; Issues and solutions. *Proceedings of IEEE/ACS International Conference on Computer Systems and Applications, AICCSA, 2019-November*. doi:10.1109/AICCSA47632.2019.9035216

Yuan, Y., & Wang, F. (2018, September). Blockchain and cryptocurrencies: Model, techniques, and applications. *IEEE Transactions on Systems, Man, and Cybernetics. Systems*, *48*(9), 1421–1428.

Yumna, H., Murad, M., Ikram, M., & Noreen, S. (n.d.). *Use of blockchain in Education : A systematic Literature Review*. Academic Press.

Yumna, H., Murad, M., Ikram, M., & Noreen, S. (n.d.). *Use of blockchain in Education: A systematic Literature Review*. Academic Press.

Yu, Y., Chen, R., Li, H., Li, Y., & Tian, A. (2019). Toward data security in edge intelligent IIoT. *IEEE Network*, *33*(5), 20–26. doi:10.1109/MNET.001.1800507

Yu, Y., Wang, X., Zhong, R. Y., & Huang, G. Q. (2016). E-commerce Logistics in Supply Chain Management: Practice Perspective. *Procedia CIRP*, *52*, 179–185. Advance online publication. doi:10.1016/j.procir.2016.08.002

Yu, Z., Yan, Y., Yang, C., & Dong, A. (2019, March). Design of online audit mode based on blockchain technology. *Journal of Physics: Conference Series*, *1176*(4), 042072. doi:10.1088/1742-6596/1176/4/042072

Zarreh, A., Wan, H., Lee, Y., Saygin, C., & Janahi, R. A. (2020, February). Risk assessment for cybersecurity of manufacturing systems: A game theory approach. *Procedia Manufacturing*, *38*, 605–612.

Zhang, J., Xue, N., & Huang, X. (2016). A Secure System for Pervasive Social Network-Based Healthcare. *IEEE Access: Practical Innovations, Open Solutions*, *4*, 9239–9250. https://doi.org/10.1109/ACCESS.2016.2645904

Zhang, K., Zhu, Y., Maharjan, S., & Zhang, Y. (2019). Edge intelligence and blockchain empowered 5G beyond for the industrial Internet of Things. *IEEE Network*, *33*(5), 12–19. doi:10.1109/MNET.001.1800526

Zhang, Y., Xu, X., Liu, A., Lu, Q., Xu, L., & Tao, F. (2019, December). Blockchain-based trust mechanism for IoT-based smart manufacturing system. *IEEE Trans. Comput. Soc. Syst.*, *6*(6), 1386–1394.

Zhang, Z., Xiao, Y., Ma, Z., Xiao, M., Ding, Z., Lei, X., Karagiannidis, G. K., & Fan, P. (2019). 6G wireless networks: Vision, requirements, architecture, and key technologies. *IEEE Vehicular Technology Magazine, 14*(3), 28–41. doi:10.1109/MVT.2019.2921208

Zhao, Q. (2020). Presents the Technology, Protocols, and New Innovations in Industrial Internet of Things (IIoT). In *Internet of Things for Industry 4.0* (pp. 39–56). Springer. doi:10.1007/978-3-030-32530-5_3

Zhao, S., Li, S., & Yao, Y. (2019). Blockchain enabled industrial Internet of Things technology. *IEEE Transactions on Computational Social Systems, 6*(6), 1442–1453. doi:10.1109/TCSS.2019.2924054

Zhao, S., Li, S., & Yao, Y. (2019). *Blockchain Enabled Industrial Internet of Things Technology. IEEE Transactions on Computational Social Systems.*

Zheng, Z. (2020, April). An overview on smart contracts: Challenges, advances and platforms. *Future Generation Computer Systems, 105*, 475–491.

Zheng, Z., Xie, S., Dai, H. N., Chen, X., & Wang, H. (2018). Blockchain challenges and opportunities: A survey. *International Journal of Web and Grid Services, 14*(4), 352–375. doi:10.1504/IJWGS.2018.095647

Zhong, S., Zhong, H., Huang, X., Yang, P., Shi, J., Xie, L., & Wang, K. (2019). *Security and Privacy for Next-Generation Wireless Networks.* Springer International Publishing. doi:10.1007/978-3-030-01150-5

Zhou, R., Zhang, X., Du, X., Wang, X., Yang, G., & Guizani, M. (2018). File-centric multi-key aggregate keyword searchable encryption for industrial internet of things. *IEEE Transactions on Industrial Informatics, 14*(8), 3648–3658. doi:10.1109/TII.2018.2794442

Zhu, Z. T., Yu, M. H., & Riezebos, P. (2016). A research framework of smart education. *Smart Learning Environments, 3*(1), 4. doi:10.118640561-016-0026-2

Zhu, M., Cao, J., Pang, D., He, Z., & Xu, M. (2015, August). SDN-based routing for efficient message propagation in VANET. In *International Conference on Wireless Algorithms, Systems, and Applications* (pp. 788-797). Springer. 10.1007/978-3-319-21837-3_77

Zhu, Q., & Kouhizadeh, M. (2019). Blockchain technology, supply chain information, and strategic product deletion management. *IEEE Engineering Management Review, 47*(1), 36–44. doi:10.1109/EMR.2019.2898178

About the Contributors

Subhendu Kumar Pani's main area of interest includes data mining and its applications using machine learning techniques. Other areas of interest include Software Engineering, Big Data Analytics, Semantic Web, Web Intelligence, Distributed Data Mining, and Decision Support Systems.

* * *

Sini Anna Alex is working as Assistant Professor in Computer Science and Engineering at M. S. Ramaiah Institute of Technology, Bangalore.

Bharat Bhushan has gracefully worked as Network Engineer in HCL Info systems Ltd. for a year. He is an alumnus as well as a Ph.D. scholar of BITs Mesra. He got numerous international certifications like Cisco Certified Network Associate, Cisco certified network professional Trained, Cisco Certified Entry Networking Technician, Microsoft Certified Technology Specialist, Microsoft Certified IT Professional, Red-hat Certified Engineer. He has published over 100 research papers in highly renowned National/International Journals and Conferences. His publications include 3 SCI Indexed Journals, 3 SCOPUS Indexed book chapters and 37 International conferences indexed by IEEE and Springer. He is currently in the process of editing 4 books to be published by the most famed publishers like Elsevier, IGI Global, and CRC Press. Due to his philosophical vision, he has been given the opportunity of chairing sessions in as many as 7 International conferences of high repute indexed by IEEE and Springer. He has also been invited as a speaker in various national and international conferences.

Megha Bhushan is an Assistant Professor in the School of Computing, DIT University, Dehradun, India. She has received her Ph.D. degree in Computer Science and Engineering from Thapar University, Punjab, India. She has 4 years of research experience as Junior Research Fellow and Senior Research Fellow under University Grants Commission (UGC), New Delhi, Government of India. She was awarded with fellowship by UGC, Government of India, in 2014. In 2017, she was a recipient of Grace Hopper Celebration India (GHCI) fellowship. She has filed 4 patents and published many research articles in international journals and conferences of repute. Her research interest includes Software quality, Software reuse, Ontologies, Artificial Intelligence, and Expert systems. She is also the reviewer and editorial board member of many international journals.

Carlos Cavalcanti is a Full Professor of Computer Systems at the Federal University of Ouro Preto (UFOP). BEng in Electrical & Electronic from the Pontificia Catholic University of Minas Gerais (PUC-

MG), MSc in Computer Science from the State University of Campinas (UNICAMP) and PhD degree in Computer Science from the Department of Computer Science at Federal University of Minas Gerais (UFMG) all in Brazil. Visiting researcher at Networks Research Group in the Centre for Communication Systems Research at the University of Surrey (UniS) working on the TEQUILA European project in 2001. Coordinator of several research and innovation projects. Research interests include cryptographic algorithms and applications, secure embedded systems and blockchain for Industry 4.0.

Suchismita Chinara received his Ph.d degree in Computer Science from National Institute of Technology, Rourkela and is currently working as an Assistant Professor in Department of Computer Science and Engineering at National Institute of Technology, Rourkela and has an experience of more than 2 decades in teaching various subjects of computer science. She has been an active contributor for more than a decade and has authored and co-authored some of the top journals SCI/SCIE/ESCI/SCOPUS/WoS , Book Chapters and Conferences and also has many publications to her credit. She has guided more than 20 M.Tech students and is currently guiding 2 M.tech and 2 Ph.d students. Her current research interests include Computer Networks & Data Communications, IoT, Wireless Sensor Networks, E-learning.

Mevlut Ersoy obtained his B.S. degree in computer engineering from Gazi University Ankara, Turkey in 2007. He completed his Masters degree in Computer Engineering from Suleyman Demirel University, Turkey in 2012. He completed his Ph.D. degree in Suleyman Demirel University Department of Computer Engineering in 2016. He works as an Assistant Professor in Suleyman Demirel University Computer Engineering Department since 2016. His research interests include New Generation Wireless Technologies, Video Streaming.

Célio Ferreira received his master's degree in Computer Science from Federal University of Ouro Preto in 2013. He is currently the CEO of LinuxPlace, and Ph.D. student in Computer Science at the Federal University of Ouro Preto. His current research interests include Blockchain, IoT, and Low Power networks using Bluetooth and LoRa.

Charles Garrocho received his master's degree in Computer Science from Federal University of Ouro Preto in 2015. He is currently a Professor of Computation at the Federal Institute of Minas Gerais and a Ph.D. student in Computer Science at the Federal University of Ouro Preto. His current research interests include 5G, D2D, Vehicular Networks, Blockchain, and Mobile Computing.

Nitin Goyal is working as Associate Professor in Chitkara University, India. He is having 12 years of teaching and academic experience. He obtained B.Tech and M.Tech from Kurukshetra University and PhD from NIT Kurukshetra, India. He has published approximately 42 research papers in various SCI/SCIE/ESCI/SCOPUS/WoS Journals, Book Chapters and Conferences. He has guided 7 M.Tech and currently guiding 2 M.Tech and 2 PhD candidates. He has delivered 2 Expert Lecture, 2 keynote speaker, 1 consultancy project completed, 7 patents filed and submitted 2 research projects also. He is IEEE, CSI member, Indian government MHRD's IIC Cell member and also Associate Editor of 1 Reputed Journal. He has recently Edited a book titled "Energy Efficient Underwater Wireless Communications and Networking" published with IGI Global and in progress of completing 2 more books. He is also handling 1 special issue. His research interests include MANET, FANET, WSN, and UWSN and always open for research projects into these areas.

Shikha Gupta has an experience of more than 2 decades in teaching computer science subjects like big data analytics, data mining, predictive analytics, artificial intelligence, design and analysis of algorithms etc. to undergraduates and post graduates . Her research interests span from algorithm designing to artificial intelligence to deep learning. She has many research publications to her credit.

A. K. M. Bahalul Haque is currently appointed as a Junior researcher at LUT University Finland. He is currently on study leave as a lecturer of North South University Bangladesh. He has completed a Bachelor of Science in Computer Science and Telecommunication Engineering from Noakhali Science and Technology University, Bangladesh. He achieved M.Sc. in Information Technology from Fachhochschule Kiel, Germany. He is a research enthusiast and his area of research interest includes Blockchain, IoT, Smart City, Cyber Security, and Cloud computing. He has published papers in reputed international conference proceedings. journals and book chapters.

Sailesh Iyer is working as Professor in Rai School of Engineering, Rai University, Ahmedabad, Gujrat. His area of interests are Computer Vision, Image Processing, Data Analytics, Artificial Intelligence and Machine Learning.

Anita Kanavalli is the Head of the department of Computer Science and Engineering at M S Ramaiah Institute of technology Bangalore.

Manpreet Kaur is currently working as an Assistant Professor in a Computer Science and Engineering Department at Guru Nanak Dev Engineering College in Ludhiana, India. She has an experience of almost 10 years in teaching subjects such as Discrete Structures, Network Security, Compiler Design, Computer Graphics and many more in capacity of UG and PG courses. Her research interests includes Blockchains, Artificial Intelligence, IoT and Network Security.

Ashok Kumar is currently an Assistant Professor in Chitkara University Institute of Engineering and Technology, Chitkara University, Punjab, India. He is a PhD in Computer Science and Engineering from the Thapar University, Punjab, India. He has number of publications in international journals and conferences of repute. His current areas of research interest include cloud computing, internet of things, and fog computing.

Hemalatha P. R., B.Tech., M.Tech (IT), working as Assistant professor in the department of computer science and Engineering in Velammal college of engineering and Technology, Madurai. I have 8+ years of experience in this field.

Kamalendu Pal is with the Department of Computer Science, School of Mathematics, Computer Science and Engineering, City University London. Kamalendu received his BSc (Hons) degree in Physics from Calcutta University, India, Postgraduate Diploma in Computer Science from Pune, India, MSc degree in Software Systems Technology from Sheffield University, Postgraduate Diploma in Artificial Intelligence from Kingston University, MPhil degree in Computer Science from University College London, and MBA degree from the University of Hull, United Kingdom. He has published widely in the scientific community with research articles in the ACM SIGMIS Database, Expert Systems with Applications, Decision Support Systems, and conferences. His research interests include knowledge-based systems, decision support systems, blockchain technology, software engineering, and service-oriented computing. He is on the editorial board in an international computer science journal. He is a member of the British Computer Society, the Institution of Engineering and Technology, and the IEEE Computer Society.

Sushree Bibhuprada Priyadarshini (Ph.D in Computer Science and Engineering) is currently working as an Asst. Prof. in Dept. of Computer Science and Information Technology at Institute of Technical Education and Research..She is the recipient of Orissa State Talent Scholarship and NRTS scholarship. She has got the certificate of Merit in Brigade Talent Search Exam. She has received the "All Round the best Student of the year" . She has secured the highest marks in Computer Science and Data Processing from ITER in 2011-13 and was awarded for "Best Poster Presentation" in the Workshop on "Monitoring of Research of Ph. D. Scholars. She has received the "Best Student Paper Award" in 15th International Conference on Information Technology, IEEE at IIIT. She has been invited and selected as the Keynote Speaker of International Conference of Innovative Applied Energy, St. Cross College, Oxford University. Besides, She is the Member of IAENG, SDIWC, CSTA. She is also working as reviewer in International Journal of Engineering Research & Technology and IEEE Consumer Electronics journal. She has around 24 publications including IET, IEEE, Elsevier, Springer, IGI Global etc.

Ricardo Augusto Rabelo Oliveira received his Ph.D. degree in Computer Science from Federal University of Minas Gerais in 2008. Nowadays he is Associate Professor in Computing Department at Federal University of Ouro Preto. Has experience in Computer Science, acting on the following subjects: Wavelets, Neural Networks, 5G, VANT, Wearables and Mobile Computing.

Drishya K. Ramdas is currently pursuing her engineering degree from Ramaiah Institute of Technology in the Computer Science domain. She is also pursuing a Post-Graduate Diploma in the domains of Big Data, Analytics and Artificial Intelligence.

Kavitha S. completed B.Tech (IT) in 2010 from M. Kumarasamy College of Engineering, Karur and M.E (CSE) in 2012 from Raja College of Engineering and Technology, Madurai.

Amrit Sahani is a recent graduate in Computer Science and Information Technology from the Institute of Technical Education and Research. He served as a Summer Research Intern at the National Institute of Technology, Rourkela He is currently working as an IT analyst and his current research interests include networking, IoT, cryptography, Computer Networks and Data Communications and WSN.

Shagun Sharma is presently pursuing Masters of Techology from Chitkara University Institute of Engineering and Technology, Chitkara University, Punjab, India. She has done her Bachelor of technology from Shoolini University of Biotechnology and Management Sciences. She is one of the ten toppers in the graduation. Her area of interest includes Data Mining, Machine Learning and Artificial Intelligence.

Ranjana Sikarwar is currently pursuing her PHD in Computer Science & Engineering from Amity University, Gwalior. She has 8 years of academic teaching experience. Her areas of interest include Social area networks analysis, Image processing, Cloud computing, Internet of Things, Blockchain.

Cihan Yalcin obtained his B.S. degree in Engineering Department of IT from Kaunas University of Technology, Lithuania in 2015. He completed Masters degree in Computer Engineering from Suleyman Demirel University, Turkey in 2018. He is still studying his PhD at Suleyman Demirel University. He is working as an IT at Suleyman Demirel University Information Technology Department since 2016. His research interests include New Generation Wireless Technologies, Blockchain, Internet of Things, Artificial Intelligent.

Asim Sinan Yuksel obtained his B.S. degree in computer engineering from Ege University Izmir, Turkey in 2006. He completed his Masters degree in Computer Science from Indiana University School of Informatics and Computing, Indiana, USA in 2010. He obtained his Ph.D. degree in Istanbul University Department of Computer Engineering in 2015. He worked as a research assistant in Suleyman Demirel University Department of Computer Engineering between 2012-2015. He is currently working as an Assistant Professor in Suleyman Demirel University Department of Computer Engineering. His research interests include Mobile Computing, Social Networks, Software Engineering, IoT, Machine Learning and Deep Learning.

Index

A

B

C

D

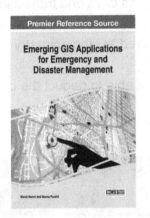

Printed in the United States
by Baker & Taylor Publisher Services